# A VIEW
*from a*
# TALL HILL

## Also by Terry Wieland

*Great Hunting Rifles: Victorian to the Present*
*Dangerous-Game Rifles*

*Spiral-Horn Dreams*
*The Magic of Big Game*

*Spanish Best: The Fine Shotguns of Spain*
*Vintage British Shotguns*
*A Shooter's Guide to Shotguns*

# A VIEW
*from a*
# TALL HILL
## ROBERT RUARK IN AFRICA

# TERRY WIELAND
### FOREWORD BY THOMAS McINTYRE

Skyhorse Publishing

Skyhorse Publishing books may be purchased in bulk at special discounts for sales promotion, corporate gifts, fund-raising, or educational purposes. Special editions can also be created to specifications. For details, contact the Special Sales Department, Skyhorse Publishing, 307 West 36th Street, 11th Floor, New York, NY 10018 or info@skyhorsepublishing.com.

Skyhorse® and Skyhorse Publishing® are registered trademarks of Skyhorse Publishing, Inc.®, a Delaware corporation.

Visit our website at www.skyhorsepublishing.com.

10 9 8 7 6 5 4 3 2

Library of Congress Cataloging-in-Publication Data is available on file.

Cover design by Tom Lau
Cover photo credit: Terry Wieland took the front cover photograph in the Okavango Delta in Botswana, in 2008.

Print ISBN: 978-1-5107-3712-9
Ebook ISBN: 978-1-5107-3714-3

Printed in the United States of America

To gallop up a hill in the sunshine and stand at the top gazing over the limitless spaces of Africa with the glorious wind blowing the delicious mimosa scent against my face and wonder if I haven't got the best possible life after all.

Lady Francis Scott
Nanyuki, 1922

# ROBERT RUARK

## ESCRITOR

*NACIO EN CAROLINA DEL NORTE*

*EL 29 DE DICIEMBRE DE 1915*

*FALLECIO EN LONDRES*

*EL 1 DE JULIO DE 1965*

*GRAN AMIGO DE ESPAÑA*

*E.P.D.*

Robert Ruark's Epitaph
The Municipal Cemetery
Palamós, Spain

# TABLE OF CONTENTS

*Foreword by Thomas McIntyre*     *i*
*Preface to the 2020 Edition*     *vii*
*[Ruark Column]*     *xvii*
*Preface to the First Edition*     *xxiii*
*Acknowledgments*     *xxix*
*Introduction*     *xxxiii*

1. Life Among the Giants     1
2. The University of North Carolina     11
3. Learning the Ropes     19
4. Gone to Sea     33
5. Trials of Babylon     69
6. The Hard True Life     97
    Safari: *Horn of the Hunter*     109
7. Kenya in Black and White     119
8. Robert Ruark Among the Mau Mau     147
    Mau Mau: *Something of Value*     187
9. Home No More     199
10. Miles and Miles of Bloody Africa     231
11. Ruark & Hemingway     255
12. Exploration & Farewell     269
    Winds of Change: *Uhuru*     281
13. Bwana Bob     293
    Other Days: *The Old Man and the Boy* &
    *The Old Man's Boy Grows Older*     305
14. The Lion at Twilight     315
    Self Portrait: *The Honey Badger*     337
15. Ruark & Selby     365
16. A Tusk and a Book     379

*Epilogue: A View from a Tall Hill*     *391*
*Bibliography*     *417*
*Index*     *423*

# FOREWORD

## BY THOMAS McINTYRE

Famous before the internet ("FBI"), columnist, novelist, product of a Carolina boyhood, Big Apple roisterer, and big-game hunter, Robert Chester Ruark was the author of *Horn of the Hunter* (1953), *Something of Value* (1955), and *The Old Man and the Boy* (1957). He also, for better or worse, shaped at least some of my life. Now, my friend Terry Wieland is telling the story of Ruark in the book you are holding, *A View from a Tall Hill*.

Terry can explain why he was drawn to Africa, and in these pages why Ruark may have been drawn, too. My own obsession with Africa predated even my ability to read, to an indelible childhood impression of an actual person I knew who had come back from what must have been, based upon his tales of buffalo, elephant, and the people he met, the most enthralling place on earth. In time I did read about Africa, but before Roosevelt or Hemingway, before Pete Capstick became "Peter Hathaway Capstick," it was Ruark I read first when I was barely a teenager and Ruark was still alive and something of a Papa *manqué*. One might take the position that it was the ruination of a young life. Or not.

Time has not been generous to Ruark's reputation. A country lad who learned a love of the outdoors from his two grandfathers, he was something of a prodigy, entering college at fifteen, then venturing

*i*

from Chapel Hill to the bright lights and big city and newspapers. By the time of his far-too-early death in the mid-1960s he had become a fading ember, disarrayed philanderer, and victim of strong drink and guttering talent. Yet for some ten years from the start of the '50s to the start of the '60s he was a genuinely estimable bestselling author; had a money-losing A-list movie, starring Sidney Poitier and Rock Hudson, made from one of his books; was a one-shot actor in television's *Playhouse 90*; and in what may or may not have been the golden age of magazine journalism, a certifiable celebrity of the first order, all of it accelerated by Africa.

"Bestselling" and "author" is a rather dismissive coupling of words today; but it was hardly a ringing endorsement even half a century ago. On top of that, Ruark found his subject in Africa and, worse, hunting, though far from entirely that. Only one writer of the day was, as we know, permitted to write about those two subjects with any hope of being taken seriously. Yet Ruark's coming to Africa can be seen as a direct-line product of an American tradition begun with Roosevelt and carried on by Hemingway—Roosevelt in emulation of the British hunter-explorer Frederick Courteney Selous, Hemingway in emulation of Roosevelt, Ruark of Hemingway, and more of us than we might care to say in homage to Ruark. The three American men and writers came to Africa almost exactly twenty years apart, each after his own war, in Cuba, Italy, and the North Atlantic, each very much a product of his own generation. Today, the power in the kind of Africa the three were drawn to can be seen in its anti-generational attraction for many of us still, in the twenty-first century.

Though initially something of a lesser hunter than either of his predecessors, Ruark went on to spend more time in Africa than the other two combined, as well as hunting in more far-flung regions, including beyond Africa, and for more charismatic game, Hemingway never hunting elephant or tiger; Roosevelt never tiger or leopard; neither hunting Alaska, as Ruark did for brown bear. Of the three, Ruark wrote arguably the most vividly and entertainingly about Africa, Hemingway more intent on *belle lettres* pontificating around campfires, and Roosevelt a serviceable, utilitarian writer with a tendency to read like a penny-a-liner, yet not without agreeable grace notes.

Ruark, more than either, was a true working writer. Professional hunters, most now dead, recalling Ruark on safari, remarked on how the day would come when he uncased the manual typewriter from the looming *massif* of impedimenta he brought and, waving away all distraction, sat at a deal table in the yellowish shade of the fever trees, doubtlessly with a large glass of iced gin near at hand, producing a stack of manuscripts to be sent back to the offices of the Scripps-Howard syndicate *par avion*. With his bank balance thus on the way to being replenished, he could return to hunting with something like a clear conscience.

Ruark's being drawn to Africa and his sensitive insights into, and love of, it and Africans, black and white, would seem to belie his superficial biography. A product of the Depression-era Jim Crow South, Ruark would seem an overwhelming candidate for prejudice, yet was anything but. Roosevelt had a vexingly conflicted regard for black people, mingling progressive politics (he praised the "buffalo" soldiers—"We're fighting bulls of the Buffaloes"–who reinforced his Rough Riders at crucial moments during their battles in the Spanish–American War, only later to say of them, "Negro troops were shirkers in their duties and would only go so far as they were led by white officers," and even later unjustly ordering the dishonorable discharge of one hundred sixty-seven black troops after a racial incident in Brownsville, Texas, in 1906, the troops being pardoned sixty-six years later when only one survived). Of the Africans he met on safari, he contended they were "strapping grown-up children." With Papa, what I would deem affected hardboiled talk came all too trippingly to his tongue, along with his exhibiting an open disdain for many of the Africans working diligently and skillfully to find game for him. (In fairness, Hemingway did feel a genuine warmth for some Africans, in particular those he perceived as regarding him as the uber-hero he hankered to be.)

It's difficult to discover similar inclinations in Ruark, perhaps because he knew hard times growing up or recalled the alienation of being a loner, and so an outsider, as a child. He may have associated, as an ordinary seaman on ships in the Merchant Marine in the 1930s or as a gunnery officer in the World War II Navy, with blacks on equal footings. Or it may simply be that as a Southerner he grew up in far closer association, and with deeper empathy for, blacks than Northerners like Roosevelt and Hemingway ever could experience.

Ruark was a full-time stop-the-presses journalist, an occupation which was mostly a part-time one for Roosevelt and Hemingway. For Ruark, as such, getting the story straight was, indeed, something of value. It also sent him, when he made Manhattan his headquarters, into an endless rounding of the nightclub circuit to forage for material for his columns (I came across a photo of a scrum of mid-century men in coats and ties laughing a little too heartily at the bar at 21, one of them, not identified by name, unmistakably a rather florid Ruark, who was probably in his head cataloging a story; Hemingway, on the other hand, is said to have had after-hours sex with a gangster's moll in the club, having met her only that night and never getting her name for the record).

Ruark's alcoholism was apparently well-established before he ever stepped foot in Tanganyika (he'd been marked for it, both of his parents substance abusers). A story from a reliable source tells how Ruark, before his first safari, took his new and unfamiliar rifles to the shooting range at the Camp Fire Club near Chappaqua, New York, of which Roosevelt was one of the earliest members. He was, however, far too worse for the drink to sight in his rifles himself, and the *Field & Stream* shooting editor, Warren Page, another club member, got all of them zeroed for him. (Another story, which may or may not have involved alcohol, was his accidental shooting of a native Indian during a tiger beat and having to flee the country with his wife to escape a charge of homicide.)

The once young, now deceased, professional hunter Harry Selby, whom Ruark made renowned, commented on the air of dissipation and sallowness he saw in Ruark upon his many rearrivals in Africa. And how within a week or two on safari, he appeared far more healthy and alive. Hemingway meant to return soon after his first time, and told how he would in the thoughts he had during his drive back to the main camp in *Green Hills of Africa* after taking the kudu he had been fixated on throughout his hunt:

I'd make some money some way and when we came back we
would come to the old man's village in trucks, then pack in
with porters so there wouldn't be any damned car to worry
about, send the porters back, and make a camp in the timber
up the stream . . . and hunt that country slowly, living there
and hunting out each day, sometimes laying off and writing
for a week, or writing half the day, or every other day, and get
to know it as I knew the country around the lake where we
were brought up. I'd see the buffalo feeding where they lived,
and when the elephants came through the hills we would see
them and watch them breaking branches and not have to
shoot, and I would lie in the fallen leaves and watch the kudu
feed out and never fire a shot unless I saw a better head than
this one in the back, and instead of trailing that sable bull . . .
all day, I'd lie behind a rock and watch them on the hillside
and see them long enough so they belonged to me forever . . .
I would come back to where it pleased me to live; to really
live. Not just let my life pass.

Of course, it never came to pass. Divorcing the rich wife whose family funded the first safari, it took Hemingway almost twenty years before *Look* magazine and the colonial government of Kenya provided
him with another African hunt, when it was too late for him to be
saved. Ruark's situation was different; and while you might wish to
imagine that a life in the African bush could have been Hemingway's
salvation, it seems less likely that it could have been Ruark's (he tried
it), who had perhaps been too long bound to his sinecure in Manhattan high society—at least the sort of high society that made it into the
inside pages of the papers—for there to be true hope of redemption.

Yet Africa is where Ruark said he had to go "to meet God" (and
perhaps of no lesser consequence, to learn to love food). With campfires and canvas it displaced *boîtes* and a grand hacienda in Spain, for
interludes, and almost certainly granted him more honest words to
put down on paper and more years to put them there, perhaps merely forestalling a London surgical theater and death at forty-nine, but
forestalling it all the same. Whatever his possible outcome—none

ideal—no better gauge of Ruark's powers as an author, fired by his miraculous discovery of Africa, may be evidenced by the thousands of others he beguiled into following him to the tall hills he had found, as if no one else had ever set foot on them.

Almost thirty years ago, when my son was born, I wanted to give him something he could keep in a pocket, as it were, knowing it was there to draw some strength from if needed, but not to have to broadcast it to the world at large. It was his middle name. Long after I may or may not have been ruined by that name, long after the name might have gone out of fashion, I thought my son could have it for whatever power it might contain, and as a possible way of explaining something about his father to him. So, of course, there was nothing else to be done but to give him the imperfect yet enduring "Ruark" for such a name.

*For forty years and more, Thomas McIntyre has written about the world of hunting, with a special regard for Africa. He has been a contributing editor to* Sports Afield *and* Field & Stream *throughout those decades. He is the author of numerous books, most recently* Augusts in Africa. *As well, he has written more than eight hundred scripts for outdoor television. Currently, he is at work on a book about the African buffalo,* Thunder Without Rain, *and a television series about an alternate history of the North American Indian.*

# PREFACE TO THE 2020 EDITION

Technically, this is not a second edition of *A View from a Tall Hill*, simply a reprint of the book that first appeared in 2000 published by Thorn Tree Press, and which was reprinted in 2003 by Down East Books. Everything that appeared in those two printings is included in this one.

Twenty years have passed since the book was written, however, and the world has changed. Public attitudes towards such subjects as racism, Africa and the Africans, and even journalism itself, are quite different now than they were in 1998. Things the author took for granted then, such as the role of newspapers and journalistic ethics—even such basic principles as seeking truth in journalism—are being questioned or dismissed as outdated.

As with most things in the world, nothing is simple. There are complex interrelationships involved. A radical change in one area often leads to changes in another, which in turn provoke changes—some good but more owften bad—in a third. One such interrelationship is the internet, the age of internet vigilantes and "viral" videos, and their influence on game management. The "Cecil the Lion" incident in Zimbabwe in 2015 is the classic example. We shall come back to this.

\*\*\*

Several people who are prominent in this book are no longer with us. Michael McIntosh died in 2009 of a heart attack, followed by Eva Monley in 2011 at the age of eighty-eight. Robert M. Lee died in 2016, and Mark Robert Selby—Ruark's reluctant namesake and purported (by Ruark) godson—in 2017. Mark's father, Harry Selby, died a year later at the age of ninety-two. His memoirs, which were supposedly in the offing for decades, have never materialized. Most of his recollections of his time with Robert Ruark, which he guarded so religiously with those memoirs in mind, apparently went with him to the grave.

Immediately, I am bound to correct one series of errors which were included in the original book, and which are included, unaltered (for various logistical reasons) in the reprint. In several places, I questioned Robert Ruark's personal relationship with Ernest Hemingway. I could find no mention of Ruark in any of the many biographical works on Hemingway, nor were there any letters between them in biographer Carlos Baker's *Ernest Hemingway Selected Letters, 1917–1961.* As of 1999, none had surfaced in Ruark's own correspondence, which is housed at the University of North Carolina in Chapel Hill.

In 2018, writer W. Baxter Byrd, a fellow Ruark admirer, contacted me with the news that he had unearthed some letters from Hemingway in the Ruark papers, and "had held them in his hands." As well, Mr. Byrd drew my attention to mention of Robert Ruark in Mary Welsh Hemingway's memoir, *How It Was.* This was one semi-biography I had not read (and there are others, including Hemingway's own posthumously published work on Africa, *True at First Light*). One cannot study everything, and in Hemingway's case, it pays to be selective. At any rate, my apologies both to Mrs. Hemingway and to the shade of Robert Ruark. It appears that he and Hemingway did, indeed, get gloriously drunk in Pamplona that time.

\*\*\*

Shortly after *A View from a Tall Hill* was reprinted in 2003, I received a letter from a reader that was highly critical of my treatment of the war in the Atlantic from 1939 to 1943, and especially the convoys. To correct my misjudgments, he wrote, shipping losses declined dramatically in 1944 because the convoy system was abandoned in favor of lone merchantmen skillfully eluding the U-boats. He insisted that, had the Allies followed American inclinations from the beginning, rather than following British experience with convoys, the whole Battle of the Atlantic could have been different. This, he added, he had learned from things he read on the internet.

In fact, the convoy system was reduced in late 1944 and 1945 because the Battle of the Atlantic had been largely won, the U-boat fleet had been reduced to a shadow of its former self, and lone merchantmen could now brave the big waters alone in relative safety. The Battle of the Atlantic had been won by the convoy system.

The internet is many things, but it's certainly not a force for truth. Online "encyclopedias" and reference works are vulnerable to almost effortless manipulation by people with a particular belief or ax to grind. You do not need to have any qualifications to represent yourself as an expert and propound views that are nothing short of hare-brained. Here, several modern trends come together. One is the general vilification of colonialism as the source of all the developing world's woes. Any African politician, no matter how crooked or venal, can blame all his country's problems on the British, French, or Belgian colonizers, and be supported in his claims by internet "authorities." Combine this with a penchant for rewriting history, either to present it as it "should" have been, or to aggrandize a particular group, and you have a potential for propaganda worthy of Dr. Goebbels or Joseph Stalin at their worst. For example, Idi Amin invented a Ugandan "war of liberation" in which he, as the hero, drove the British out of the "jewel of Africa." In reality, the Protectorate of Uganda was dragged to independence kicking and screaming (in the words of one historian) by a British government that wanted to wash its hands of all its East African possessions. Amin created a special medal to commemorate his fictional feat, and gave himself the title "Conqueror of the British Empire." Such hogwash has found its way into various histories. A similar rewriting of the Mau Mau Emergency in Kenya characterizes it as Kenya's war of liberation, in which they drove the British out. Certainly the British left in 1963, but it was only indirectly because of the Mau Mau.

This general demonization of colonialism has become a mainstay of political correctness in the modern world, aided and abetted by internet self-styled experts. A few years ago, an opposition politician in South Africa was imprudent enough to suggest that colonialism actually had some benefits. The resulting furor led to her resignation. These days, making such a suggestion is unthinkable, and retribution by the politically correct is swift and absolute.

Presumably, the benefits she was thinking of included the establishing of universities, spreading literacy, combating malaria, reducing infant mortality, and attempting to eradicate female circumcision. Of course, all of these contributed to an exploding human population in Africa that threatens everything from wildlife species to the water supply, so perhaps the anti-colonialists have a point.

As for the state of things in Africa today, would that I could apologize for having been so pessimistic and report that things have improved. Alas, such is not the case. In fact, in the last twenty years, although the superpower tug of war between the Soviet Union and the West has ceased to be a consideration, it has been replaced by the dual threat of Islamic extremism in the North, and the encroachment of the Chinese in search of raw materials virtually everywhere else. And, of course, there is the limitless greed and corruption of African politicians in more countries than one can list.

In 2000, in Zimbabwe, Robert Mugabe embarked on a program of land seizures, without compensation to white farmers, that destroyed the country's economy. Mugabe hung on for almost another twenty years before he was finally forced out but, a few months after his successors took power, very little seems to have changed. The motivation for getting rid of the criminal Mugabe was not to make things better for the country, only to allow a new generation of crooks and thugs to elbow their way to the trough.

Around the same time, the president of South Africa, Jacob Zuma, announced that his country would begin similar land expropriations from white farmers, also without compensation. The result has been a crash in property values. One can only assume that South

Africa's leaders looked on Zimbabwe's actions, liked what they saw—in Mugabe's lifestyle and bank accounts, at least—and determined that this was worth emulating. It's too early to tell exactly how this will play out, but erring on the side of pessimism has proven to be a winning strategy everywhere in Africa since 1960, and there is no reason this case should be any different.

Since this book was published, the wildlife industry in South Africa mushroomed into the dominant force in big-game hunting on the continent, at least in terms of number of visitors every year. A two-week hunting trip in South Africa—I refuse to call it a safari—became less expensive than an elk hunt in Montana. With big money, naturally, came big abuses, from keeping tame lions in enclosures to allow them to be shot, to deliberately in-breeding to create freak antelope "subspecies" in an attempt to have them recognized by the record books and propel their breeders to wealth and fame. These perversions of big-game hunting, so far outside any concept of ethics that they can hardly be mentioned in the same sentence, have been largely condemned by such organizations as Safari Club International (SCI), but most continue just the same—under cover of darkness, as it were.

Now, apparently, the crash in South African property values, as the result of looming land confiscation, is damaging the wildlife industry to the point where at least one close observer believes it will not recover. One can argue cause and effect, and relative benefits to this group or that, but it always seems to come back to the same thing: There will undoubtedly be winners, but the game animals will be the losers. They always are.

In 2008, Botswana announced it was closing the Okavango Delta to big-game hunting, and pious pronouncements were made about turning the country into a "green" paradise and oasis of New-Age environmental responsibility. This, it was hoped, would draw ever more eco-tourists to the photo-safari camps. Botswana was already enduring the effects of a couple of wildlife imbalances; in parts of the Okavango, there were simply too many lions—partly the result of a moratorium on lion hunting. In other areas, especially the Kwando district north of the delta, there were vastly too many elephants and they were destroying their own ecosystem.

Nothing short of a massive cull would have curbed this, but the authorities were deathly afraid to do anything of the sort because of the inevitable negative publicity of the type that accompanied the death of Cecil the Lion in Zimbabwe. Had the government attempted an elephant cull, it was feared, various international animal-rights groups would invoke a boycott and the tourist industry would collapse. While game managers wring their hands and politicians issue mealy-mouthed statements, the elephants continue to destroy the forests.

The internet is one more proof of mankind's ability to take anything, no matter how beneficial it might seem at first, and turn it into a force for evil. The internet today is the greatest repository of lies, hogwash, and crack-brained theories in the history of mankind. While social media, phone videos, and the like may have contributed to the liberation movements of the "Arab Spring" in 2011, allowing self-appointed internet vigilantes to dictate wildlife and conservation policy is a blunder of unbelievable proportions. If politicians can mobilize the internet to get themselves elected, then others can mobilize it to manipulate those same politicians. Fear of such an internet campaign alone now seems sufficient to shape government policies.

For two years, as I write this, there has been talk of big-game hunting being reopened in Botswana. We shall see. Particularly, there are demands from those Botswanans, living cheek-by-jowl with the ever more destructive elephants in Kwando, to have their numbers reduced. The new president of Botswana is in favor, for this and other reasons, but there is great fear that any move to reopen elephant hunting will result in an international furor from conservation groups, "green" foreign governments, do-gooder actresses, and similar molders of public opinion.

There is a popular belief that elephants are an endangered species. They are not. In some areas, they have been wiped out, but in others (like Kwando) there are too many for the habitat. This being the case, so goes the popular belief, elephants from areas of over-population should be transplanted to areas where numbers are few. There is a popular image of Dumbo being carried in a sling beneath a helicopter, trumpeting with glee, being transported to his new home of greenery and plenty. In fact, transplanting elephants in any meaningful numbers presents a logistical problem that defies belief, from simple transportation requirements (huge flatbeds travelling hundreds of miles on non-existent roads) to veterinary concerns (keeping a drugged elephant alive and able to recover) to the views of the locals who may not welcome elephants back to trample the mealie crop. Then, of course, there are the ever-present poachers who would immediately shoot anything with tusks. And who would pay the immense sums required for all this, even assuming it were physically possible?

When the white man came to Africa, there were islands of humanity in a sea of elephants. Today, there are ever-shrinking islands of elephants in an ever-expanding sea of humanity. In the old days, elephants were a force for natural regeneration. They meandered along their migration routes, which stretched from the Cape to the edge of the Sahara, pausing here and there to push over a few trees and generally stir things up, then moving on. The fallen trees provided cover for other animals, birds, and new plants, and life was renewed. Now, with migration routes blocked, elephants are confined in small areas, increasing in numbers and gradually destroying their habitat. This, in turn, is bad for other species which depend on that same habitat. The secretive bushbuck, for example, has been wiped out in some parts of Botswana by habitat loss, and they are just the tip of the iceberg.

In South Africa's Kruger National Park, one of the continent's greatest repositories of wildlife of all kinds, elephant numbers have been a problem for years. Mozambican ivory poachers have made some inroads, but in a bizarre twist, National Public Radio (NPR) in the United States, a little while back, ran a lengthy piece on how poaching ivory and coming back to their village with money to spend gave the young poachers status with their families and friends. Evidently, in the warped view of NPR, a Mozambique poaching-gang member's self-esteem is more important than the welfare of the animals.

The efforts of SCI and other hunting organizations to promote the genuine conservation benefits of trophy hunting—the current *bête noir* of the Humane Society and the internet vigilantes—bears fruit in some places (usually in negotiations behind closed doors) but often seems like King Canute versus the tide when it comes to public opinion at large.

Unfortunately, press releases from SCI get swamped by the tide of negative publicity that results from issues like "canned lion" hunting in South Africa. Ethics, it seems, will always be trumped by greed and egotism. When Rowland Ward, the London taxidermist, established its big-game record book in 1892, it did so with the best of intentions. Seeing the decline, and sometimes extinction, of one species after another, from bison in North America to the springbok in southern Africa, Rowland Ward wanted to create records for posterity of what animals had existed, and the size they achieved. Since then, however, shooting an animal that "makes the book" has become a mania and, in some instances, the only reason for hunting at all. Big-game awards, such as the Weatherby Trophy (later renamed the Weatherby Award) are examples. Jack O'Connor, the second recipient, wrote in 1977 that, since its inception in 1956, the Weatherby Trophy had become distorted even from its original purpose, and candidates "campaigned for it like Nixon running for president." In the forty years since, that situation has only become vastly worse.

Naturally, the oversized egos that demand places in the record book will pay huge amounts to shoot an animal that gets them in, by hook or by crook. Game ranchers then take advantage of this by inbreeding animals to create artificial subspecies and lobby to have them recognized by the record books, which in turn creates new No. 1 and No. 2 places in the book for so-called big-game hunters. And this is leaving aside the despicable practice of deliberately breeding and raising spectacular animals like greater kudu, for example, then keeping them confined and auctioning them off as a new "guaranteed No. 1" to the highest bidder.

The ultimate goal of ethical trophy hunting is the good of the species that are hunted, not to catapult the lucky hunter to undying fame. As Robert Ruark pointed out, many times a top trophy was collected by a farmer who didn't realize what he'd shot, or by a first-timer who got lucky with little effort. Serious trophy hunters who train and practice, plot and plan, and then invest big money only to come up short, are left gnashing their teeth in frustration. If nothing else, this proves the Red Gods have a healthy sense of humor.

In the face of this, one can only return to Robert Ruark's own comments about trophy hunting, written late in his life when he had spent literally years on safari and had seen it all. If Ruark stood for one thing—as a man, as a journalist, and as a novelist—it was for telling the truth regardless of political fashion, whether it was tribalism in East Africa or the ethics of hunting.

"Man can as easily be debased as ennobled" by trophy hunting, he wrote. "Nothing is worthwhile unless you work for it, and if the work is hard enough, you don't need to possess the trophy to own it."

Today, with few exceptions, there is far more debasing taking place than ennobling. Ruark's words grow more true—and more relevant, and more important—with every passing year. That is not something that can be said of many writers.

*This column first appeared in* Gray's Sporting Journal, *in July, 2016.*

## DATELINE: NAIROBI, AS IT WAS
### *Or, as we like to think of it*

Robert Ruark, Esq.,
Cottage #7, Norfolk Hotel,
Government Road, Nairobi,
Kenya Colony, British East Africa

Dear Mr. Ruark,

It is the 29th day of December, 2015. You would be one hundred years old today, had you lived, which of course you did not. Not being sure just where you ended up, or what the wire services might be like there, I can only assume your shade is inhabiting cottage #7, and send this missive by ghostly cleft stick to bring you up to date on the last 50 years.

Frankly, it ain't been good since you left us in 1965, but that would hardly surprise you. Those last few years, you saw pretty plainly the way the world was going — especially the world you valued most. Everything you predicted for Africa in *Something of Value* and *Uhuru* has pretty much come to pass, and for the reasons you foresaw.

For your 100th birthday, the Wilmington newspaper despatched a reporter to write a feature. Naturally, being a modern journalist, he apparently didn't bother to read anything you wrote. He found some old people who remembered you from the 1950s, and they made the usual comments about your drinking and your "Hemingwayesque bravado." A couple of local novelists no one ever heard of were asked for their opinions, and they admitted you'd done pretty well there, for a while, but your "tales of Africa" had been, and I quote, "supplanted by modern African novelists."

I guess those would be the modern African writers who present the Mau Mau as a noble band of freedom fighters, instead of murderous criminals, egged on by Moscow. The reporter ended the piece by accusing you of "Jim Crow racism."

After reading what passes for journalism in the Wilmington paper, I went back and reread your newspaper columns about civil rights. If I recall correctly, some Southern newspapers cancelled your column, and there were even a few dark mutterings about lynching you as a traitor to Dixie. That would certainly be an ironic fate for a Jim Crow racist, now wouldn't it?

The basis of the accusation seems to be the fact that you raised some objections to the headlong rush to decolonization of the early '60s. Apparently, now, any good word said for British colonial rule (as opposed to tribal wars, dictatorships, and corruption) is rejected as "racism." As it turned out, your predictions about the future of Africa were dead on in most cases: The Congo, Nigeria, the Sudan, Uganda, Angola, Mozambique, Rhodesia.

To be honest, though, Mr. Ruark, all of that matters less to me (and probably to you) than the state of the wildlife, which ranges from dire to not bad. Black rhinos are all but gone, but elephants are healthy in most areas, and Cape buffalo thrive wherever they're given half a chance. The traditional tent safari, that great African adventure you made us all hunger for, no longer exists. Hunting today is mostly from permanent camps. You don't move around much, so you don't get to see much country, which was the real joy of an old-time safari.

There are animals all over South Africa now, which was a big-game wasteland in your day, so that's a definite plus. The fact that most of the animals shot there require about as much real hunting as a Hereford in a meadow is beside the point. Better to have animals than no animals.

We won't dwell on the state of trophy hunting, which you rightly believed could debase a man as well as ennoble him. The debasing has almost completely eclipsed any ennobling. You may recall that you wrote "Nothing is worthwhile unless you work for it, and if the work is hard enough, you don't have to possess the trophy to own it." Well, today's attitude is to get the biggest trophy with the least work, get it on video, and make up a bunch of lies about how tough it was. And the most important thing is that it make "the book."

Trophy hunting today is like the Church of Rome, complete with indulgences, about the time Martin Luther nailed his 95 theses to the church door. Alas, there is no Martin Luther of Hunting anywhere in sight.

Wingshooting's doing okay, but you'll be sad to hear the wild bobwhites are all but gone from the South. You can still shoot quail, but they're pen-raised birds. They let them go just before you head out with the dogs. Pen-raised quail are to real wingshooting what a stay at the Venetian in Las Vegas is to a week in Venice, overlooking St. Mark's Square. There's a vague resemblance, but that's where it ends.

It's hard to believe it's 50 years since your death. You know, I discovered *The Honey Badger* a couple of months after you died, and proceeded to devour everything else you wrote that I could get my hands on. *Something of Value, Uhuru, Horn of the Hunter.* It's also hard to believe that, six years later, I was sitting on the veranda of the Norfolk Hotel, sipping a Tusker, and reflecting on my second trip to East Africa.

Looking back, I can hardly believe I did it. Twenty-two years old, with three years on small-town newspapers under my belt, and I bought a one-way ticket to London with $210 in my pocket and an ambition to be a foreign correspondent. I ended up in Uganda, purely by chance, and from there into the Sudan. The next year I was back, with a hand-shake newspaper contract, working out of Nairobi and telexing collect.

That's when I managed to spend some time in cottage #7. I scraped up the dough for one night at the Norfolk, drank Gordon's gin with Schweppes Indian Tonic Water, raised a toast, and tapped out a dateline on a portable typewriter: NAIROBI, Kenya (Special). Those were the days.

Cottage #7 is gone now, along with the others. Torn down to make room for a highrise addition to house all the game-park tourists. At least I got to see it before it went. That, and the last vestiges of British colonial Africa, in Kampala, and Nairobi, and Fort Portal. The Mountains of the Moon and the Albert Nile and refugee camps and Nile barges with the piles of bananas and the striped towel stretched over the cockpit like the *African Queen*. Hitchhiking north to Moyo, and crossing into the Sudan in the moonlight, and the Anyanya with his Lee-Enfield accepting a cigarette with such grave politeness. There was that trip down the Tana River, too, in the dugout canoes, and the African girl with the headscarf dancing in the firelight. A headscarf meant she was married, alas. I can still see her.

Thanks to you, Mr. Ruark, I've been chased by elephants and woken up with more hangovers in more mud huts than I ever thought possible. I came *this close* to getting nailed by a Cape buffalo on a mountaintop, of all places, and got PI-ed from Uganda for black-marketing currency. We were pretty poor there in Kampala for a while, selling off our clothes to the Indian rag dealer until the day some newspaper money arrived and we got drunk on *waragi* in the City Bar.

It's intriguing to trace the lineage. Selous read Baker, and Roosevelt read Selous, and Hemingway read Roosevelt, and you read Hemingway, and a bunch of us read you, and everybody tried to emulate those who went before. But, as your contemporary (and fellow Chapel Hill alumnus) Thomas Wolfe observed, you really can't go home again.

The problem is that where you went no longer exists. I can go and stay at the Savoy in London, but it's not the Savoy of 1942 and the Blitz. I did do one thing, though, that first trip. We were near the Mountains of the Moon, and I went and climbed for a day, getting higher and higher, watching the ground fall away, and the years with it. The country gradually changed back into what you'd seen years before: Thatched huts, herds of cattle, smoke from distant fires, intertwining rondels of thornbush bomas to keep out the lions, all disappearing into a haze where the horizon becomes the sky.

That was your "view from a tall hill." Sorry for stealing your title like that, but I figured you weren't using it at that point and might be happy to see it published. I never got to be you, but I didn't drink myself to death in despair, and when I close my eyes, I can smell the smoke from those distant fires, the eternal, burning-grass smell of Africa. And I need to thank you for that.

Y'r ob't serv't, etc., etc.,
TW

# PREFACE TO THE FIRST EDITION

On July 1, 1965, Robert Ruark died, ostensibly of a ruptured liver, in a hospital in London, England. There is no doubt that his liver was, indeed, hemorrhaging terribly, a result of advanced cirrhosis and Ruark's refusal to stop drinking.

Those are the surface facts. The underlying truth about Ruark's death, however, is just as elusive as the underlying truth about Ruark's life, and it would not be overstating to suggest that the real cause of his death was a broken heart. After a lifetime of striving to succeed, and to find his place in the world, he instead found himself, at the age of forty-nine, strangely adrift.

At the time of his death, Ruark was one of America's best-known and most controversial writers. Already a top-notch reporter, after World War II he became an enormously successful syndicated columnist, then an authority on Africa, and finally a novelist whose major works were all best-sellers. As a columnist, he was frequently described as a "gadfly," and he referred to himself, on occasion, as "a professional wiseguy." When he went on his first safari in East Africa in 1951, however, he began a professional transition that would turn him from a journalist into a novelist whose major works (*Something of Value* and *Uhuru*) ranked him with James Jones (*From Here to Eternity*) and Herman Wouk (*The Caine Mutiny*). When he died, he was — on paper, at least, or so he claimed — a millionaire with a Rolls-Royce and a villa in Spain, and another major novel (*The Honey Badger*) about to be published.

Ten years after his death, however, a friend of mine walked into one of the largest used-book stores in North America and enquired about the availability of any titles by Robert Ruark. The pony-tailed clerk, with his first whispy attempt at a beard, replied, "Who?" When it was explained who Ruark was, and what the titles were, the answer was a disdainful "We don't have any demand for that sort of thing anymore." It was as if Ruark and his memory had been quietly slipped overboard, to sink from sight in the wake of a departing ship. The reason for this, at least, was fairly simple: Ruark was, like Socrates, a man who spoke unwelcome truths. During the 1950s, when Africa's many colonies were slipping toward varying degrees of independence, Ruark took up a decidedly unpopular cause — that of the white settlers, especially in his adopted country, Kenya, the place he felt "more at home than anywhere on earth." The unpleasant truths that he spoke concerned the readiness of the average African to embrace independence in a modern world. The vast majority, Ruark wrote frankly, were simply not ready for l'indépendence. Yet selfish superpower interests (the United States and the Soviet Union) were combining with anti-imperial sentiment everywhere to pressure the colonial powers (especially Britain, France, and Belgium) to get out of Africa — immediately if not sooner, and regardless of the consequences. The result of their premature departures, as Ruark foresaw, would be decades of tribal warfare, murder, corruption and economic exploitation of the common people of Africa that far exceeded the colonial powers at their worst.

This opinion was objective and realistic, and certainly not without compassion for the various African peoples, but it was a far from popular viewpoint in the late 1950s, as the Civil Rights movement in the United States heated to a boiling point. While Robert Ruark was unquestionably not a racist, and his writings on segregation in the U.S. and on apartheid in South Africa confirm this, there was still a wide view that "the poor African" was oppressed and exploited, and must be set free. The liberal guilt of the 1950s and '60s has since been translated into the current environment of political correctness, in which only certain things can be said and certain other things (including, in many instances, the stark, naked truth) must never be said.

By 1965, the battle had been all but lost. Kenya, Tanganyika, Uganda, the Congo, the Sudan, Zambia — all were independent under governments that swiftly became very undemocratic. Ruark himself had been barred from Kenya, and American attention was turning to other parts of the world, especially Southeast Asia. When Ruark died, a lonely but high-profile voice of dissent on African affairs fell silent, and the politicians, diplomats, fellow-travelling journalists, and — let's be frank — crooks and thugs and tyrants and aid agencies were left to turn Africa into what it is today. In all likelihood, that is where the career of Robert Ruark would have ended. The books would have gone out of print, the newspaper columns used to wrap fish, and his name forgotten even in his home town. The shelf life of departed journalists is short at best.

\* \* \*

Ernest Hemingway once wrote, "When you describe something that has happened that day the timeliness makes people see it in their own imaginations. A month later that element of time is gone and your account would be flat and they would not see it in their minds nor remember it." So it is with books by journalists describing, in perishable depth, the news of the day or of past weeks or months; so-called journalistic works lose their value quickly and become little more than historical or academic curiosities. Hemingway went on to say that if, on the other hand, "You make it up instead of describe it you can make it round and whole and solid and give it life. You create it, for good or bad. It is made, not described. It is just as true as the extent of your ability to make it and the knowledge you put into it."

On Africa, Ruark combined deep and extensive knowledge with an extraordinary writing ability that allowed him to create a world in literature, and the results were his greatest works: *Horn of the Hunter*, *Something of Value*, *Uhuru*, and *The Honey Badger*. As well, for almost nine years he wrote a monthly column in *Field & Stream* called "The Old Man and the Boy." It ran for 106 issues and was based on Ruark's remembrances of his childhood in North Carolina, hunting and fishing with his grandfather. The best of these columns was collected in an anthology of the same name in 1957, and this was followed, in 1961, by a second volume, *The Old Man's Boy Grows Older*. The subject matter was timeless, and as a result the stories themselves are immortal. It may well be that, a hundred years from now, the only book by Ruark that is still being read will be *Old Man*, which would not be surprising. Like a fine wine, these stories grow better with age.

Ruark once referred to himself as the "godfather of the modern safari business," and while that may be overstating, it is essentially true. With *Horn of the Hunter* he inspired much of the post-war migration to hunt Africa, and his subsequent writing about safaris in Kenya, Uganda, Tanganyika, and Portuguese East Africa (Mozambique) kept interest at a high level. Between his safari writing and his columns and articles in *Field & Stream*, Ruark established a firm base of admirers completely independent of his general-interest syndicated newspaper column.

When he died, and his celebrity faded away to almost nothing, the hunters and fishermen who loved his work and admired the man for his many good qualities kept the flame alive. By the late 1980s, this specialized interest in Ruark had driven up prices of his books on the used-book market to the point where various publishers began to reprint his most popular works. As well, many of his previously uncollected articles were gathered into two anthologies (*Robert Ruark's Africa*, edited by Michael McIntosh in 1991, and *The Lost Classics of Robert Ruark*, edited by James Casada in 1995) and in 1992, Hugh Foster published a biography of Ruark entitled *Someone of Value*.

You would think, then, that perhaps there are enough words already in print by and about Ruark. As an admirer of Robert Ruark from the age of seventeen, and with an admiration that grows the more I come to know Africa from travelling and hunting there myself, I felt there was at least one more book to be written, one that concentrated on his time in Africa and on the books that were the result of his deep love for the Dark Continent, for its people — all its people, black, white, and brown — and most of all, for its animals.

This is not intended to be a biography in the conventional sense; Hugh Foster has already done that. Instead, this is a portrait of Ruark seen in the context of events in Africa in the 1950s and '60s, of the places he went and the people he knew, and of his influence even after his death.  To a great extent, Hugh Foster built his biography on an exhaustive examination of Ruark's newspaper columns on contemporary topics such as American politics, Civil Rights, the Cold War, and African affairs, and gave relatively little weight to the one thing that makes him of serious interest today:  Africa and big-game hunting.

The real key to Robert Ruark lies not in his journalism so much as in his major works of fiction, especially in the posthumously published novel, *The Honey Badger*.  For reasons that completely elude me, this book, an autobiography in everything but name, has been largely ignored, if not dismissed outright, by others who have studied Ruark. But it is an omission for which I am grateful because it allows me to approach his life from a completely different direction.

✻ ✻ ✻

# ACKNOWLEDGMENTS

This book is not a formal biography of Robert Ruark and was never intended to be. It is as much a book about Ruark's time as about the man himself. However, I owe a great debt to Hugh Foster, who did write a biography of Ruark (*Someone of Value*, published by Trophy Room Books in 1992) and performed a great service for Ruark admirers by preserving information that otherwise would have been lost. In writing this book, I have relied heavily on Foster's work, especially his detailed accounts of Ruark's frenetic travelling in his later years, and the general facts and figures related to his life. While I disagree with some of his conclusions about Ruark's life and character, Hugh Foster's diligence and attention to detail must be acknowledged.

The editor of this book was Bill Buckley, a freelance photographer, editor, and writer, who was passionate in keeping the author on the straight and narrow. No dubious conclusion went unchallenged and no faulty construction uncorrected. If eternal vigilance is the price of coherence, then Bill deserves much of the credit for whatever literary virtues the book possesses. I really cannot thank him enough. Bill is, incidentally, no relation to the Bill Buckley who was Ruark's editor at Henry Holt & Co. This strange coincidence I took to be a good omen.

The number of people who knew Ruark well has, naturally, decreased steadily during the thirty-five years since his death. Because of this (to say nothing of fading memories) much information has been lost. I discovered in some people a strange reluctance to talk about Ruark; in oth-

ers, there was an odd insistence on recounting, over and over, tales of
Ruark's drinking and his behavior while he was under the influence.
Why people would take such pleasure in seeing the bad side of a man's
character so many years after his death is a mystery to me, but then
Ruark engendered strong emotions in people. Many people loved him,
but more than a few disliked him intensely. Much of what I was told I
have condensed or left out, for the simple reason that I did not want to
belabor some points, such as his drinking or his many love affairs.

The two people who knew Ruark best who are still alive are Eva Monley and Harry Selby. I wish to thank both of them for the assistance they
did offer. In collaboration with Joe Coogan, Selby is in the process of
compiling his own autobiography and we can only hope he sees fit to
write at length about his adventures with Ruark. Only Selby knows the
details of many of those safaris, and of such significant events as the
death of the old elephant of Illaut. For her part, Miss Monley was helpful and encouraging but left the impression she should really write her
own memoirs.

In Kenya, there remains a handful of professional hunters who knew
Ruark. John Sutton, Ruark's close friend, is dead, but his widow, Angela
Sutton, was very generous and helpful. Through Finn Aagaard and Joe
Coogan, I met Joe and Simonne Cheffings, who were extremely hos-
pitable and generous in arranging for me to meet such people as Angela
Sutton and Tony Archer, as well as providing a great deal of information
about Kenya as it is today. Finn and Joe, needless to say, were the kind
and generous friends they have always been.

In Kenya, I would also like to thank Esmond and Chrysee Bradley
Martin, Keith Mousley, Tony Seth-Smith, Tony and Betty Archer,
David Mead, Felicity Williams, Frank Sutton, Ian Parker, and all the
other modern-day Kenyans who were so generous in sharing their memories and their understanding of the country.

In Botswana, John Dugmore was extremely helpful and spent considerable time reminiscing about the Mau Mau, as well as his days with Ker
& Downey and years of professional hunting since.

My great private source of information on military history, Derek Nelson, went out of his way to provide me with insight into events of the

second world war and also kept me from misinterpreting some of the more arcane aspects of that conflict.

Michael McIntosh, as always, was a great source of encouragement. As an admirer of Ruark, and one who has anthologized his work and written about his life, Michael was invaluable as a sounding board for some of my theories about Ruark.

Finally, there is Richard Sanders. This book is being published largely because of Richard's faith in me and his willingness to set aside his own business and prod me into writing what I believe. Richard and Gail Sanders have been a great moving force behind this book in many ways and I only hope the effort as it stands repays them for all they have done.

* * *

# INTRODUCTION

Throughout his career Robert Ruark found himself being compared with Ernest Hemingway. Usually it was done in a negative way; every distasteful reaction that Hemingway, the quintessential masculine writer, evoked in critics and literati was transferred to Ruark, who was referred to more than once as "a poor man's Hemingway." In a review of one of his early books, the *Time* critic asked, "If Hemingway had never existed, could Robert Ruark ever have been invented?"

Ruark was accused of imitating Hemingway's lifestyle, his interests, his approach to life, even his writing style, but except for some obvious parallels, the accusations are mostly absurd. Considering that, since 1925, every writer who produced a serious novel or short story involving hunting or fishing has encountered the same bias, it becomes obvious that critics are quick to compare and categorize. Literary criticism tends to be a herd activity, and many critics are reluctant to contradict others, for fear of showing ignorance, which is how shallow, and often ill-founded, accusations become accepted wisdom.

When it came to spawning imitators, Ernest Hemingway was, without a doubt, the single most influential writer of the twentieth century. He possessed an extraordinary magnetism that has kept alive the public's fascination with his life, even forty years after his death. Hemingway was a giant in many ways, not only in his writing but in his appetite for life, and many writers since have met their downfall trying to equal him — in literary output, drinking, even divorces and marriages. In

Ruark's case, the accusations were based primarily on his love of Africa and of big game hunting. Once established, they were extended to include his hard-drinking lifestyle, his tendency to brag as he got older, and virtually every other quality where a comparison, however far-fetched, might be drawn.

\* \* \*

In the 1920s, when Ernest Hemingway was living in Paris, the writer Gertrude Stein acquainted him with her theory of "art as therapy for life." For a true artist, she maintained, work provides catharsis. It does not matter whether you are a painter, a sculptor, or a writer; art is a means of exorcising anger and guilt, of expressing your deepest emotions in a way no conversation ever could, even the most intimate conversation with your wife or closest friend. A writer can put into a work of fiction his deepest beliefs and fears, exposing emotions and vulnerability that he would never dare express otherwise.

Once, many years ago, I rather irritated a news editor by expressing the view, half in fun, that "fiction is the only truth." By that I meant two things. One was that only in a work of fiction would you find great truths as opposed to mere facts, which change with the times and eventually become completely irrelevant. *The Brothers Karamazov*, for example, contains timeless truths about such things as family ties, madness, and obsession. As Hemingway himself once stated, a thousand years makes economics a joke, but a work of art endures forever. My second meaning was that only to a work of fiction could the artist entrust his deepest, truest feelings, because there is always the escape clause, "But after all, it's only a story."

Hemingway took Gertrude Stein's advice to heart, and it helped shape everything he wrote. All his novels, and many of his short stories, contain a strong autobiographical element, and some could almost be considered pure autobiography. Every injury he sustained, every hurt he inflicted, every bit of guilt he felt for betrayal, infidelity, lack of loyalty, or his perceived failure as a son, father, or husband, eventually found its outlet in a piece of fiction. As well as the cathartic effect of writing, there is also the feeling that any hurt, no matter how intense, is actually worthwhile if it contributes to the creation of a piece of art. Most non-writers (especially the writer's family) find this attitude callous, but it is part of what makes an artist an artist.

* * *

Robert Ruark, writing about Hemingway after his suicide in 1961, said that one of the things he admired most was his ability to show "how it was," whether it was baiting a fishhook or describing a countryside. In this, Ruark was consciously or unconsciously echoing Hemingway himself, who praised Herman Melville's *Moby Dick* for its depiction of whales and life aboard the whaling ships as no mere history could. Great literature is rooted in journalism; not journalism of the daily "who, what, where" variety, but in the acute observation and description of real events and real people. Hemingway brought this understanding to his work, which he then combined with his own emotions.

Robert Ruark's greatest literary works are also rooted in the best kind of journalism — journalism that recreates reality in a larger and more solid way. Whether he was writing non-fiction (*Horn of the Hunter*), pure fiction based on fact (*Something of Value*) semi-fiction (*The Old Man and the Boy*) or virtual autobiography (*The Honey Badger*), Robert Ruark was practicing his lifelong craft of journalism. And, as a journalist, he was one of the finest America has ever produced. What these four books share is a remarkable ability to touch a chord in people many years after they were written, after the events of the day have long since faded from the headlines and all that is left is what Ruark created, as Hemingway put it, "round and whole and solid. Made, not described."

Literature as catharsis takes many forms, and writers use it in a wide variety of ways, not all of them pretty. A novel can be used as a thank-you note, a farewell, or a love letter. Just as easily, it can be a bludgeon and a means of getting even with a person, a town, or the world. One advantage of being a novelist is that you always have the last word, and a character based on a real person assumes a life of his own that often overshadows the model. Such a character lasts, it seems, forever — as long as there is one book left in print, as long as there is a Library of Congress. And so a moment of petulance can become an eternity of revenge. Hemingway, for example, created the thoroughly dislikable Robert Cohn in *The Sun Also Rises* from a model provided by the real-life

Harold Loeb, who never lived it down. Similarly, Karl in *Green Hills of Africa*, whose blind luck as a hunter continuously overshadows the protagonist's skill, was based on Hemingway's friend Charles Thompson.

Any author who writes about real places and bases his plots on actual events will unavoidably use friends and acquaintances as models for his characters. This is usually quite harmless, but it can backfire when people study the text searching for "their" character. Inevitably, they find characters they think are themselves and then either crow or cringe depending on whether these characters are admirable or despicable. Ruark encountered this problem in every major novel. It is generally conceded that Peter McKenzie, the hero of *Something of Value*, was modeled on professional hunter Harry Selby, Ruark's one-time close friend and guide on his first safari in 1951. Other characters in that book are actual people, portraying themselves so to speak. While the book itself caused a considerable stir because of the graphically shocking nature of the events it described — all brutally honest, according to those who were there — it did not foment a great deal of back-biting and jealousy by people wishing to see themselves in its pages. Selby may have squirmed a little, but no one could be insulted by being portrayed as Peter McKenzie who, although he had his faults, was an admirable man overall.

It was after Ruark had achieved nation-wide stature as a novelist with the publication of *Something of Value* that the problem became acute. His next novel, *Poor No More*, was published in 1959, and is unquestionably his weakest major effort. This book makes you wonder why he would take the time and make the considerable effort to write it. When it came out, Ruark told Harry Selby, very simply, "That is my autobiography." At that moment he may actually have meant it, although in a symbolic sense more than in the portrayal of actual people and events in an actual place and time. The hero, Craig Price, certainly has an early life that parallels Ruark's in some ways, although their paths diverge as soon as Price goes into business. The underlying theme, Price's determination to escape poverty regardless of what it takes, was also a driving force in Ruark's own life. No one would have objected to the novel had it not been for the auxiliary characters who were drawn from Ruark's childhood in Wilmington and Southport, and portrayed with a level of invective that is almost puzzling. At the beginning of the book, Ruark even acknowledges that many of the characters are drawn from real life, but "working out just who is who is bound to be difficult." His acquaintances back home in Wilmington, however, seemed to have no difficulty at all. According to Hugh Foster, at that point, "Many of them resolved not to talk to Bobby again." It was also at that point, perhaps, that Wilmington ceased to be "home" for Robert Ruark. He had paid off a debt, using the novel as his currency, and he no longer needed to go home again.

The stories of the Old Man notwithstanding, there was an essential rootlessness about Robert Ruark, a feeling of being an outsider, of not being accepted, and of having to prove that he belonged, not just once, but over and over. After *Poor No More*, his next novel was *Uhuru*, which returned him to Kenya, the land he loved above all. It is a far more complex work than *Something of Value*. It is a novel of nuances and shades of grey, rather than blacks and whites or rights and wrongs. Again, it is peopled with characters drawn from real life. The major family is based on his friend Eva Monley's own, who lived on a farm in Kenya. That was a harmless connection; a damaging one was naming Chief James Gichuru of the Kikuyu as a Mau Mau leader when in fact he had been cleared of any involvement. Gichuru's subsequent lawsuit led to Robert Ruark's final departure from Kenya in 1962. He never returned.

Once again, Ruark found himself without a country, so to speak. By that time he had cut himself off from North Carolina, abandoned New York, and was living in the town of Palamós, east of Barcelona on the Spanish Mediterranean coast. Kenya, however, was his spiritual home, the one place he had found worth defending, and he had defended it to his utmost. After *Uhuru*, however, that too was gone, and his personal life crumbled as well. His long-standing marriage to Virginia Webb Ruark ended in early 1963, and he was beset by financial and legal difficulties. It was then that he turned to writing the novel that is his most autobiographical, the distillation of everything he had learned in his life as a writer.

*The Honey Badger* was published in October, 1965, three months after his death. It is considered a posthumous novel — which it is, technically, although that term is usually reserved for a work published after the writer's death that he may or may not have ever intended to publish (Hemingway's *Islands in the Stream* and *The Garden of Eden* are prime examples). There is no doubt Ruark intended to publish the book; he just happened to die around the same time. The unfortunate result was that, since he was dead, critics who disliked him personally, or objected to his political views, felt free to assail him by attacking the book, and the reviews were almost universally negative. *Time, Newsweek* and *The New York Times* all savaged *The Honey Badger* with such abandon that one wonders if any of the critics actually read it — or, if they did, whether they thought about what they had read instead of about what they would say about it. If, as writers themselves, they had reflected upon its content, they would have seen beyond the surface story to the truths Ruark was presenting. The hero of the novel, Alec Barr, is Robert Ruark in everything but name. His childhood is Ruark's childhood, his family Ruark's family. They went to the same college, shipped out on the same tramp steamer, served in the same war, married the same woman. They had the same agent and drank with the same friends, hunted the same animals, and, insofar as can be determined, slept with many of the same women. That being the case, it is logical to assume that Alec Barr's innermost thoughts are, in reality, Robert Ruark's. And so it is in *The Honey Badger* that one can look not just for the facts about Ruark's life, but the truths as well.

* * *

A star that burns twice as bright lasts half as long. Robert Ruark was not even fifty years old when he died. His career as a famous writer lasted barely fifteen years. Yet he had a profound effect on many of the people he met, and an almost fatal effect on some of the women in his life as well as his close friends. Ruark's own terminal engagement with alcohol is legendary in Kenya, even today. His wife, Virginia, became just as much an alcoholic, to the point that he saw fit to upbraid her for it at a time when he himself was on a one-way trip to oblivion. Harry Selby, his close friend and professional hunter during the early years in Kenya, also became an alcoholic, and it took him many years to get over it according to those who know him well.

How much of this can be attributed to Ruark, and how much to the fashions of the day in which people drank more heavily than they do now, is difficult to assess. One facet of his character on which everyone who knew him agrees was his appetite for living, his exuberance and enthusiasm and desire to go places and do things. His close friend, Eva Monley, was quoted by Hugh Foster as calling Ruark "fat and lazy and wonderful." He may have been overweight, and many thought him wonderful, but no one in their right mind would ever describe him as lazy. His output, both literary and journalistic, was prodigious. He wrote reams, and he wrote it everywhere — on airplanes and tramp steamers, in hotel rooms and safari camps. If he shared any traits at all with Hemingway, they were his desire for life and his need to write. Near the beginning of *The Honey Badger*, an introspective Alec Barr surveys his bookshelves and the long row of titles "by Alexander Barr" and wonders, "When did I ever have time to make the trips, shoot the animals, drink the booze, chase the dames? Christ on a crutch, when did I have time to go to the post office to send the second carbon? Been a long time since I worried about the second carbon."

Sometimes it seemed as if Robert Ruark was everywhere at once — on a sheep station in Australia, fishing in New Zealand, bear hunting in Alaska, on a tramp steamer bound for Genoa, or on the fourth leg of a three-day plane trip to get from Rome to the Congo to cover the fighting. Constant travel and constant deadlines were his companions, and he spent hours hived up in hotel rooms with a shaky portable and a bottle of gin. The words that poured out of that portable became his newspaper columns, episodes of *The Old Man and the Boy*, or parts of novels. All of them display his propensity for living life at warp speed. But even when he was at his weariest, writing that he had logged two million air miles and it was time to take it easy and eschew deadlines, he had a knack for making you wish you were right there with him, tired, hungover, worn out, and happy.

This was, perhaps, one more way in which he shared something with Hemingway: To a great extent both lived dangerous lives on our behalf, and we glimpsed the way they lived through their writing. They were not just recording events; they were living them. They were not just covering the story; to a great extent they *were* the story. Hemingway set this example and killed a whole generation of writers who tried to live up to it, and it could be argued that Ruark was one of those who died trying. But even if that is so, he produced a powerful legacy before he left us, and very little of it is owed to Hemingway — not in style and not in content. If, in the end, he used literature as Hemingway did, in the way Hemingway learned from Gertrude Stein, then his works are that much more valuable for giving us the only real remaining insights into what made Ruark the Man into Ruark the Writer.

* * *

*Chapter One*

# LIFE AMONG THE GIANTS

Robert Ruark's childhood on the coast of North Carolina is often depicted as a Huck Finn-like idyll of hunting and fishing with his grandfather, reading the classics in the shade of a magnolia tree, and dragging a hand-cut Christmas tree home to a house redolent with the aromas of home-cooking and a crackling fire. Based on the tales that make up the series "The Old Man and the Boy" in *Field & Stream*, that is certainly the impression Ruark leaves — no doubt intentionally. But if those stories are read with an eye toward what is *not* there, then something quite different emerges.

Two people are missing: Ruark's father and mother. It is as if they do not exist, as if the only people close to Ruark the boy are his grandfather, Captain Ned Adkins, and his grandmother, Miss Lottie. The stories are the pleasant memories of childhood recalled forty years later, excluding all the nastiness and all the pain. In Robert Ruark's actual childhood, there was more than enough of both. He grew up in a turbulent family in a turbulent time, born as the First World War was beginning in Europe, living as a child through the '20s, watching those close to him die, and economic depression bring financial ruin to the people around him.

The facts of Ruark's family and childhood are a matter of record. He was born in Wilmington, North Carolina, on December 29, 1915. His full name was Robert Chester Ruark, Jr. Many years later, when his name was appearing regularly in major newspapers, and attached to books on the bestseller list of *The New York Times*, the name was pared. First he dropped the Jr., then the initial C. By the time of his death, and his greatest stature in the literary world, he was known simply as "Robert Ruark," and he had achieved the dubious distinction of his name being printed much larger on the dustjacket than the title of the book itself.

To non-literary people, that may seem an arcane distinction, but it carries considerable significance. It means the author himself is now bigger than his work, and that his name alone is sufficient to sell a book regardless of what lies between the covers. It is a distinction many authors think they would enjoy, but usually come to rue once they have achieved it. Generally, it means their lifestyle is upstaging their work. For Ruark, that is exactly what happened. As for the trimming of the byline — discarding the pompous "Jr." and the middle initial — any number of explanations are possible, from the factual (that he disliked his middle name) to the fanciful (that by getting rid of the Jr., he denied the existence of the Sr., a father he despised). And of course, some would point out that Ernest Hemingway never used his middle initial; therefore Ruark would not, either.

Perhaps there are elements of all of the above in his transition to Robert Ruark, literary giant. Certainly he disliked his middle name, despised his parents, and rejected his own origins. If Wilmington never accepted its most famous native son, for his part the native son outgrew the town and eventually came to hate the memory of it.

Readers of *The Old Man and the Boy* sometimes insist that the stories it contains are strict autobiography, and they point to Ruark's note at the beginning — "Anybody who reads this book is bound to realize that I had a real fine time as a kid" — as evidence of an idyllic childhood in pre-war, small-town America. There is some truth in that: Robert Ruark did not, by all accounts, have a terribly unhappy childhood in the sense of suffering dreadful privation or abuse. But it was hardly idyllic, either. For the first fifteen years of his life he was, in a sense, a fugitive, finding respite in make-believe, and that make-believe was reflected, many years later, in *The Old Man and the Boy*.

\* \* \*

Ruark's parents were Charlotte Adkins and Robert C. Ruark, Sr. Charlotte's parents were Edward Hall Adkins, a retired sea captain, and his wife, Charlotte (the Miss Lottie of the *Old Man* stories). On his father's side were his "literary" grandfather, Hanson Kelly Ruark, and his wife, Caroline. Grandfather Adkins lived in Southport, a small coastal town at the mouth of the Cape Fear River, and it was in his house that Ruark spent much of his time as a child. It was that house, with its magnolia tree and its wide veranda, that Ruark immortalized in his stories, and later repurchased when he had made it big as a writer in New York. The tale of how he bought back the house in 1949 is told in "The House Comes Home."

Ruark wrote of his childhood in three main works: *The Old Man and the Boy*, *Poor No More*, and *The Honey Badger*. As well, in a long interview in early 1964, quoted at length in Hugh Foster's biography, *Someone of Value*, Robert Ruark talks about his family and background. From these sources, it is possible to assemble a picture not just of the facts about his childhood, but his memories of it, the pain that it inflicted on him, and his reaction to it later in life. According to Foster, the Ruark family came from a lower social stratum in Wilmington and as such were not regarded as social equals by the "better" people. He might play with the other children, but neither he nor his parents would be invited into their homes on important occasions. This may well be true — certainly there is no evidence to refute it — but the real problems with Ruark's early life originated within his own family and his problems (he himself used the word "hatred") with his mother. The picture he paints, of a drug-addicted, domineering, nagging hypochondriac is completely at odds with Foster's description of Charlotte Adkins Ruark as a "gentle, sweet person."

If the recollections in *Old Man* are pleasant memories called up years later, the deliberate and bitter portrait of family life in *The Honey Badger* is the clear view of an observant man who has moved far from his origins and now sees his parents — "those people," as he refers to them — confined to mental institutions, running up bad debts, drinking, taking drugs, and flinging endless accusations of disloyalty, neglect, and generally unfilial behavior.

Ruark's picture of childhood is one of almost endless conflict: between his mother and father over who was head of the family (his mother won), between his mother and paternal grandmother over who was chatelaine of the house (again, his mother won when his grandmother died), and between Robert's sense of propriety and the ugly reality of his family having to take in boarders. The boarders were nurses in one story, teachers in another, and barely disguised prostitutes in Ruark's own mind.

Robert C. Ruark Sr. was a bookkeeper for a wholesale grocer. According to every portrait, he was a shy, diffident man with a receding hairline, unsure of himself and completely dominated first by his mother, then by his wife. Robert Ruark described him as "that strange father of mine," and said he was a lifelong drunk who never took a drink until he was forty-seven, then became an instant drunkard. With the onset of the Depression in 1929, he was fired from his job and never found steady employment again. He discovered, according to his son, that he preferred reading poetry and playing his father's violin; later he was diagnosed (incorrectly as it turned out) with tuberculosis and sent to the state sanitarium. He was later released and returned home, but spent the rest of his life as a depressive hypochondriac, alcoholic, and sometime drug addict.

This contradictory portrait of Robert, Sr., becomes understandable when you look at his origins. His father, Hanson Ruark, spent his life being nagged by his wife and taking refuge in books and whiskey; having learned to read and write late in life, Hanson then tried to make up for years of deprivation by compiling a large library and spending every waking moment buried in a book. He made a violin and taught himself to play it; he became Registrar of Deeds, but gave up steady work because he preferred reading. Which he did, to a background of Miss Caroline's nagging, until he died of cancer in 1927 at the age of seventy-eight. In the meantime, they had shared a house with their son and daughter-in-law, and Miss Caroline and Charlotte Ruark had fought a running battle to determine who would be top bitch in that particular kennel. Every encounter was a skirmish, every meal a battle, with Ruark's father "stammering as he asked for the biscuits" or his grandfather "dribbling food into his beard," until the menfolk could make their escape to the blessed silence of the woods where they could fish, or hunt quail, or read under the shade of a tree.

Such is the portrait Ruark paints in The Honey Badger, and insofar as the facts are known, such was his childhood. Under the circumstances, it is not surprising he would find refuge whenever possible in the house of his maternal grandparents in Southport. Miss Lottie, although portrayed rather sardonically, is never doused in vitriol, and while she nags the Old Man occasionally, as in "The Women Drive You to the Poolrooms," he generally manages to do as he likes. Throughout the *Old Man* stories Ruark's parents are mentioned only once or twice, and then just in passing. It is almost as if he was orphaned, and raised by his grandparents.

While Ned Adkins is the namesake of the Old Man, and provides the basis for his character, in reality the Old Man was a composite of the two grandfathers. Like Adkins, the Old Man was a retired sea captain who lived in Southport with Miss Lottie and was a devoted hunter and fisherman. But, like Hanson Ruark, he was also bookish, intellectual, and introspective.

Hanson Kelly Ruark died in 1927, when Robert was twelve; his maternal grandmother, Miss Lottie, died the following year, and Ned Adkins in early 1930. When Adkins died, the bank called the mortgage on the Southport house. About the same time the Depression struck, and Robert Sr. lost his job. Then came the tuberculosis episode. Meanwhile, his mother contracted measles, which gave rise to asthma, for which she began taking morphine, which grew, in turn, into a "full-blown addiction." To make ends meet they took in boarders, and the boarders — young women of imaginative means — took in work of another kind. As young Robert saw it, the whole thing was a desecration of his childhood and his home.

* * *

Robert's paternal grandmother, Caroline, may have been a nagging woman, as he later wrote, but given his description of Hanson Ruark, she appears to have had more than sufficient reason. Whatever her faults, she taught her grandson to read at the age of three. This is not a skill widely admired by other boys, especially boys who are older and bigger, and Robert acquired a reputation as a bookworm. Such a reputation carries with it the necessity of disabusing others, usually with fists, and Robert's childhood was an endless stream of encounters with children he describes as "louts who liked to turpentine cats when they weren't breaking windows or beating up colored kids."

Like many other children with an inborn academic bent, Robert took refuge in isolation. With his grandfather as a tutor, he learned to shoot and fish and became a "hardened recluse" by the time he was twelve. He spent as much time as he could off in the woods by himself with a book or wandering with a shotgun and a bird dog. Together, he and his grandfather built a small boat, and Robert would ship out by himself to become "Captain Blood, Columbus, or Vasco da Gama," poling through the swamps. Ruark spent his childhood avoiding his family, and in the course of it learned how to be happy by himself. He also learned to put up a wall to shield himself, not least of all from his mother. If Ruark's father was ineffectual, his mother was anything but.

"My mother would have made a good lesbian, if lesbians had been popular in those days," he recalled in his 1964 taped interview. "She rode astride, she was great big and hearty. We declared war on each other as soon as I was able to walk. Mother had a lot of strange ideas; she wanted to be a doctor. She was well-educated, had taught school..."

In *The Honey Badger*, Alec Barr's mother is described thus: "Perhaps the only person Alec Barr had ever really thoroughly hated was his mother." And thus: "She had been a big hearty woman who prided herself on the fact that she rode astride when proper ladies rode side-saddle. She worked when proper ladies did not work." Emma Barr and Charlotte Ruark are not just interchangeable, they are the same person. They are Robert Ruark's mother seen by her son through forty years of bitterness.

Robert Ruark was an only child, but it was not for lack of trying. What he described as the "regular confinements" invariably resulted in still-born children for Charlotte — three brothers lost, according to Ruark in 1964. All three were "mangled with high forceps that hurt Ma as well" and contributed, he said, to her morphine addiction. One thing that puzzled Ruark was how these regular pregnancies even came about, given the atmosphere of sexual warfare that pervaded the Ruark household. Presumably his father, diffident to a fault, simply did what he was told, when he was told.

The status of the Ruark family as outsiders in Wilmington may have been, as Hugh Foster would have it, because they lacked the proper bloodlines of the town's upper class. But Charlotte's overall behavior —

her nonconformist ways, her drug addiction, the behavior of her "board-ers" — would certainly not have endeared her to the upper crust of Wilmington or any other conservative small town of the 1920s. By all accounts, the Adkins family, headed by grandfather Ned, was highly respected and well educated, and being a sea captain in a coastal town is a position that carries considerable social status. Ruark emphasizes, time after time in the *Old Man* stories, how Ned Adkins was widely respected, how people looked up to him, listened to him, and deferred to him. He was not wealthy but he was not poor either, at least not until the end of his life when his illness had drained away much of the family money. And, in "All He Left Me Was The World," the Boy describes how Adkins' funeral procession stretched for many blocks through the town and included everyone who was anyone, black and white. This is not a description of a social outcast.

Young Robert and his parents were, however. It is pointless to specu-late exactly what made them so, but it is significant that, in *The Honey Badger*, Alec Barr says that his mother's behavior caused him such embarassment as a child that he showed little enthusiasm for athletics or any of the "other social gatherings of the young." In all likelihood, that was Alec Barr speaking for Robert Ruark. His mother was the most influential figure in his young life. Ned Adkins and Hanson Ruark may have taught him what he wanted to be, but Charlotte Ruark made him what he was.

\* \* \*

So Robert Ruark spent the first fifteen years of his life in the towns of Wilmington and Southport, with occasional forays farther afield with his grandfather. He hunted quail and deer, as well as wild turkeys, ducks and geese. He fished in the Cape Fear River and along the coastal beaches. As he tells it, he was raised by a variety of men, both black and white, and many are lovingly described in *The Old Man and the Boy*. This was the Deep South, post-Civil War, pre-Civil Rights. While there may have been deeply entrenched inequalities, that did not preclude whites and blacks recognizing each other's good qualities and getting along well on a day-to-day basis. According to Ruark, his grandfather Ned was loved and respected by everyone in town, both black and white, and when he died his funeral procession stretched for half a mile. Robert grew up playing with "colored kids" and hunting quail on sharecroppers' property where they reserved their "buhds" for "their white folks" — meaning Ned and young Robert.

It would take a person of abnormally heightened racial sensitivity to find anything racist in Ruark's descriptions of these black people, although the terminology is not politically acceptable by today's morbidly sensitive standards. Some might read the dialogue and find evidence of Uncle Tom stereotypes, because they have never listened to the way folks actually talk. A stereotype, like a cliché, begins life as a recognized truth and becomes a cliché because it is so truthful. Ruark's fond feelings for, and his writings about, the black people of his home town are important to keep in mind because of later accusations when he began writing serious pieces about emerging Africa. For someone who disagrees with a political view, it is always convenient to lay charges of racism, and Ruark faced more than his share. His childhood experiences with black people in North Carolina — some of whom worked for his family cooking and cleaning, others who were friends like the share-cropper Abner — were evoked many years later in a series of columns he wrote for Scripps-Howard at the time of the civil-rights movement, race riots, and school integration. As a Southerner then living in New York City, he was admirably placed to see both sides of the issue, and there is no doubt that he disapproved of segregation on every level — humanitarian, political, and practical. This did not mean he was color-blind, nor that he viewed relations between the races through rose-colored glasses, nor denied the realities that had given rise to many of the problems in the first place. Perhaps his real difficulty lay in the fact that he was writing from a vantage point of first-hand knowledge, with all the contradictions that brings, rather than pontificating from the easy certainties of an ivory tower on how far-away people should behave.

Ned Adkins died when Robert was fifteen. Not particularly well-off to begin with, the family endured serious hardship because Adkins' last illness, cancer, had eaten up what financial resources he had. When he died, the bank foreclosed. The house in Southport with its magnolia tree passed into other hands. If Robert Ruark had any other close friends in town, he does not mention them. A year earlier the New York stock market had crashed, and economic depression now enshrouded the country. Robert Ruark Sr. lost his job, and the family was forced to take in the boarders who Robert later viewed with such a jaundiced eye.

Like many children who learn to read early on, and use reading as an escape, Ruark found he was able to glide through school effortlessly. While his bookish bent may have caused him social problems with other children, it paid off academically, and he graduated from high school early. Already he had a burning urge to shake the dust of Wilmington from his heels, and the first step to fame and fortune, as he saw it, was a university degree. Over his mother's objections, he enrolled at the University of North Carolina in Chapel Hill and began his college career when he was just fifteen years old.

❀ ❀ ❀

*Chapter Two*

# THE UNIVERSITY OF NORTH CAROLINA

If Ruark's later writing is to be believed, he left for college with no clear idea of what he wanted to do in life beyond the simple desire to make money. Coming from an impoverished family, in a poor part of the country, with no family business to inherit or professional tradition to adhere to, he went to Chapel Hill with the idea that "pants were unimportant if you had some, but very, very important if you did not," and that in the business world to come, a man without a degree would stand "pantless in the halls of commerce." It was a very perceptive view for 1930, when even high school graduation was a notable feat in small southern towns, but Ruark had already set his sights high. He may not have known exactly what he wanted to become, but he certainly knew what he did not.

The first obstacle, however, was to get through four years of college on almost no money. His family was chronically unable to contribute, and he set off that first year with fifty dollars in his pocket, the proceeds of a summer spent working in a parking lot.

The picture he later painted of Chapel Hill in 1930, first in *Poor No More*, later in *The Honey Badger*, is both loving and resentful — loving in the sense of what it was and what it represented, but resentful in that much as he might want to, he did not fit in there any more than he had in Wilmington. First, he was very young. Even in 1930, starting college at fifteen was unusual. Second, he was poverty-stricken, yet he was forced to rub elbows with students who were going to college riding on their fathers' bankrolls. The children of wealthy people have a way of looking down on those who are not, and young Ruark felt the full weight of their disapproval. He managed to get into a fraternity, but then paid his dues by waiting on tables at meals. He held down one or two jobs, pinching pennies endlessly, enduring humiliating interviews with the dean, pleading for one more student loan — going through college, as he put it, on one threadbare suit.

That, at least, is the picture of the Chapel Hill that Ruark's alter ego, Alec Barr, attended. It is a poignant picture, to say the least, but not completely true in Ruark's own case. He was not rolling in money, but nor was he starving. Alec Barr, having left home (Kingtown, South Carolina) never looked back; in the novel, he goes home for a visit one time with a classmate and flees after being humiliated by his mother's behavior, never to return. Ruark looked around him at Chapel Hill and saw a bastion of privilege; he saw, even in "the teeth of the Depression," students from wealthy families driving cars and drinking mint juleps on the veranda. He heard, from a distance, the music of Hal Kemp and Ray Noble. Although he formed a couple of lasting friendships at Chapel Hill, Ruark's college career only deepened his already intense desire to make it big and then rub everyone's nose in it.

The question was, make it big at what? Medicine and the law were equally unattainable given the shortage of funds. Teaching was, as he put it, too long a road with not enough money at the end. And so he worked his way through the first three years cramming in as many courses as he could, studying when others were socializing, working when they were relaxing. His natural ability in English garnered him an "A" in a course whose professor had never before given an "A" to anyone "including Thomas Wolfe."

\* \* \*

In truth, Robert Ruark had a somewhat checkered college career, in the sense that he was nagged by money problems, family problems, and the demands of fitting into a society where he felt like an outsider.

Ruark had completed one year of university when the financial situation at home became so severe that he was forced to drop out and return to Wilmington. There he found things going from bad to worse.

By 1931, only one of his grandparents, his paternal grandmother Caroline, was still alive; she was living with his parents, was very ill, and required constant, expensive medical care. For their part his parents continued their feckless ways with drugs and alcohol. There were still boarders in the house, which had been expanded into a "nursing home" and now included convalescents. Ruark missed one semester, then went back to university.

Charlotte Ruark, who is at best an enigmatic character in Ruark's life, decided she wanted to be near her son and took a room in a boarding house in Chapel Hill. She became a source of eternal embarassment. Occasionally Ruark would be forced to stay with her, sleeping on a cot in the front hall of the boarding house.

Ruark had become a member of a fraternity and was living, for the most part, in the fraternity house. According to Hugh Foster, he acquired a reputation for drinking and carousing, and even helped with the home-made gin when the legitimate supplies ran out. In interviews later in life, Ruark claimed he made money hustling anything that moved, including women for his fraternity brothers. How much of that is true, and how much is nostalgic fantasy, is impossible to determine. It is apparent Ruark was neither as ascetic nor withdrawn as Alec Barr in *The Honey Badger*, but he was not a highly social student either, mainly because of financial constraints.

In his fourth year, an event occurred that determined the course of his life: He met a girl and fell in love. Her name was Nan Norman; she was a year behind him and financially considerably better off, coming from a well-to-do family in the western part of North Carolina. She even had her own car. Since she was a journalism major, Ruark decided to sit in on her journalism classes, which were run by a professor named "Skipper" Coffin. Ruark wrote a couple of trial articles for Coffin, one of which the professor sold on his behalf to the newspaper in Raleigh for twelve dollars. It was Ruark's first income as a freelance writer.

Here again, the events of Ruark's life and those described in *The Honey Badger* are so close in all their details that the novel is almost autobiography: Nan Norman becomes Fran Mayfield, Skipper Coffin becomes Skipper Henry, and the twelve-dollar check becomes twenty dollars. And, oh yes — Alec Barr loses his virginity to Miss Mayfield in the bushes one balmy spring evening, whereas there is no indication Ruark was so blessed. In fact, there is ample evidence that while Ruark may have been in love with Miss Norman, she was definitely not in love with him. His subsequent portrayal of Fran Mayfield as a half-breed coed with "decidedly nymphomaniac tendencies" may have been an effort by Ruark to distance the fictional character from her real-life counterpart. More likely, Fran may have been the weapon through which Ruark, thirty years later, finally got even for being brushed off.

The end result of his relationship with Nan Norman and, through her, Professor Coffin, was Ruark's decision to become a writer. He would begin by going into the newspaper business. Reporting, advised the professor, taught a writer the nuts and bolts of the business, how to meet deadlines and write under pressure, and allowed him to eat while he learned. Unfortunately, 1935 was not a good time to look for a newspaper job; the Depression was weighing upon the country in full force, and most newspapers were laying off people, not taking on new ones — especially people with no experience. Professor Coffin, however, had at least a partial solution: He arranged a job for Ruark on a small country weekly in Hamlet, North Carolina. It did not pay much — only ten dollars a week — but it offered one great advantage: the opportunity to learn every aspect of the newspaper business, from the ground up.

Again, the parallels with *The Honey Badger* are almost absolute. The Hamlet, North Carolina *News-Messenger* became the weekly in Center City, N.C. Ruark later quoted Professor Coffin as saying "the owner don't wash but once a week, got bad breath and yellow teeth, the town is owned lock, stock and barrel by the Seaboard Railway." Ruark became managing editor, advertising manager, ace reporter, and subscription salesman. He covered council meetings, wrote editorials, and then set them in type himself. Skipper Henry tells Alec Barr there are just as many stories in a small town as there are in a big city, and says he will learn how to hush up abortions and overlook rushed wedding dates. According to Ruark, that is exactly what happened. Hamlet may not have been the "little Sodom, a solid concentration of small-bore evil" Skipper Henry described to Barr, but it was certainly an education.

Ruark lasted three months before he quit and headed for Washington in search of a real job on a real newspaper.

In *The Honey Badger*, Alec Barr quits because Fran Mayfield jilts him and marries someone else; he goes on a short binge, then heads for Washington in disillusionment. Ruark, on the other hand, claimed he quit because of "a problem with the daughter of a railway engineer" and said he got out of Hamlet one step ahead of the enraged father. He did indeed end up in Washington, but instead of working for a newspaper he lied his way into a job with the Works Progress Administration. The WPA was a creation of the federal government under Franklin D. Roosevelt's New Deal. Ruark claimed to be an accountant. He was hired and sent to work on a project in Florida. When his employers discovered a few months later that his accounting skills were nonexistent, he was fired. This episode does not show up in *The Honey Badger*; instead, Alec Barr leaves Center City, hitch-hikes east, and gets a job on a tramp steamer — which is exactly what Ruark did after leaving the WPA. Again, there are contradictory accounts of how it came about, depending on whether one believes Ruark's interviews or his written recollections.

In the 1964 interview, he says he got his job on the S.S. *Sundance* by challenging the first mate and fighting him to a standstill. Yet in his *Old Man and the Boy* episode "Life Among The Giants," he credits his cousin Victor Price, an executive for the shipping company. In 1936, seamen's jobs were harder to come by than reporting jobs, the docks were ruled by the unions, and desperate master mariners were shipping out as ordinary seamen. As well, Ruark was a college graduate — definitely not an advantage in the blue-collar world of merchant shipping. His later story of challenging the mate to a fight has a strange ring to it, much like Ernest Hemingway's legend of riding the rods during his youth, hopping trains and living in hobo camps. Hemingway never actually did those things, nor did he ship out on the Great Lakes freighters, moving "as a boy in the company of men" and knowing how to use a knife to kill, if necessary, not to be "interfered with," as he claimed many years later. Ruark's suggestion that a kindly relative ran interference, helped him get the job, and kept a benevolent eye on him as he roamed the world before the mast rings with considerably more truth.  At the time, Robert Ruark was barely twenty years old.

The *Sundance* became, in a sense, a third *alma mater*, after the University of North Carolina and the Hamlet, N.C., *News-Messenger*.  It taught Ruark a great deal about real life.  The ship was captained by a man who had, from Ruark's description, many of the endearing personal qualities of such other great marine executives as Queeg, Ahab, and Bligh.  Ruark's stories of shoveling sheep manure in the hold, of cleaning the paintwork with lye, and of standing eight-hour watches across the freezing Atlantic show up over and over, in the *Old Man* series, in *Poor No More*, and finally in *The Honey Badger*, where:

> *(Alec Barr) wound up eventually in Hamburg, Germany (and) reflected, as he drank with the painted women in the Grosse Freiheit, in the company of two Russian female sailors and a Negro mess cook, that in one way he was following Skipper Henry's advice.  He was seeing life, and if you were going to be a writer, life was something you had to see.*

\* \* \*

*Chapter Three*

# LEARNING THE ROPES

The newspaper business gets into your blood and, once there, is there forever. As Robert Ruark put it many years later, long after he had departed from the business of daily newspapers, "You never really get that reporting monkey off your back." Once a reporter, always a reporter.

Newspapers are a magic business — never just a job, never nine to five. It is a magic compounded of many things. When you look back, you remember it in terms of the different sounds and smells. You crawl into work an hour before dawn, on three hours sleep with a quart of harsh black coffee the only thing standing between you and oblivion, and as soon as you walk through the door you can feel it. There is the smell of hot linotype, a metallic, burning odor that seeps into every corner of the building, but always seems to be strongest in the stairwells. There is the quiet clack-clack of the linotype machines, as their operators key in copy and see it come out in little lines of type set in metal as bright as a new dime. Most of all, there is the sound — the feel, really — of the press as it begins to roll. Wherever you are in the building, you can feel it start up, slowly at first, beginning as a tremor through the floor and ending as a pounding throb when you can't hear yourself think in the press room, and the newly printed papers are rolling up the conveyor belt a thousand a minute. And then there is the smell of those newspapers, the first ones off the press, in black, damp ink, that the copy boy grabs and carries up to the city room at a run.

No other business ever combined so many sensual aspects, building up to the pounding climax of the press run and the delivery trucks backed up to the loading dock with their engines running.

It is a business built on adrenalin. The adrenalin of late-breaking stories and tight deadlines, of shouting editors, flying typewriters, occasional fistfights. Of politicians invading the newsroom, threatening libel suits. Of weeping women, some better dressed than others. Of the smell of fresh paste and tired photographic fix, seeping out under the darkroom door. Of idealistic young men, and tired old has-beens, and crusading editors, and money-grubbing publishers, all crammed in together with one object only: To beat everybody else to the punch — for the glory of it, for the money, or just out of long unbreakable habit.

Nowhere else do you find so many conflicting emotions, so many different ambitions. No one ever goes into the newspaper business with the intent of staying in it. To do what? Become a copy editor some day? A dead-end thankless job. To run the place? Who would want to? To become publisher, and maybe run for office, and see and be seen at all the cocktail parties in town? Never happen. And anyway, to a real newspaperman that is an unworthy ambition. No, the first and truest ambition of any young, would-be reporter is to see his name in type, in those little agate letters, where it says "By So-and-So, Staff Writer." But that is just the beginning.

Scratch any reporter, in any newsroom in the world, and what you find is a novelist, or a playwright, or a poet. At the very least, you find a foreign correspondent just itching to dodge bullets and sit in a sweltering tiny office with the flies buzzing, typing the words "Dateline: Khartoum." The thing about the newspaper business is that everyone loves it, but everyone is just there for a short time, on their swift way somewhere else — up, down, or out.

It is an ephemeral business. The old joke is that today's top story is being used to wrap fish tomorrow, or to line a birdcage. There is no permanence in newspapers, not for the stories and not for the people who own the bylines.

In the 1930s, the newspaper business was at its all-time peak in America. Television was not even a rumor, and, while it was widespread, radio had not established itself as a serious news medium. Newspapers were the source of news, opinion, analysis, and entertainment. Every major city had at least two, and some had four or five. There were morning papers and evening papers, and all of them had several editions, and so the deadlines just kept on coming and the newspaper hawkers in the streets were always unwrapping a fresh bundle. New York City was the major newspaper town, but Chicago and Los Angeles were not far behind. Washington was a special case. It was a company town, really, a small town at heart, and in the 1930s, still a small, segregated Southern town, regardless of what anyone said. Except for the federal government, there was really nothing there. Hamlet, N.C., had the Seaboard Railway, and Washington, D.C., had the federal government; the difference was merely one of scale. In the economic disaster of the 1930s, however, the federal government was just about the best kind of company to have running a town, because at least it had money coming in, and its employees were not likely to be laid off in waves.

There were a half-dozen newspapers in Washington then. The *Star*, an evening paper, was known as "Washington's official mother-in-law." It was a staid, establishment paper that erred on the side of pomposity and rarely stooped to compete with the lesser papers, at least overtly. The *Post* was a morning paper and, in those pre-Watergate days, did not particularly stand out. The *Daily News* was an afternoon rag, a brash young upstart that took equal glee in enraging the police commission or tweaking the nose of its afternoon rival, the boring old *Star*.

Robert Ruark arrived in town in the fall of 1936, not yet twenty-one years old. He had a college degree, three voyages to Europe under his belt, and a knowledge of the newspaper business gleaned from three months of putting out, singlehanded, the Hamlet, N.C. *News-Messenger*. It was not a resume that was going to batter down any managing editor's door. And so, like just about everyone else in the newspaper business in those halcyon days, Robert Ruark started at the bottom: He was hired on by the Washington *Post* as a "detail boy."

\* \* \*

"If minus-nothing were to be perpetually multiplied by ten," Ruark later wrote, "the sum still would not adequately connote the position of a detail boy on a large metropolitan newspaper."

A detail boy (sometimes known as a "proof boy") is the advertising department equivalent of a copy boy. In any other business, they would simply be called "office boys." Even that term has disappeared in the modern world, replaced by weird designations like "intern" or "trainee." One advantage of the term "office boy" is that, since it is so demeaning and devoid of status, the holder of such a title is determined to either move up or move out as quickly as possible.

Traditionally, a copy boy — literally, someone who runs copy from the reporters to the copy desk to the composing room — is a first-step position for a young man (or woman) starting out in the newspaper business and aspiring to make "staff." The duties are menial at best: mixing paste, back in the days when paste was used to cobble stories and layouts together, fetching coffee for the editors on the rim, running the thousand errands back and forth between the city room, where the reporters and editors toiled, and the composing room, where their words were set in type.

A copy boy has one other duty: Every day, it is his job to be in the press room when the presses start to roll, to grab the first ink-wet pristine newspapers as they come marching up the conveyor belt and get them up to the editorial offices as quickly as possible. For one fleeting moment each day, as he comes through the door into the city room and every head turns to look at him expectantly, the copy boy feels like he has a job of supreme importance. That, and the adrenalin rush you get, standing there, when the press room foreman pushes the button and the presses lumber smoothly into motion, vibrating every rivet in the building, is what makes being a copy boy worthwhile. But that's *all* there is.

A detail boy, on the other hand, has all the menial aspects of such a job and none of the glamor. The most you can look forward to is being promoted to advertising salesman. For Robert Ruark, that was reason enough to hand over the detail boy's job and move into a copy-boy position as quickly as possible. It meant taking a two-dollar a week pay cut, from fourteen dollars down to twelve — a huge chunk of income in 1936. But at least it put Ruark where the editorial action was, and even if he was not immediately in line for promotion to a staff reporter's job, it did allow him the consolation of knowing he was rubbing elbows with what he wanted to be.

* * *

When Ruark arrived in Washington, he moved in with Jim Queen, his old friend from college, and four other young men who shared an apartment. Queen was in transit, working in Washington temporarily while preparing for law school. Ruark settled into the typical existence of a single, broke young man without family, living on a scant income that was totally absorbed by the bare necessities of living.

Having taken a pay cut to move from the advertising department to the city room, he then had to make the toughest leap in the newspaper business — getting his first reporting job.

In the old days, it seemed, there was an inviolable rule that copy boys were never routinely promoted to staff reporter. Once you made reporter, of course, the sky was the limit. You would be shifted from news to sports and back again, sent to city hall or the White House, assigned to cover fires or congressional hearings. Occasionally, a reporter would be put on the rim for three months of penance, coping with other reporters' grammatical shortcomings, then be back on the street chasing fire engines. A reporter even moved, seemingly effortlessly, from one paper to another, burning a bridge one day, rebuilding it the next. To a great degree it was a democratic business of nomads, roving restlessly from paper to paper and town to town. And once you had been a reporter, there was little practical limit on what you could do, barring, of course, your own lack of talent or predeliction for alcohol. But getting to be a reporter the first time — *that* was tough.

Ruark's first step was leaving the advertising department at the *Post* and signing on as a copy boy with the *Evening Star*. The *Star* was renowned for never, ever, promoting a copy boy to staff, and Ruark moved from there to the *News*. Hugh Foster says he was fired, but Ruark insists that, technically, he was not. According to Ruark, he had a disagreement with one of the owners over whether "a quest for a certain type of dog biscuit constituted journalism," and he was out-voted.

The usual approach an ambitious copy boy would take to get the editor's attention, and perhaps someday be promoted, was to volunteer for all kinds of assignments outside normal working hours — small-time news events the paper did not have enough staff people to cover. This included everything from meetings of the Optimists' Club to house-league baseball games. Then, the copy boy would return to the newsroom and, working at someone else's typewriter, sweat over the story long into the night trying to make it letter-perfect before it came up for critical assault. If he was lucky, the next day he might see two or three column inches in print, and some of it might actually be the words he wrote.

The Washington *Daily News* was different than other papers of the time in that it regularly promoted copy boys to staff; in fact, it viewed the job as a training program for would-be reporters. After a few months on the job, Robert Ruark was duly promoted and given his first full-time reporting job in the sports department.

In *The Honey Badger*, Alec Barr follows a tougher route (although the trail from the *Post* to the *Star* to the *News* is identical) and finally gets his big break when a major fire erupts on Christmas Eve and he happens to be the only person in the newsroom available to cover it. This kind of situation often actually happened, although the formula has found its way into so many stories and movies that it is a cliché. Ruark's own progress was less spectacular.

As he later admitted, he went into sports reporting at a decided disadvantage, since he had played very few sports as a youngster and had little interest in baseball, football, or boxing (his alleged fight with the first mate of the *Sundance* notwithstanding).

It is a truism of the newspaper business that, if you want to find the best writers, the place to look is the sports department. Sports is the one section of the newspaper where writers are encouraged to be colorful and imaginative in their presentation of the facts. The best writers often become columnists, where they are given even greater leeway. At the same time, there are the ever-present constraints of space, so a sports writer is required to be colorful and imaginative, yet still get all the facts into a very limited number of words. As a training ground for a magazine writer, newspaper columnist, or novelist, a newspaper sports department is better than any university. This is especially true if the sports editor is a good one, and Robert Ruark was uncommonly lucky in that regard: His first editor was a man named Rocky Riley, who was reputed to be, in the newspaper world of Washington in the 1930s, the very best around.

It is difficult to overstate the lasting influence a good editor can have on a young writer. Habits become ingrained early, never to be broken or discarded. For example, at one time I was working for a small daily and stringing for a big-city newspaper, hoping to land a reporting job. I crawled home from some sort of public meeting in the small hours, after writing the story for my own newspaper, and sat down to write a couple of paragraphs to file, dateline "Oakville (Special)." In newspaper parlance, (Special) is as opposed to (Staff), although sometimes it means a story is "Special To," and no one else has it. These little shorthand messages are a hold-over from the early wire-service days and are significant to people in the business, if not to the average reader. At any rate, I filed the story, stating that "over a hundred people had turned out," and staggered off to bed. It was four-thirty in the morning. At exactly six-oh-five the telephone jangled, I groped it to my ear, and a voice barked,"More than, you idiot, more than!" and hung up with a bang. To this day I always write "More than a hundred..."

By coincidence, I got my own start in the newspaper business as a detail boy in the advertising department of a medium-sized daily and spent my off-hours freelance sports reporting. The sports editor was a man named Lew Fournier, who went on to fame, if not fortune, on the copy desk of a major daily. He was a lousy writer but a first-rate editor who demanded strict adherence to all the arcane rules of daily journalism, and to this day, more than thirty years later, I can pick out my own stylistic quirks that I owe to him.

In Robert Ruark's case, Rocky Riley was like a refugee from central casting, headed for an off-Broadway production of *The Front Page*. As Ruark later told it, Riley wore his hat in the office, so Ruark wore his. Riley talked out of the side of his mouth, so Ruark did likewise. Most important, Riley had certain immutable rules Ruark did not dare break for fear of wearing Riley's typewriter as a fedora, and it stood him in good stead for many years of newspaper writing.

Reading a newspaper from the 1930s today, much of the writing seems stilted, slangy, abrupt, and dated. Yet most of the basic rules are still good. Perhaps the most important principle was a deep distrust of adjectives. Ernest Hemingway came up through the same school, albeit a little earlier, and learned his craft first on the Kansas City *Star*, later with the Toronto *Daily Star* and some European wire services. Hemingway's rule, and the basis of his terse writing style, was that adjectives and adverbs waste space. A writer is better to find the right noun, and couple it to a tough verb, than to try to paint a picture with a dozen adjectives and adverbs. This was the Rocky Riley school of journalism as well, and he forced Ruark to follow it to the letter, on pain of, well, pain.

Outside the office, Ruark applied a "harsh hand on his own rein" as well. In his copy-boy days, he had skipped lunch, and occasionally breakfast, to save the money for a matched set of Somerset Maugham, a second-hand dictionary, and a library card. If he came upon a word he did not know, he immediately looked it up and "memorized the tiny type." A vast vocabulary is not a necessity for good writing; in fact, it can be a drawback. But a writer has to know the nuances of each word in order to avoid using the wrong one. A sidebar to the Hemingway school was what Ezra Pound called the *mot juste*, the belief that, in English, there are no synonyms, and that in any given situation there is only one word that is absolutely correct. If a writer believes this and applies it, it forces him to search for exactly the right word and, to a great extent, makes adjectives and adverbs superfluous. If you have the right noun and the right verb, you do not need to embellish.

As well as his use of English, Ruark worked on his knowledge of sports. He borrowed books on baseball, boxing, football, and any other realm he might be asked to cover, cramming a knowledge of the arcane aspects of games he did not know firsthand.

While Riley ruled the sports department with an iron pencil, the life of a sports reporter outside the office was not without its moments. Sports writing is a fun way to make a living, by and large, and Ruark entered into the spirit of it as if he were auditioning for a role in *Guys & Dolls*. This led to one celebrated incident resulting in Ruark's first taste of being a celebrity. He got into a fistfight — well, not actually a fistfight, but almost one — with a professional baseball player.

Louis Norman "Buck" Newsom was a pitcher for the Detroit Tigers — a hefty Southern lad who chewed tobacco and drank beer and had a largely unremarkable career, except for this one year when he was compiling a great record and leading the Tigers to a pennant. One night, returning to his hotel, Newsom got into an altercation with a considerably older man. Ruark wrote a scathing article about Newsom. Newsom responded by letting it be known that if Ruark showed up in the clubhouse, he would be eating his words, and the paper they were printed on. Hearing of this, Ruark gulped and headed down to face Newsom, figuring that getting it over with was the only way out.

What followed was a comedy of deliberate errors, with Newsom blustering, Ruark taking a swing at him, a couple of other Tigers stepping in to save Ruark, and all of it witnessed by a reporter from another paper. The next thing anyone knew, the *News* was running a picture of their young employee, posed like a heavyweight with his dukes up, ready to take on all comers. The whole episode was a tempest in a concocted teapot, but it gained Ruark a little temporary fame and a taste for being in the limelight. A decade later, when he was a successful syndicated columnist, Ruark summed up the whole affair: "Chiefly, it richened my life because all the rest of it I am allowed to remember that in my youth I once had the temerity, while stark sober, to take a cuff at 230 pounds of successful athlete. It is a beautiful memory, and I will never have to be brave again."

* * *

Ruark's five years on the sports desk at the *News* made him into a competent, self-confident — and cocky — newspaper reporter. Eight years later, when he published *One for the Road*, an anthology of his postwar syndicated columns, the dedication read, "This One Is For Rocky Riley," and the foreword was titled "Life With Riley."

"I was the nineteenth straight cub to pass through Mr. Riley's orbit in something under a year," Ruark wrote. "The other eighteen are now happily engaged in selling shoes, peddling marijuana, speculating in the market, and other salubrious, remunerative pursuits. Mr. Riley was not the easiest man to work for...

"Rocky was an intolerant, intemperate, wonderful man. He had a voice like a foghorn with the croup. When he was exasperated, which was often, he would smack his desk with the flat of his hand. Then he would scream like a tortured horse. Rocky was the greatest free-style screamer I ever heard. He screamed at me for four years."

If Galbert Rockford Riley was all of those things, he was also a great teacher of tough journalism. He allowed no self-congratulation, no simpering praise. Self-indulgence, the great trap of conceited writers, bought you a one-way ticket off the staff, and he believed a good journalist never stopped snooping and never stopped learning.

"He was a great teacher," Ruark said. "He was extremely generous with his own time, and even more so with mine. On one occasion he flung the same story back at me seven times, and the edition went fifteen minutes late, because he was dissatisfied with my handling of the piece. He hated fancy words and windy circumlocution. He said florid adjectives were for the exclusive use of Henry L. Mencken.

"For four years Riley held a daily catechism class, after the first edition, during which time the chinks in my newspaper knowledge were painfully explored and filled, much as a dentist calks a leaking tooth."

Aside from his rules on grammar and diction, Riley laid down a few basics on how a reporter should behave. Today, all university journalism courses include classes on journalistic ethics, but you would be hard-pressed to come up with a better, or more succinct, set of rules than Ruark put into the mouth of Skipper Henry as he sent his protegé, Alec Barr, out into the world:

*There ain't but a few rules to this racket. Don't write what you don't know. Don't start out to write it until it's clear in your head and you know what you're writing. Don't listen to anything off the record; it only confuses you. Don't rat on your sources. Don't take no cheap little gifts from nobody. Take it easy on the booze, and kiss no man's ass, however big he is. That's about all. You already know how to spell.*

\* \* \*

If Rocky Riley was pivotal in Ruark's professional life, there was a young lady who played just as important a role in his personal life.

Virginia Webb was the daughter of Polly and Benton Webb of Chevy Chase, a suburb of Washington. The Webbs were a respectable, middle-class family. Benton Webb had a successful printing business in Washington, and if they were not socially top-rung, they were not far below it. Most of all, to Robert Ruark, they represented everything he craved, everything he had not known as a boy growing up in Wilmington, with a drug addict for a mother and humiliation at every turn.

Ruark met Virginia through his best friend, Jim Queen, who had been dating her off and on until he prepared to leave Washington to return to law school. By all accounts, including Alec Barr's introduction to Amelia in *The Honey Badger,* Jim Queen bequeathed the girl to Ruark, knowing he was both lonely and chronically hungry. The Webbs were reputed to have a well-stocked refrigerator.

At that time, Ruark was leading a decidedly threadbare existence in Washington. He lived in a rooming house whose denizens were mostly, like himself, broke, single, and recently emigrated to Washington in search of work. Whether Virginia and Jim Queen were lovers, as Amelia and Jim James are in the novel, is a matter of speculation. Ruark's description of Barr's early life in Washington, his climb up the newspaper ladder, and especially his engagement, marriage, and early married life, are presented in exquisite and authentic detail.

For Robert Ruark the writer, what is important is the effect meeting and marrying Virginia had on him at a time when so many young men lose sight of their ambitions in the glow of sudden prosperity. Subsequent events would suggest that if Robert Ruark got some lucky breaks, meeting Virginia was probably the luckiest. She turned out to be a woman of considerable merit who was the almost perfect support for a man like Ruark. He came to depend on her greatly in his professional life, even though his marital fidelity was measured in months, if not days. While they had many serious disagreements over the years, they stayed together for the better part of three decades, and when they finally divorced, Ruark was like a ship that had slipped its anchor and was drifting before the waves.

\* \* \*

When she met Robert Ruark, Virginia was a student at George Washington University. She was tall, pretty if not beautiful, and well-proportioned, a member of the Chi Omega sorority, and had reached her senior year with excellent grades. Washington was a town awash in young men in government jobs, from FBI types to senatorial aides, and Virginia was more accustomed to dating older career men than her fellow college students. And her dance card was always full.

Unlike Amelia, Virginia Webb was not an only child. Her brother, Jack, told Hugh Foster many years later that his parents were happy when Virginia began dating Ruark, because she had been seeing a young man who was "as wild as he could be." They were happy, he said, when she settled down "to dating Bobby," even though he was then only a copy boy "making $21 a week."

The romance progressed normally. Robert Ruark was a charming young man, and his Southern manners stood him in good stead with the Webbs. He proposed to Virginia over dinner at the Webbs' house, and they were married in August, 1938. The groom was twenty-two years old, the bride a year younger. By that time, Ruark had been on staff with the *Daily News* for a year and a half and was making good money as a reporter, with more on the side as a freelance advertising copy writer. The Webbs were well enough known to warrant coverage of the wedding in the *Evening Star* (the *News* did not cover society events). The detailed description ended with the note that the groom's mother, Mrs. R.C. Ruark Sr., had been unable to attend "because of illness."

The Ruarks first moved into a flat in Washington near Wisconsin Street. Virginia went to work at a department store. She was intent on pursuing a career in interior decoration. With two good incomes they were able to live very well, compared with other people in their age bracket. As soon as they could afford it, they moved out of Washington and rented a house in Maryland. All the social stability and acceptance Ruark had craved as a child, as a college student, and later as a copy boy gnashing his teeth in frustration, were now his. He was one of the top reporters on an up-and-coming newspaper, married to a lovely girl from a well-to-do family.

Altogether, Robert Ruark had managed to take his native charm, talent, and capacity for unremitting hard work and put himself solidly several rungs up the ladder of success at an early age, in a very tough environment. A colleague in 1940 described Ruark as "brash, ambitious, cocky, fast, and good." Like most writers, there was a strong dash of chameleon in his make-up. He was an actor who could change roles effortlessly, fitting in wherever he happened to be, whether it was the hard-boiled newspaper reporter, the Southern charmer, or the dedicated career man "on his swift way up." Like most natural actors, however, there was also a strong element of insecurity. From childhood Robert Ruark was insecure, no matter how successful he ultimately became. There was always the nagging suspicion, the fear, that he would be found out and unmasked as a fraud.

As well, there was another contradictory element.

For years leading up to 1939, there were signs that a war was coming in Europe. In his last visit to Chapel Hill, accompanied by his fiancée, Amelia, Alec Barr meets with his old professor, Skipper Henry. Henry asks if he will go to the war when it comes, and Alec says he will, but not as a reporter. As they are driving back to Washington, Alec reflects on the fact that in a strange way he has a yearning for that war as a means of escape from all the things he now had, that were so important to him, and that he had worked so hard to attain. Barr's dominant trait as a "compulsive truant" began to emerge before he had even settled into married life.

Robert Ruark was exactly the same.

❋ ❋ ❋

*Chapter Four*

# GONE
# TO SEA

Given his family's nautical background and his own experience as a merchant seaman, it was only logical that when war broke out, Robert Ruark would join the navy. After all, his favorite grandfather, Ned Adkins, had been a sea captain and his uncle Rob the master of a cargo boat on the Cape Fear River. As a boy he had spent much of his time aboard a Coast Guard cutter, occasionally chasing rumrunners when they were not fishing, and two of his boyhood heroes were Vasco da Gama and Blackbeard the Pirate. Where else to go but the navy?

The bombing of Pearl Harbor, on December 7, 1941, sparked a flood of volunteers to all the services, and there were lineups outside recruiting stations. As a university graduate in his late twenties, Ruark was a natural for a commission, which he duly received and, as he later put it, "we all went shopping for sailor suits." Considering his age, marital status, and occupation, Ruark could easily have obtained either a deferment, a war correspondent's job, or, if he insisted on wearing a uniform in the service of his country, at least a comfortable billet in Washington doing public relations for the service of his choice or working in the censor's office. Robert Ruark, the not-so-reluctant warrior, waived all of these options in favor of full and unpreferential sea duty. He was dispatched for training and then assigned to an obscure, patched-together branch of the U.S. Navy that delighted in the name "Armed Guard." It consisted of regular navy types whose commanders wanted to get rid of them, unskilled new recruits who fitted nowhere else and whom no other branch wanted, and of officers such as Ruark, who had no marketable military skills beyond an eagerness for duty and a life that could be sacrificed if need be.

The purpose of the Armed Guard was simple: To man the cannons and antiaircraft and antisubmarine defenses on merchant ships that were carrying supplies and war materiel in the convoys across the North Atlantic, to Murmansk for Russia and to Great Britain, which was standing alone in defiance of the Third Reich, kept alive by a tenuous lifeline of fragile ships running a gauntlet of U-boats.

## THE BATTLE OF THE ATLANTIC

The Battle of the Atlantic began on September 3, 1939, the very day Britain declared war on Germany, and it continued almost without pause for the next four years. It was a battle fought mostly between the Royal Navy and the German Navy, with its surface fleet and U-boats. The prize was the tonnage of supplies coming from America that was keeping Britain alive against all odds. For the British it was a life-and-death struggle, and the events of those early years in the war at sea have passed into myth just as the Battle of Britain, with its first and second blitz, has become a symbol of the days when Britain stood alone against Hitler. It has been said that the war produced one winner (the United States), one loser (Germany), and one hero, Britain. If the Royal Air Force, gallant and outnumbered, and London's civilian population were the heroes of the Battle of Britain, the Royal Navy in all its traditional magnificence was the undisputed hero in the Battle of the Atlantic. The aviation fuel that went into those Spitfires in the skies over London arrived in tankers from America protected from the U-boats by ships flying His Majesty's battle ensign.

When war broke out in 1939, the Royal Navy vastly outnumbered the German fleet in all the traditional measurements of naval might. The British had eighteen capital ships (battleships and battle cruisers) to the Germans' four, outnumbered them in aircraft carriers ten to one, in heavy cruisers fifteen to four, light cruisers sixty-two to six, and in destroyers 205 to twenty-five. While these look like overwhelming odds, several factors favored the Germans. For one thing, the Royal Navy was stretched thin. It had the task of protecting British outposts and shipping lanes throughout the entire world, from Hong Kong to Suez, including India and the entire Mediterranean, as well as the supply convoys from America in the north and south Atlantic. What's more, many of the British ships were old, while almost all the German ships were new and modern. And, in one vital area, the German navy outnumbered the British: It had ninety-eight U-boats in September, 1939, and an industrial capacity that could turn out new ones like cookies in a bakery.

To properly understand the Battle of the Atlantic, a little background in naval terms and definitions is necessary. The battleship, that most evocative of terms, applies to the heaviest of sea-going gun platforms. Typically, a battleship weighed 30,000 tons and was armed with at least eight large guns of fourteen to sixteen inches in bore diameter; it was heavily armored to withstand punishment, and the hull was wide in the center to make it stable enough to take the recoil from its guns when they were fired, in unison, in a broadside. The weight of the armor and the shape of the hull made the battleship, by definition, relatively slow, but it was slow only in the sense that a heavyweight boxer is slow. A battle cruiser was a different animal: It was just as big as a battleship, and often bigger, but its hull was long and slim, and its armor light. It sacrificed protection for speed on the theory that it could outgun anything faster, and outrun anything more powerful. The most famous example of this was the H.M.S. *Hood*, the darling of the Royal Navy in the years between the wars. The *Hood* was big, fast, and beautiful. She weighed more than 41,000 tons, carried eight fifteen-inch guns (each of which weighed a hundred tons), and was capable of speeds of up to thirty-two knots. She was named after an illustrious English naval family that included two rear-admirals, the most recent of whom had died commanding battle cruisers in the Battle of Jutland and had gone down with the *Invincible*. In theory, at least, the *Hood* could fight it out with any ship in the German fleet — including its two largest battleships, the *Bismarck* and *Tirpitz*. The *Hood* had two sister ships, the *Repulse* and the *Renown*, both smaller, slower, and more lightly armed, but still formidable opponents for anything else afloat.

Under the terms of the Washington Naval Treaty of 1922, restrictions were placed on how many ships each nation could build, and on how heavy they could be. This led to a number of innovations in warship design intended to get around the intent of the agreement without violating the letter of the treaty itself. For example, the British had laid the keels for two new, ultra-large battleships that were to weigh in excess of 48,000 tons and be armed with three turrets of three sixteen-inch guns each. When the treaty made these ships illegal, the British shipyards merely cut them short, relocated the superstructure, rounded off the stern, and left three, three-gun turrets forward. The result was an odd-looking hybrid which, for lack of a better term, they called simply a "capital ship." There were two of these, H.M.S. *Nelson* and H.M.S. *Rodney*, both named, like the *Hood*, for famous admirals of the past. Both ships were to play pivotal roles in the naval war — the *Nelson* in the Mediterranean and the *Rodney* in the North Atlantic.

Until the H.M.S. *Dreadnought*, which was launched in 1906 and revolutionized naval warfare, a battleship was armed with a variety of guns in different sizes for different purposes. The *Dreadnought* was the first to have a large number of big guns — in her case, ten twelve-inch guns. Her appearance rendered all older battleships obsolete and sparked the pre-1914 naval arms race. The reason was the increased power and range of her guns. By 1939, even twelve-inch guns had been superseded. Battleships were armed with fourteen, fifteen or sixteen-inch guns, and their power and range were awesome. For example a sixteen-inch gun (such as the *Rodney* carried) was vastly more powerful than an eight-inch gun. A sixteen-inch shell weighed 2,048 pounds, had a muzzle velocity of 2,600 feet per second, and a range of almost 40,000 yards — or more than twenty-three miles. An eight-inch gun, such as those carried by heavy cruisers, fired shells that weighed only 256 pounds and had a range of 30,000 yards. A battleship with heavy guns could make mincemeat of anything smaller long before it got within range, and even then the smaller gun's projectiles could not penetrate the heavy armor of the battleships, which was sometimes eight inches thick. These were the logistical concerns that dominated any question of facing, fighting, and ultimately sinking, any large surface ship.

For their part, the Germans met the limitations of the Washington

Naval Treaty by developing the "pocket battleship." These were small but very heavily armed. In reality, at 14,000 tons they were merely small battle cruisers, but with their six eleven-inch guns they were much more powerful than a typical heavy cruiser with eight-inch guns. They were capable of twenty-six knots and had a cruising range of 20,000 miles on full tanks. With the exception of the battle cruisers *Hood*, *Renown*, and *Repulse*, there was no ship in the Royal Navy that the pocket battleships could not either outrun or outgun. The most famous of the pocket battleships was the *Graf Spee*. After *Bismarck* and *Graf Spee*, the most notorious German heavy ships were the *Scharnhorst* and the *Gneisenau*. Both were battle cruisers.

As soon as war broke out, the British imposed a naval blockade intended to keep the German surface fleet bottled up in the Baltic Sea. The image of a fast, powerful surface raider loose in the sea lanes of the Atlantic was the recurring nightmare of the Admiralty from 1939 through 1943. Those sea lanes were heavily traveled by convoys of tankers and merchant ships carrying aircraft, tanks, ammunition, fuel, and food supplies. Without that lifeline, Britain would be starved out of the war in short order, and the havoc that a surface raider could create was substantial. The need to prevent this became the dominant strategic consideration and, to a great degree, dictated British naval policy during those years.

The Germans, on the other hand, wanted nothing more than to do exactly that — sink convoys — but they had no desire to put their big ships to sea to engage the Royal Navy in gun-to-gun combat. This was partly due to an innate inferiority complex dating back to the Battle of Jutland, in 1916, and partly due to the fact that they could not afford the losses. As well, the German admirals realized that, while they might defeat one British battleship, all they would gain would be a breathing space until the next one came along to throw down the gauntlet.

Instead, the Germans used their big ships predominantly as decoys — potential threats whose very existence kept the Royal Navy's hands tied — and coupled this with periodic forays to keep the tension high while unleashing their U-boat fleet to attack the convoys. German naval strategy was summed up in two words: commerce destruction. Britain's naval blockade could certainly hinder Germany's war effort on land in Europe and later in Russia, but it was incapable of a knockout blow. Germany, on the other hand, could strangle the island nation if it could cut off the supply line from America.

These, then, were the strategic considerations on both sides that helped mold the tactical approaches they used to combat each other, move for move, in the chess game that ensued.

Ships sailing alone were obviously vulnerable to attack by U-boats lurking along the shipping lanes, and the convoy system was adopted early, immediately after a U-boat sank the *Athenia*, a passenger liner bound from Liverpool to Montreal with 1,400 passengers aboard. She was sunk without warning, 200 miles west of the Hebrides, and 112 people died. The action took place on September 3, the very day war was declared. For a convoy system to work, however, escort ships are needed — destroyers and destroyer escorts to provide a screen and anti-submarine defenses, with a few larger ships included to defend against powerful surface raiders like the *Graf Spee*, plus aircraft carriers for air cover and reconnaissance. Very quickly, the Royal Navy established convoy escort groups, families of ships and sailors and Royal Marines that lived, sailed, and as often as not, died together in the waves of the frigid North Atlantic.

The backbone of the escort group system was the destroyer, and Britain simply did not have enough of them. Winston Churchill ordered an accelerated construction program, but it could not turn out destroyers fast enough. By August, 1940, the U-boats had sunk two and a half million tons of shipping. The American president, Franklin D. Roosevelt, braving criticism at home, decided that in spite of its neutrality, the United States had to help combat fascism. He sold Britain fifty old American destroyers under the "Lend-Lease" program, in return for the use of British naval bases in the western hemisphere. The process of drawing America into the war had begun. Meanwhile, the desperate engagement continued between the convoys on the sea and the U-boats beneath it.

* * *

The early months of the war brought about some of the most famous engagements and naval battles. When war broke out, there were two

German pocket battleships at sea, the *Graf Spee* and the *Deutschland*. The *Graf Spee* had a brief and spectacular career as a surface raider before she was sunk in the Battle of the River Plate, off South America, in December, 1939. After the Battle of Flanders, the German blitzkrieg against France, and the British evacuation from Dunkirk in May, 1940, the naval war took on even greater importance. The Royal Navy once again became the "wooden walls" behind which Britain sheltered, as it had since the days of the Spanish Armada. Meanwhile, the Luftwaffe turned its attention on London and the other English cities in an attempt to pound Britain into submission without having to mount a sea-borne invasion.

The Royal Navy's blockade of Germany was seriously hampering the flow of vital war supplies, especially steel from Sweden; to protect the supply lines down the coast, Hitler seized Norway and Denmark in the spring of 1940. Holding Norway gave Germany a springboard for aerial attacks against the blockading British ships, as well as bases from which to fly bombing missions against the British Isles.

Supply convoys from America faced a formidable array of threats between New York and Liverpool. The German submarine commander, Admiral Karl Doenitz, had countered British antisubmarine efforts with the concept of the "wolf pack," as many as fifteen to twenty submarines operating in concert, spread across the sea lanes approaching Britain. A convoy could range far to the north and south in the mid-Atlantic, but eventually they had to come in close to the British Isles, and that was where the U-boats lay in wait. Reconnaissance subs would spot a convoy and then shadow it, giving its position and course by radio and allowing the U-boat command to assemble a wolf pack. At the same time, land-based bombers in France and Norway could attack any ships that made it past the U-boats, while still staying out of range of R.A.F. fighter planes themselves. When the British mobilized their own bombers to send out long-range patrols from Northern Ireland to attack U-boats and help protect the convoys, the U-boats simply moved farther out to sea, beyond the reach of even the high-flying, long-range bombers.

For a merchantman on the North Atlantic run, there was no shortage of dangers — from beneath the sea, from beyond the clouds, even from fearsome surface ships with guns so powerful they could open fire from almost beyond the horizon. Added to this was the prospect — a dead certainty in some months — of fierce winter gales and mountainous waves that were an enemy in themselves. Still, both the navy and the merchant seamen welcomed bad weather; it kept the submarines far below torpedo-launching depth, the long-range bombers at home, and the battleships hidden from view. It was a tough choice, all the same.

Throughout this period, the Admiralty was haunted by the prospect of a break-out into the North Atlantic of any of Germany's big ships. In late October of 1940, the pocket battleship *Admiral Scheer* slipped through the blockade. In early November, she encountered a thirty-seven-ship convoy escorted only by the auxiliary cruiser *Jervis Bay*, armed with just four six-inch guns. After ordering the convoy to scatter, the *Jervis Bay* turned and deliberately took on the *Admiral Scheer*. It was a hopeless contest from the start, but the British ship bought enough time for thirty-two merchantmen to escape before she was sunk.

In January, 1941, the battle cruisers *Scharnhorst* and *Gneisenau* also made a short foray into the Atlantic under the command of Vice-Admiral Günther Lütjens and sank five unescorted merchantmen. For two months they searched for a major target — a convoy worthy of their big guns — but were not successful until the night of March 18, when they encountered a convoy just as it scattered from a submarine attack. In a two-day running battle, the pair of German raiders sank sixteen merchant ships, then made for safety at the French port of Brest as British battleships closed in. This established a pattern: break out, take targets of opportunity, then make for home and safety to refuel, resupply, and repair any damage. Meanwhile, the Royal Navy was stretched to breaking point, always forced to react to German initiatives and never able to take the initiative itself.

In May, 1941, the greatest German ship of all, the huge battleship *Bismarck*, set sail from Gdynia on the Baltic Sea and made for Denmark, accompanied by the new heavy cruiser *Prinz Eugen*, with the redoubtable Admiral Lütjens in command. On paper, the *Bismarck* was 35,000 tons, to conform with treaty requirements; in reality, she weighed 42,000 tons and was armed with eight fifteen-inch guns. The

*Prinz Eugen* displaced 15,000 tons and was armed with eight-inch guns. They were a formidable pair.

R.A.F. reconnaissance planes spotted them off Bergenfjord, and the Royal Navy mobilized every ship and aircraft it could muster, from Gibraltar to Scapa Flow, to try to stop them. Admiral Lütjens, fox that he was, was in no hurry. He bided his time off Bergenfjord; when a heavy fog closed in, the grey colossus and her escort quietly weighed anchor and slipped out, making for the Denmark Strait. The Admiralty's nightmare had become a reality — and there were, at that moment, eleven supply convoys scattered across the Atlantic, sitting ducks for the *Bismarck* if she could get out into the sea lanes. There were four possible routes into the Atlantic, the Denmark Strait being one. As the *Bismarck* entered the strait, she was spotted by two British cruisers, H.M.S. *Norfolk* and H.M.S. *Suffolk*, which radioed the news, and her position, to the Admiralty; then the two cruisers lay back out of range, shadowing the raiders and waiting for reinforcements. Fortunately, the *Hood*, the one British ship capable of handling the *Bismarck* on her own, was close by.

Accompanied by the new battleship *Prince of Wales* (so new that she was ordered to sea with some shipyard workmen still aboard, and without proper training for her crew), the *Hood* steamed north on an intercepting course. On the morning of May 24, 1941, they came within range and opened fire on the *Bismarck* and the *Prinz Eugen* at a range of 25,000 yards. Within minutes of the first shot being fired, it was all over: a fifteen-inch shell from the *Bismarck* plunged through the *Hood's* light deck armor, penetrated her main magazine, and blew the pride of the Royal Navy to bits. Broken in half, the *Hood* sank in a matter of seconds, taking all but three of her 1,500-man crew to the bottom. *Bismarck* then turned on the *Prince of Wales* and damaged her so badly she was forced to withdraw. The German ships continued westward into the Atlantic, with the *Suffolk* and *Norfolk* shadowing them like a pair of determined but helpless sheep dogs.

The loss of the *Hood* was the greatest single blow the Royal Navy endured in the entire war, partly because she was so famous and was considered invincible. Yet this very myth of invincibility contributed to her death. It had been recognized that she had a few design weaknesses, most notably insufficient deck armor to withstand plunging fire. She was scheduled for a refit, but it was postponed when war became imminent and refitting older, less battle-worthy ships was given priority. The chances of a large enough shell hitting her at exactly the right angle was considered a relatively small risk.

What followed was a running battle in fog and bad weather, with the *Bismarck* attempting to slip away from her followers and the British attempting to bring large ships within range. The *Prinz Eugen* was detached and headed for Brest, while the *Bismarck* shook off the two British cruisers. She was not lost for long, however: Almost immediately she was spotted by a land-based patrol plane. On May 27, planes attacking from the aircraft carrier *Ark Royal* inflicted some damage, slowing her down, and a flotilla of destroyers managed to seriously damage her further with torpedoes. One of them struck the *Bismarck's* steering mechanism, jamming her rudder and forcing her to sail in a wide arc far to the west and north, away from Brest and safety. The *Rodney* and *King George V* then closed in and engaged the great German battleship on the morning of May 28. Finally, on fire and with all her guns out of action, the *Bismarck* was sunk by torpedoes from the cruiser *Dorsetshire*. Of her crew of almost 2,500 men, only 110 survived. Admiral Lütjens was among those who accompanied the great ship to the bottom.

The loss of the *Bismarck* was as great a shock to the Germans as the sinking of the *Hood* was to the British, the difference being that the Germans became doubly reluctant to take risks with their ships thereafter, whereas the professional sailors of the Royal Navy simply went about their appointed task of patrolling the world's oceans with renewed confidence.

Less than four weeks after the sinking of the *Bismarck*, Germany invaded the Soviet Union and changed the whole complexion of the war. Most especially, for the British (and their uneasily peaceful and unofficial allies, the Americans), it transformed the war in the Atlantic.

## THE NORTH ATLANTIC CONVOYS

The war on the eastern front removed any threat of a German invasion of Britain and began to drain away German manpower and air power as the three German army groups drove deep into the Soviet Union. In the opening days of Operation Barbarossa, the Red Army was pounded mercilessly, losing tens of thousands killed and wounded, and hundreds of thousands captured. Barbarossa involved almost three million men, along a 2,000-mile front, and was undoubtedly the greatest invasion that has ever been, or ever will be, mounted. By comparison, the Normandy Invasion three years later was a lighthearted raid. The Red Army, outgunned and outmaneuvered, fell back toward Moscow and came within a hair's breadth of losing the war in the first few months.

While conventional wisdom today says there was never any real doubt, that no invasion of Russia could possibly succeed because of its vast size and the inevitability of a winter campaign, the fact is that Stalin could have — and really should have — lost the war. He was saved by a fortuitous combination of circumstances, including interference by Hitler at critical moments. The German war machine ground to a halt, finally, almost in the suburbs of Leningrad in the north and Moscow in the center, and Stalin was given breathing space to recruit new armies in the east and rearm his surviving divisions. The key to keeping the Soviet Union alive and fighting — which was, at that point, the key to any hope of an eventual allied victory — was to keep Stalin supplied with war materiel. Most especially, the Russians needed aircraft, aviation fuel, and every type of military equipment from tanks to small-arms ammunition. Supplying Russia became as important as supplying Britain itself. The problem was, how to do it?

Shipping goods through Siberia from the far east was one possibility, and in fact about half of all the materiel shipped to the USSR during the war went across the Pacific, then by train from Vladivostok. This was possible as long as the Soviet Union was not at war with Japan. From the other direction, across the Atlantic, convoys could go through the Mediterranean, but the Mediterranean was itself a battleground involving the British in North Africa, the Italians with their substantial navy and air force, and German involvement from France to Crete. Supplying Malta, Britain's hard-pressed outpost in the Mediterranean, was hazardous enough; getting supplies through to Russia would be impossible, even if the German forces invading Russia were not threatening the Crimea on the south flank, which they were. The only other answer was the sea route to the north, high above the Arctic Circle and around the North Cape to the Russian port city of Murmansk and, in the summer months, Archangel. It was a relatively short route, it was direct, and it provided Winston Churchill with the symbolic gesture of helping the Russians that he desperately needed.

Although at this time the United States was still officially neutral, it was moving steadily toward war with Germany. The invasion of Russia made American entry into the war all but inevitable, and while the official declaration did not come until after Pearl Harbor, the U.S. Navy was actively involved from April, 1941, onward. First, President Roosevelt put Greenland (a Danish possession) under American protection. He then landed American troops in Iceland, freeing the British garrison there to return to combat duty elsewhere. In August, after a meeting in which Roosevelt and Churchill pledged to preserve world freedom after the war, Roosevelt announced that henceforth American warships would escort all convoys west of Iceland. The United States became an informal belligerent in the war, and some of the pressure was taken off the Royal Navy. Germany responded by attacking the American escorts, and the first serious casualty was the destroyer U.S.S. *Reuben James*, sunk while on convoy duty on October 31, 1941.

By June of that year, German submarines had sunk almost six million tons of British shipping, and British shipyards were able to replace only 800,000 tons. The entry of the U.S. Navy, albeit unofficially, did allow the Royal Navy to move some of its fighting units farther into the eastern Atlantic to help combat the U-boats. But the decision to supply the Soviet Union by convoys to Murmansk and Archangel high above the Arctic Circle put renewed pressure on both the British and the Americans. As if it were not difficult enough to protect convoys between Halifax and the British Isles, now they had to protect merchant ships in the even more dangerous North Atlantic and Arctic Ocean, where they were threatened not only by submarines, but by land-based aircraft from Norway and German surface raiders such as the *Tirpitz*, sister ship to the *Bismarck*, which had been based since 1942 in Norway's Alta Fjord.

With the entry of America into the war in December, 1941, Germany concentrated its naval efforts on blocking the sea lanes by which the convoys could supply both Britain and Russia. Sixty-four U-boats were scattered across the Atlantic and posted off the American coast from New York down to the Gulf of Mexico. While the American shipyards laid on extra shifts to increase production, tankers loaded up in the Gulf and made their way up the coast to join the convoys that were assembled in New York. As they sailed north, nervously searching the sea for periscopes, they were joined by other tankers and freighters. A favorite tactic of the U-boats was to torpedo ships as they were silhouetted at night against the glow of the bright lights of America's coastal cities and resort towns.

When it came to waging war, America was downright nonchalant. In his *History of the Second World War*, B.H. Liddell Hart reported:

*The Americans were slow to take other precautions (in addition to adopting convoy tactics). Lighted channel markers and the unrestricted use of ship's radio gave the U-boats all the help they wanted. Coastal resorts, such as Miami, continued to illuminate their sea-fronts at night with miles of neon-lighted beaches — against which the shipping was clearly silhouetted. The U-boats lay submerged offshore during the day, and moved in to attack, with guns or torpedoes, on the surface at night time.*

The entry of America into the war removed many of the restrictions on Germany's freedom of operation. They moved as many U-boats as they could into the westernmost reaches of the Atlantic, to prey on shipping along the American east coast, and although only a small number could be diverted to this duty, they achieved results out of all proportion to their numbers. There were never more than a dozen German U-boats operating there, but during the first four months of 1942, they sank eighty merchant ships along the American coast — half a million tons of shipping, of which more than half were tankers. That four-month period of the war became known, among the sailors of the German U-boat fleet, as "The Happy Times" — a time of good and carefree hunting along an almost undefended coast. For the merchant ships, the run up the coast, however harrowing as it must have been at the time, was but a hint of the terror and hardship that was to come.

Through the summer of 1942, more and more submarines put to sea, and more and more tons of shipping were lost. In June alone, the U-boats sent 700,000 tons to the bottom, bringing the total for the year to more than three million. Altogether, the Allies lost more than four million tons from all causes, and ninety per cent of the losses were in the North Atlantic and the Arctic.

Just as the war in Russia claimed most of Germany's military attention on land, halting the convoys to Murmansk that supplied the Russians became a priority for the German navy. Major surface ships were concentrated along the Norwegian coast, including the *Tirpitz*, the *Scharnhorst*, the pocket battleship *Admiral Scheer*, and the heavy cruiser *Hipper*. The major ship-sinking duties were left to the screen of submarines and land-based bombers that could fly from Norwegian bases, but the constant threat of a sortie by the big ships forced the Royal Navy to keep comparable forces nearby, and a heavy squadron that included both battleships and an aircraft carrier was posted permanently near Bear Island, 400 miles above the Arctic Circle. Supplying Murmansk became a game of cat and mouse, in which some of the convoys were used by the Admiralty as bait in an attempt to lure the *Tirpitz*, especially, out of her safe harbor to, they hoped and prayed, her doom. That exact scenario never came to pass, but the mere presence of the *Tirpitz* at Alta Fjord dominated British naval strategy in the North Atlantic for more than two years.

The Murmansk convoys typically assembled in New York or Halifax and moved northeast to Iceland, protected by a screen of American and Canadian destroyers, destroyer escorts, corvettes, and similar small anti-submarine warships. Off Iceland, they would be taken over by one of the escort groups of the Royal Navy, which would shepherd them the remaining hazardous 1,500 miles north into the Arctic. An escort group typically consisted of a cruiser or two, a half-dozen destroyer escorts and frigates, and (if they were lucky) a few escort carriers. The escort carrier was developed in 1940 to counter the threat of both submarines and bombers by providing fighter air cover. An escort carrier was a converted merchant ship with a fitted flight deck that would carry a half-dozen aircraft. The carriers were small, vulnerable, usually slow, and hazardous in the extreme for the pilots flying off their makeshift flight decks, but they played an invaluable role in protecting convoys through the worst years, 1942 and 1943, when the U-boat menace was at its height.

The convoy system was an evolving military technique, first developed during the First World War to counter threats from early U-boats and surface raiders. From 1939 onward, it was developed and refined both to counter new German techniques and to make use of technological innovations such as Asdic and radar. A convoy could be as many as a hundred merchant ships and cover hundreds of square miles of ocean. There were slow convoys (those that traveled at less than eleven knots) and fast convoys (eleven knots and up). Each convoy had a close escort, whose job was to provide both anti-aircraft fire and a screen against U-boats. A covering, or shadow, force was there to pursue and destroy any U-boats that were found, while the convoy and its close escort continued on. Air power was found to be a particularly effective anti-submarine tool, and land-based aircraft from North America and the British Isles helped cover the convoys across the Atlantic; there was one stretch of ocean that was out of range of either side, however, which became know as "The Gap." Needless to say, the Gap was a favorite hunting ground of the German wolf packs.

In 1955, Alistair Maclean wrote a novel of the Murmansk convoys called *H.M.S. Ulysses*. It is one of the great sea stories of all time. It tells of the voyage of one fictional convoy, FR77, and her escorts led by the *Ulysses*, a modern, fast, light cruiser. FR77's role in life was to be the irresistibly tempting bait that would draw out the *Tirpitz*. That the scheme fails, and the convoy is destroyed, and the *Ulysses* herself is sunk by the *Hipper*, does not take away from the novel itself, which is perhaps the finest account ever written of the naval war in the high Arctic.

First of all, there were the normal hazards of convoy duty: Long hours at action stations, and days upon days without sleep or proper nourishment (because the cook was also at action stations). But the Arctic convoys added new dangers: cold, frostbite, and exhaustion; nerve-stretching tension and the certain knowledge that if your ship was sunk, your chances of survival in the freezing water were measured in minutes; and the other ships were under orders not to try to pick up survivors since a stationary ship was a sitting duck for a submarine.

Winter in the Arctic brought freezing gales and mountainous waves that could kill a ship as effectively as any torpedo. There were stories of gunners found dead and frozen solid, still at their action stations; stories of ice building up on the superstructure of a ship, making her top-heavy enough to capsize (the escort carriers, with their flat flight decks, were especially vulnerable to this); and there was even one instance of a freak wave so high that an escort carrier climbed up one side, plunged down the other, and bent her flight deck into an "L." In another case, a destroyer climbed a similar wave, teetered, plunged down the other side, ruptured her plates and just kept on going, straight to the bottom. Keeping the decks, rigging, and guns free of ice was a never-ending struggle — and on top of all this there was the constant threat of submarines below, and bombers above, and the vision of the *Scharnhorst* looming out of the fog.

In summer, the Arctic convoys faced a different and, in some ways, far worse situation. They were at their most vulnerable when they rounded the North Cape, and in the months of June and July, there was good weather and almost constant daylight. With excellent visibility and no blanket of darkness, the convoys were easy to spot and could be attacked twenty-four hours a day.

The most famous of all the Murmansk convoys was PQ17, which consisted of thirty-six merchantmen and tankers escorted by a dozen destroyers and smaller craft. The covering force consisted of several cruisers and a destroyer squadron, shadowing the convoy at a distance. To the north, lying in wait, was an Anglo-American battle group of two battleships, one aircraft carrier, three cruisers, and a flotilla of destroyers. PQ17 put to sea in June, 1942; on July 4, off Norway, the convoy was heavily attacked by submarines and aircraft. That same day, the escorts received a signal from the Admiralty that the *Tirpitz* had put to sea. They were ordered to withdraw, which they did at high speed, leaving the ships of PQ17 to scatter and make their way to Russia as best they could.

As it turned out, the *Tirpitz* never came, but the submarines and aircraft flocked to the scene like vultures. Slow and unprotected, the dispersed ships were easy pickings: Twenty-three ships out of thirty-six were sunk, taking to the bottom 430 tanks, 210 aircraft, 3,350 other vehicles, and almost 100,000 tons of supplies. PQ17 was the lowest ebb of the Arctic convoys — and the lowest ebb of the Royal Navy's reputation, although in retrospect it is hard to place blame on anyone. The next convoy did not sail until September; PQ18 had forty ships and a much stronger escort, and twenty-seven of them made it to Archangel. A few smaller convoys were sent the following winter, but after March, 1943, the Admiralty was unwilling to risk further losses in the lengthening Arctic days. The situation in the Atlantic was critical at that point anyway, and some convoys intended for Murmansk were diverted to Great Britain.

The spring of 1943 was the most critical phase of the war in the Atlantic and resulted in a decisive defeat for the U-boats. When the Arctic convoys were resumed late that year, they were bigger and much better armed, and the U-boats and the Luftwaffe were weaker. The final tally for the Murmansk run was forty convoys from 1941 onward; out of 811 ships that sailed, 720 got through, delivering almost four million tons of supplies to the Russians. This included 5,000 tanks and 7,000 aircraft. On the debit side, the Royal Navy lost eighteen warships. When the Mediterranean was finally opened to convoys, the Murmansk run was suspended and supplies to Russia went through the Black Sea and then overland from there.

The last act of the Arctic drama took place in December, 1943. The *Scharnhorst* left Alta Fjord with five destroyers to attack an Allied convoy 400 miles northwest of Trondheim. Instead of the easy victims they expected, however, they encountered two British task forces that included the battleship *Duke of York*, sister ship to the *Prince of Wales* and *King George V*, which had fought the *Bismarck*. The Battle of the North Cape, as it is known, was one of the most thrilling naval engagements of the war, taking place as it did high above the Arctic circle in continuous darkness, with the sky illuminated by star shells as the two great ships exchanged fire during the long chase. In the end, the *Scharnhorst* went to the bottom fighting and took all but thirty-six of her 1,900-man complement with her.

The fate of the *Tirpitz*, on the other hand, was anticlimax. To the British, she was too powerful for any one ship to fight alone; to the Germans, she was too important to risk losing, and after the sinking of the *Bismarck*, the German Navy's inferiority complex was redoubled. As a result, the *Tirpitz* never participated in a major naval battle; she was damaged by torpedoes from a midget submarine at her berth in Alta Fjord, then by bombs from carrier-borne aircraft, and was moved south to Tromso in late 1944 for repairs. There she was within reach of the British Isles and was finally sunk by Lancaster bombers flying from airfields in Scotland.

## LIEUTENANT RUARK, R.C. JR., USN

On the afternoon of December 7, 1941, Robert Ruark was a sports reporter for the Washington *Daily News* covering a Washington Redskins football game at Griffith Stadium. When word of the Japanese air attack was flashed to the press box, the reporters immediately lost any interest in the game, but Ruark did not immediately rush out to enlist. History records that the Redskins won the game, but the news stories that were filed that day dwelt more on the reaction of the crowd than on the play on the field. With a reporter's impatience at being where the news is not, Ruark wrapped up his story and left Griffith Stadium for the White House, where he hung around looking for angles and stories the beat man was too busy to go after. A couple of weeks later, he was transferred off the sports desk and through the early months of the war wrote features on topics such as the effects of blackouts. From there he left the *News* altogether to work directly as a syndicated feature writer for the NEA Service, a Scripps-Howard subsidiary.

Nineteen forty-one became 1942, and winter turned to spring before Ruark's commission papers in the Navy came through. He was posted to Dartmouth for eight weeks' training. By his own account, Ruark possessed no mechanical aptitude whatsoever; he could, he said, barely change a typewriter ribbon, and he was "frightened out of his skin" at the prospect of indoctrination school and the complex subjects naval officers are expected to master. Mechanical aptitude he may not have had, but Ruark was a natural student and a quick study. He "memorized his way through navigation and gunnery and seamanship," as he put it, and graduated with no difficulty. Early in the process, officers were assigned their future duties, then sent for specialized training. Ensign Robert C. Ruark Jr. volunteered for duty in the Armed Guard, a branch of the U.S. Naval Reserve that filled an unglamorous but decidedly hazardous duty: manning the guns on armed merchantmen on the Atlantic and Murmansk convoys. Dangerous and essential it may have been, but it was a job that was unlikely to make the cover of *Life*.

"'Fish food' was what they called the Armed Guard in the early days of the war, when the Luftwaffe owned the skies and the Nazi submarine wolfpacks were bold enough to hang around American river mouths to blast Allied shipping before the ships actually put out to sea," Ruark wrote in *The Honey Badger*, describing its hero, Alec Barr, and his wartime naval career. Barr's fictional experiences roughly paralleled Ruark's own and are the closest he ever came to writing a novel about the war. One difference is that Barr makes it to Murmansk on one run, whereas Ruark never did. But in other ways his description of Barr's war at sea is, in reality, his own.

Although technically a naval officer and no longer a reporter, during his months of training Ruark managed to get permission to write about the service in several magazine articles. Since all branches of the military were hungry for publicity, partly for recruiting purposes and partly for the greater glory of their commanders, and since Ruark was known even at that stage of his career, he had no difficulty with censors or reluctant superiors. Given what he wrote, it is unlikely the censors would have done anything except tone it down, out of deference to truth in advertising. To read any of Ruark's half-dozen published pieces, the Navy, and the Armed Guard in particular, was a great way to see the world free of charge.

Ensign Ruark's training took him down the Mississippi, and at one point ensconced him in a whorehouse in Gulfport — temporarily requisitioned as an officers' quarters — where, he said, "the whores babysat for the officers' wives, lent them money when the eagle forgot to scream, and never, ever, made a pass at the boys in blue." His training ended at the United States naval station in New Orleans, from where, in the early months of 1943, Ruark was posted as officer commanding the Armed Guard on the S.S. *Eli Whitney*, a 7,100-ton freighter with a top speed of eleven knots. The ship made her way up the East Coast, loading cargo at Charleston and other points in the Carolinas and Virginia before joining her convoy off Delaware. Ruark, busy training his green crew, practiced gunnery with a five-inch naval gun using the masts of sunken ships along the coast as targets. He credited his skill with a shotgun, honed since childhood, with giving him at least the rudimentary theories of lead required to hit a moving target, a concept that was lost on his unsophisticated crew of "Iowa farmboys, street fighters from Brooklyn, and bully boys from New Jersey."

On board the *Eli Whitney*, Ensign Ruark coped with one problem after another. One was an episode involving a rating from New Jersey named Zabinski, a slouching, thick-headed, sullen insubordinate. Ruark wrote about the situation twice, most eloquently in *The Honey Badger*. There, Zabinski was Alec Barr's cross. If anyone was drunk on duty, smoking in the powder magazine, or overdue from leave, it was Zabinski. Barr tries reason, he tries punishment, he tries confining him to the ship, but nothing works. Finally, with his men losing respect and discipline going to hell, Barr tries a desperate move. He challenges Zabinski to a boxing match "for recreation," and they stage the contest on number-three hatch with the rest of the Armed Guard and the merchant crew as an audience. With a sinking heart, Barr (who, as a former sports reporter, knew a thing or two about boxing) watches Zabinski shuffle and weave and throw shadow punches, and realizes he is "in an unroped ring with a semiprofessional." Zabinski, it turns out, had been runner-up middleweight in the New Jersey Golden Gloves. Although he could have dispatched Barr at any time, he toys with his commanding officer, landing punches at will and opening cuts. Occasionally, to show his contempt for Barr's punching power, he allows him to land a blow, which he laughs off. Barr calls time out to repair some cuts, goes to the safe in his cabin (he is also paymaster for the freighter's naval contingent) and inserts a heavy roll of coins into his right fist, then ties his glove back on and returns to the boxing match. The next time Zabinski contemptuously gives him an opening, he swings a punch from the ground up and breaks Zabinski's jaw with a crack that could be heard "from Norfolk, Virginia to Archangel, Russia." The episode ends all disciplinary problems with his gun crew, and the men "chipped seconds from the time it took to get the guns manned when the horn blew General Quarters." The Zabinski affair from *The Honey Badger* exactly parallels Ruark's account of his actual problems with the actual Zabinski, taken from newspaper articles he wrote after the war.

Gradually, Ensign Ruark learned his job and his gun crew learned theirs. The *Eli Whitney* took on a cargo of ammunition, and on March 25, 1943, Ruark, the *Whitney*, and the rest of the convoy weighed anchor in New York and sailed out into the wintry Atlantic, bound for England.

## MARCH, 1943

By 1943, convoy planning had evolved into an art. There were troop convoys, individual ships carrying troops, and the supply convoys carrying food, fuel, and equipment. The individual troop ships were the fastest passenger liners available, able to outrun the U-boats easily. Next came troop convoys, which were assigned extra antisubmarine escorts. This left the supply convoys on the short end in terms of protection. A typical convoy of forty-five ships had a perimeter of more than thirty miles to protect. An escort ship equipped with Asdic, the forerunner of radar that was used to detect submarines, could sweep an arc of one mile. Simple arithmetic indicates such a convoy would need an absolute minimum of fifteen escorts, yet in 1941 convoys left with an average of only five. Obviously, large gaps were left through which U-boats could penetrate the defences, and many a U-boat surfaced in the middle of a convoy to open fire with its deck gun, causing havoc as ships scattered, fired upon each other by mistake, or collided. As well, a supply convoy was only as fast as its slowest ship, and a shortage of merchant tonnage forced the Allies to use any ship they could find, regardless of speed. Although the specially built Liberty ships were fast, averaging eleven knots, many pre-war freighters and tankers were not. Creeping across the Atlantic at a speed of seven or eight knots, and stripped of escorts, the supply convoys were a juicy target. Finding the troop convoys too heavily protected, the U-boats concentrated their attention on the freighters and tankers, and the toll was frightening.

The first months of 1943 were a critical stage in the Battle of the Atlantic. Britain and Germany had now been at war for three and a half years, and in many ways the situation in the Atlantic resembled a heavyweight boxing match in the late rounds, when the two sluggers are evenly matched but nearing exhaustion, desperate but determined, knowing that sooner or later one will go down. Although Germany's U-boat fleet was still formidable, and, in fact, had more boats at sea on any given day than in 1939, many U-boats had been sunk and taken their experienced crews with them. Since there was insufficient time for training, many of the U-boat crews were relatively raw.

The terrible strain of the war was also showing on the British and their allies. Morale had become a serious problem on the merchant ships, and such was the carnage that some officers in the Admiralty were questioning whether the convoy system should even be continued. Unfortunately, there was simply no alternative. And so the merchantmen kept putting to sea, in spite of the fact that, at times, their crews were bordering on mutinous. The month of March, 1943, was the worst of all. In fact, the first twenty days are singled out in Admiralty records: "The Germans never came so near to disrupting communications between the New World and the Old as in the first twenty days of March, 1943."

In January, Grand Admiral Erich Raeder had been replaced as German naval commander by the U-boat specialist, Karl Doenitz. The wolf-pack campaign, already in high gear, was given even greater priority. Through this period, there was an average of 116 operating U-boats on any given day, spread out along the East Coast of America from the Gulf of Mexico to Newfoundland, right across the Atlantic, and up into the frigid waters off Norway. They crisscrossed the shipping lanes, taking their toll of every convoy in what amounted to one continuous battle. In January, the U-boats sank 200,000 tons of shipping, and in February, they doubled that. During the first twenty days of March, it reached a peak of 108 ships totaling 627,000 tons. Mid-month, two homeward-bound convoys that happened to be close together were attacked by thirty-eight U-boats, and twenty-one ships were lost. By the end of March that year, the United Kingdom was down to a "hand-to-mouth" three-month supply of food and fuel. To make matters worse, the winter of 1942-43 brought with it the worst winter storms in living memory. Gales lashed the seas into rolling mountains of liquid ice, while wind-blown spray coated decks and rigging and froze guns solid.

This was the overall situation on March 12, when three convoys assembled and prepared to make the passage east from America. They were SC 122, HX 229, and HX 229A — approximately 125 ships in all, plus their escort groups. Their voyage across the Atlantic in March, 1943, was such an epic that two books were devoted entirely to their crossing — Convoy: The Battle for Convoys SC 122 and HX 229, by British historian Martin Middlebrook, and The Critical Convoy Battles of March 1943, by Jürgen Rohwer. Historian John Terraine, in his work Business in Great Waters, The U-boat Wars 1916-1945, describes the departure of the three convoys as part of a relentless cycle which, by that time, had been continuing for three and a half long years:

The cycle was inexorable; no sooner had a convoy passed, some on their way into history but the majority unnoticed, than another followed. After SC 121 came SC 122; after HX 228, HX 229; and with 100 U-boats at sea, these east-bound ships, laden with war-material and essential supplies, could depend on a reception committee. SC 122 and HX 229 were destined to provide the whole Atlantic battle with what has gone down as its ultimate climax, and is commonly regarded as a high peak of U-boat warfare never before or afterwards matched.

Convoy SC 122 left New York on March 5 and immediately ran into a violent storm that scattered the ships, damaging several so severely they were forced to return to port. Sailors are great ones for omens, and the British ore freighter Clarissa Radcliffe provided it. She was one of eleven ships missing after the storm, but was sighted two days later by a Canadian corvette searching for stragglers and given a course to catch up to the convoy. The corvette continued on its way, and neither the Clarissa Radcliffe nor any of her fifty-five crew members was ever seen again. To this day, her fate remains a mystery.

Convoy SC 122 left St. John's on March 12, followed two days later by HX 229, and HX 229A the day after that, each traveling at its own speed and on its own course. Almost immediately the two lead convoys were caught in a terrible storm blowing from the west. The winds were Force 9-10 (gale and strong storm), and the seas were described as "very high and precipitous." "The great seas were pounding up astern of the ships with the effect of 'pooping'," wrote Terraine, "which is something that sailors prefer not to experience: waves breaking on the ship's stern with tons of water tearing along the decks." Such was the force of the storm that several ships, both merchantmen and escorts, were damaged and forced to return to port. To add to their problems, the ice floes were farther south that year than usual, and as the convoys moved north toward Iceland they encountered icebergs and banks of fog.

As bad as the storm of March 15 was, it was preferable to what happened next. The German U-boat command, anticipating the convoys' crossing, had assembled two wolf packs, the *Stürmer* group and the *Dranger* group. On March 16, the main action began when thirty-eight U-boats "threw themselves like wolves," as Admiral Doenitz quaintly put it, upon the convoys. That night, HX 229 lost five ships to torpedoes; the next day, SC 122 also lost five, and HX 229 another two. By the 18th, the two convoys had lost a total of eighteen ships, and another full gale was blowing from the north-northwest. There was no end to the misery.

Morale aboard the merchantmen was quickly becoming a major factor in the North Atlantic convoys. The relentless combination of storms, high seas, and attacking U-boats was having a devastating effect. As well, there was the problem of picking up survivors. Some convoys had rescue ships, but these were a mixed blessing: A rescue ship, by definition, would become a sitting duck every time it hove-to to pick up survivors, and the casualty rate among such ships was high. By 1943 the custom had evolved that the last ship in line had the responsibility of trying to pick up survivors, but this order was impossible to enforce and, as often as not, was ignored by the merchant captains, who made the difficult decision that the safety of their own ship and crew was more important than a handful of men in the icy Atlantic. John Terraine described the problem:

> The only ones left for rescue work were the escorts. An escort hove-to, perhaps with boats out, or hauling in drowning men and pitching rafts, probably silhouetted against the glare of a raging tanker fire, was an escort both extremely vulnerable herself and also lost to the convoy's protective screen until the work was done (which might be a matter of hours).

HX 229 had no rescue ship, but its escort group, B4, was known for its tenacity in hunting subs and also for its diligence in trying to rescue survivors. The ships of B4 were even more willing than usual to put themselves at risk in this way, not out of compassion for the drowning men, but because, as an officer later told it, "Our conclusion was that rescue was very important at a time when the worst disaster in the Atlantic battle would be a failure of morale in the merchant ships. In the absence of a rescue ship and with the failure of the last ships in the column to stop and pick up survivors, the Escort Group Commander had an almost impossible decision to make." (Middlebrook).

Exactly how close they were to such a failure of morale is illustrated by the actions of one merchant captain in HX 229 and his ship, the *Mathew Luckenbach*. She was a light, fast freighter, capable of doing fifteen knots. During a lull in the action, the captain called a meeting of the crew. He told them the ship was better off on its own, steaming at full speed, than limping along in a nine-knot convoy whose escorts were ineffective. After a show of hands, the ship slipped out of the convoy under cover of darkness. The escort commander tried to persuade him to change his mind, but he was determined to proceed on his own. By the next morning, the *Mathew Luckenbach* was forty miles ahead of HX 229 — and right in the middle of the wolf pack that had been attacking SC 122. She was torpedoed and sunk, becoming, ironically, the last casualty of convoy HX 229.

In March, 1943, eighty-two ships were lost in the North Atlantic, bringing the total of ships lost in the forty-three months of war to 4,486. Of these, 2,385 were sunk by submarines. The SC 122/HX 229 convoy battle cost the lives of 292 officers and men. Both figures were, to quote John Terraine, "appalling." That was the situation on March 25, when convoys HX 230 and SC 123 left New York. They included the *Eli Whitney*, with Ensign Robert Ruark, riding shotgun.

Ruark described life aboard the convoys:

*Flares lit the night into ghoulish noon. Depth charges thumped shockingly against the fragile bottoms of the eight-knot merchantmen that plowed through dense fog, scraping bows against sterns and butting into one another like milling cattle. It was cold beyond belief; the machine guns and Oerlikons were thawed with blowtorches. Beards clotted into icicles — everyone was bearded, because the touch of steel on skin stripped patches in its path.*

*No night or day passed that failed to record the massive display of exploding ammunition ships or the flaming, greasy-smoking destruction of tankers. Slightly hit ships and vessels two-blocking the blackball for engine trouble drifted back and out of convoy and were left sorrowfully to be picked off at leisure by the submarines. There was no attempt to rescue the survivors of stricken ships. In that ice-floed water, life expectancy was something under five minutes.*

Life was an endless succession of rolling waves and action stations, of blowing snow and drifting icebergs. At one point Ruark went seven days and seven nights without sleeping, catching five-minute catnaps in the wheelhouse as the sky was lit with flares, the terror punctuated by the explosion as a sister ship went up. "I had not washed for days. I had not slept for days. The convoy was under semi-constant attack by submarines," he wrote. "I stank — chiefly from fear. The smell of fear was separate from the smell of dirty body. The fear smelled worse." On that day, he and his crew had been at General Quarters for several hours without any action, and he decided to grab a fast shower. Stripping off his Arctic parka and long underwear, he lurched into the shower cubicle; the hot water rolled over him and lulled him into a great sense of peace and tranquillity, and he stood there in the steam for many minutes. "And then there was a crash and a boom and a hoarse screaming of the ship's general alarm."

Ensign Ruark jumped out of the shower, grabbed his pistol and helmet, and scrambled up to his gun station on the flying bridge. A ship, hit by a torpedo, was losing station and drifting slowly astern, smoke pouring out of her. Ruark, clad only in a helmet with the battle phones attached, was reflecting on the fact that he was on the bridge in the middle of an action, naked, with 7,000 tons of high explosive underneath him, when a submarine surfaced in the middle of the convoy. Every gun turned on the sub and blew her out of the water. Escorts raced about, dropping depth charges, and Ruark felt the hardening frost in his beard and reflected that it was cold up on the bridge with no clothes on. "What, I said to myself, in the name of Holy Christ am I doing out here?"

Scraped, battered, and bruised, the *Eli Whitney* and the other survivors of Ruark's first convoy limped up the Thames Estuary and docked in London on April 14, 1943. They had fought their way through the absolute height of the Battle of the Atlantic.

Two weeks later another convoy left New York. Under Commander Peter Gretton of the Royal Navy, Convoy ONS-2, consisting of forty-two slow and heavily laden merchantmen, fought a running battle across the Atlantic with fifty-one U-boats. Thirteen ships of the convoy were lost, but Gretton's escort ships sank five submarines, and two more were destroyed by aircraft. The voyage of Gretton's convoy, within a few weeks of Ruark's, was the high-water mark for the U-boats and the turning of the tide in the Atlantic. Never again would they be able to mount such a threat, and never again would the convoys suffer such hideous losses. In fact, between May and September that year, history records that 3,546 tankers and freighters crossed the Atlantic, in sixty-two convoys, without the loss of a single ship; Allied merchant construction hit full stride and exceeded all enemy destruction by six million tons. The food crisis in the British Isles was averted. Ensign Ruark, the men of his Armed Guard unit, the *Eli Whitney* and her crew, and all the other ships of Ruark's first convoy were part of that epic action. Winston Churchill:

*The Battle of the Atlantic was the dominating factor all through the war. Never for one moment could we forget that everything happening elsewhere, on land, at sea, or in the air, depended ultimately on its outcome, and amid all other cares we viewed its changing fortunes day by day with hope or apprehension.*

\* \* \*

Military service, especially in a hazardous duty involving real gunfire, real danger, and real fear, affects individuals in different ways. For those who live through a terrifying time, where the mere act of waking up every day constitutes a feat of bravery and heroism becomes routine, the experience often leads to introspection and reluctance to talk about it, partly because it is so intensely personal and partly because no one who has not been through it could possibly appreciate it. After the Battle of Gettysburg, a Confederate captain, Praxiteles Swan, described what happened: "We all went up to Gettysburg, the summer of '63. Some of us came back from there. And that's all, except for the details." The Atlantic convoys had much the same effect on the sailors and merchant seaman who survived them: Most did not want to defile the memory by talking about it.

Discussing it in terms of personal heroism, when so many of their friends had died in the icy waters of the Atlantic, was sacrilege; conversely, men who came back from war bragging about their exploits, by and large, were the ones who saw little action and less real danger.

Robert Ruark was one of the former: He never based a novel on his experiences in the navy, although he certainly could have. After 1945, war novels were *de rigueur*, and both Ruark and his fictional hero, Alec Barr, professed openly that they went to war as warriors, not as war correspondents, because they wanted to see the conflict from the inside as participants and not cheat the postwar literary public of the benefit of their own observations and experiences. In *The Honey Badger*, a young Alec Barr is advised by his former university professors about the value of war to a writer; one calls it too big an experience to be seen from the outside, that it must be seen from within and is not a spectacle for casual strangers to view from a distance. Another adds that no writer can afford to miss a war, especially if he intends to write books; it is "the most basic research." All agree that "war is more intimate than marriage."

Intimate and intense as it was, and for once participating and not just observing and reporting, Ruark found later that the memory was something to keep to himself and share only with those who knew what he was talking about. He never took his experiences and turned them into literature, except as background in *The Honey Badger* and for a few brief reflections in *Horn of the Hunter*. Alec Barr experiences some "early and rather frightening" activity, after which he becomes a staff officer in the Pacific. He never makes himself out to be a hero; he is self-deprecating about his own role in the war and is tolerantly amused at the attitudes he sees in others — the "ring-tailed *wunderkind*" who actively hated the enemy.

Ruark's silence may also be explained by the fact that his closest friend from college and the early days in Washington, Jim Queen (in *The Honey Badger*, Jim James) is killed in the war. In *Horn of the Hunter*, Ruark is sitting in a cathedral-like grove of trees somewhere in an untraveled, untrammeled part of unspoiled Tanganyika. "I was very grateful to be here, all by myself with a bottle of cool beer and some peaceful thoughts," he wrote. "I was especially glad that ship didn't blow up that day in the Mediterranean. I felt very sad for my best and oldest friend, Jim Queen, who loved this sort of stuff as much as I did but who was never going to be able to do it with me because a JU-88 came over a hill at Salerno one day and laid one into Jimmy's stack and that was all there was of Jim, then and forevermore. I was grateful that it hadn't worked that way with me, because the opportunity was equal." For his part, in a moment of savage introspection, Alec Barr thinks to himself, "Maybe you should have got your dear little self killed in line of duty. All the better ones did. Jim James gets killed, and you just get richer, so you can work in a rich room writing rich pieces for rich readers. Personally, I think you stink, *Mister* Barr." Under the circumstances, any suggestion of personal gallantry would be unseemly in the extreme — for fictional hero or real-life naval officer.

* * *

The *Eli Whitney* left London and put back to sea in late April, made New York a month later, and on May 28th set sail again, this time in convoy to the Mediterranean and the Middle East. By then, America and her allies had split up the responsibilities for convoy escort: Canada and Great Britain took sole control of the northern routes to Murmansk and the United Kingdom, while the U.S. covered convoys on the southern routes to the Mediterranean and North Africa.

The Mediterranean Sea had been a major battleground from the beginning, pitting the Royal Navy against the Italians, who had a formidable navy at every level — from submarines to battleships. When war broke out, the Italian fleet had six battleships and battle cruisers and 115 submarines — more than Britain, France, or Germany. In the close confines of the Med, the Italian undersea fleet was a considerable menace. While Italy had no aircraft carriers, she really did not need them: With the Italian boot extending out into the Mediterranean, and with Sicily and her colonies in North Africa serving as bases, Italian land-based aircraft were a threat from Gibraltar to the Holy Land, and high-level bombing became a specialty of her pilots and a constant nightmare for the British.

For its part the Royal Navy had the responsibility of keeping the convoy routes in the Mediterranean passable, if not exactly safe. She had to maintain access to the Suez Canal, which meant protecting Britain's hold on Egypt, and there was the island of Malta, a British colony that served as a base for British aircraft and warships. The siege of Malta and the need to keep her supplied with food and ammunition was the focus of British military activity in the Mediterranean, as was the need to disrupt German ships supplying Rommel's Afrika Korps with ammunition and reinforcements. British ships had two main bases, Gibraltar and Alexandria, and fought a continuous war with Italy. There were triumphs on both sides, and losses were heavy.

By the time Robert Ruark first ventured into the Mediterranean, the Royal Navy had the upper hand. Rommel had left North Africa, and his Afrika Korps was finally defeated by British and American forces in early May in the Battle of Tunisia. Plans were underway for the invasion of Sicily, which began in July, 1943.

The *Eli Whitney* sailed into the thick of the invasion plans, reaching the Mediterranean in early June and off-loading her cargo, which again consisted largely of ammunition and explosives, in Casablanca, Gibraltar, and Tunisia. The voyage was no more hazardous than usual and considerably warmer than the North Atlantic run. By August, the ship was back across the Atlantic, and Ruark and his crew were given a couple of weeks leave in Baltimore. After seven months of convoy duty, mostly ferrying ammunition "to tough places," they were overdue to be relieved. Rotation supposedly came after six months, but no replacements appeared, and they re-embarked for one more run to the Mediterranean.

Ruark's third and last Atlantic convoy weighed anchor in September and was, for him personally, the most hair-raising. Not counting the escorts, Convoy UGS 42 was ninety ships strong — ninety ships loaded with ammunition, high explosives and aviation fuel. A little east of Oran, they were attacked by the Germans with submarines, low-level aircraft and torpedo bombers ("long, sharky-looking Heinkels"), which came up from German bases in occupied France. On the bridge of the *Eli Whitney*, directing the efforts of his gun crews, Ruark felt naked: "There were about seven thousand tons of bombs under me, and tetryl detonators, and another two thousand tons of aviation gas in one hold of my ship, and if we got hit that was all she wrote." Almost immediately, a ship in the column just to the left of the *Eli Whitney* was hit by a bomb square amidships and she "blew like a firecracker." A gun crew on another ship, panicking, lost control of their gun and raked the bridge of a sister ship. "The air was suddenly full of iron and fire, and the shrapnel was rattling down like hailstones," Ruark said. Destroyer escorts were racing about dropping depth charges, and occasionally a plane, hard hit, would fall lazily into the sea and explode in a column of water.

The attack was almost over, and British Spitfires from their African bases were chasing off the last of the torpedo bombers, when one Heinkel made a final run and unleashed its torpedo. Ruark's starboard gun crew yelled up that there was a torpedo off the starboard bow. Ruark shouted to the captain to turn hard to starboard, into the oncoming torpedo, and allow it to slip past the fantail, but the *Eli Whitney* was fully-laden and sluggish, and had barely started to answer the wheel when the torpedo struck her right under the number two hatch. There was a "great crash" when it struck, the deck plates popped and flames appeared — but there was no explosion.

"I had seen so many ammunition ships catch the big horn and I knew what happened to them," Ruark wrote. "Pinwheels and skyrockets and one big boom. But the ship did not blow. She listed, moaned, and some fires flickered and went out, but she did not blow. Nobody knows why. For the longest thirty seconds of any man's life she was potential explosion and she didn't explode. I was an older man when I went round to the ladder and yelled down at the Old Man..."

The Old Man, in this case, was the quiet-spoken Dane who commanded the *Eli Whitney*. In response to Ruark's query as to whether they should get off and walk, he replied that the ship was still answering the wheel, and she was still underway, and she was not blowing up. So they would stay aboard and see what happened. In a newspaper column six years later, Ruark described Captain Karl Peder Olsen as "about the calmest old gentleman I ever saw, and certainly one of the bravest. As long as she answered the wheel, he would have driven the ship to hell and back again. He regarded bombs and mines and torpedoes as minor hindrances to navigation."

They continued on to Malta, getting bombed along the way, then from there through the Adriatic Sea to the port of Bari, dodging mines and getting bombed. This was one of the first Allied convoys into Bari, which became the major supply port for the British and American armies fighting up through Italy. From there Ruark's ship returned to Bizerte, where she survived another encounter with a submarine and got hit by lightning. Off Oran, the Germans sank another ship as she sailed out to join the homebound convoy, and the *Eli Whitney* finally reached Philadelphia on Thanksgiving Day, 1943. Because it was Thanksgiving Day, no one in the United States was working, and so the bruised and battered old ship, with her bruised and battered crew, was forced to heave to and wait offshore, fuming at the delay after two months of convoy duty in a very hot war zone.

When Ruark finally disembarked, he reports, he was "a little mad" for a while. He drank too much and slept too little; he had "noisy trouble with waiters" and hit a Pullman conductor for some offense, real or imagined. "It was going to be a long time before I could hear an airplane in the night without coming full awake and reaching blindly for tin hat and pistol," he wrote. One afternoon he was at his mother-in-law's house taking a nap, while she held a bridge party for her friends downstairs. A commercial plane came in low over the house, and Ruark "hit the stairs, running. That I was entirely naked seemed to disconcert the female guests."

A few weeks after the *Eli Whitney* unloaded her cargo and departed from Bari, the Germans mounted a major air attack on the town. On the night of December 2, the JU-88s came over and attacked the ships anchored in the harbor. A single bomb hit the ammunition ship *John Harvey*. There was a moment's hesitation and then a momentous explosion that destroyed the *John Harvey*, sank sixteen other merchantmen, and damaged half a dozen more. Some of the ships were carrying bombs charged with mustard gas; these detonated and sent a wave of mustard gas rolling across the harbor. More than a thousand Allied servicemen were killed, and another thousand Italian civilians. The harbor was unusable for months.

"Researching the convoys that Ruark was on in the Atlantic, you come to the conclusion that he was immensely lucky. All around him ships were sinking, people were dying, ammunition ships were exploding, and he came through it all without a scratch," said military historian Derek Nelson. Ruark himself agreed.

\* \* \*

Ruark and his crew were finally relieved. A month later, he was promoted to lieutenant (j.g.). While he waited for his next posting, he and Virginia moved to New Orleans. She returned to Washington in March, 1944, and Lt. Ruark assumed command of the Armed Guard crew of a new ship, the S.S. *Afoundria*. The *Afoundria* was 6,000 tons, a fast troopship capable of doing fifteen knots, and with considerably more serious armament than the *Eli Whitney*. Her assignment was ferrying troops to Guadalcanal in preparation for the final Allied assault on Japan. The war in the Pacific was not at that stage nearly so concentrated as the U-boat peak in either the Atlantic or the Mediterranean, and the voyage was uneventful.

While the *Afoundria* was refitted for the return voyage, Ruark and some fellow officers went on a tour of the nearby Russell Islands. Their jeep overturned on a muddy road, and Ruark suffered a severe shoulder injury. A naval surgeon repaired it as best he could, and Ruark returned with the *Afoundria* to Treasure Island Naval Station near San Francisco. There he was relieved of his command and underwent several months of therapy in Oakland before being transferred back to Washington where he could be treated at Bethesda Naval Hospital. As he recovered from the injury, he passed the time doing some reporting. Summer came and went. He applied for, and was granted, war-correspondent status, but the Navy was not about to let him go. Instead of discharging him or giving him inactive status, he was ordered instead to Hawaii. Lt. Robert Ruark's next assignment was in the U.S. Navy's public-relations office. His career as an active naval officer in the thick of battle was over.

\* \* \*

For his part, Alec Barr later reflected that the war had been "the greatest single boon of a short and very lucky professional life."

*Through no real aim of his own, quite a lot of exciting things had happened to Alec Barr in the war, and he was seldom able to bring himself to speak of them. Somebody had asked him once: 'But what did you do in those four years?' and he had answered, not meaning to be rude: 'Nothing very much.'*

*'But where did you go?' if the questioner was determined to persist.*

*'Oh, places,' Alec Barr would say. 'North Atlantic. Mediterranean. South Pacific. Islands. England. Australia. Hawaii. Just places. Sometimes scared out of my wits when I wasn't being bored to death.'*

*And dismissed it all with a short, entirely insincere laugh.*

Like his creator, however, Alec Barr found something in the Navy that he had been looking for all his life. It can be described in many ways: a sense of security, of belonging, of knowing what would happen tomorrow without having to make decisions, of moving from day to day without the need for ambition or to out-do rivals and competitors, of having people around doing their jobs just as you are doing yours — them helping to keep you alive, you doing your best for them, and knowing that you can all depend on each other, regardless of what happens. The closeness and the intimacy of a military unit is rarely appreciated by those who have not experienced it, and there is really nothing like it in civilian life.

For a man like Robert Ruark, who had an unsettled childhood, had been a loner, and had been on his own more or less since he left home, at fifteen, to go to university, such a feeling of belonging was immensely gratifying. In many ways, Ruark found a home in the Navy. It may not have been fashionable to feel affection for the Navy (or the Air Force, Army, or Marines) but Ruark did, nonetheless, and this affection stayed with him for the rest of his life.

In later years he would tell himself that, if all else failed, "I can always go back to sea."

\* \* \*

*Chapter Five*

# TRIALS
# OF BABYLON

In later years, Robert Ruark delighted in telling the tale of how he was discharged from the Navy in 1945. By the end of the conflict he was in a "semi-civilian" job in the censor's office in Australia, attached to the Royal Navy. Ruark loved Australia at first sight, not least of all because of the Australian women. His natural charm, combined with his admirable war record, took him a long way in a country whose able-bodied menfolk were mostly off fighting the Japanese. As the war drew to a close, however, Ruark wanted to get home more and more, the various fascinations of Australia notwithstanding; when Japan surrendered, he realized, there would be a rush for the boats, and he did not relish the idea of standing in line with the other about-to-be-discharged servicemen.

Having a desk job, with access to a typewriter, all the necessary forms, and a knowledge by this time of exactly how the service worked (and more important, how it did *not* work), Lt. Ruark cut himself a new set of orders, bumped a ranking general off a flight, and flew home to Washington. His reception at naval headquarters was less than ecstatic, since his superiors believed he was still in the Pacific. By Ruark's own account, he was unable to get an audience with an admiral to arrange his (legal) discharge, so he stood in the street outside the building and threw rocks at the admiral's window to attract attention. Because the war was over and Ruark had an excellent service record of duty under fire, it was considered expedient, rather than court-martialing him for desertion, to quietly process him out of the Navy and back into what he called "the grey oatmealy realities of the peace."

Like many servicemen returning home, what he expected and what he found were two completely different things. The utter lack of personal responsibility in the service — in the sense that you go where you are sent, and you do what you are told to do, and you cope with what you find when you get there — becomes a warm and happy memory when you are faced with decisions such as where to live, where to work, and what to pursue as a career. Returning to his pre-war job as "meek morning editor of the Washington *Daily News*" did not, by itself, appeal to a man who had commanded other men under fire, who had travelled the world and seen ships sink and his friends die, often horribly. From now on, Robert Ruark decided, he was going to live his life on his own terms.

* * *

Ruark was, by instinct and inclination, a newspaperman, and the years immediately after the war and before the advent of television were, in many ways, the heyday of newspapers. Radio, while a powerful medium in some ways, had failed to dislodge the printed word as the primary source of news and opinion — opinion that was molded by columnists who enjoyed nationwide celebrity status. The syndicated columnists of that time wielded considerable power and influence, to say nothing of freedom. Walter Winchell, Heywood Broun, and Walter Lippmann were household names, and a columnist who caught the public's attention, who was read religiously regardless of subject matter, and who helped sell newspapers, was, to a great extent, free to write his own ticket. The freedom to go where he wanted and to cover the stories (and only those stories) that seized his imagination, appealed to Robert Ruark, and he set his sights on getting a syndicated column.

Post-war America certainly did not lack for news stories, so finding something to write about was no problem. The atomic bomb, the Cold War, the activities of the House Un-American Activities Committee, the beginnings of new wars in Indochina and Malaya, the dismantling of the British, French, and Belgian colonial empires — all of these guaranteed a steady diet of headlines. The problem was not news, it was getting attention. As any reporter can tell you, there is a big difference. For Robert Ruark, returning serviceman, the competition was rather heated;

established columnists and returning war correspondents, replete with anecdotes and high-level contacts, dominated the news wires. Going back to work for the Washington *Daily News* was easy enough; elbowing his way into the ranks of the syndicated columnists was not.

The one thing Ruark could offer that big names like Edward R. Murrow could not was the perspective of a man who had seen the war from the inside — who had actually fired the guns and been shot at, had frozen on eight-hour wheel-watches in the North Atlantic, and had faced death on a daily basis. The Edward R. Murrows might have the ears of the mighty, but Robert Ruark could reach the imaginations of twelve million returning servicemen, and they were the people who bought the newspapers. As he figured it, anything that made him "glad, sad or mad" probably did the same for those twelve million other men who were in the same boat; all he had to do was put his finger on it. And what does a man alone in a foxhole think about when the bullets aren't flying? Women. And what does he look for first when he comes down the gangplank in New York? Women. And what were the returning men actually finding? *Not* women, according to Ruark — at least not the women they had been dreaming about for the past four years. He looked around, as he put it, for the biggest window he could find and prepared to lob a rock through it. The window that grabbed his attention was the one through which the returning servicemen viewed, with increasing horror, disappointment, and dismay, the vision of American womanhood that greeted them as they got off the boat.

"During the war, since I was almost perpetually attached to lonesome ships and chained to lonelier islands, I had considerable opportunity to dwell upon dames and their place in our time," he wrote later, in a piece that was included in a posthumous anthology called, simply, *Women*. While on watch in the Pacific off the island of Espiritu Santo in the New Hebrides, Ruark concluded that the key to his future prosperity as a columnist was to play upon the vanity of women. Men were sure to love it and women were sure to hate it, but either way it was sure to sell newspapers. He began with a column that on the surface appeared to be about women's fashions, but which he later insisted was really a piece about "S*E*X." In Ruark's view, women's fashions, from hairstyles to padded shoulders to spike-heeled shoes, were a conspiracy designed to cause those men to run back up the gangplanks and set sail once more for the South Pacific. He presented that opinion in a feature that appeared in November, 1945, and (Ruark commented innocently) "oddly, made the newspaper front pages." The world was never quite the same again, and Ruark's career as a syndicated columnist was launched amid a mob of nodding heads on the one hand and infuriated letters on the other.

Many years later, Ruark remarked that he had been a "professional wiseguy" as a columnist, and that phrase sums him up as neatly as anything. Reading his columns today, they are mostly dated, not only in subject matter but in their writing style as well. They are, for the most part, mildly amusing but eminently forgettable. The style of the day, as epitomized by Walter Winchell, was short, snappy, opinionated, and laden with slang; it was designed to grab attention first, to inform a distant second. There were political columnists, who ranged from the thickly ponderous to the thunderingly partisan; there were comic columnists, who wrote about their home life, their difficulty with income tax forms, or with getting the car started on a cold morning. Those who wail about the influence of television today, which seeks the lowest common denominator of intellect and then caters to it, should take a close look at the newspaper columns of the 1940s and '50s. Nostalgia aside, they were not much better, and in some ways, such as blatant libel and character assassination, they were considerably worse.

Robert Ruark's columns fell somewhere in the middle. He wrote about politics, southern cooking, and the atomic bomb; he wrote about his dog, and living in Greenwich Village, and the mob. In one instance, he wrote about a mobster, walking his dog for him, in Greenwich Village. When it later became an issue, he wrote about civil rights and the attitudes of politicians in the Deep South. New York taxicabs, child rearing, and women's fashions became staples — and there is nothing a daily columnist needs more than tomorrow's sure-fire topic. Early on, he hit on his own domestic life as a winner, in that he could present Virginia as wife, feminist, autocrat, villain, heroine — but always, ultimately, the winner in any domestic squabble. It was formula writing to be sure, but it is a formula that predated Ruark by several centuries and will outlast him by several more.

To a working journalist, writing a daily column seems like a holiday. You write about what you want, offer your opinions, then knock off and go for a drink. Anyone who has written a column, however, knows the dictatorial deadline is a constant enemy, and life is one long search for the next topic. A truism of the business is that everyone in the world has three months' worth of columns in him, waiting to pour forth; what separates the would-be columnist from the genuine article is how you fill that newspaper space, on time and every day, in the months and years after the easy topics run dry. There is a limit to how many times you can write about the same thing. Variety is an absolute necessity of survival, and a columnist is only as successful as the newspapers he helps to sell on any given day.

It is an ephemeral business — literally. Today's triumph is forgotten if tomorrow's column is boring, obscure, or in some way fails to touch a chord with various editors and is relegated to a back page. Then as now, there were means for polling readers and finding out if they read a column regularly, and if so, why. Ruark admitted that, even after he was an established columnist, the arrival of each day's paper was torture. The first thing he would do was look to see where his column had been placed, how it had been treated, and whether his picture was, in fact, at the top beside the headline. In his perceptive foreword to *Robert Ruark's Africa*, Michael McIntosh says of him, "His success was entirely of his own making, and yet he never believed it could last. At the core, he was a deeply fearful man, lacking all but the merest shreds of confidence in his own ability." This hard-core insecurity stayed with Ruark throughout his entire professional life — as reporter, columnist, and novelist. No matter how great his success, he always feared it could be snatched away from him at any moment.

In *The Honey Badger*, commenting on the writing business generally in New York, Alec Barr's agent, Marc Mantell, says "This is a forgetful business in a forgetful town." Nowhere is that more true than in the business of daily newspaper column-writing. Columnists spend their early years elbowing their way into the ranks, and their later years trying to keep from being elbowed aside by newcomers.

Like most of his contemporaries, Robert Ruark mined the news wires for material. He stockpiled clippings and every so often would present a grab-bag column of funny titbits with suitable comment. Lightweight it might be, but it helped fill the gaps when ideas would not come. More than that, however, Ruark did actually go out and search for news. He was, like Winchell (to quote Hemingway, who had a very low opinion of newspaper columnists) "the most working of working newspapermen." Ruark defined a columnist as "a reporter with a point of view." This was an era in which a columnist, if he was a working newspaperman, dug up stories and broke them in his column. Ruark did that more than once during his early years as a columnist, and in a very high-profile way.

His first column, the "rock through the window" feature, had its desired effect: It caught the attention of Roy Howard, of the Scripps-Howard newspaper empire, and he hired Ruark as a feature writer, working out of head office in New York City. In January, 1946, Robert Ruark left Washington and moved to New York, checking into the Elysée Hotel on East 54th Street in Manhattan while he looked around for an apartment. Back in Washington, Virginia packed up the household effects and prepared to join him, which she did in June of that year. They found an apartment in Manhattan and settled in to become New Yorkers.

The Scripps-Howard chain, like most of its contemporaries, owned individual newspapers but also ran its own syndication service, employing both columnists and beat reporters. Its two major newspapers were the New York *World-Telegram* and Ruark's *alma mater*, the Washington *Daily News*. When he went to New York, the managing editor of the Scripps-Howard News Service was Dick Thornburg, who was later replaced by Ruark's old friend from Washington, Walker Stone. On hearing that Ruark had been hired, Thornburg was enthusiastic about having him aboard, but offered some advice as to how he should approach his column: Don't be a clown, he said, and write what you see and hear, not what you think. Most of all, Ruark should have fun and let it show in the copy. It was a wide-ranging mandate in one way, but it required considerable self-discipline as well.

The newspaper business is built on self-discipline, because with few exceptions, editors care about two things, and two things only: Getting good copy, and getting it on time. Of the two, meeting deadlines is the more important. The daily newspaper business and the wire services are ruled by deadlines, and because their products — news stories — are transitory at best, what really counts more than literary quality is having copy that is accurate, that is the right length with the names spelled correctly, and that lands on the editor's desk with minutes to spare. In the era before television, there were both morning and evening newspapers. Most major cities had one of each, and a metropolis like New York would have at least two of each. The morning papers competed with each other, and the evening papers competed with each other, and the two solitudes fed off one another, cannibalising stories for fresh copy and new leads.

On top of this, most papers would have more than one edition, and some had as many as six. The "bulldog edition" of a morning paper might appear on the streets as early as ten o'clock the night before, and the last edition hit at seven in the morning. The first edition of an afternoon paper would roll off the press at nine, and the last one late in the afternoon to catch people on their way home. In those halcyon days there were also the "Extras," special editions printed on a moment's notice, that were generally replates of the latest edition with a new headline shouting the news of events like the explosion of the *Hindenburg* or the bombing of Pearl Harbor. Competition — for readers, newsstand sales, and advertising — was as intense as it has ever been in any medium. Reporters were under constant pressure to deliver, and no one cared very much how they did it.

A columnist who had free rein, such as Robert Ruark, was allowed to work pretty much as he pleased, as long as he met his deadlines. By definition, a reporter is rarely in the office except when he is waiting for an assignment, writing his copy, or picking up his check. If you are not required for spot assignments on a moment's notice, as a reporter is, most editors are quite happy to let you work wherever you are most productive. Early on, Ruark's apartment became his office as well, a practice he continued for the rest of his life.

New York City, especially Manhattan, was the postwar Mecca for anyone seeking the big time, whether in newspapers, advertising, sports, or show business. Joe DiMaggio was playing for the New York Yankees, and the Brooklyn Dodgers were still ensconced at Ebbetts Field. It was a late-night town, and Damon Runyon was its wise-cracking chronicler. On

Broadway, Rogers & Hammerstein competed with Nathan Detroit and Harry the Horse. For those who did not deal with them personally, even the gangsters had a certain panache and included such legendary names as Lucky Luciano and Bugsy Siegel. Black shirts with white ties, snap-brimmed hats, and loud-checked sports jackets were in. Flying to Havana was a popular weekend pastime, and there was always the chance of seeing Ernest Hemingway seated in a corner of the Floridita reading El Diario.

Robert Ruark stepped off the train in Grand Central Station in January of 1946 and instantly became a New Yorker. In later years, everyone from critics to biographers would describe Ruark as a boulevardier, a quaint term that evokes images of Maurice Chevalier and, in Ruark's case, was not a compliment. New York is, like Paris and London, a society town. There are places to go and places to be seen. Its social life is a living, breathing entity, something you do not find in cities like Pittsburgh or Chicago. For Robert Ruark, a small-town boy from North Carolina who had spent his professional life in Washington, New York City was like a vast candy store — and Ruark was a small boy with an insatiable sweet tooth. The deprivations of his childhood, his years at university during the Depression, the tough climb up the newspaper ranks in Washington, eating the local diner's blue-plate special every day for lunch, and his time cheating death in the Atlantic — all compounded to give him an insatiable appetite for everything New York was and what he aspired to be. The city's pounding rhythms appealed to him. The same forces that shaped Guys & Dolls, that inspired Runyon and Frank Loesser and Leonard Bernstein, had their immediate effect on Robert Ruark, and he began to shape his life to the city around him.

One of the strongest characteristics of a good writer — of any good journalist, in fact — is the ability to blend into the scene around you like a chameleon. It allows you to see something from the inside, while remaining on the outside. In The Honey Badger, in a conversation with actress Barbara Bayne, Alec Barr compares writing with acting. We're both hams, he tells her. "You adopt the protective coloration of a country or a situation or a group just like a chameleon changes his color. Yours is surface — Smithfield ham. I soak up my contact with situation,

76

and store it away. That makes me a Serrano ham." Used carefully, it is a very useful attribute, but carried to extremes it can be harmful. Robert Ruark employed this ability to great effect throughout his life, from the Navy to New York to Nairobi, but nowhere was it as destructive as in his efforts to become part of New York's "saloon society." His self-destructive tendencies, especially in alcohol consumption, were always there, but Manhattan provided the perfect environment to make them develop with horrifying ease.

According to Hugh Foster, Ruark's daily schedule reads like something out of Damon Runyon. He would get up at noon, or later. His schedule was managed by his secretary, Leila Hadley, "a 19-year-old divorcee," according to Foster, who "arrived for work around ten in the morning and worked sometimes until midnight. Though he seldom arose before noon, he would leave written instructions for her before retiring at night and there was always work to be done. She typed his daily column, answered the mail, and researched the topics that interested him. She also made his phone calls, booked his lunches, and kept track of his social schedule."

Ruark's actual working day does not look overly arduous — a few hours late each afternoon and an hour or so more after he got home in the wee hours, usually around four a.m. In fact, he was working very long hours: From the time he got up until he went to bed shortly before dawn, he was working — gathering material for his column, making contacts, jotting things down, following things up. That most of this work got done in a saloon does not mean it was not work. An inescapable truth of life in Manhattan is that it can be a great life, if you survive Manhattan. New York City is filled with hangers-on, people who claim the attention of working writers, novelists, playwrights, columnists, painters, and sculptors. There are so many, in fact, that it is a wonder any novels, plays, or columns ever get written, paintings painted, or sculptures sculpted. The distractions that make Manhattan such a fascinating place also make it exceedingly difficult to do anything that requires concentration, time, attention, and most of all, solitude.

From all appearances, Robert Ruark applied his chameleon-like qualities to fitting in all too well. He adopted a lifestyle that gave new meaning to the term "frenetic," as if his liver had absorbed entirely too little punishment during his years at sea and he was determined to make up for lost time. His haunts were Toots Shor's and Twenty-One for lunch; P.J. Clarke's, The Stork Club, El Morocco, and Eddie Condon's late into the night. He moved through Greenwich Village and Harlem like a prowling alley cat, exploring the darker caves with all the relish of a country boy who steps off the bus with a fistful of banknotes and not much time to live. All accounts of Ruark's life in Manhattan, from his own rueful but boastful recollections to Hugh Foster's disapproving judgments, suggest a breathtaking pace, as if he simply could not wait for his own destruction.

* * *

What is sometimes forgotten, although it never was by Ruark himself, is that he was an immensely successful columnist and journalist throughout it all. His renown as a columnist does not rest on his turn of phrase describing New York taxicabs, but on two stories in particular that he broke as exclusives and pursued to the bitter end. The first involved Frank Sinatra and Lucky Luciano, and the second was about a prominent U.S. Army general in postwar Europe. As triumphs of investigative journalism, neither was quite Pulitzer Prize material, although Ruark was justifiably proud of them at the time.

Charles "Lucky" Luciano was a New York mobster of considerable notoriety in the 1940s, being a cohort of Benjamin "Bugsy" Siegel (of Las Vegas *Flamingo* fame) and Meyer Lansky, as well as former luminaries like Dutch Schultz. At one time, Luciano's main business was brothels, and he was finally convicted on a vice-trafficking charge, sent to prison, and, on his release, deported to Italy. From there he migrated to Havana, Cuba, which became his base for running his part of the New York mob and its expanding interests in places like Las Vegas. Frank Sinatra was then in the early years of his career, a slender young crooner from New Jersey who was the heart-throb of millions of teenage girls but not much else. Still, he was a popular public figure who was idolized, and who, at the time, made a great show of trying to direct young feet onto the straight and narrow path. Consorting with known mobsters was not, as Robert Ruark repeatedly pointed out, much of an example to the young.

When Ruark arrived in Havana in early 1947 as part of a trip around the country to visit friends and gather column material, he happened to see Sinatra in the company of Luciano and his bodyguards, as well as various other unidentified notables of the underworld. Ruark then unleashed a series of columns, condemning Luciano's activities, applauding his deportation from the United States, and repeatedly asking what Sinatra was doing in his company. Shortly after these appeared, Luciano was deported from Cuba, which was reacting to a threat by the American government to halt shipments of pharmaceutical drugs if Luciano was allowed to stay. Ruark later claimed he "ran Lucky Luciano out of Cuba." His columns probably did have some effect in marshalling public opinion on the matter and maybe even goading Washington into doing something, but Ruark was not solely responsible. Back in New York, his columns drew considerable criticism in the form of threats, both from Luciano's fellow mobsters (as Ruark would have it) and Frank Sinatra's fans.

Sinatra himself suffered little from the attack. He insisted he just happened to meet Luciano in a casino in Havana and could hardly be held responsible for the character of everyone who approached him in a bar. Even as early as the 1940s there were rumors about Sinatra's mob connections, although Ruark was the first reporter to come up with some solid evidence and put it in the newspapers. For their part, the newspapers knew good copy when they saw it and splashed Ruark's columns on Sinatra and Luciano all over the front page. News stories about Sinatra and the mafia have always had an air of self-righteousness about them that completely ignores the fact that, if you grow up of Italian heritage in an Italian neighborhood, chances are you are going to know a lot of different people, some good, some bad. Some childhood friends grow up to be famous mobsters, others become famous singers. This is not to justify "consorting with known mobsters," as the phrase quaintly goes, but simply to point out that it is a fact of real life.

Robert Ruark, however, saw the impact he was having and homed in on Sinatra personally. In his last column on the affair, he called Sinatra "a menace to the mental and moral welfare of several million adolescents." Obviously, the publicity did not hurt Sinatra one bit, and it most definitely helped the career of one R. Ruark, Esq. The impact on Luciano is not known. Ironically, by the early 1960s, Sinatra was a global superstar and Robert Ruark was a big fan of his music. Both had moved on to bigger and better things.

Ruark's next splash as a muck-raking columnist involved a man who was not then, and never would be, a household name. And so, many years after the fact, reading Ruark's lip-smacking description of how he brought down Lieutenant General John C.H. "Courthouse" Lee, the immediate reaction is, "Huh?" Here is what happened.

In the early summer of 1947, fresh from his triumph over Luciano and Sinatra, Ruark set out for Europe on a trip down memory lane: A series of visits to seaports he had known when he was in the Navy, on convoy duty to the Mediterranean. The itinerary included Gibraltar, cities on the North African coast, and, of course, Italy. At the time, there were still large standing armies in Europe, and the U.S. Army was a major presence in what had been the Mediterranean theatre of operations. The commander-in-chief of the United States Armed Forces in the Mediterranean was Lt. Gen. J.C.H. Lee. His headquarters were in the Italian city of Leghorn. There had been for some time bits and pieces of stories leaking out about abuses in the armed forces in Europe, which is not surprising when you consider the situation. The continent was only just beginning reconstruction, and there were occupying armies everywhere you looked, from the Russians in eastern Europe, to the British, Canadians, Australians, and Americans in Italy and Germany. The military establishments were still huge, because it takes time to dismantle a major military machine. As well, there were areas of the continent that were still under, if not martial law, then at least a form of benevolent military government.

During the war, Lt. Gen. Lee had been on General Eisenhower's staff in Britain, in charge of supply. When the war ended and the big-name generals either retired, returned home, or were promoted to senior positions in the Pentagon, Lt. Gen. Lee was given a major command in Europe. He appears to have been the kind of rear-echelon warrior who strides forth to assume command when the fighting is done, his chest resplendent with ribbons denoting nothing except accidents of time and place. Such officers can be found in all armies at all times, but nowhere can their questionable talents bloom so fully as right after a war, when the fighting is done but the budgets are still huge, civil government is weak or nonexistent, and the senior generals become a law unto themselves. Even so, Lt. Gen. Lee seems to have set new standards of self-aggrandizement and abuse of authority.

Robert Ruark went to Italy, saw the HQ, talked with the men, and went home to write a series of exposés. What he saw in Italy had enraged him; as a former officer who had spent a good part of his military career in the thick of some of the fiercest fighting of the war, the posturing of peacetime martinets like Lee naturally infuriated him. Some of the accusations against Lee seem trifling now; his actions were irritating and silly, perhaps, but hardly court-martial material. For example, it was said that Lee had military policemen from a black unit specially outfitted and polished to a high sheen, then stationed throughout the town specifically to stop other traffic and salute him as he passed. If so, Lee was only following military tradition: A hundred years earlier, Lord Cardigan, one of the most infuriating martinets the British Army ever produced (and the man who led the Charge of the Light Brigade at Balaclava), did the same thing with men from his regiment, the 11th Light Dragoons, nick-named the "Cherry Pickers" because of their flamboyant red breeches. The smartest-looking soldiers were given a day's leave and five shillings, and were stationed throughout London with orders to snap to and salute when Lord Cardigan passed. One difference, of course, was that their pocket money came from Cardigan's personal account, not from the military budget.

Other charges against Lee were more serious, otherwise the whole thing would have been dismissed as civilian carping. Lee's men, it was said, were deprived of such essentials as proper food and washing facilities, and the money spent instead so Lee and the other officers could live in luxury. The general had special staff cars, special aircraft at his disposal, and strode around in polished boots and spurs. If that were the case, he may have been modeling himself on Gen. George Patton, whose home-made uniforms made Lord Cardigan's men look drab. The difference, of course, was that Patton fought the battles and won the wars, and so could be forgiven his eccentricities; Lt. Gen. Lee was merely an elevated poppinjay (to use a Cardiganesque term). One other difference was that Patton never neglected his men, who worshipped him, whereas Lee's men hated him and ultimately gave Ruark the material to blow the whistle. Which Ruark did, with a vengeance.

The series of columns appeared in August, 1947. In them, Ruark exposed the excesses of the officers, the deprivations of the rank and file, and the idiosyncracies of Lee himself. The first column appeared on August 11; on August 14, Scripps-Howard reported that a congressional subcommittee was looking into Ruark's charges, and after that events unfolded with astonishing alacrity. Lt. Gen. Lee issued the usual denials, the army began an investigation, and the general decided that honorable retirement was in order. Meanwhile, other newspapers and magazines had picked up the story and were in full cry. As Ruark later commented, "many of them were covering me." He was, he said, the complete expert on the story, and even had aircraft laid on to allow other reporters to cover *him*. As a journalistic triumph it belonged more to the wild and woolly days of Ben Hecht and crusading newspapers than it did to the Watergate affair and the advent of investigative journalism a quarter-century later, but for Ruark personally it was the story that turned him from a columnist who wrote about things, into a man about whom things were written. He made *Time* and *Newsweek*, and later that year was described by *Life* as "the most talked about reporter in the U.S. today." Ruark also became a syndicated columnist for United Features, a Scripps-Howard subsidiary, which allowed him to be published in any newspaper that subscribed to the syndicate.

In 1948, John Freeman, managing editor of United Features, nominated Robert Ruark for the Pulitzer Prize in National Reporting and submitted the Lee series to the Columbia School of Journalism for consideration, along with other examples of Ruark's work. He did not win the Pulitzer, but that hardly mattered. As a national columnist, no more proof was needed that he had, indeed, arrived.

Fifteen years later, Robert Ruark had achieved sufficient status that *True* Magazine asked him to write an autobiographical piece, published as part of its continuing series titled "The Man I Know Best." In it, Ruark reviewed his own life from start to finish and summed up his post-war journalism career this way: "You get started with a gimmick. Mine was a simple gimmick. I came out of the war looking for an easy way to make a living, and maybe some largish money as well..." He had, he pointed out, established himself as a magazine writer before the war, and during the latter stages of the conflict when he was on staff duty, or kicking his heels at home waiting for a new posting, he had written various pieces for *Collier's, the Saturday Evening Post,* and *Liberty.* When the war ended, he had the contacts, the skills and, Lord knows, he had the material to write about, but doing magazine articles was "piecework." There was too much time required to prepare and sell each article for the amount of money received at the far end (a lament that any modern-day magazine writer will echo). What Ruark wanted was a steady gig — a daily column that would bring in the money, each week and every week, regardless of where he was or what he was doing.

Having decided he would write for the twelve million returning servicemen, Ruark described his ideal writing as "not as lofty as Lippmann, not as gossipy as Winchell, not as bosom-conscious as Wilson, not as angry as Pegler. I would be a cosmic columnist..." It only needed, he said, a few things: "A fast kickoff, and then a succession of attention-getters, and somebody would be coming around with a fat contract for syndication." The actual events followed the script to the letter. The first column on women's clothes, or as Ruark put it, "S*E*X," was the kickoff; Sinatra, Luciano and Lt. Gen. Lee provided the follow-up attention getters. Thus Ruark the writer, on Ruark the reporter:

These good stories only really happen when you're young, with strong arches, and the digestive processes of a goat. In those days I could use gin as a substitute for slumber and still write fifteen columns in a brisk afternoon at the portable.

It was a wondrous time of lucky reporting.

Wondrous and lucky, to be sure, and, to his credit, Robert Ruark made the most of it.

* * *

It is amazing now, looking back at Ruark's first five years in New York, to see the amount of work and travel he managed to pack in. This was in the days when trans-Atlantic air travel took sixteen hours instead of six, and when most journeying around the country was still done by train. Ruark, whatever his other faults (and in spite of written disclaimers to the contrary on his part) was never lazy, and his output in terms of words written and words printed was astounding. One time, he mentions, he wrote sixteen columns at a sitting, in a hotel room in Rome, working through the night to file a backlog of columns before he continued on to Africa.

Ruark had been a working columnist in New York for barely a year when he published his first book, a "spoof of a historical novel" titled *Grenadine Etching, Her Life and Loves*. The dust jacket copy describes it as a "hilarious and riotous lampoon," and "a brilliant burlesque." Ruark himself goes on to describe it thus:

*It is a very adequate historical novel, suitable for Hollywood, book clubs, or for lighting the fire. You want sex? Sex we have. You desire action, intrigue, discussions of food and clothes and philosophy? We have them all.*

It is, according to the dust jacket, also a book of "straight thinking and sharp satire, all very much in the tradition of Robert Ruark's enormously popular syndicated column." Alas, *Grenadine Etching* is also as eminently forgettable as most of Ruark's columns: written for today, written for the fast buck, written to grab attention, to get a laugh, and then move on. In 1947, historical novels of the Samuel Shellabarger (*Prince of Foxes*) genre were the rage. They appeared in hardcover, shortly followed by paperbacks with lurid jackets, and were made into movies starring second-tier actors and actresses. Presumably, everyone involved made a pretty good living, however, and Robert Ruark never wrote anything in his life where he did not keep an eagle eye on the money involved. Whether *Grenadine Etching* made much money is another question. It did not sell well, and Ruark ruefully advised anyone "with a book in him" to leave it right where it was. But the book certainly added a little lustre to his name as a popular writer.

The action largely takes place in New Orleans and involves a cast of characters that are larger than any life should be. Ruark brings in historical characters in outrageous situations, and while much of it may have been pretty funny at the time, very little of it is funny (or even comprehensible) now. Without the daily headlines to give context to the in-jokes, none of it makes a great deal of sense. In an odd sort of a way, the

book reminds one of Ernest Hemingway's *Torrents of Spring*, a satire on
Sherwood Anderson intended for the sole purpose of breaking his contract with his publisher, Boni & Liveright. Unless you have read Anderson's novel *Dark Laughter*, which was the immediate object of the satire,
the satire itself makes little sense. Today, *Torrents of Spring* is a Hemingway curiosity and nothing more; similarly, *Grenadine Etching*.

Reflecting on the book's reception in his column, Ruark reported that
"*Life* magazine did about seven pages on it. *Time* murdered it, but
*Newsweek* loved it good. The papers kicked it around, for good or evil,
and I went on the radio..." Ruark the columnist takes jabs at Ruark the
novelist, and the column satirizes the novel — journalistic recycling
with a vengeance, proving yet again that everything that happens in a
writer's life is bound to end up in print somewhere, eventually if not
sooner. Ruark being Ruark, beneath the surface lather of humor lies the
real truth of what it is like for a first-time author seeing his work bound
between hard covers:

> (You think) this is a real, live Book. At least it's got words in it and my
> name on it. But it's a false emotion. All you've got is a dead chicken
> around your neck, and you wear it for months. Even when it begins to
> stink you still wear it.
>
> Then the reviews flow in, and the torture starts. What you thought was
> funny ain't. You thought the book was too short. Some fugitive from a
> pawnshop thinks it was too long. You thought...

And thought, and thought: All the conflicting emotions of an
author, weighing the good reviews against the bad, lying awake nights
trying to figure which are the accurate reviews and which are merely
jealousy or sycophancy — all of these come into play. Ruark became
what he called a "victim of literary lead poisoning — a dire disease which
comes from operating outside your regular racket." He was a happy man
once, he said, before he became a book author. "Now I am merely
addicted to benzedrine, whisky, and rest homes. With quilted lounges."

As it turned out, if literary lead poisoning was a disease, it was a malady
without a cure. The one lasting value of *Grenadine Etching* was that it
showed Robert Ruark he could, and should, write books. Certainly that
was the feeling of his publisher, Doubleday & Company. The following

year, Doubleday published an anthology of his newspaper columns, *I Didn't Know It Was Loaded*, which, true to form, included his just-quoted column entitled "Authors and Ulcers." According to Ruark, the book's title has very little to do with its content. He used it because, he insisted, "someone gave it to me, *gratis*, and good free titles are hard to come by." The correct title would have been: "Food, drink, dogs, sports, radio, women, children, cosmetics, fashion, war, peace, wives, husbands, architects, actors, columnists, jugglers, Chinamen, singers, artists, houses, apartments, birds, bees, flowers, and juke boxes." But, he said, as a title, that was too long and not sensational enough, although it certainly summed up, not only the contents of the book, but Ruark's daily column besides.

From the beginning, his wife, Virginia, was a favorite column topic, whether as subject matter or alleged instigator thereof. The image of the bumbling husband whose wife allows him to revel in his own supposed superiority while, in reality, she calls the shots, was a staple not only of columnists, but of comedians, radio shows and, later, television writers. Here is how Ruark established Virginia's literary persona, Mama: "It is a damned lie that Mama writes my stuff. I write it. She just tells me what to write. I generally obey her, because she is smarter than I am. Also, she is bigger than I am."

Although *I Didn't Know It Was Loaded* mostly contains Ruark's daily columns, some chapters were written expressly for the book, and others were columns expanded beyond their original length. They were then grouped and titled by subject matter, such as "This Is New York."

A year later, Doubleday published a second volume along the same lines, *One for the Road*. Although it followed the same format as *Loaded*, for the first time Ruark allowed a hint of seriousness to creep in. The book was dedicated to Rocky Riley, the former sports editor of the Washington *Daily News*, the man to whom Ruark felt he owed a lot for the writer he had become. In the foreword he talked about Riley's views on the craft of writing, and credited him with any discipline he might have as a writer. Riley, he added, would probably have hated the fact that the book was dedicated to him, since he "had a pretty low opinion of people who committed books. He ranked them with newspapermen who wore spats." With that sentence alone, you see what a good influence Riley had been.

\* \* \*

Robert Ruark had been in New York barely four years and had already published three books, as well as close to a thousand newspaper columns. In pursuit of material, he had travelled to Europe, North Africa, South and Central America, the Caribbean, and all over North America. Manhattan was now his home, and he and Virginia were living in a flat in Greenwich Village with their boxer dog, Schnorkel. Schnorkel had become something of a celebrity himself, having been adopted by a local mobster who appeared periodically and politely asked permission to take him for a walk. He also assured Ruark that he need not worry if he accidentally left his door unlocked; no one in this neighborhood, he said, would touch the Ruark household.

For its part, the Ruark household was not exactly a nest of domestic bliss. The footloose existence of an itinerant newspaperman is not endearing even to the most understanding of wives, and Virginia was far from being that. Once in New York, she quickly abandoned any thought of a formal career in interior decorating and settled in as the wife of a celebrity columnist. She was, however, no more sympathetic to Ruark's absences as his fame increased than she had been when the *Daily News* had despatched him from pre-war Washington to cover a murder trial in the boondocks. It was not merely the absences, either: Ruark was a dedicated, almost flagrant, pursuer of other women. From the beginning Virginia had been convinced he was carrying on love affairs during every absence, and to a great extent she was right. Ruark's pursuit of other women, and his need to prove his ability as a lover, make one wonder what, exactly, he was trying to prove.

One obvious need stemmed from the fact that the Ruarks were child-less, and were destined to remain so. By 1949, they had been married for eleven years, yet they had no children and it was not for want of trying. The post-war baby boom was in full swing, with children being born left and right, yet Virginia never became pregnant. In 1947, Ruark returned from a prolonged swing through South America; exhausted, he went to see his doctor and underwent a lengthy series of tests. They proved beyond a doubt that he was sterile. This fact about their lives together became a significant part of *The Honey Badger* when it was written fifteen years later. Like Ruark, Alec Barr is sterile; like Virginia, Amelia Barr is frustrated at being deprived of having children. Reflecting on the situation in an interview many years later, Ruark opines that children really are the basis for a marriage, since there is no other sound reason for two people to live together permanently. Children become the cement that holds a couple together, and after the children are gone, the responsibility stays on. Whether this was somehow intended to justify his own behavior, which was by almost any marital standard irresponsible, is hard to say. In *The Honey Badger*, he describes the process of "baby building" with clinical brutality. Barely a dozen paragraphs into the book, Alec Barr is watching his wife as she dresses for dinner:

*Alec Barr was not seeing the fine firm breasts and the sumptuous backside. He was not seeing the thin fair skin or the dark blue eyes. He was not seeing a tall, oppressively healthy woman in her thirties. He was seeing a pretty woman drawn by Dali or Artzybasheff.*

*Alec Barr was seeing a thermometer stuck into a sumptuous backside. He was seeing a chart which logged days and hours between menstrual periods, with red checkmarks against vital dates. He was seeing taxicabs panting at the curb, waiting for the fluid of life (produced by masturbation, trapped by contraceptive, caught after swift withdrawal in a cup) so that the recipient of wishful new life might rush speedily to the gynecologist, who would inject the fluid of life into the cervix, thus avoiding vaginal acids...*

*He was seeing himself, Alexander Barr, as a sterile stallion, bought at great price, checked and crosschecked, stuffed on wheat germ until tassels grew from his ears — Alec Barr, stallion at stud who could produce no get from the willing mare.*

Hugh Foster says that the knowledge they could not have children "drove an additional wedge into the Ruark relationship. Virginia became increasingly maternal about Bob, called him 'Baby' and tried to envelop him in a blanket of expanded domesticity. He, on the other hand, increased his number of one night stands." Foster even suggests that learning of his sterility made women more accessible to Ruark, since they knew there was no danger of pregnancy if they had an affair with him, but whether that was stated by one of the participants, or was merely conjecture on his part, he does not say.

In 1964, a year after his divorce from Virginia, Ruark stated flatly, "The marriage department is for the birds unless you want to have children out of it. In the process of manufacturing them and raising them up, you have done something between you and your wife which gives you a solidity and firmness of love. Sexual love gets to be like oatmeal after one becomes divorced from the moonlight and roses and let's-fall-down-in-the-arboretum stage." This sentiment is echoed in *The Honey Badger*, indirectly, when sex between a married couple is described as "The same old trade. It lacks mystery." Perhaps Ruark was trying, with his serial seductions, to prove he was a man in spite of his sterility, or perhaps he was merely seeking to reprise the "moonlight and roses" stage of romance, by falling down in the arboretum with one new woman after another. Or, perhaps, it was simply the thrill of the chase. As with most things, the simplest explanation is the most likely. At any rate, it really does not matter what Ruark's motivations were, because his extramarital sex life had very little overt effect on his marriage over the years. No monumental love affair ever arose to cause terminal strife or a messy divorce; he and Virginia stayed married almost to the end, during which time she played a significant (if behind the scenes) role in his work, as well as providing a stable base from which to operate. Jealous she might have been, but she was just as jealous in guarding her own life as the wife of a famous writer of ever-increasing wealth, and the way to keep that life was to stay married, regardless of the indiscretions of the writer himself.

\* \* \*

Shortly after he moved to New York, Robert Ruark met Harold Matson, the literary agent who was to play an equally important role in his life, not only in promoting him as a writer but by becoming a close friend and confidante who helped Ruark over the rough spots and managed much of his private life. The Matson Agency had offices at 30 Rockefeller Plaza. Matson himself was a transplanted Californian who had emigrated to New York just before the war, and built an impressive stable of authors that included Herman Wouk, Evelyn Waugh, Richard Condon, and Arthur Koestler. Matson also has an alter ego in *The Honey Badger*, Marc Mantell. From all the evidence, it appears that Matson played a rather complicated role in the lives of the Ruarks, much more so than Mantell does with Alec and Amelia Barr. As painted in the novel, Amelia distrusts and resents Mantell from the beginning, while he plays father confessor, coach, and trainer to Barr throughout his literary career. In Matson's case, he became a close friend of both Ruarks — husband and wife — and later in their marriage, according to Foster, was at times the only link between them as their marriage drifted inexorably onto the rocks. He also looked after the management of the Ruark finances, handling the money, covering overdrafts, providing "impeccable accounting facilities," and dealing with the ever-increasing number of medical emergencies involving Ruark's parents. Marc Mantell does exactly the same for Alec Barr.

The important role that an agent can play in an author's life is difficult to explain to someone who is not a writer, but Ruark comes very close to it in *The Honey Badger*. Writing, especially writing a book, is a very lonely profession. It requires a single-mindedness of purpose. The writer is alone with his thoughts, his plots, his characters. Typically, writers are assailed by doubts about the quality of the work they are doing, which makes it even more difficult to sit down at the typewriter and immerse themselves in an exhausting labor that may, they become convinced, be a complete waste of time and effort. You have no one, really, to confide in, to bounce ideas off, or to discuss plot twists. A man's wife might, in normal circumstances, provide such a sounding board, but it is very rare to find such an animal for the simple reason that the vast majority of literary wives are already jealous of the time their husbands spend writing, instead of paying attention to them. Writing is a full-time job, "full-time" being twenty-four hours a day when you are gestating something major like a book. You walk around with your head full of facts and figures and conjectures and possible leads and improbable twists, and "even when you are there, you're not," as Ruark put it.

In *The Honey Badger*, Alec Barr does not discuss his work with Amelia, and it becomes one of the failings of their marriage; in real life, however, Ruark did discuss his work with Virginia. According to Harry Selby, his close friend for more than a decade in whom he confided at length, Virginia was a very important part of Ruark's work. Every new idea was tried out on her first, and if she did not approve, it was discarded. She read the drafts and criticized at length, and Ruark both depended on her and trusted her judgment. Such a relationship is, however, the exception. There is another kind of literary wife — the woman who tries to become involved in her husband's work but either does not know good from bad, or is afraid to say anything except positive things. Alec Barr's second wife, Penny, falls into that category: She reads everything he hands her and responds that it is "marvelous" even when Alec has already mentally marked it "rewrite." For Alec, the one constant is the guidance of Marc Mantell; for Robert Ruark, it was that of Harold Matson.

An agent's major purpose is to sell an author's work, negotiate contracts, look after the administrative chores, field complaints, and generally keep people off the author's back so that he can do what he does best, which is write. For this, the agent gets a percentage (usually ten per cent) of the money that comes in. Having an agent singing your praises and going to bat for you in the face of publishers and their legal lapdogs is a huge advantage for a writer, who usually has little interest in the arcane aspects of business and the endless legal clauses of publishing contracts. As he pointed out repeatedly over the next decade, Robert Ruark was very lucky to become associated early in his career with one of the best literary agents in New York.

Financially, Robert Ruark was doing very well indeed, and doing so in a very high profile way. His columns were printed in hundreds of daily newspapers, and his byline was frequently found in magazines like *The Saturday Evening Post*. With his column, his freelance magazine writing, and the books that he was publishing, by 1950 Ruark's income had become substantial. In an era in which a salary of a hundred dollars a week was enough to support a middle-class family, even in New York City, Ruark was very well off. Hugh Foster quotes a profile of Ruark from *Life* Magazine in November, 1949, in which he said his 1948 income totalled more than $55,000 — $40,000 from his syndicated column and another $15,000 from his book publisher, Doubleday. A thousand dollars a week is decent money today; in 1949, it was wealth.

About this time another incident occurred that was of great significance to Ruark. His grandfather's house in Southport came up for sale, and Ruark bought it, had it refurbished, and ensconced his parents in it at his own expense. They would live there most of their remaining lives. Over the next eight years, the house assumed considerable importance to Ruark's work, when he began writing about his childhood in *Field & Stream*, and it even became one of the later "Old Man and the Boy" columns under the title "The House Comes Home." Ruark's grandfather, Edward Hall Adkins, lived in the house with his wife, Miss Lottie. When he died of cancer in 1930, the house passed out of the family, along with the magnolia tree and its resident mockingbird. According to Ruark, it became the property of a real estate agent who was known throughout the town as a miser. Miser he may have been, but also according to Ruark, he refused to sell the house to anyone outside the Ruark family — all of whom were "flat busted" until little Bobby came along with his New York millions in the fall of 1949. That may be overstating what happened, although it is the impression Ruark gives in the articles he wrote about the house.

Ruark may even have entertained the idea of living there himself eventually, but it never came to pass for a variety of reasons. And if he expected that becoming a property owner in Southport would enhance his or his family's social status in the town, he was very wrong. There was a long legacy of bitterness, in Ruark at least, toward the denizens of Wilmington and Southport, and that bitterness was eventually reciprocated when he wrote about them in two novels, *Poor No More* and *The Honey Badger*. The house is still there, and the Robert Ruark name has become famous in Southport, but it is only since his death and the revival of his reputation in the 1980s that this has been so. There is now a Robert Ruark Foundation and all kinds of references to him in and around the town, according to Eva Monley, who visited Southport while trying to turn *The Old Man and the Boy* into a movie. There are now pilgrims who go to see the places Ruark wrote about, and the residents are eager enough to take the money when it is offered. But this attitude is a far, far cry from the situation that existed from 1950 until Ruark's death in 1965.

The status of the Ruark family in North Carolina was not enhanced by the activities of Ruark's parents, Robert Sr. and Charlotte, who deteriorated quickly after the war, both financially and physically because of their dependence on drugs and alcohol. What had been a worrisome situation before the war became a full-blown, family-destroying problem afterwards. The family reputation suffered, partly due to the elder Ruarks themselves, but also from public perception of how well Robert Jr. was doing in New York, what he was (or was not) doing to help his parents, and what he should have been doing instead. This is not unusual for anyone who leaves a small town and makes good, but it is worse for anyone who has a high public profile, whether actor, singer, or syndicated columnist. Every article that appeared about Ruark, commenting on his success or his income, exacerbated the situation at home. On the one hand, the elder Ruarks, chronically broke and needing money to feed their respective habits, borrowed from anyone they could, with no apparent intention of repaying the money. Their creditors loaned them money believing they were good for it, given their rich and famous son. The other citizens of Wilmington and Southport watched this scenario unfold with the usually "tut-tutting" of neighbors everywhere, and Robert Ruark found himself opening one letter after another demanding he make good his parents' debts.

From all appearances, Ruark wanted to have it both ways: He wanted to enjoy honor in his home town for his accomplishments, but at the same time have it realized that he was not made of money and was not about to shower endless dollar bills on his parents or their creditors. Since alcoholics and drug addicts are not noted for either their restraint or good sense, this problem could only get worse until the parents did the honorable thing and died. Which is exactly what happened. They became a millstone of ever-increasing weight around Ruark's neck, and a source of endless irritation for the next ten years.

In 1950, Ruark managed to get everyone concerned to agree to a reasonable course of action, at least temporarily: He would repay his parents outstanding debts on condition that they commit themselves to a sanitarium for addiction treatment. Later that year his father was released, but his mother remained in the hospital, apparently incarcerated until such time as Robert Jr. authorized her discharge. This he refused to do, in spite of his father's repeated entreaties and accusations that she was being kept a prisoner. At one point, while Robert Jr. was out of town, Virginia wrote to her father-in-law and laid down the law in no uncertain terms. He had no right, she said, either to question his son's judgment in the matter or to quarrel with the doctor's diagnosis. She ended the letter by telling her father-in-law his wife would be released when "Bobbie is damned good and ready" and that they would pay no more of the family debts, even if it meant jail for the parents. Needless to say, this was not the end of the matter, but it gives some idea of just how critical the situation had become even at this stage.

The "parent problem" was one more source of pressure on a man who really did not need any more. The demands of writing a daily column are bad enough without adding endless importuning letters from home, the mounting costs of living large in New York, and constant travel far and wide. Robert Ruark set a very high standard for himself, and it was obviously taking its toll. He was always a great one for keeping score, whether it was dollars of income or words of output. In the same *Life* profile, he was quoted as listing the number of words he was required to write in a given year. Each column was 650 words, and there were five columns a week, fifty weeks a year, for a total of 162,500 words. He threw in "another 100,000 expended in false starts" and did not even include book-writing and magazine articles.

To put this in perspective, a novel or serious nonfiction book might run 100,000 words. Ruark added that the popular conception that he could do a column in half an hour might sound good to the uninitiated, but it was like saying that a baby was born in half an hour in the delivery room, without taking into account the previous nine months. Actually, many of Ruark's columns read as if they were written in thirty seconds, never mind thirty minutes — as if they were dictated into a tape recorder while chasing kangaroos over rough ground. To say they are unpolished is putting it mildly, and it was only Ruark's innate ability with words that allowed him to pull it off. His newspaper columns are not the raw material of which immortality is made, literary or otherwise. At the same time, he was exactly right that the time required to physically write a column is but the barest tip of a very large iceberg. Figuring out what you want to write about, absorbing the information, then letting it gestate in your subconscious, is the most time-consuming aspect of writing. Trying to write something before you are really ready is a waste of time unless you are writing quick-and-dirty daily journalism, where perspective does not matter a great deal. Ruark may in fact have written sixteen columns at a sitting one long night in Rome, but the work that went into those sixteen columns was the product, probably, of weeks of observing, sifting, and subconscious consideration.

From the beginning, a major part of that material gathering was done by travelling, and Robert Ruark set a pace that is daunting even to consider. No part of North America escaped a Ruark visit, as well as the rest of the western hemisphere. As a syndicated columnist, he was writing for readers all over the country, not just in New York, and much as Manhattanites might think their island is the center of the universe, and every aspect of their lives endlessly fascinating to everyone else in the country, to his credit Robert Ruark realized such was not the case. This was probably because Ruark was not a New Yorker; at any rate, he used travel as a convenient way of coming up with new topics and new perspectives.

In 1948, he and Virginia boarded a tramp freighter (a lovely, romantic term, that) for another trip to North Africa. The following year, they headed in the opposite direction for an extended visit to Australia, with a stop-over in Hawaii on the way. On that trip they covered some 30,000 miles, according to Ruark, and he was only persuaded to leave Australia by a peremptory summons from United Features to get back to New York to do some work. This summons, naturally, became the subject of a column. As with most columnists, Ruark's daily life was becoming the real subject about which he wrote regularly, and gradually his life was being built around its suitability for literary treatment. This is another of the (many) failings of professional writers: Everything that happens, from childbirth to father's death, from a friend's betrayal to a lover's loss, becomes grist for the mill. There is no such thing as a quiet, private vacation with your wife, only the prospect of a business trip on which she accompanies you.

By 1950, Robert Ruark was financially successful enough to begin planning the really major business trip, thinly disguised as a vacation, that he had dreamed of all his life: A two-month safari in East Africa.

❋ ❋ ❋

*Chapter Six*

# The Hard
# True Life

Robert and Virginia Ruark arrived in Nairobi by air in June, 1951. For Ruark, landing in Africa to actually go on safari was the realization of a lifelong dream. While neither he nor anyone else knew it at the time, what he was about to experience was a last, fleeting glimpse of a way of life that had become almost mythical over half a century of books and films. The Kenya of 1951 would be swept away in little more than a year, when the Mau Mau struck for the first time. The Emergency was declared in October, 1952, and the colony – and, for that matter, the British Empire – would never be the same again.

For the time being, however, during the two months or so the Ruarks would be in Kenya and Tanganyika, it was still the old East Africa made famous by Karen Blixen, Ernest Hemingway, J.H. Patterson, and the Prince of Wales. They were met at the airport by Donald Ker, partner in the safari firm of Ker & Downey; Harry Selby, who was to be their professional hunter, was unable to meet them, they were told apologetically, because the game department had asked for someone to sort out a recalcitrant rhino on the outskirts of town. The Ruarks went to lunch with Donald Ker and attempted to recover from the series of flights that had taken them from New York to Paris, and thence to Nairobi down the series of legs that included, for many years, Cairo, Khartoum, and Entebbe. They had been in Nairobi for only a few hours when a report came in of a marauding leopard, and Ruark was asked if he would like to shoot it on a special license. He declined, on the grounds that he was newly arrived, his hunting clothes had not yet been delivered, and his soul needed time to catch up to his body. It was too early, he said, for him to run off and start shooting things, and observed that Ker was rather disappointed at his lack of warlike spirit. Then came the news that the American ambassador expected the famous columnist and his wife to join him for dinner. "This I need," Ruark muttered. "This I need bad."

All of the above appears in *Horn of the Hunter* by way of introducing the reader to East Africa. Mr. and Mrs. Ruark go off to Ahamed Brothers to be fitted for their safari clothes, and then to the African Boot Company to have suitable footgear made. From there they head off to the south, along the old road from Nairobi to the Tanganyika border, to cross at Namanga and make their jolting, jouncing, painful way to Arusha, the small town in northern Tanganyika, under the brow of Mount Meru, to sign in with the Tanganyika game department and get their licenses. This was the standard course of events in the days before the mobile safari fell victim to cost-cutting and was replaced by permanent camps and company concessions. In 1951, as in 1933 when Ernest Hemingway arrived, the colonial authorities treated East Africa in many ways as one big game field. Although they were separate colonies, protectorates, and territories, with their own game departments and licensing systems, safaris moved easily among Kenya, Tanganyika, Uganda, and even up into the Sudan. A hunter like Harry Selby would be licensed to operate in all three colonies, and safaris moved around by vehicle. Hunters went to the best area for pursuing a particular species, rather than being stuck with whatever was available in one or two concessions.

The hunting areas of East Africa were divided into hunting blocks, numbered and coded by the game departments, and safari companies booked the blocks in advance. If a client especially wanted, for example, a lesser kudu, then the company would ensure it had a booking around Mount Longido, the premier lesser kudu area of northern Tanganyika. For a sable, you might head toward Tabora in western Tanganyika. Big rhino were found near Lake Manyara, and so on. In the course of a six- or eight-week safari, more or less the standard even as late as 1951, you would drive thousands of miles – from Nairobi down into Tanganyika, down as far as the Ruaha River, over to the Moyowasi, up to the Serengeti, from there up through the Masai Mara and farther north, pushing into the Northern Frontier District (NFD), where you could hunt various desert species as well as rhino and big elephant. There were national parks, game reserves, and areas the game department opened and closed, depending on such vagaries as the rains, or the effect of a drought, or poaching levels, or the warlike tendencies of the resident tribes.

A man going on safari in 1951 could expect to see a lot of country in the course of collecting his Big Five (lion, leopard, rhino, elephant and Cape buffalo), to say nothing of a greater kudu, a sable, and a Hunter's hartebeest. Some species were found only in remote and concentrated areas. The Uganda kob, for example, a relative of the lechwe, is peculiar to northwest Uganda around Murchison Falls, and the Mrs. Grey's lechwe is found only in the southern Sudan around Lake No. A man like Ruark, not a collector of rare game trophies nor at the time a particularly keen big game hunter, went on a safari for the overall experience, to see the country and the animals and the people. Some, like Ruark, became completely enamored of safari life and came back again and again; others acquired a taste for big game hunting, or an interest in a particular family of animals – the spiral-horned antelope, for example – and returned to try to collect them all. On a less admirable note, some hunters found they just liked to kill, and Africa was the one place left on earth where you could go out on a given day and slay animals in large numbers.

The hunting-block system was administered by the game departments, headed by a chief game warden with a hierarchy of game wardens for different districts, descending finally to the game scouts who patrolled the parks and reserves, dispatching problem animals, dismantling traps and snares, arresting poachers, moving squatters off the protected land, and preventing cattle-herding tribes like the Masai from encroaching on grazing land reserved for the game. A district game warden might have responsibility for an area of twenty to a hundred thousand square miles, to be patrolled by a couple of assistant wardens and a dozen game scouts.

The men who filled these jobs were stalwarts of the colonial administration, individuals who devoted their lives to preserving the species, protecting the animals, and to a great degree standing guard over a land and a way of life that was doomed to change, if not disappear altogether. In his later writings, Ruark tended to idealize the hunting profession and make its practitioners into latter-day Lancelots. Some of them may well have been that, but others were out-and-out rogues who would poach an elephant or cheat a client as quickly as drink a beer. By and large, however, the men who staffed the game departments were honorable people who did an admirable job. Because the game herds were such a major part of life in the colony, other game-management tasks had to be carried out. For example, the colonial administration might open up a particular area for farming or want to resettle members of one tribe or another. Professional hunters would then be sent in to reduce the herds of rhino or Cape buffalo, or to eliminate cattle-killing lions. This was known as "shooting on control," and most professional hunters of the "taking-out-clients" variety learned their trade carrying out these duties for the game department.

There was a tremendous amount of lateral movement among control hunters, professional hunters – white hunters, as they were generally called until the politically correct 1980s – and game wardens. Tony Henley is a good example. He was a licensed professional hunter in Africa for more than fifty years, from the 1940s until his death in 1994. During that time he shot on control, worked as a game warden in Kenya and Uganda, founded Kidepo National Park in northeastern Uganda and was its first warden, and later emigrated to South Africa, where he finished his career as a professional hunter for Safari South in Botswana. There were very few professional hunters in East Africa who had not hunted on control at one time or another, and the system was very good in many ways. In East Africa an applicant for a professional hunter's license had to have experience hunting dangerous game, and there was no better way to learn the ways of elephants and lions than by shooting them on control, living with them on a daily basis and hunting them under all conditions. This kind of training is very hard to come by in modern Africa and is a continuing problem for would-be professional hunters in countries like South Africa, where the opportunities to hunt dangerous game are limited. J.A. Hunter, of *White Hunter* fame, killed thousands of lions, Cape buffalo, and rhino during his career, which consisted mainly of shooting on control. Tony Henley said he had either killed or been involved in the killing of at least 1,500 Cape buffalo during his career, and many of those were killed for the game department.

Then, of course, there were the professional ivory hunters who existed right up until the second world war. These were men like John Taylor, who never worked as a professional hunting guide or in any game department capacity, but made his living killing elephants for their ivory or hunting other big game like Cape buffalo for whatever money could be made. It was a tough way to make a living, and very few professional ivory hunters got rich from their activities. But there is no question they were superbly skilled hunters and shooters; those who were not simply did not survive. Again, there was a certain amount of lateral movement, with ivory hunters becoming game wardens, then going back to ivory hunting again.

Finally, there were the Kenya farmers who worked as either ivory hunters or game wardens or shot on control to make ends meet when drought ravaged the land, disease killed off the cattle, or the market for pyrethrum collapsed and the bank was calling the loan. In the pre-war, cash-starved years, it was common for a farmer to take out all the ivory licenses he could afford and trek off into the bush, leaving his wife to manage the farm, while he shot all the ivory he could in the hope of getting some actual money. Almost all the professional hunters operating out of Nairobi when Ruark first arrived either came from farm families, or were part-time farmers. Professional hunting was woven into the fabric of Kenya life in 1951 just as much as cattle ranching is a part of Texas. It was not merely something you did. It was something you were.

* * *

Harry Selby, Ruark's professional hunter on his first safari, came from such a background. He was actually born in South Africa, of old South African stock, and his parents emigrated to Kenya when he was very young. He apprenticed with Philip Percival, who at the time was widely perceived as the dean of professional hunters in East Africa. Percival was the younger brother of Blayney Percival, long-time head game warden of Kenya, who wrote *A Game Ranger's Note Book*. Philip Percival was

Ernest Hemingway's white hunter in 1933. When he retired, according to legend, Harry Selby inherited his "string of blacks," the safari crew of cooks, camp boys, skinners, trackers, and gun bearers that were the backbone of the safari industry.

Selby's contemporaries were men like Tony Henley, Tony Dyer, Andrew Holmberg, Frank Bowman, John Sutton, John Dugmore, and many others who became famous, partly thanks to Ruark's writing. Most came from a Kenya farming background. The usual story was that a boy, raised on a farm, who learned to hunt and shoot at an early age, would reach his teens and start chafing at the restrictions and the tedium of farm life. He would yearn for the glamor of professional hunting, or the adventure of ivory hunting in the Lado Enclave or the Karamoja. After finishing school, he would either sign on with a safari firm like Ker & Downey as an apprentice hunter, or go to work for the game department as a game control officer and work his way up from there. Typically, his parents would sigh at his lack of enthusiasm for treating hoof-rot or shearing sheep, but they would finally give in to his incessant demands, secure in the knowledge that he would eventually grow weary of American clients or recalcitrant Cape buffalo, and return to marry, settle down, raise children, and take over the family farm. This scenario has become a cliché of novel and feature film, for the same reason most clichés come to be: Because they are so often true.

In 1951, Nairobi was the unchallenged capital of the safari world, and was a very nice town to boot. Accounts of it from that period generally decry its deterioration from what it had been ten years earlier, but writers who disliked what it had become by then should have seen it twenty years later. Right after the war, and before the Mau Mau Emergency, Nairobi was a pleasant city, at a high enough altitude (4,000 feet) to have a temperate climate. It had the Norfolk Hotel, its social hub since 1906, the New Stanley Hotel, and a handful of good bars and restaurants. It was a great place to return to after a tough two-month safari, and the lives of professional hunters "in town" consisted, according to legend, of one long round of pink gins and pinker stewardesses off the in-bound airliners.

Joe Coogan, for many years a professional hunter in Botswana who spent much of his early life in Kenya, once said that if he could be reincarnated to any period, anywhere, he would probably choose Kenya in the early 1950s. There were still big tuskers roaming vast areas of unhunted, untrekked territory, and South African Airways and BOAC conveyed a steady stream of adventure-seeking stewardesses to Nairobi, stopping over for a few days until the return flight departed, at which point a white hunter would drop off one girl, have a quick drink in the bar, and meet one of the new stewardesses as they came through customs. After a couple of weeks of this, worn out and hungover, he would load up and head back into the bush to recuperate by chasing lions and walking twenty miles a day in the hot sun on the trail of an elephant. As a way of life, it was bound to be wearing after a while, but it certainly appealed to the imagination of a man like Robert Ruark, to whom chilled gin and warm girls were the two finest things life had to offer.

* * *

Ruark was introduced to this way of life over the course of the first safari, which ventured initially down into Tanganyika and later back up into Kenya, into the inhospitable climes of the NFD.

Ruark had licenses for the full list of game animals then available. He shot a couple of lions, a couple of Cape buffalo, and a leopard; he was unsuccessful at greater kudu, which was high on his list, and he did not shoot an elephant. He did, however, take a waterbuck that scored very high in the Rowland Ward record book. Overall, the safari was a success in terms of animals taken and animals scored. At that time in East Africa, leopards were much more difficult to come by than they are today in South Africa and Zimbabwe, for example, where they come readily to baits and entire game ranches are devoted to delivering leopards to clients. The same could be said of greater kudu, a common species in southern Africa today but which were almost mythical in East Africa half a century ago.

One unfortunate event part way through the safari was the theft of all the Ruarks' camera equipment from the safari car. They had both still cameras and a movie camera, and all were full of partially exposed film. This explains the shortage of photographs from that trip, which is the most famous single safari of the latter twentieth century. They lost many of the photos already taken, as well as the means of taking any more. All the existing photographs come from film they had already exposed and tucked away.

Ruark regarded the entire adventure as a business trip, despite his insisting over and over, in print, that it was his first real vacation since before the war. He wrote newspaper columns while on the safari and posted them from various points in East Africa. He had his portable typewriter along, naturally, and even made a point of going on ahead to a new camp that was being set up and spending the afternoon writing while the others looked after breaking camp and moving.

At first, the safari was treated by Ruark and his New York pals in the same breathless terms that he would refer to a trip anywhere in the world. His name appeared in gossip columns, reporting on his preparations for the trip and the fact that he was driving everyone around him crazy with his incessant chattering about Africa. He announced his departure in his own columns, again in terms that are typically New York: a combination of wise-cracking and condescension, with a scattering of mangled Swahili thrown in. Ruark let his intentions be known to Trans World Airlines, and made a deal with the New York office to provide them with reprints and photographs that were taken on the safari, for TWA's own promotional purposes. The practice of columnists and journalists getting discounts or free accommodation in return for mentioning the name of an airline, or a hotel, or a cab service, is as old as journalism itself. Today, it is standard practice for writers to be given various benefits, including an occasional free hunting trip, in return for the publicity they can provide.

Significantly, Ruark did not ask Ker & Downey for any kind of break of that kind, and he said so explicitly, not only in the book that resulted from the safari but in columns and articles written from Africa many years later. "Nobody was paying my way," he said. As safaris go, it was not cheap even then. The number Ruark quotes is ten thousand dollars, which seems about right for a two-month safari in 1951. Whatever his motivation for paying the full price, he seems to have known instinctively that the trip could have long-term benefits for him professionally, and that it would be to his advantage even at that early stage to be seen by the safari industry as a good client and by his readers as a man beholden to no one.

Behind the scenes, there were other considerations related to the safari. One was that Ruark's health was starting to give him problems. His life in New York, with its odd hours, long evenings spent in saloons, and liquid lunches, was starting to have its effect. His relationship with Virginia was also suffering because of his extramarital affairs. So, even though he wrote in his column that he was undertaking the trip to fulfil a lifelong dream, there were other reasons as well. From all indications, Virginia saw it as a possible way to repair their marriage, and as a respite from the destructive lifestyle they had adopted in New York.

Ruark's biographer, Hugh Foster, concentrated on his developing physical ailments while Michael McIntosh, in his introduction to his 1991 anthology, *Robert Ruark's Africa*, stresses the psychological problems that were beginning to afflict Ruark. McIntosh described Ruark as a man "pursued by demons" as he flew the various legs from Manhattan, to Paris, to Cairo, to Nairobi. The implication is that something was starting to weigh on Ruark's mental well-being, beyond the stresses of working, making a living, and supporting his wife and himself in Manhattan, outlandish and expensive as that lifestyle might have been. Of course, there was already the added expense of supporting his parents and their weird and wonderful peccadiloes back in Southport, but even taken together, and severe as they were, these stresses are the normal wear and tear of everyday life.

What was apparently happening to Ruark, what one writer described as "worshipping false gods," was a developing realization that the goals he had set for himself, and which he had now largely attained, were not really worthwhile. Such trappings of success as a penthouse on the upper east side, being called "ya bum" by Toots Shor, and having your picture in the newspaper every day, were not enough. With the exception of the four years of war, Robert Ruark had been striving, struggling, and working long hours since the day he left home at the age of fifteen to go to university. By 1951, he had achieved professional success and a degree of financial security, but he was discovering the unfortunate truth that, if that was all there was, it was not enough. The question was, what was missing? An obvious answer was children. The Ruarks were childless and, thanks to his sterility, destined to remain so. An endless succession of one-night stands for him, girl lunches for her, and back-to-back hangovers for both of them were no substitute. Both Robert and Virginia Ruark needed something more. In his case, at least, Africa was the answer.

Very early, hints crept into his writing that he had found something of lasting importance and value, although he couched it in deceptively simple terms. Drinking, for example, was a subject he touched upon fairly frequently, and in *Horn of the Hunter* dealt with at length. Now he began to approach it as a possible source of serious trouble. He contrasted the way he drank in Manhattan versus the way they drank in Africa, and the effect of gin while in New York as opposed to how he felt when he drank under the stars on the Little Ruaha River in the wilds of Tanganyika. One major criticism of *Horn of the Hunter* is that it dwells at length on the drinking Selby and the Ruarks indulge in during that safari. Each page, it seems, finds them popping a cork to celebrate, to drown their disappointment, to quench a dry-mouth Cape buffalo thirst, or to wash away the taste of defeat. Ruark writes about warm martinis and ice-free whisky in plastic cups with an infectiously boyish enthusiasm that would make Carry Nation reach for a bottle and a corkscrew.

More than once he writes that hangovers had never been a problem for him, but in other places he alludes to them with something approaching dread. At one point he claims that in almost any place except Manhattan, he could drink wine with lunch, have a couple of brandies afterwards, martinis in the evening, and feel "marvelous all day." Such a regimen in New York, however, would put him to bed for a week. He then goes on to present his own explanation for why New Yorkers of that era drank so much: They did it "to stay sober" and to kill the boredom and nervousness and strain of merely being New Yorkers.

Everyone who knew Ruark well insists he was not prone to depression. Harry Selby says the only time he saw Ruark despondent in the twelve years he knew him was during a nine-month period when Ruark was on the wagon. In spite of this, however, his attitude toward life, drinking, and the direction his life seemed to be heading points to at least a subconscious despondency at his own lack of purpose. In writing about Africa and safaris and the lives of white hunters, he referred occasionally to "the hard true life," and that seems to be what he found in

Kenya that beckoned to him for the rest of his life, like a flickering beacon in a distant lighthouse. From 1951 until the day he died, Africa reached out to him with a promise that there he would find something that was worth having – something that did not exist in Manhattan. Even if he could never articulate exactly what that something was, it was solid and tangible to him.

During that safari, Robert Ruark got his first view from a tall hill, and what he saw out there on the African plain was of incalculable value to a writer: He saw a subject that was truly worth writing about.

\* \* \*

Ernest Hemingway once wrote that "the most difficult thing to do in life is to write honest prose about real people."

Until the fall of 1951, Robert Ruark's prose had been artificial and his people superficial. His newspaper column was a diverting grab-bag designed to amuse today and wrap fish tomorrow. That he accomplished this purpose very well is undeniable, but even a quick leaf through the three books he had written up to that point, two anthologies and a satirical novel, shows just how forgettable this writing really was. Ruark, perceptive as he was, realized he was pouring his life into work that was of little lasting value. When he and Virginia returned to New York from Kenya, he resumed his column writing with the old verve and familiar side-of-the-mouth wisecracking brittleness. In between the daily column writing, however, he began working on a book on his recent experience in Africa. It was a book that would set out what he had seen and what he had felt, honestly and sincerely, with no gimmicks. It would be honest prose about real people. The result was Ruark's first serious book, *Horn of the Hunter*.

\* \* \*

# SAFARI:
# *Horn of the Hunter*

It is very likely that Robert Ruark intended all along to write the non-fiction account of his first safari that eventually became *Horn of the Hunter*. To a writer, anything and everything that occurs in his life is potential subject matter, whether for a book or a newspaper column. So it is hard to imagine that Ruark, the freelance writer, would embark on such a major undertaking without planning to turn it into a book; at the very least, the safari would become tax deductible. No matter what he had in mind when he left New York with his wife, Virginia, in June, 1951, it is unlikely that Ruark imagined in his wildest dreams that he was embarking on a whole new chapter in his life — that the account of the safari would become a hunting-world bestseller and the catalyst that would transform his career and inspire thousands of other Americans to travel to Africa. But that is precisely what happened.

The history of African hunting can be traced back, link by link, through a chain of men who traveled, hunted, explored, and returned home to write about it, to be read by young men who traveled in their turn, and wrote themselves, and were read themselves, and inspired the next generation. This chain goes all the way back to William Cornwallis Harris, the English army officer who hunted in southern Africa in the 1830s, wrote *The Wild Sports of Southern Africa*, and was read by Frederick Courteney Selous. Selous's books inspired Theodore Roosevelt, Roosevelt's *African Game Trails* enchanted Ernest Hemingway, Hemingway hunted in East Africa in the 1930s and wrote about the adventure in *Green Hills of Africa*, and that caused Robert Ruark to add himself to the list. The study of who inspired whom, and to do what, is a fascinating pastime in itself.

*Green Hills of Africa* is a book that is largely misunderstood. Professional hunters hate it, because they think it portrays Philip Percival poorly and glorifies Hemingway's own accomplishments when in fact he was merely one of that despised breed, the client. Hunters who read it as a hunting story find endless fault with it, for reasons geographical and zoological. The fact is, however, Hemingway never intended it to be a factual account of an African safari *per se*. It was a piece of experimental literary writing, an attempt to portray fact in novel form and to see if reality could be made into literature. Hence the reason the characters are not named: The professional hunter becomes Pop and the wife becomes P.O.M. (Poor Old Mama), while the real-life hunting partner, Charles Thompson, becomes Karl and the second professional hunter is known only as Dan. If the book fails, it fails as a piece of experimental writing. Conversely, some critics in the hook-and-bullet press who hail *Green Hills* as one of Hemingway's greatest works really need to get out more. It is neither a great hunting book, nor a great piece of literature, nor a particularly successful piece of experimental writing. It has been, on the other hand, a perennial bestseller, for which the Hemingway estate is undoubtedly grateful.

This, however, was the competition Ruark was facing as he left for his first safari, and it was formidable competition indeed. Ernest Hemingway was then at the peak of his career, in spite of the poor reception accorded *Across the River and into the Trees*, his first postwar novel, which appeared in 1950. Two years later, he rebounded with *The Old Man and the Sea*, for which he was awarded the Nobel Prize for Literature. All of this literary heavy-hitting occurred around the time Ruark published *Horn of the Hunter*, and comparisons with Hemingway were inevitable.

Throughout his later career, Ruark was forced to endure constant comparison with Hemingway for his lifestyle, his subject matter, his interests in life, even his physical appearance. Almost without exception, he came out on the short end and the resentment built up. To a great extent, however, Ruark helped fuel this, and it began with *Horn of the Hunter*. For example, in the book he makes a major point of the fact that he was following in Hemingway's footsteps, that he was on safari with Harry Selby, who had apprenticed with Philip Percival, Hemingway's professional hunter, and about having "the same basic string of blacks" with whom Hemingway had traveled twenty years earlier. From the tone of the writing Ruark's references read more like homage than competition, but with hindsight he would have been better off going on safari, writing his book, and saying nothing.

At that time, of course, Robert Ruark was best known as a wise-guy syndicated newspaper columnist and author of two anthologies of that column, as well as one rather forgettable spoof of an historical novel, *Grenadine Etching*. In 1951 he was neither literary man, nor outdoor writer, nor serious novelist; it could be argued that he was not really a serious anything, professionally speaking, until he wrote *Horn of the Hunter*. It was a book that made Harry Selby, for good or ill (there are conflicting opinions), but it undoubtedly also made Robert Ruark: It was the cornerstone of his career and set the stage for everything he was to become.

In a note at the beginning, Ruark says *Horn of the Hunter* is "a book about Africa in which I have tried to avoid most of the foolishness, personal heroism, and general exaggeration which usually attend works of this sort." To a great extent he succeeded. Ruark the hunter learns as he goes along; Ruark the shooter improves with practice. He stands his ground when he has to and earns the respect of his young professional hunter, Harry Selby, who turns twenty-six during the safari; Ruark was just ten years older, although the tone of the book implies that, even then, Ruark was an old man compared to the boyish Selby.

Anyone who has read any of Ruark's newspaper columns from the late 1940s, or any of the three books he had published by 1952 (*Grenadine Etching, I Didn't Know It Was Loaded,* and *One For The Road*) will immediately notice the radically different writing style in *Horn of the Hunter*. It is simple and sincere, with an easy style that is eminently readable. It is witty, occasionally hilarious, sometimes serious, sometimes philosophical, but never heavy or ponderous. Occasionally, Ruark delves into his memory to recall incidents from his childhood, or from the war; in fact, until *The Honey Badger*, this is the only place where he wrote much about his experiences in the Navy, on the North Atlantic convoy run or in the Mediterranean. He reflects on the meaning of fear and on the need to earn respect. Very little of his own personal circumstances, his psychological state, or the precarious state of his marriage intrude on the almost idyllic account of his first safari.

In the introduction to his anthology *Robert Ruark's Africa*, Michael McIntosh described Ruark on that safari as a man "pursued by demons," whose physical health was failing from the strains of a life of living hard, drinking lots, and staying out late in Manhattan. Harry Selby, reading McIntosh's description many years later, said he had hit the nail on the head. Although Ruark himself does not give any details about his physical and psychological condition when he stepped off the plane in Nairobi, he certainly explains with considerable satisfaction how his weight dropped, his endurance increased, and his overall well-being improved on a steady diet of angry Cape buffalo, hard-biting tsetse flies, and a regimen of walking many stony miles up hill and down dale. By implication, if he was that much improved at the end, he was that much in need of improvement at the beginning.

During the safari Ruark becomes unapologetically worshipful of Selby and reports, almost with satisfaction, that Virginia was half in love with this paragon of PH-ing virtue. *Horn of the Hunter* received very little in the way of negative criticism when it appeared, and none at all in the years since except for the odd excerpt used in anti-hunting works to condemn the killing of animals for recreation. One of the strangest examples is a case where Ruark reported the effects of a .220 Swift on a hyena in a blunt and unvarnished account, and was then taken to task by Roger Caras in a book published in 1970 called *Death as a Way of Life*.

Robert Ruark was one of the best newspaper reporters of his time, and he employed his talents as a journalist to the utmost in *Horn of the Hunter*. This alone sets it apart from most hunting books, which rarely care about such journalistic virtues as telling the whole story, reporting both sides, or getting the names spelled right. Ruark the journalist cared about all of the above and went to great lengths to do so. As a result, the book is almost a manual on how safaris functioned, how they were organized, and who is responsible for what. He examines the role of everyone from the kitchen *mtoto* to the head skinner and explains the social hierarchy of what was, in effect, a small, mobile community.

This was all very new and fascinating to Ruark. Just as new to him, if not as fascinating, were the rifles he took on that safari: he had a .470 Nitro Express, a .375 H&H Winchester Model 70, a Remington .30-06, and a .220 Swift. Having never fired a rifle at anything except a target at the Campfire Club, or so he wrote, he was apprehensive about his ability to hit anything. When it came to shooting, he was a shotgunner and wingshooter first and foremost. It is hard to imagine any cartridge less suited to any practical purpose in Africa than a .220 Swift, especially with the light, fragile bullets with which the factory ammunition was loaded in the early 1950s, but Ruark, in his innocence, carted one along on the advice of some well-meaning friend.

His experience with the hyena, which is a heavy animal the size of a timber wolf, was exactly what should be expected: a ghastly, gory travesty of wounding and suffering. After nine or so shots, Ruark finished the animal off with the .470. He then committed a cardinal error: He told the truth, in print. It was an honest mistake on his part, taking the .220 Swift in the first place, and he reported the incident exactly as it happened. He condemned the cartridge as a "wounder." In his book, Roger Caras quotes the gruesome passage as a frontispiece and later in a chapter on the effect of bullets on wild animals. He never explains the context of the incident, nor does he bother to mention its effect on Ruark — that he swore never again to use the .220 Swift "on any animal I respect." Ironically, although the passage appears first in *Horn of the Hunter*, it was reproduced in *Use Enough Gun*, and it was from there that Caras lifted it. Had he paid attention, or been interested in the truth, he would have seen that that was Ruark's whole point.

At any rate, journalistically *Horn of the Hunter* is a highly successful work, which is probably the secret of its enduring popularity. It is a book that anyone can learn from, whether he is interested in the nuts and bolts of safari organization, the tribal traits of different Africans, the personal habits of hyenas and Cape buffalo, or the mechanical skills of professional hunters. Ruark never consciously tries to be profound — at least not obviously; profundity is better when unplanned anyway, and there is a considerable amount of truth conveyed in the simple descriptions of people and events Ruark presents. It is a frank book in which mistakes are made on occasion by all concerned. These are reported fairly and honestly, without judgment, and there are regrets — for wounded animals that escape, for easy shots missed, for difficult shots that are attempted when they should not be and the results are hard to live with. Anyone who professes to hunt, but who has not endured all of the above at some time or another, has not hunted very much. Bad things happen. What you have to do is learn to forgive yourself and then do your best to ensure they do not happen again.

The central theme of *Green Hills of Africa* was Hemingway's pursuit of a greater kudu, and not surprisingly, Ruark makes the greater kudu — or rather, the hunting of same — central to *Horn of the Hunter* as well. In the end, Hemingway shoots two wonderful kudu, only to return to camp to find his friend Karl has killed one that makes his look like dwarves. In Ruark and Selby's case, they stalked a greater kudu and shot him with the sun behind him, only to find that they misjudged the horns and shot a kudu that would have been magnificent when he reached maturity, but was now just an immature bull with one and a half curls. The meat will still be good, and the hide will make a nice coat for Virginia, Selby says lamely; in bitter atonement, Ruark dines on pork and beans out of a can, and that afternoon they go out with the shotguns to shoot sand grouse.

If Ruark has an obsession in the book to match Hemingway's, it is for the Cape buffalo, of which he shoots two. And it is while he is on his knees in the long grass, frightened out of his mind because of the proximity of numerous buffalo, that he mutters the immortal words, "God *damn* Ernest Hemingway." Interestingly enough, although he hunted buffalo for the rest of his African career, the animal that became his personal favorite was the leopard.

\* \* \*

*Horn of the Hunter* was published in 1953 by Doubleday & Co. It contained thirty-two pages of photographs and thirty-two original drawings by the author. Most, if not all, of these drawings were copies of photographs, many of which were also reproduced in the book. It was later printed in paperback and remained in print in softcover until at least the late 1960s. By any measure, it is one of the most successful non-fiction hunting books ever written. As Ruark's fame as a novelist waned in the 1970s, his reputation as a hunting writer gained lustre, and his non-fiction works became highly sought-after by hunters, readers, and collectors. First editions of *Horn of the Hunter* commanded a premium on the secondary market. In 1987, Safari Press reprinted the book with the permission of the Ruark estate.

As a hunting book, it has had a serious, long-lasting influence. More than any other book, it inspired hunters to go to Africa to hunt in the 1950s and 60s. Even today, according to photo-safari guides in Kenya and Tanzania, their clients often arrive with a copy of the book in their luggage, and almost everyone who goes on safari has read it. In his later years, Ruark occasionally referred to himself as the godfather of the postwar safari industry; the statement was mostly true, and it was mostly due to *Horn of the Hunter*.

Not all of the book's influence was good, however. The law of unintended consequences kicked in, most obviously in the case of Harry Selby. At the time, Selby was just one more young PH working with the respected but not extraordinary firm of Ker & Downey, a company that was started after the Second World War by Donald Ker and Sydney Downey. In the early 1950s the crop of young professional hunters in Kenya included many names that became famous, including Selby, Andrew Holmberg, Tony Henley, Tony Dyer, and John Sutton. When Ruark booked his safari, he could just as easily have gone with anyone on that list, and just as easily written most of the same things about them as he did about Selby. His descriptions of Selby, from his physical appearance to his mastery of every situation, whether it was replacing a broken axle, facing down a charging lioness, or driving at full speed across a plain strewn with pig-holes, is frankly hero-worship. There is not a single negative word about Selby in the entire book. What's more, having written *Horn of the Hunter*, Ruark went on to write about Selby in various magazine articles. Selby himself went to New York the year after the first safari to visit the Ruarks on their home ground. Altogether, Harry Selby became an international celebrity courtesy of Robert Ruark's prolific pen.

"Harry Selby made Ker & Downey, and Robert Ruark made Harry Selby," was a line I heard more than once while interviewing people in Kenya who are still associated with the safari business. Many of them are still guiding for Ker & Downey, which is now the pre-eminent photo-safari company in East Africa and one of the most famous names in safari history. Much of this renown is due to Robert Ruark.

The effect on Harry Selby was a mixed blessing. While his bookings increased dramatically, and going on safari with him became a status symbol for international hunting clients, there was no little amount of resentment from his colleagues in the business. More senior professional hunters resented the fame and fortune that he had been handed, as they saw it, by fortuitous circumstance; what's more, the attention and acclaim drove a wedge between Selby and the other young hunters of his age group, men that he went to school with, apprenticed with, and with whom he would normally have remained friends and colleagues throughout his career. Harry Selby himself says the benefits were a two-edged sword and that he sometimes feels he would have been better off, overall, had Ruark never written the things he did. His close friend, Joe Coogan, a professional hunter with Safari South during the 1980s, reflected that Harry Selby was cut off from the other young hunters of his age group by the Ruark connection, and that personally (as opposed to professionally) it did Selby no good.

All of this, of course, is speculation — what might have been instead of what was. Aside from the publicity that made Selby one of the most sought-after guides in Nairobi, Ruark later took a hand in the management of Selby's career. He persuaded him to leave Ker & Downey and form his own safari company in partnership with Andrew

Holmberg; many young hunters left with him and went to work for Selby & Holmberg, including John Sutton, Reggie Destro, and Mike Rowbotham. Some years later, Selby left that partnership and returned to Ker & Downey, using the leverage of his considerable prestige to have his name added to the marque. The venerable company became Ker, Downey & Selby — and that also added to the resentment, this time on the part of older, more experienced hunters who felt they had just as good a claim to partnership. It can be argued that Harry Selby enjoyed the most fabled career of any postwar professional hunter because of Robert Ruark, but it can be argued just as strongly that, in the final analysis, Robert Ruark did him no favors.

\* \* \*

Late in life Robert Ruark referred to *Horn of the Hunter* as a particular pet of his, even after his major novels. This may have been due to the unpretentious, thoroughly honest, and highly personal nature of the book, or because it was his first really serious venture into book writing. Whatever the reason, it occupied a special place in his heart.

As a book about an African safari, it is the most influential by far of the post-war period, and one of the best of this century. In fact, there are not many books on hunting in Africa that can compare with it journalistically, and certainly not in writing style. As a book about Africa, it is better than Hemingway's *Green Hills* (although that is comparing two books with completely different aims); as a book about hunting, and what it is really like to seek and kill an animal, it is better than Roosevelt's *African Game Trails*. Where it really shines, however, is as a book about a man's budding discovery of himself, and in that sense it compares creditably with some great works of literature. It may not be as lofty as *Lord Jim*, but still it ventures into a different realm than the vast majority of African hunting books.

More than anything else, *Horn of the Hunter* shows how Ruark discovered those things in life that were genuinely important. He then wrote that story simply, truly, and well, and created his first work of literature.

\* \* \*

*Chapter Seven*

# KENYA IN BLACK AND WHITE

The Kenya Robert Ruark saw on his first safari in 1951 was the last glimmering of a unique and tiny civilization that existed in East Africa for barely half a century. Yet in that time it managed to capture the world's imagination out of all proportion to its size.

It was a civilization made up of an exotic combination of wild animals and glorious mountains, forbidding deserts, vintage wine under the stars, Mozart on gramophones, man-eating lions, and poverty-stricken younger sons of the nobility, trying to create a working farm from dangerous bush and coming into town to beg more loans from the banks and get drunk at the Norfolk Hotel. It was a civilization that welcomed Scottish gamekeepers, Jewish peddlers, Polish soldiers of fortune, and the Prince of Wales. Its denizens inspired literature, created literature, and set a standard for rampant adultery that has never been equalled. Given its huge reputation, it is amazing to realize now just how small and short-lived that Kenya actually was.

Kenya Colony, as it was known for most of its transition from untamed bush to uneasy independence, was unlike any other British colony. The country was different, the native tribes were different, and the white settlers were different. It was a candle that burned with a very special flame, but like all candles that burn too brightly, it did not last long.

Many histories have been written of Kenya, from many points of view. A history written from a native viewpoint would be vastly different than one from an impoverished white settler, from a liberal social historian, or from a member of the upper class. Depending on what picture the writer wishes to present, various aspects of Kenya's kaleidoscopic history can be magnified and others ignored. An apologist for black terrorism of the 1950s might concentrate on the degeneracy of the white settlers, as exemplified by the inhabitants of "Happy Valley," the drug-taking connoisseurs of serial adultery who gave Kenya much of its scandalous reputation. Yet that would ignore the suffering, privations, and exhausting efforts of the average white settler in the highlands, far from the bright lights of Nairobi. An anthropologist enthralled with Kikuyu customs would describe a different country than would an expatriate English gentleman, in the mold of Lawrence of Arabia, who worshipped the wild ways of the unspoiled Masai.

\* \* \*

To a European or American the modern history of Kenya really begins with the explorations of Sir Richard Burton and John Hanning Speke, searching for the source of the Nile in the 1850s. Until then, the region was populated exclusively by primitive black tribes and throngs of wild animals, with the occasional Arab trader working established routes inland from the sea. Along the coast, there were Arab settlements that dated back a thousand years. The Portuguese, especially, had battled back and forth with the Arabs for hundreds of those years. The coastal city of Mombasa, with its white walls and palm trees, was already old when Burton landed, and of course, the island of Zanzibar, to the south, was a long-established slave-trading center. Inland much beyond the first line of hills, however, was *terra incognita*. Columns of shackled slaves wended their way down to the Indian Ocean, and the slave traders disappeared back into the bush, but few outsiders ventured more than a few miles from the sea.

The journeys of Richard Burton and John Speke, and later of Henry Stanley and Samuel Baker, and the books they wrote about their travels and the country they had seen, with its black tribes, its herds of animals, and the wonders of the Mountains of the Moon and the Nile River and the great inland lakes, stirred the imaginations of people in England and Scotland. The years from 1860 to 1900 saw the initial flowering of the

great age of books. For the first time in history, people were widely literate and books were available in large numbers. They rolled off printing
presses with seeming abandon, heavy volumes bound in leather to last
forever. Everyone who went anywhere, it seemed, returned home to write
a book about it. Young ladies devoured books, both novels and nonfiction works about far-off lands, wild tribes, exotic plants, birds, animals,
you name it. To look at some of these books today, one wonders what the
publishers saw in them or who, exactly, they expected to buy them.

One such is a two-volume work titled *The Uncivilized Races of Men in
All Countries of the World, being a Comprehensive Account of Their Manners and Customs, and of Their Physical, Social, Mental, Moral and Religious
Characteristics*, written by the Reverend J.G. Wood, M.A., F.L.S. It was
published in 1877, totalled 1,530 pages, and purported to deal with every
"uncivilized" tribe on the globe. The book is surprisingly comprehensive, including extensive tracts on tribes which, at the time it was written, were still in the process of being discovered and catalogued. The
great African explorer, missionary, and self-promoting egotist, Dr. David
Livingstone, published his *Travels and Researches in South Africa* in 1857,
and the book became and stayed an all-time best-seller. Africa was still
the Dark Continent — "dark" in the sense of being unknown — and
there was great public curiosity about it. Names like "The Mountains of
the Moon" (Uganda's Ruwenzori Range, although that was not known
at the time) pervaded conversation. King Solomon's Mines were a reality, in the public's mind if not in fact, and readers eagerly gobbled up any
and all stories about them that could be published.

The source of the Nile was a mystery that had enthralled men for
thousands of years. Where, exactly, did this river of life originate?
Attempts to navigate the Nile from Egypt to its source had ended, sometimes in tragedy, but always in failure. Expeditions up the Nile compounded the mystery rather than solving it. The major physical obstacle was the great inland swamp called the Sud in central Sudan. A boat
might get as far as the Sud, but once in this vast, spreading marsh, with
visibility limited by its towering reeds and little or no discernible channel of flowing water, explorers could get no farther. Add to this the
intense heat, mosquitoes, malaria, hostile tribes, madness, and death.

Even years later, explorers who knew where the Nile began and ended and how to get through the Sud, in theory at least, had difficulty actually doing it.

When Richard Burton and John Speke landed in East Africa, their plan was to cut inland in search of a great lake that would prove to be the source of the Nile. Such a lake existed in mythology and was even marked on ancient maps. Once into the interior, Burton reasoned, such a lake would be well-known by the inhabitants. The story of Burton and Speke, their enigmatic relationship, and subsequent betrayal (by Speke) and tragedy, laced with triumph that turned bitter for both men, is one of the great real-life dramas of all time. In Victorian England, with all its contradictions, with its prudery and love of erudition and fascination with the occult and the mysterious and the frankly erotic, the rivalry between these men assumed Shakespearean proportions. It was more than merely a *cause célèbre* that provided conversation at Victorian breakfast tables, however; the saga of Burton and Speke cast a spell that drew people to East Africa for decades after both were dead.

The story of what actually happened is well known. Richard Burton was one of the greatest Victorian heroes, a man of such erudition and accomplishment that it defies belief. He was perhaps the greatest linguist of all time, a man who acquired new languages "like other people change socks," according to one biographer. Eventually, he spoke three dozen languages and dialects; he could gain a working knowledge in a couple of weeks and be fluent in a month. Burton combined this extraordinary ability with a far-ranging curiosity and scholarship, and a love of adventure that was right out of *Boys' Own Annual*. After a brief military career in India, he set out to explore Africa. Penetrating forbidden cities was almost a specialty, and he accomplished this both in his famous expedition to Mecca, disguised as a Persian physician, and later to the Abyssinian city of Harar.

On one of his early expeditions he took on John Hanning Speke, another young British Army officer, to replace a member who died unexpectedly. Speke was as unlike Burton as it is possible to get: A man of limited intellect but overwhelming ambition, he was blond where Burton was dark and satanic, he spoke no language but English, and wanted to explore to gain fame, not to learn. To Burton, the journey was more important than the end; to Speke, the end was everything.

In 1857, they set off into the interior of East Africa in search of the mythical lake thought to be the source of the Nile. After months of hardship, they found Lake Tanganyika (not exactly a discovery, since it was known to the Arabs from their trading activities) and Burton suspected it might be the source of the Nile. On their return journey Burton fell very ill and they halted for several weeks to allow him to recover. Natives told of a great lake to the north of their camp, and Speke set out alone to find it. What he found was Lake Victoria — Victoria Nyanza. On nothing more than intuition combined with wishful thinking, Speke decided he had found the real source of the Nile — as indeed he had. He returned to tell Burton of his find. Speke's blurted, bald announcement that he had discovered the Nile's source — "the Nile is solved!" he is reputed to have said — infuriated Burton. Speke had no real scientific evidence, much less definitive proof. Had he circumnavigated the lake? No. Had he seen a great river flowing out of it, or even a small one? No. Well then, Burton said, you have seen a great body of water from a distance, and that's all you have seen. Speke, however, was adamant. Their relationship, already strained, deteriorated further over the next several months as they struggled across Tanganyika. They were barely on speaking terms by the time they made it back to the coast and boarded a ship for England.

Burton's health did not improve, and he was forced to stop over in Aden to recuperate. The two explorers made an agreement that neither would make any announcement about their findings until they could do so together and let them be judged on their merits. As soon as he landed in London, however, Speke went straight to the Royal Geographical Society to announce his discovery. Burton eventually returned to find Speke the lion of the hour, heralded as the man who had discovered the source of the Nile.

Burton continued to champion Lake Tanganyika, and the two men became bitter enemies. Speke returned to Africa to enlarge on his explorations and did, in fact, follow the Victoria Nile from its source at the Uganda town of Jinja. Burton, meanwhile, went on to other things. The argument continued to rage, however, and in 1864 they were scheduled to meet in a debate to settle who was right; on the eve of the event, Speke died in a shooting accident — an accident many still contend was suicide. His death inflamed passions on both sides, and Burton himself was distraught with grief for the man who had been, at one time, like a brother. Public fascination with the controversy and its tragic ending has kept the story of Burton and Speke alive for 140 years, and transferred itself from the men to the country they had explored.

Burton lived another twenty-six years — he died in Trieste in 1890 — and wrote many more books (forty-three in all) on such disparate subjects as swordsmanship (he is considered one of the greatest swordsmen in history), falconry, the Mormon settlement in Salt Lake City, and classic Eastern eroticism. Burton was truly one of the great intellects of all time. It is said that if each of his published books were placed in a pile, the stack would be four feet high; if books written about him were added, the stack would be forty feet high. His two most influential works on East Africa were *First Footsteps in East Africa* (the story of the Somali expedition) and *The Lake Regions of Central Africa*. The latter dealt with the exploration for the source of the Nile that led to both Lakes Tanganyika and Victoria, and while his conclusions were incorrect about which lake drained where, the overall account of the journey, and what they discovered along the way, has become one of the great classics of African literature. Like Livingstone's book, *Lake Regions* has been printed and reprinted for more than a century and played a great part in inspiring people to visit East Africa, and even to settle there.

The inspirational value of literature in the settling of Africa went beyond tales of the explorers. By the 1860s, all kinds of hunting books were also being published. The first was William Cornwallis Harris's *The Wild Sports of Southern Africa*. Harris hunted in South Africa during the time of the Great Trek and was in the vicinity of what is now Zimbabwe when the Afrikaner *Voortrekkers* came into conflict with the Matabele, an offshoot tribe of the Zulus. Harris's book inspired other men to emulate him, and they too returned home to write books that encouraged others. Roualeyn Gordon Cumming, a wild Scot if ever there was one, wrote *A Hunter's Life in South Africa*. William Cotton Oswell came out to hunt and stayed to finance Livingstone's journey across the Kalahari to locate Lake Ngami. Oswell wrote sections of *The Badminton Library* series on big game hunting. After that came Frederick Courteney Selous, the most famous hunter and author of them all. While most of this activity was in southern Africa — what is today South Africa and Zimbabwe — it spilled over into East Africa when that area opened up in the latter half of the century.

\* \* \*

By this time, South Africa had been settled for more than two hundred years, and the great game herds were being killed off rapidly. The European countries were engaged in what history now refers to as the "Scramble for Africa," planting their flags up and down the continent. From unproductive goat paradises like Somalia, to the fever-ridden coastal swamps of Mozambique, to the mineral-rich Belgian Congo, there was a frantic drive to colonize every square inch of the Dark Continent. When the scramble was over, Africa had been divided up among Great Britain, France, Portugal, Germany, Italy and Belgium.

The greatest single power was Great Britain, which ruled the Cape of Good Hope and points north as far as the Zambezi; it controlled Egypt and the Sudan, and British East Africa, as well as Nigeria and other parts of west Africa. The same European rivalries that led to the colonization of Africa played a part in the first world war, although what was cause and what was effect is still being debated. In his book *The Scramble for Africa*, English historian Thomas Pakenham summed up the unseemly party:

*In half a generation, the Scramble gave Europe virtually the whole continent: including thirty new colonies and protectorates, 10 million square miles of new territory and 110 million dazed new subjects, acquired by one method or another. Africa was sliced up like a cake… By the end of the century, the passions generated by the Scramble had helped to poison the political climate in Europe, brought Britain to the brink of war with France, and precipitated a struggle with the Boers, the costliest, longest and bloodiest war since 1815 — and one of the most humiliating in British history. As for the pieces of the colonial cake, they have now become, ninety years later, for richer or for poorer (mainly for poorer) the forty-seven independent nations of Africa.*

Today there are more than forty-seven independent nations, and it would be pointless to even state a number. By the time this book goes to press, there will almost certainly be more. The artificial boundaries that were drawn by the colonial powers have imposed unbelievable hardship on native African peoples in the forty years since they began embracing independence, mainly by dividing homogenous tribes between two neighboring countries. The Masai of Kenya and Tanganyika are a classic example. A line on a map, drawn in London or Berlin or Paris, or wherever the latest treaty was negotiated, means little to a Masai herdsman in search of fresh pasture, or to a wandering goat, or a migrating elephant.

Many conflicting interests motivated the scramble, although the whole episode is still puzzling to historians, much like the South Sea Bubble or the Dutch tulip mania of the 1700s. Bismarck referred sardonically to the whole affair as *Kolonialtummel* — the colonial whirl — as in, "give it a whirl." To a great extent, the motivation of newly united countries like Germany and Italy was the desire to be seen as the equal of other European states, traditional colonial powers like Britain and France. Britain itself had a mix of motivations, some of them highminded (at least at the beginning), some purely avaricious, and a few strategic. Starting out with that mix, a politician can always find some excuse that is acceptable to a majority of the electorate.

To start with the strategic, Britain as a great sea power, with colonies spanning the globe, had a vital interest in keeping the sea lanes open — hence its interest in Egypt and the Suez Canal at one end of the continent, and the Cape of Good Hope at the other. Its high-minded subjects, including such ego-driven do-gooders as David Livingstone, felt it was Britain's responsibility to halt the slave trade, a traffic in black Africans that had existed for thousands of years. Slaves were shipped from both coasts, some heading west to the Americas, others east to the Arab emirates. The Sudan was then (and is today) the focal point of that trade, and Britain was drawn into a lengthy war with the Arab slavers of the Sudan that led to the death of General Charles George "Chinese" Gordon at Khartoum, the eventual defeat of the Mahdi by Kitchener at Omdurman, and a colonial administration in the Sudan that lasted until 1956. Coincidentally, there was the exploration of the

Nile, both up from its mouth and down from its source, involving such luminaries as Henry Stanley and Samuel Baker as well as Burton and Speke. This determination to stop the slave trade drew Britain and the Royal Navy into such disparate locales as the Gold Coast of west Africa and Zanzibar on the east coast, both of which were slave-trading centers.

The discovery of gold in the Transvaal in the 1880s, and the great diamond strikes in southern Africa, eventually led to the activities of adventurers such as Cecil Rhodes, the Boer War (the greatest armed robbery of all time), and the penetration of British soldiers of fortune into Bechuanaland and the Rhodesias. Where British adventurers led, the British government inevitably followed — either to protect them from the inhabitants or to protect the inhabitants from them. As a rule, especially under Liberals like Gladstone who were essentially anti-imperial, the British government did not want to add colonies; they were expensive and few contributed anything to the treasury. The Sudan, for example, was a money-sink, imposing endless costs with little to show except frustration and failure. The problem was, there always seemed to be some good reason for getting involved — whether it was the slave trade, gold mines, diamonds, or protecting settlers — and never sufficient reason to pull out. Great Britain did not set out to colonize the world. Mostly it just happened.

The third great item of trade in African history, after slaves and gold, is ivory. Elephant tusks have been used as currency for millenia, and there has been a thriving ivory trade from East Africa to the Far East almost as long as there has been trading. By 1900, the great elephant herds were gone from South Africa, and the Belgian king, Leopold, had locked up the heart of Africa and the ivory trade down the Congo River. That left the elephants of East Africa. Their ivory was not the prime motivating force for Britain becoming involved in Kenya, but once there, ivory played a pivotal role in the region's colonization.

Although there were all kinds of motivating factors, the European invasion of Africa was always one of people. Colonies require settlers; otherwise they remain merely conquests, lonely flags planted on distant shores. The Portuguese and the Dutch began the white colonization of Africa in the 1500s and 1600s. The largest and most enduring white settlement was that of the Dutch Boers of South Africa, who first landed at the Cape in 1652. So entrenched did they become that they eventually became known, and largely accepted, as a "white tribe" of Africa, with their own culture, language (Afrikaans), and traditions. The word "Boer" is Dutch for farmer, and farming was (and is) their primary focus. The Portuguese in Angola and Mozambique tended more toward mining, hunting, trading, and plantations, while the old-world farming of the Boers centered on cattle.

Where the British went, they went to hunt, farm, explore, mine, and trade. Often they were led by visionaries, whether of the David Livingstone missionary stamp, determined to save the heathen and eradicate slavery, or of the Cape-to-Cairo imperialism of a Cecil Rhodes. There always seemed to be some eccentric, magnetic Brit out in front, waving a flag, wearing a tie to dinner in the middle of the jungle, or mowing down hordes of savages in the name of Christ. The image of "mad dogs and Englishmen, out in the midday sun" is more than just a music hall parody. A more accurate image, however, is the kind of men who defended Rorke's Drift against the Zulus in 1879. In her colonial wars, Britain more often than not faced overwhelming odds, and preferred to depend upon the resourcefulness of one man to win through, rather than sending a dozen battalions. For one thing, it was cheaper. And if the one resourceful man failed and paid with his head, as Chinese Gordon did at Khartoum, the government could always depend on the newspapers to whip up public opinion to approve of sending the big battalions later.

As foreign policies go, it was one of the more successful, and certainly most economical, in history. Occasionally, the resourceful visionary would cause unwelcome problems for the government by stirring up public opinion when it was not wanted, but that is one of the risks of trying to run an empire on a budget.

In the scramble for Africa, Britain was different from the other European powers in one significant way: It was a democracy, with politicians who were both pro- and anti-imperial. During the late 1800s, the Liberal Gladstone was in and out of power, alternating with Benjamin Disraeli, Lord Palmerston, and finally Lord Salisbury, Tories all, who were more or less pro-imperial. And so, as governments changed, a period of imperial expansion would be followed by one of contraction or neglect or fretful hand-wringing, either by the civil servants at the Exchequer at the enormous cost of saving the heathen, or by missionary societies at the evils of slave traders and the other, less enlightened, European powers. Germany immediately comes to mind in that regard. Germany seized two large chunks of territory — German South-West Africa (later Namibia) and German East Africa (later Tanganyika). These colonies were governed with the fairness and enlightenment for which the Germans later became famous in Belgium, Poland, and the Ukraine. The image of the shaven-headed, bull-necked German overseer, lashing slaves to build roads and bridges, is no more far-fetched than the effete Englishman dressing for dinner in ninety-five-degree heat. Both existed. Fortunately, the English model prevailed.

\* \* \*

It is difficult to write a brief history of Kenya because it was a most unlikely colony that grew out of a series of unlikely events, each of which needs to be explained if the rest is to make much sense. One of the most improbable factors was the building of the Uganda Railway — the "Lunatic Line" — in the 1890s. This was an expensive, controversial venture undertaken to accomplish one particular goal, but not completed until some considerable time after the reason for building it in the first place had already disappeared. Like so many odd occurrences in British history, it came about because of the death of one of the "resourceful men" upon whom Whitehall habitually depended to save the day. In this case, it was the death of General Gordon at Khartoum. Gordon had been dispatched by Gladstone with orders to evacuate the city, which was being threatened by a fanatical Muslim force under the Mahdi. In 1885, Khartoum fell to the Mahdi, Gordon was killed, and his head severed and put on display, enraging the British public. They demanded a relief force be sent to re-conquer the Sudan. The ensuing war was pursued sporadically until 1898, when a British expeditionary force under General Kitchener defeated the Mahdi's forces at Omdurman. In the thirteen years between Gordon's death and the Mahdi's final defeat, however, various approaches had been suggested as alternatives to sending an army up the Nile from Egypt, which was a difficult and expensive undertaking and one that was anything but a guaranteed success.

One suggestion was building a railway from Mombasa to Lake Victoria to carry troops, weapons, and supplies, which would then be shipped down the Nile into the Sudan, to invade the territory from the south. There were other reasons for building the railway, but this was a major one. Over all opposition, on August 13, 1896, a bill was passed in the House of Commons authorizing construction. Over the next five years, the project would cost five and a half million pounds and the lives of hundreds of workers, many of them killed by the infamous man eaters of Tsavo. By the time the line was finished, however, the war in the Sudan had already been over for three years. The British were left with a railway going, essentially, from nowhere to nowhere. There were no products to be carried out from Lake Victoria and no trade goods to be sent in. The government was left with a costly white elephant for which it now needed a use. The answer? Create a colony, settle the land, and give the rail line a reason to exist.

The five-year construction project had produced more than merely a railway. The man-eating lions that delayed its construction by killing and eating the Indian coolies working on it had finally been killed by Col. J.H. Patterson, and Patterson wrote a book about the ordeal. The book, *The Man-Eaters of Tsavo*, was published in 1907. It became one of the best-selling African hunting books of all time and ignited the imaginations of thousands of young British men and women, many of whom settled in Kenya.

Meanwhile, in 1897, a young hunter named Hugh Cholmondely (pronounced CHUM-ley), later Lord Delamere, came to Africa to hunt in Somaliland and almost accidentally wandered into the highlands of Kenya around Laikipia, north of what is now Nairobi. He was entranced by the mountains and streams and returned to England determined to settle in British East Africa. In 1903, he and his wife, Lady Florence Cole, arrived and established Equator Ranch. A few other white settlers were already in Kenya, but Delamere was one of the very few who had enough capital to finance a serious venture; as well, he was a man of great energy and vision, and utterly ruthless in getting what he wanted, whether the enemy was the tsetse fly, the Kikuyu, or the British Colonial

Office. Delamere became a legend in East Africa. The main street of Nairobi was named Delamere Avenue, and there was a statue of him at the head of the street near the Stanley Hotel. Today, the street is Kenyatta Avenue, and a statue of Jomo Kenyatta stands in Delamere's stead. But that does not lessen Delamere's contribution.

Nairobi was founded in 1899 and became the capital in 1905. Its location was chosen because the railway passed through; otherwise it was situated in about as inhospitable a spot as is imaginable. The settlement was established in a swampy area renowned for its mosquitoes and fever. Dr. Boedeker, one of the earliest settlers who later became a government medical officer, skirted the area on his trek to Fort Smith and described it as "the worst possible choice for any sort of urban center by virtue of its swamps alone." He pointed out that the early Arab trading caravans had given it a wide berth for that reason. Regardless, Nairobi took root, grew, prospered, and is today one of the major cities of Africa, known (by name at least) to people who otherwise have only the vaguest idea where Kenya is.

At a height of 4,000 feet above sea level, however, Nairobi had other virtues. Its climate is very pleasant most of the year, and mosquitoes aside, it is not as congenitally fever-ridden as such coastal areas as Dar es Salaam. By 1901, the East African Protectorate, as Kenya was originally known, had a coastal port (Mombasa), a 582-mile rail link from Lake Victoria to the sea, and a city (Nairobi) taking shape in the interior. All it needed, in the eyes of the British government, was people.

Of course, the region already had people. It had several dozen black tribes, including the two largest that would play a major role in the events that were about to unfold: the Kikuyu and the colorful, photogenic Masai. With their red cloaks, their haughty good looks, and their free-spirited lifestyle, the Masai seized the romantic imaginations of many Europeans. The Kikuyu, mortal enemies of the Masai, fought a brief war with the British which ended, predictably, with their defeat. Kikuyu, Masai, and European then entered into a long period of settlement, resettlement, and mounting resentment, most of it based on land or the lack thereof. As in South Africa with the Boers and the Zulus, land ownership was to play a pivotal role in shaping Kenya Colony. In the case of the Masai, land is largely communal property, held by the tribe as a whole but grazed by everyone. For the Kikuyu, land ownership is also a tribal concern but in a different way; not being a tribe of nomadic herdsmen, they require individual plots of ground to raise crops. One man may have several wives, and each wife requires her own *shamba* on which to raise her crops. When the British arrived, to a great extent they put an end to inter-tribal warfare, and over the course of the twentieth century black populations increased dramatically. As the number of people rose, demand for land became greater, and that, in turn, became a source of friction.

When he first arrived in the 1890s, Lord Delamere saw the highlands north of Nairobi and dubbed it "white man's country." This phrase was seized upon over the next few years as an indication of racism — that Delamere intended Kenya to be for white people only. In reality, the term stemmed from the fact that the highlands were country in which a white person could survive, unlike the fever-ridden lowlands or coastal areas. There was a great European fear in those days, almost a supernatural dread, of the tropical sun's effect on northern peoples. This is the reason you see, in old photographs, men and women bundled up without a square inch of skin showing, wearing huge hats and solar *topis*. They treated the sun almost as a living adversary, and it was many years before most Europeans dared to venture outdoors in the tropics without a hat.

The first settlers came to Kenya and followed the railway inland, settling in the "white highlands" north and west of Nairobi. They established towns whose names became famous in books and novels — Thomson's Falls, Fort Hall, Nyeri. They lived a hard life. Although they were allotted land by the government, there were mixed feelings about the benefits of settlement. Some government officials supported the idea of white colonization; others felt the land belonged rightly to the Kikuyu, Masai, and other tribes. The colonists, led from the start by Lord Delamere, fought a running battle with the colonial administration. The Kenya settlers gained an early reputation for being combative, quarrelsome, even mutinous. At times, it seemed the colonial administration was practically at war with its own people, and this antagonism and mistrust would play a significant role decades later.

\* \* \*

The appearance in 1907 of *The Man-Eaters of Tsavo* was a milestone for the protectorate. The book received rave reviews: *The Times Literary Supplement* called it "overpoweringly dramatic;" *The Spectator* said the tale was "simply amazing." The book was reprinted twenty-six times by 1945. It was required reading for anyone "going out" to East Africa, and one of its greatest admirers was Theodore Roosevelt, the President of the United States who, in 1908, passed up the chance for a second term in the White House in order to go to Kenya and fulfill a lifelong dream: a full-scale African safari. The Roosevelt safari was one of the pivotal events in early Kenya history because it helped put the place on the map. Already Kenya was becoming known as a shooter's paradise, with a seemingly endless supply of big game of every kind. Roosevelt's arrival and the subsequent publication of his book, *African Game Trails*, set more hunters' hearts a-flutter. The company that arranged Roosevelt's safari, Newland & Tarlton, set a standard for opulence that stood for years.

In the early part of the century, men in Kenya hunted for many reasons. The most obvious was food, and game meat was a staple on many of the farms being hacked out of the highland forests. They also shot lions and leopards to protect their cattle, and Cape buffalo, elephant, and rhino to protect their crops; zebras and wildebeeste were shot by the thousands to remove their grazing mouths from land needed for cattle and goats. As well, money could be made directly from animals like the elephant. There was a continuing demand for ivory, and a hunter could make serious money coming back into Nairobi with a long string of porters, weighed down with tusks. Men like Karamoja Bell and Arthur Neumann hunted elephant professionally, but many farmers hunted elephant in their spare time to pick up cash, which was then used to buy equipment, seed, or to pay off a bank loan.

From there it was a short step for farmers to use their hunting skills and fieldcraft to guide visitors from abroad who came to Kenya to go on safari and hunt. Roosevelt's guides were also farmers, and the civilian farming industry of the East African Protectorate grew alongside the commercial safari industry, each feeding off the other.

In 1913, there was another literary milestone: the arrival of Karen

Blixen and her husband, Baron Bror von Blixen-Finecke. They purchased a coffee plantation at the foot of the Ngong Hills, southwest of Nairobi, in what is now the town of Karen. The Baron became a famous white hunter, Karen became the lover of another hunter, Denys Finch Hatton, and eventually the author of the book that will forever be associated with Kenya, *Out of Africa*. The tangled multiple love affairs of the Blixens *et al* were just a part of what became practically a national trait; two of the affairs became famous, and later played a part in the further unfolding of the literary history of Kenya, through the works of Ernest Hemingway.

\* \* \*

Life in the East African Protectorate changed in 1914 when it was forced to go to war with its neighbor to the south, German East Africa. The war was fought almost entirely on Tanganyikan soil, after British forces invaded. The first battle was on the plain between Mount Longido and Kilimanjaro, and the outnumbered forces of the German general, Paul von Lettow-Vorbeck, fought a legendary campaign of hit-and-run which only ended in 1918, with von Lettow's surrender after a fighting withdrawal to Northern Rhodesia (now Zambia). The most noteworthy event of the war, from a hunting and literary standpoint, was the death of F.C. Selous, in 1917, shot by a German sniper. On hearing the news, Kaiser Wilhelm, an admirer of Selous, sent a note of condolence to the British.

The war ended with German East Africa in British hands and from 1918 onwards, Kenya, Tanganyika, and to a lesser extent Uganda and the southern Sudan, were the hunting Mecca of the world.

For Kenya, the war brought one bounty: more people. Under the Soldier Settlement Scheme of 1920, demobilized British soldiers came out from the United Kingdom by the boatload. Many were given land in the highlands, and Nairobi grew quickly. By this time outfitting safaris was a major industry, and publishing safari books was a minor but influential offshoot. The Roaring Twenties and the Jazz Age had their effect on Kenya in the sense that a society that had always been iconoclastic exhibited a tendency toward outright lawlessness. The so-called Happy Valley Set became notorious as far away as London and New York, with newspaper articles appearing that gave all the delicious, devilish details of their drug-taking, bed-hopping, weekend parties. There was the famous hostess who interpreted "dressing for dinner" as meaning removing every stitch of clothing before making her entrance, to the delight of her guests. Another uttered the memorable line, as she rose with the latest in a series of crushing hangovers, walked out onto her bedroom terrace, and snarled: "Another goddamned beautiful day." Eventually, there was a standing joke in London: "Are you married, or are you from Kenya?"

Such behavior was not typical of British colonies. Kenya was different, and it was different because of the people it attracted. It is over-simplifying to say that it was settled by the nobility, while other colonies attracted lower-class or middle-class Englishmen, but to a great extent it is true. Rhodesia, for example, presented a distinct contrast with Kenya. Both were settled in the immediate aftermath of the Second Anglo-Boer War (1899-1902), and both drew their early settlers from South Africa and from veterans of that war, both British and Afrikaner. Eventually, Southern Rhodesia (later Zimbabwe) had a white population of about a quarter-million. They were storekeepers, railway men, drovers, engineers, ranchers, hunters, miners, prospectors. Many of them were drawn from the working classes of industrial British cities like Sheffield and Birmingham, and most skilled jobs were filled by white settlers, not by natives or Asian immigrants.

Kenya, on the other hand, took its tone from Lord Delamere, who was heir to a substantial estate in Cheshire. Kenya was a place to go to shoot, to be a landowner, a gentleman farmer (although most quickly found that life was anything but gentlemanly, for the most part). Although the white highlands eventually were carved up into large, white-owned farms, the total white population of Kenya never exceeded 60,000 people. Kenya also had a large Indian population. At one point, there were 35,000 Indians employed building the Uganda Railway, and many stayed on in East Africa. The Asian population developed a vibrant community in its own right, and Indians formed Kenya's major commercial class. Asian businessmen became a third pillar upon which Kenyan society was built; if the white farmers and professional ivory hunters were the men who killed the elephants, the Asians were the people who provided the market for the ivory.

During the 1920s a rash of safari books appeared, written by men who had traveled to East Africa after the war. In those days a safari was typically three months or more, not counting the many weeks spent in transit. A shooter might board a ship in Southampton for a lengthy cruise through the Mediterranean to the Suez Canal, then down the coast to Mombasa with stops along the way at such intriguing places as Port Sudan or Aden, unaffectionately known as the "Coal-Hole of the East." By the time a big game hunter disembarked at Mombasa, he had likely been at sea for several weeks. He would then board the Uganda Railway for a journey of several days up-country to Nairobi. Altogether, a safari was a major undertaking involving great sums of money and vast amounts of time. Only the very serious, or the seriously wealthy, could contemplate doing it.

When Roosevelt hunted in East Africa in 1908, the camp and supplies were carried by a long string of porters, five hundred or thereabouts, and the organizing and marshaling of these men was a full-time job. There were porters to carry the camp, askaris to guard the porters, and hunters to provide game meat to feed them all. Needless to say, this was not cheap. From the beginning, an East African safari was a considerable financial commitment. By the 1920s, foot safaris had given way to vehicles, much to the chagrin of some traditionalists, who pronounced it "the end of the game." They predicted the motorized safari would bring ruin, but it had the advantage of providing greater mobility at lower cost and offered the possibility of reaching areas that otherwise would have been out of the question. As with so many things technology changed safaris, but it did not wipe them out and in many ways made them more accessible.

In 1927, for example, an American physician, Thomas Arbuthnot, arrived in Kenya with two young friends for a safari. Their guides were the Trichardt brothers, Carl and Fannie, Afrikaners who had emigrated to Kenya after the Boer War. Over the next several months they hunted throughout Kenya and Tanganyika. The finale, after the hunting was over, was a drive to the headwaters of the Nile, where they embarked on a river steamer for the long voyage down river to Khartoum; from there they travelled by boat and railway to Cairo, and from there back to the

United States. In 1954, Arbuthnot published an account of the journey called *Grand Safari*. Neither the safari nor the book is particularly noteworthy except for the fact that the trip took place, Dr. Arbuthnot wrote a book about it, and publishers in several countries saw fit to publish it. No one was killed, no one was eaten, and nothing new was discovered, but it was a great adventure all the same, and the world agreed.

In 1928, the Prince of Wales went to Africa on safari and was guided by Denys Finch Hatton and Bror Blixen. Naturally, the event was one of the social highlights of the year, covered in detail (if at a distance) by all the London newspapers.

The glitz and glamor of safari life, as reported by the *Daily Mail*, tended to obscure the colony's less newsworthy daily life, which consisted largely of a struggle to survive by the farmers who had settled the highlands. For them, life was an endless round of crop failures, unexplained livestock deaths, problems with recalcitrant labor, battling the strange religious beliefs of the tribes living on and around their land, watching children come down with various diseases, and making once- or twice-yearly trips to Nairobi to buy supplies and beg a further extension from the bank. To read books like *Out of Africa*, you would think the Kenya settlers lived permanently on the brink of bankruptcy, and to an extent this was true. While the highlands were spectacularly scenic, with Mount Kenya jutting its snow-covered fist to the skies, the land itself was not particularly well adapted to growing anything anyone wanted to buy. Experiments with cash crops like coffee, tea, and wheat had a boom-or-bust quality; chances are the crop would fail, eaten by some heretofore unsuspected fungus, or if there was a bumper crop the market would collapse. At which point, Father would pick up his .470 Nitro Express and head off into the bush to hunt ivory, to make ends meet, while Mother supervised the planting of next year's failure.

In 1933, a young American writer named Ernest Hemingway disembarked at Mombasa, accompanied by his second wife, Pauline. Hemingway was recognized even then as one of the most significant modern novelists. He was only thirty-four but had already published two of his best works, *The Sun Also Rises* and *A Farewell to Arms*, as well as several collections of short stories and an enigmatic non-fiction masterpiece on bull-fighting, *Death in the Afternoon*. A hunter and fisherman since childhood, Hemingway had dreamed of going on safari for many years, and now here he was, in spite of the onset of the Great Depression, with the great (and expensive) adventure bankrolled by Pauline's wealthy Uncle Gus. Their professional hunter — still called a "white hunter" in those pre-politically correct days — was Philip Percival. The term "white hunter," by the way, came into being very early in the game; at one time, there were two professional hunters employed on a particular ranch to control predators and crop-trampling herbivores. One hunter was white, the other black. The white one, believe it or not, was named Alan Black, who became the very first "white hunter," to differentiate him from the "black hunter." Or so the story goes. At any rate, Philip Percival, brother of Kenya's long-time chief game warden, Blayney Percival (author of *A Game Ranger's Note Book*) was a renowned professional hunter even before he became associated with Hemingway.

Hemingway hunted with him for the better part of three months, then took ship from Mombasa with his head filled with memories of Africa and plans to come back. These ideas spilled out later onto the pages of *Green Hills of Africa*, one of the modern classics of safari writing. More important than *Green Hills*, however, were two short stories Hemingway wrote. One, *The Short Happy Life of Francis Macomber*, may be, from a technical point of view, the finest short story ever written,. It is a tale of a classic love triangle involving a wealthy American client, his beautiful straying wife, and their white hunter, Robert Wilson. The client, Macomber, finds himself but loses his life, shot by accident or design by his lovely wife as he faces a charging Cape buffalo. The plot is loosely based on an actual incident Percival related to Hemingway. It involved J.H. Patterson, killer of the maneaters of Tsavo, when he was guiding an Englishman and his wife on safari. The Englishman shot himself with a revolver (or did he?) after which Patterson and the wife blithely continued with the safari. The affair caused a monumental scandal, and Patterson left the colony in disgrace. He died in 1947. When Hemingway was there, the affair was still a *cause célèbre*, a current issue rather than an ancient incident. He took the theme and made it into a great short story, which was read by millions of Americans. It was later made into the usual dreadful movie, as with so many of Hemingway's works, but the movie reinforced the general rather distorted (albeit romantic) view of life in Kenya.

There was an indirect connection with another love triangle — that of the Blixens and Finch Hatton. Robert Wilson, the PH, was modeled on Bror Blixen (a renowned philanderer), and Hemingway armed him with Blixen's favorite rifle, a .505 Gibbs. This also served the purpose of distancing Wilson from Philip Percival, who always used a .450 No. 2.

The other important short story was *The Snows of Kilimanjaro*. Although it takes place in Africa, it is not about Africa in any overt sense. A writer is dying of gangrene, after being scratched by a thorn during a safari. He and his rich wife are in camp, waiting for a plane to take him to a hospital in Nairobi. The writer, Harry, reflects on his life and all the things he failed to do, all the responsibilities he had neglected, preferring to travel in his wife's circles, on his wife's money. Regardless of its plot, the story captured imaginations. At the beginning, there is a reference to a "dried and frozen carcass of a leopard" found near the summit of Mount Kilimanjaro, and the statement that no one knew what the leopard was seeking at that altitude. If *Macomber* fixed forever the public's perception of safari life, *Kilimanjaro* cemented the image of the snow-capped volcano dominating the horizon, looking out over the African plain, and the notion of mystical adventurers coming to Africa to seek if not to find.

* * *

Behind the glamor of safari life, Kenya Colony, as it had become in 1920, was a developing society that combined the real hardships and dawn-to-dusk labor of farmers battling the elements with undercurrents of racial tension. There was never a formal system of apartheid in Kenya as there came to be in South Africa, and never the race-based antipathy of Rhodesia. In the early days, however, there was at least a partial color bar — places where blacks were not allowed to go — but it never became a major issue on the scale of apartheid.

Kenya was settled about the time of the first major international conference on game conservation, the International Convention for the Preservation of Wild Animals, Birds, and Fish in Africa, which convened in London in 1900. The colonial authorities moved quickly after that to ensure that the great game herds of East Africa did not go the way of the springbok and the quagga of South Africa. Over-hunting and out-right policies of game extermination in South Africa had eradicated the huge migrating herds of springbok, and driven a few other species to extinction, and by the early 1900s wildlife in much of South Africa was but a memory. The Cape Province, the Orange Free State, Natal, and much of the Transvaal were farmland, as devoid of wild beasts as if they had never existed.

In Kenya, huge tracts of land were set aside early as national parks, in name or in fact, and a game department was established with strict licensing provisions and bag limits. These measures did not have the same impact on the native peoples as a similar system would have on, for example, the Cheyenne, if all of South Dakota had been set aside as a park and the shooting of bison had been prohibited. Major tribal groups in East Africa did not depend on hunting for survival; there were a few individual hunters who lived by snaring or shooting animals for the meat, but they were not a large consideration, political or economic. The Kikuyu were farmers, the Masai were herdsmen, and both could get along quite nicely without man-eating lions, goat-eating leopards, or maize-trampling elephants. What they could not do without, however, was land. Land set aside for wild animals was land that could not be tilled or grazed. Game preserves and parks became one more bone of contention in what was already a serious issue: the availability of land for a growing black population.

The British and the colonials have always pointed out the benefits they brought to native people. One was medical care, and the other an end to tribal warfare. The end result of both, however, was population increase. Infant mortality rates dropped, but fertility rates did not, and without raids back and forth to thin out the adult warrior population, numbers naturally increased. Tribal raids were not light-hearted outings; they were bloody affairs costing many lives. In his memoirs, Philip Percival noted that had the British not arrived and put an end to tribal warfare, the Kikuyu "might easily have been exterminated by the warlike Somalis from the north and the Masai from the South."

Had this happened, Percival said, "Kenya would have lost its hardest working tribe, but might have been spared a lot of political headaches from which we now suffer."

The Kikuyu had a highly formalized social structure even before the British arrived, and like most aboriginal societies, it was both pragmatic and practical. A man could have as many wives as he could afford, each of which would bear children; he would spend time with each wife, week by week, and in between his visits, they would each cultivate their own crops, raise their own children, herd their own goats, make their own beer. Brides were purchased, and a daughter's future bride price was a significant part of a man's social security. As populations increased, so did the need for land to provide a *shamba* for each wife. As land became harder to come by, because of strictures imposed by the colonial government, young Kikuyus drifted away to the towns and cities. Nairobi developed a large native quarter to go along with its Asian quarter, its market quarter, and so on. At the same time, more and more young Kikuyu and other blacks were attending mission schools, becoming educated, and even going to university. Some went to England for their education. One such was Jomo Kenyatta, who studied at the London School of Economics and later wrote a book, *Facing Mount Kenya*. Very early he became involved in some of the budding nationalist movements advocating a policy of Kenya for the Kenyans — meaning black Kenyans — and the overthrow of white rule.

These pressures were building in every colony and protectorate in the British Empire during the 1930s. Kenya was no different than any other colony, except it was one of the few where the British government (albeit half-heartedly and sporadically) had encouraged settlement by whites. In Uganda, by contrast, there was very little European settlement and no land restrictions on blacks, and hence no political pressure from settlers to keep blacks from wielding power. Even in India, the crown jewel of the Empire, there was no significant white voice in the move to independence, which was achieved in 1947. In colonies like Kenya and Rhodesia, however, the settlers were a force to be reckoned with — a thorn in the side of the colonial office, whose servants came to wish, fervently, that the settlers did not exist, and a thorn in the side of the black nationalists, who wanted them off the land and out of the country.

Aside from their social structure, the Kikuyu were highly political and politicized, and both accepted and embraced formal education. Although they resisted white settlement, they were defeated in a series of short, sharp battles and thereafter settled down to be ruled by the British colonial authorities. Very early on, however, the Kikuyu began to organize politically. One of the first groups was the Kikuyu Central Association; Jomo Kenyatta became secretary general of this group in 1928 and went to London in 1931 to represent the KCA at the Colonial Office. He lived in England for the next fifteen years, studying, writing, and lecturing, and even married a white woman.

The disintegration of the British Empire began in a major way with the first world war. The financial cost of that horrible conflict ate up much of Britain's wealth. The process continued with the second world war, but for another reason. Between 1939 and 1945, Britain called up troops from almost all her colonies and overseas possessions and deployed them in far-flung battlefields against the Germans and the Japanese, from Europe to Burma and everywhere in between. The native troops saw things they had never suspected, including the near-defeat of the heretofore invincible British. If they could come so close to defeat at the hands of the Japanese, it was reasoned, then they could just as easily lose to the Indians, the Pakistanis, the Malayans — and the Kenyans. Many young Kenyan men, including the Kikuyu, were called up to serve in the army, mainly in the King's African Rifles (KAR). The KAR was organized along traditional British regimental lines, which meant there was one regiment, with one set of colors, badges, insignia, and so forth, but it could have anywhere from one battalion to a dozen. The KAR was the catch-all regiment for British East Africa, with battalions drawn from Kenya as well as other parts of the region.

Between 1939 and 1945, KAR battalions were sent around the world and saw combat in many theaters of war, especially the bloody hand-to-hand jungle fighting against the Japanese in Burma. Having been given their initial military training by their British officers, KAR soldiers then received post-graduate courses in jungle warfare, guerrilla tactics, and survival, with the Japanese as unwitting tutors. As well, the KAR soldiers saw that their white officers were human, just as they were, and not at all invincible. The Kikuyu veterans of the KAR returning to Kenya at war's end were an invaluable asset for a movement that sought to use military force, if necessary, to liberate Kenya from British rule.

Kikuyu tribal organization is built around traditions and customs, among which are the circumcision ceremonies for both young men and women. Young men of the same age, who are circumcised at the same time in the same ceremony, share a special bond. A class of young men, later known as "The Forties," were those who had been circumcised together in that year, and many of them joined the KAR, saw wartime service, and became, on their return, a mainstay of the black Kenyan liberation movements.

The second world war brought major changes to Kenya, for many reasons. Between 1939 and 1941, the British not only fought the Germans in North Africa, they also fought the Italians, who had conquered Ethiopia in the mid-1930s. The initial tank battles in North Africa were between the British and the Italians, and only when the Italians had been decisively defeated did Adolph Hitler despatch the Afrika Korps under Erwin Rommel to bail them out. Meanwhile, the British had been busy dislodging the Italians from Ethiopia, with invasions mounted from the Sudan to the west and Kenya and Somaliland to the south and east. Many of the Kenyan white hunters were involved in these military adventures, including John "Pondoro" Taylor, Donald Ker, and Sydney Downey. Thousands of Italian soldiers taken prisoner in the battles in the desert, and in Ethiopia, were incarcerated in prisoner-of-war camps in Kenya for the remaining years of the war. They were put to work building roads and bridges, among other things, and more than one Kenyan noted it was not until then that the colony enjoyed anything like a respectable road system.

Because Kenya also produced commodities, mainly agricultural, the war brought prosperity for its farmers. Many a Kenyan farmer who had been hanging on the lip of bankruptcy through the 1930s found himself, for the first time, *persona grata* with his bank manager. When Kenya's soldiers returned home in 1945, the young white men found family farms prospering and bank balances bulging. The young black soldiers saw things differently: They now looked at their homeland with eyes that had seen other ways of life. They now saw prosperous white farms on what once had been their tribal land; they looked at the prosperity around them with a large measure of resentment combined with a new sense of nationalism and self-confidence, and a determination to take back what they saw as a heritage that had been stolen from them. Far from bringing an end to conflict, for Kenya 1945 was really just the beginning.

* * *

*Chapter Eight*

# ROBERT RUARK AMONG THE MAU MAU

Depending on who is telling the story, the Mau Mau Emergency in Kenya was a war of independence, a revolution against racism, a Communist-inspired terrorist action, or a reversion to primitive bestialism. In truth, there is evidence to support all of these views and more. Even today, some people contend the Mau Mau were simply criminals and thugs bent on looting, while others insist they were sadists, tanked to the eyeballs on hemp and home-made gin.

Even allowing for a generous portion of historical revisionism and twenty-twenty hindsight, however, the facts indicate that Mau Mau was primarily political, with roots going back many years, deep into the fabric of Kikuyu tribal life. It is tempting to begin the story with the first bloody attack, describe it in lurid detail, then fill in a little background and continue on to the climax. For a white settler, the climax would be the final destruction of the Mau Mau forces in the mountain forests; for a black activist, it would be Kenya's independence from Britain in 1963. This story has something for everyone. That fact alone says much about the Mau Mau movement: It was not a crystal-clear series of events that can easily be judged in terms of right and wrong.

For one thing, there were many non-Kikuyus included in the political movements of which Mau Mau was a part, including Asians and whites. Most notably, two early participants were British veterans of the second world war, who had settled in Kenya after 1945. Similarly, there were the "loyal" Kikuyu, those who sided with the colonial authorities and refused to take part in the Mau Mau movement. These Kikuyu comprised the majority of those who died on the government side. Regardless of whose count you believe, one fact is irrefutable: The vast majority of casualties during the Mau Mau Emergency were Kikuyu. And there were casualties: At least 11,000 people died in the Emergency, of whom only a tiny percentage were white — fewer than a hundred people. Declared wars have been fought from start to finish with less bloodshed.

\* \* \*

Perhaps the best place to start is with the global political situation after 1945, because what happened in Kenya can really only be explained — at least the international reaction to it — in terms of what people believed was happening at the time.

After 1945, there was a massive movement of people. Emigrants left Europe, especially, and settled in countries like the United States, Canada, Australia and South Africa. Many from England went to Kenya. These later settlers were noted for one thing: They were often considerably more right-wing and racist than whites who had lived in Kenya for a long time. As well, a significant number of Italians settled there, especially former prisoners-of-war who had been interned in Kenya, liked the country, and decided to stay. There were even German immigrants. This puzzled the Kikuyu, particularly ex-KAR soldiers who saw their former enemies arriving in droves and being welcomed by the settlers as fellow whites. They were allowed to take up land in areas reserved for whites, while Kikuyu war veterans were barred. Such an anomaly would puzzle anyone.

At the same time, with the Iron Curtain having descended across Europe, the first Communist insurgencies were springing up around the world in conjunction with wars of independence. There were stirrings in Indochina and Malaya. India became independent in 1947, and many whites departed. A considerable number of these ex-Indians migrated to Kenya, including Jim Corbett, who became famous as the author of *Man-Eaters of Kumaon*. While these expatriate Anglo-Indians might not have been particularly right-wing, they certainly distrusted and feared native nationalism, and the memory of the riots and massacres that had swept the Indian subcontinent after partition were kept alive in Kenya. Their twin fears were nationalism and Communism, and they tended to see both, even where they did not exist.

Almost one hundred thousand black Kenyans served with the British Army during the war, and they returned home with a different view of the world. They also returned to find prosperity for the white settlers and an increasing flood of white people into a country which already had shortages of arable land for its black population. This was a problem that had been simmering, really, since the end of the Kikuyu wars. The Kikuyu had resisted British settlement for fourteen years, from 1890 to 1904. One of the officers who commanded the British forces was Richard Meinertzhagen, a career soldier who became famous as a writer about both Kenya and big game hunting. In spite of his Teutonic surname, Meinertzhagen came from an upper-class English family. The battles he describes with the Kikuyu, and the actions on both sides, could have been lifted from later accounts of the Mau Mau in terms of atrocities, torture, and massacres. The Kikuyu wars and the Mau Mau Emergency were only fifty years apart, so there were still people alive for the second who had vivid memories of the first. Meinertzhagen emerged from the experience with a great affection for Kenya and admiration for the Kikuyu.

Very soon after the Kikuyu were subdued, the colonial authorities began to impose rules and regulations regarding land management and overall administration. Tracts of the best land in the highlands — the region with the best climate, if not the most arable land — were set aside for whites. The Masai were resettled in the southern part of the colony, and the Kikuyu Reserve was established. This consisted of an area of several thousand square miles of territory, but very soon became overcrowded as Kikuyu numbers grew and pressure on land increased. Eventually, as many as a thousand people tried to coax a living out of each square mile of arable land on the reserve. Naturally, many left to work on European farms or find a new life in Nairobi; inevitably, those who did not find work became squatters on white farms, or big-city slum-dwellers. White demands that the squatters and "city spivs" be returned to the reserve, by force if necessary, became a tedious refrain. It reached a crescendo toward the end of the Mau Mau Emergency, when more than ten thousand Kikuyu were transported back to the reserve.

The Kikuyu way of life was based on farming and multiple marriages. With tribal wars stopped and the introduction of modern medicine, death rates declined, but birth rates continued at a high level. Soon the black population was climbing. With more and more Kikuyu, and relatively less land, there was increasing rootlessness. A system of identity cards for natives — the *kipande* — was imposed, and this was the basis of a series of "pass laws. " The *kipande* was carried in a metal container worn around the neck, and it allowed white employers to write comments about the wearer's character and work habits. This became a form of permanent letter of recommendation (or the opposite) and a source of growing friction and resentment among black Kenyans. At the same time, the British set up a system of tribal chiefs. Modern authorities insist the Kikuyu were traditionally ruled by councils of elders and never recognized any one individual as a chief, but there is no doubt they had them after 1910. The early chiefs accumulated wealth in the form of land, goats, and wives, and were noted for their loyalty to the British.

Another stress on Kikuyu tribal life was the proliferation of missions, missionaries, and religious schooling. Especially, there was white disapproval of the traditional custom of female circumcision. There are conflicting accounts of exactly what this entailed. Those who oppose it insist it is a barbaric custom in which large portions of the female genitalia are removed, preventing any pleasure in sex (thereby eliminating a desire to stray when one's husband is inattentive) and reducing women to the status of beasts of burden. The custom's apologists say it is no more harmful than male circumcision, in which the foreskin is lopped off. Regardless, controversy over female circumcision led to a split within the Christian Kikuyu. One faction broke away and formed its own church. Years later, the pro-circumcision faction sided largely with the Mau Mau, while the anti-circumcision Kikuyu stayed loyal to the British.

The Kikuyu became politicized very early in the life of the colony. Meinertzhagen predicted that once the Kikuyu learned to read and write they would become a political force, and he was right. The Harry Thuku affair of 1922 was a precursor of the problems that were to surface with a vengeance after 1945. Thuku was a 24-year-old government employee and member of the Young Kikuyu Association who organized a series of protests against the *kipande* system as well as related pass laws, and hut and labor taxes. Thuku urged black people to throw away the *kipande* containers and made various incendiary statements naturally interpreted as seditious. Thuku was arrested and placed in the jail of the Nairobi central police station, across the street from the Norfolk Hotel. A crowd gathered outside the jail, which was surrounded by 150 black policemen armed with rifles and fixed bayonets. The protest began peacefully but quickly turned ugly. A prostitute named Mary Nyanjira began to taunt the policemen, urging the crowd to rush the jail and release Thuku. For reasons never fully explained — the exact flash point is unknown — the police opened fire, killing the woman and several others in the crowd. White settlers drinking on the veranda of the Norfolk heard and saw what was happening and joined in, shooting into the panicking mob.

How many were actually killed remains a point of debate. The next day, the *East African Standard* reported twenty-five killed, twenty-seven wounded. A black eyewitness stated categorically that he had counted fifty-six bodies in the morgue, yet the Corfield Report, the official Kenya Government investigation into the causes of Mau Mau published in 1960, said only three people died. Other estimates range as high as 250 dead. Whatever the real number, the Harry Thuku riot of 1922 is evidence of the political unrest among the Kikuyu many years before the Mau Mau Emergency. Ironically, Harry Thuku was never put on trial. He was exiled to Somalia, where he remained for the next nine years.

In the crowd outside the police station that day was the man who would become Jomo Kenyatta. Kenyatta had many names during his lifetime. The first was Kamau Ngengi, the name he gave when he first appeared at a Scottish mission in 1909 as a naked herd boy of about twelve years old. He was baptized as "K.N. Johnstone" and spent five years at the mission school. From there he drifted to Nairobi, where he became a meter reader. He wore a beaded Masai belt, called an *akinyata*, and took to calling himself "Kenyatta."

In 1925, Harry Thuku's organization was replaced by the Kenya Central Association. Kenyatta was a member and soon became a full-time employee. In 1929, calling himself "Johnstone Kenyatta," he went to England, where he would spend the next fifteen years. Kenyatta's career in England was somewhat checkered. Although he was already married with two children and had promised not to marry a white woman, he married a governess and sired two more children. Later, when he returned to Kenya, he abandoned his English family for good. While in England, he travelled to both the Soviet Union and Nazi Germany and attended one of Adolph Hitler's earliest mass rallies. He was also furthering his education at the University of London and acquiring considerable political sophistication to go along with his natural magnetism and commanding presence. Kenyatta's transformation into the acknowledged leader of his people was completed with the publication in 1938 of his book, *Facing Mount Kenya*, a defense of the Kikuyu, their culture, and customs. The book lent Kenyatta a stature few black African leaders have ever enjoyed. It was then he dropped the name "Johnstone" as being inappropriate for a tribal leader, and began to call himself "Jomo," a name he invented as sounding suitably revolutionary.

In writing about Kenyatta in the early 1950s, Robert Ruark zeroed in on the name as evidence of Kenyatta's crude nationalism. In the Kikuyu language, he said, Jomo is a common diminutive, and Kenyatta was derived from the country, so his name was the equivalent of "Joe Kenya." This, however, was not true at all. Oddly enough, many people today believe the country of Kenya is named after its first president, while others think he named himself after the country in order to secure greater prominence. The *akinyata* he wore as a badge throughout his adult life, which was the original source of his surname, is forgotten.

The second world war began in 1939, and the first two years were disastrous for the British in most parts of the world. In Kenya, a series of emergency measures was instituted as part of the war effort. In 1940, the KCA was banned because it was considered a threat to security. At that time, Kikuyu nationalism was mounting. As the war progressed, however, tribal sentiment changed and tens of thousands of Kikuyu, including members of the radical "Forties" circumcision group, volunteered to serve in the armed forces. When they returned home in 1945, they brought with them new ideas about their proper place in the world, and the military skills to force changes.

In 1946, Jomo Kenyatta came home from England. He stepped off the boat in Mombasa to the cheers of hundreds of supporters, and a new era began in Kenya. Throughout the Mau Mau Emergency, it was generally believed that Kenyatta was the movement's guiding light. The colonial authorities certainly thought so. They arrested him in 1952, as soon as the Emergency was declared, and he spent nine years in prison. In fact, while Kenyatta was widely considered the natural leader of the Kikuyu, and the man most likely to assume command when the British were eventually driven out (as the Mau Mau and their sympathizers devoutly believed), he was not part of the inner decision-making circle. If anything, he was almost a stalking horse for the movement, or a lightning rod — someone on whom the authorities were welcome to concentrate their attention, leaving the real leaders free to organize the insurgency.

Kenyatta's political efforts were genuine, however. Shortly after his return, he set up a new organization to replace the KCA. The Kenya African Union (KAU) was intended to attract the support of all blacks, Kikuyu and non-Kikuyu, and very quickly grew to a membership of 150,000. It became, and remained, Kenyatta's power base. By this time he was a middle-aged man of great presence and skill as a demagogue. He was called *mzee*, which means "elder" in Swahili, and was known for wearing a large signet ring with a huge red stone, and for carrying an ebony walking stick with a carved elephant's head on the end. Kenyatta had a Van Dyke beard, and his piercing eyes were enough to frighten the most hardened settler. Part of this was reality, part was theater, and part was settler paranoia, but it all added up to the Kenyatta myth. When the Mau Mau revolt began, the white settlers were more than prepared to believe Jomo Kenyatta was the evil mastermind behind it all.

\* \* \*

Between 1945 and 1952, many factors combined to bring Kenya's political situation to a boil: There was the influx of new white settlers, including the addition of many frankly racist whites; the growth of black trade unions and militancy among young blacks, especially the Kikuyu;

various plans by white minorities to ensure white supremacy in the country; and communist-inspired unrest among the black and Asian communities. One issue, however, overshadowed all the rest: Land.

"In 1948, the most burning issue was still the unavailability of agricultural land," wrote Robert Edgerton in *Mau Mau*. "As the rising Kikuyu birthrate made the land shortage increasingly acute, the Kikuyu looked more and more to the 'white highlands' for relief. They could readily see how crowded people were in the reserves and how vast stretches of land in the highlands remained undeveloped. In fact, 3,000 European families owned more arable land in the highlands than was available to the more than one million Kikuyu in their reserves. Many landless men were ready to use violence to free Kenya from what they called 'white settler' rule." In short, when Robert Ruark arrived in Nairobi in June, 1951, to set out on his first safari, Kenya was, on the surface, a peaceful, sunlit land. In reality, it was a pot waiting to boil over.

The prime movers were militant young Kikuyu who had lost all patience with Kenyatta's Kenya African Union, which they saw as weak and old-fashioned. Armed revolt was the fashion of the early 1950s, but Kenyatta let it be known he favored peaceful solutions and control of the independence movement began to slip into other hands. Kenyatta reacted by drinking heavily and becoming more and more moody. By the time he was arrested in 1952, Kenyatta was considered by many, especially militant young blacks, to be yesterday's man.

The radical leaders who organized what became known as Mau Mau were people like Fred Kubai, the trade-union leader, and Bildad Kaggia, a former clerk who was mission-educated and had spent some years in England. Although the KAU was intended to be multi-tribal, the radicals built an organization in which the Kikuyu and their traditions were central. These traditions provided a sound base on which to build. The taking of oaths, for example, is central to Kikuyu tribal life. The KAU recognized this and adopted a traditional oath of obedience. The radical group did likewise; as it grew, and events moved at an ever-faster and more violent pace, the oaths changed and became increasingly bloody and repugnant. Robert Ruark made a point of researching the Mau Mau oathing ceremonies, and his descriptions are among the most wrenching parts of *Something of Value.*

\* \* \*

Even now, it is difficult to pinpoint the exact beginning of the events that were later characterized as the Mau Mau Emergency. As a secret organization, the Mau Mau had many small beginnings. Its leaders took pains to ensure their activities did not become public, and even to provide red herrings to mislead the authorities. Many of these diversions were reported as true and the stories have been retold down through the years. Sorting out the facts has been a difficult process, and even today historians in Kenya disagree on exactly what roles were played by whom. Not surprisingly, when the Emergency ended and Kenya became independent — and after the danger and bloodshed had passed — many emerged from the shadows to claim credit, rightly or wrongly. This was true on both sides of the conflict.

If any one man can be credited as the founder of the Mau Mau, it would have to be Fred Kubai, the trade-union leader. Kubai was a half-Kikuyu, born in Mombasa, who worked in Nairobi as a telegraphist. Throughout the war he stayed in Kenya and became a leader of both the Forties circumcision group and various trade unions. By 1947 he was already organizing underground independence movements and was recognized as one of the most militant and influential activists. In 1948, Jomo Kenyatta's more moderate KAU conceded that it was not attracting the more militant elements it needed to be fully effective, and, as a result, was in danger of losing leadership of the independence movement. The KAU invited Kubai and several others to join. This was a distinct concession for the KAU, because Kenyatta distrusted men like Kubai, whom he feared as having "dark and uneducated minds." Kubai and John Mungai, another trade-union leader, joined KAU and brought with them eight cohorts. These ten men became the "action group" that created the Mau Mau. In 1949, Kubai became president of the East African Trades Union Congress, which further extended his influence. The action group swiftly recruited followers, administered stronger and stronger oaths, and set out on a campaign to steal the weapons they needed, suborn Kikuyu government employees to obtain information, and establish a network of agents throughout the colony.

Robert Edgerton went to some lengths to determine the origin of the name Mau Mau, which is perhaps the most hazy question of all. No one really knows how it originated. The words, as such, have no meaning in either Kikuyu or Swahili. Various explanations have been advanced, most based on the assumption that *mau* is a corruption of a Kikuyu word like *muma*, which means "oath." Regardless, the name *Mau Mau* was of incalculable value to the movement because it gave focus to the fears of the settlers. Instead of a hodge-podge of legal, semi-legal, and secret independence movements, Mau Mau came to represent the forces of darkness in white Kenyan minds. Although it allowed the government a convenient shorthand excuse for jailing thousands, it also gave focus and identity to the independence movement. It may have lent short-term benefits to the former, but it helped guarantee the long-term success of the latter. Any modern political strategist or public-relations guru would kill to come up with such a mesmerizing symbol, yet this one seemingly grew out of nowhere.

For a so-called secret society, however, Mau Mau was remarkably visible to the authorities. In 1949, Richard Meinertzhagen, by then an elderly man, visited an old Kikuyu chief that he had known many years before, during the Kikuyu Wars. The chief warned him of an impending resurrection by a group he called "maw maw." Meinertzhagen's letter to the governor apprising him of the warning was one more indication to the authorities that something serious was afoot. As the practice of oathing spread rapidly, the government moved to contain it. They arrested oath-givers and sought to infiltrate the movement.

The activities of the Mau Mau were directed and coordinated by a central committee, which included Fred Kubai. According to Edgerton, from 1947 to his arrest in 1952, Kubai was the chief oath-giver for Nairobi, as well as being responsible for executing anyone who violated their oath. "He was perhaps the most militant of the Mau Mau leaders," Edgerton says, "and the one most feared within Mau Mau inner circles."

From 1948 to 1950, tension mounted and violence increased. As oathings spread, the government banned the Mau Mau, closed more than three hundred Kikuyu Independent Schools, and arrested oath administrators. Politicians and government leaders, acting from fear, ignorance, or willful disbelief, characterized the Mau Mau in many ways, mostly as terrorists, criminals, or primitive thugs, but rarely in terms of a modern political or revolutionary movement and never with any claim to legitimacy. Whether this was to help justify their own reaction to it, or to head off international sympathy, is open to question. From the beginning, Mau Mau was a shadowy organization, impossible to pin down and difficult to characterize.

The violence began early but slowly. At first it consisted of beatings and cattle maimings, as well as the execution of "traitors" within the organization and the systematic murder of black policemen for their weapons. It was difficult to differentiate some of these activities from the more normal crimes of passion, robbery, or inter-tribal raiding, but the authorities quickly found that by labeling any activity as "Mau Mau," they had a ready-made justification for the most arbitrary of counter-measures.

A hundred thousand Kikuyu may have returned in 1945 with well-honed military skills, but against the British they would need them all. In challenging Britain, they were taking on a nation that was the world's most experienced, competent, and ruthless in dealing with insurgent, nationalist, or terrorist organizations. Virtually non-stop for the previous century, the British Army had been fighting anti-guerrilla actions somewhere in the world, from the northwest frontier of India to the back streets of Dublin. Not only could the British field thousands of officers and men who, after four years in Burma, were skilled jungle fighters, they could also call on any number of the kind of men like Richard Burton, men who had invented the "Great Game" Kipling made famous in *Kim*, and who had turned counter-espionage and counter-insurgency into an art form.

Whether the British could muster the political will to bring this to bear against the Mau Mau was another question. Exhausted and near-bankrupt after the second world war, successive governments in London were not only reluctant to engage in another armed conflict, but in many ways even sympathized with the aims of the insurgents. On the other hand, the Cold War was just getting underway, and there was the constant threat of spreading Russian or Red Chinese influence. This, of course, had to be contained for larger, global reasons. Britain's Labour politicians might want to see black African nations become independent, but they wanted to see them as social-democratic countries, not as Bolshevik tyrannies.

For their part, Kenya's white settlers had no such qualms, and no doubts about what they wanted or how to get it. Like their Kikuyu enemies, most young settlers had spent the years 1939 to 1945 acquiring military skills. These, coupled with their natural abilities in the bush honed by years of big game hunting, game control, and anti-poaching missions, and the fact that they grew up with a gun in their hands, made them formidable opponents. By 1951, the stage was set for a small, local, but unbelievably bloody battle that would astonish the world with its viciousness.

* * *

There was, of course, another side to Kenya in the years 1945 to 1950. That was the world of the glamorous big game safari, as written about by Hemingway and portrayed by Hollywood — a world symbolized by the most famous safari company of all, Ker & Downey Safaris Limited.

Sydney Downey was one of the all-time great Kenya professional hunters, and Donald Ker not far behind. They met first in the 1930s, hunted together off and on, and decided to go into business at a chance meeting in, of all places, the Imperial Hotel in Addis Ababa at the end of the Ethiopian campaign in 1941.

If Kenya was a small and insular society, the hunting community was even smaller, and their lives were intertwined through the years in business associations and partnerships of one kind or another. To say everyone knew everyone else is a gross understatement. There were never more than a few dozen top-notch, full-time professionals, and the same names run like threads through a succession of books written by and about them.

Sydney Downey is an excellent example. He was an Englishman who spent his boyhood on his family's cattle ranch in Argentina, went back to England to school, and on graduation boarded a ship for Kenya. Having spent much of his childhood in the bush, Downey had already decided he wanted a career working outdoors, doing something with wild animals. Once in Kenya, he went to work on a coffee plantation near Nairobi. Much of his spare time he spent in the bush, however, and in 1933 he was taken on as a professional hunter with Leslie Tarlton's company, Safariland. This was the same Leslie Tarlton who had formed Newland & Tarlton and guided Theodore Roosevelt in 1908. One of Tarlton's professionals was Philip Percival, and Downey acted as Percival's second hunter on several safaris. Percival, of course, had guided Ernest Hemingway.

Donald Ker was also a professional hunter of considerable renown. In 1911, at the age of six, he arrived in Kenya with his family, grew up on a coffee plantation, and killed his first lion while in his early 'teens. In 1928, he accompanied Denys Finch Hatton on safari with the Prince of Wales. During the 1930s, Donald Ker and Sydney Downey opened up much of the Masai Mara country of southwestern Kenya. When war broke out in 1939, both enlisted in the British Army. Downey was posted to Intelligence, Ker to the Scouts, and they took part in the campaign against the Italian Army occupying Ethiopia. According to legend, they met by chance in a bar in Addis Ababa when the city was liberated in 1941. On seeing Downey, Ker let out a whoop that brought several other professional hunters running to see what was happening. They included Philip Percival, Tom Murray-Smith, and Pat Ayre, whereupon the whole group sat down and held an impromptu meeting of the East African Professional Hunters' Association. That, at least, is the legend.

It was at that meeting Downey and Ker decided to go into business together, which they did as soon as they were discharged in Nairobi in 1945. They started with one operable vehicle, and Donald Ker managed to cobble together a second one from random parts. Their very first client was London Film Productions, which was coming to Kenya to make *The Macomber Affair*, based on Ernest Hemingway's short story. It was Kenya's first post-war commercial safari.

Many years later Verity Williams, the widow of professional hunter Dave Williams, told me the saying in Nairobi was "Harry Selby made Ker & Downey, and Robert Ruark made Harry Selby." There is enough truth to that rather bald statement that it bears repeating, but it suggests that without Ruark and Selby, Ker & Downey would not have amounted to much.  In fact, however, the two founders were among the best-known and most respected names in the industry when they formed the company, whereas Harry Selby was a young unknown.

Certainly Ker & Downey attained (and retained) a stature head-and-shoulders above everyone else, but it was not solely due to Ruark by any means.  Ker & Downey began operations working out of a room at the Norfolk Hotel and later moved to the New Stanley, which was more central.  Both hotels were owned by the Block family, and Jack Block eventually joined the partnership.  The Blocks were astute businessmen (Abraham Block having been one of the founding fathers of Nairobi), and Jack Block saw the obvious connection between outfitting safaris for the global jet set and providing hotel accommodations for them before and after.  As well, neither Donald Ker nor Sydney Downey was a natural office manager, and Block offered the administrative support that would allow them the freedom to do what they did best, which was guide safaris.

Ker & Downey began hiring, and the list of professional hunters they employed in the early years reads like Who's Who:  Tony Henley, Andrew Holmberg, Stan Lawrence-Brown, Frank Bowman, Kris Aschan, and Tony Dyer, to begin with.  Harry Selby and Myles Turner joined the company in 1948, and a few years later, John Sutton, Eric Rundgren, Reggie Destro, and Bill Ryan.  John Kingsley-Heath, Tony Archer, John Dugmore, and Fred Bartlett came in the mid-1950s.

Jack O'Connor, the shooting editor of *Outdoor Life*, went on safari in East Africa several times, and his professional hunters included Downey, Turner, Kingsley-Heath, and Aschan.  His accounts of these trips appeared not only in *Outdoor Life* but in various of his books, and the names became familiar to American hunters.  Robert Ruark and Jack O'Connor were probably the two most-read and widely travelled hunting writers of the 1950s and '60s, and between them they helped to construct the legend of Ker & Downey — or "K&D" — into the dominant name in big game safaris anywhere in Africa.  It was a case, really, of the best helping the best:  K&D's reputation caused Robert Ruark, looking for a top-flight safari, to book with them in the first place.  He then spread their fame far and wide, causing others to follow in his footsteps.  The moment *Horn of the Hunter* was published in 1953, it became a game of catch-up for every other safari company in Nairobi.

\* \* \*

For Kenya, the summer of 1952 was a period of impending turmoil. Events were moving rapidly, for good and ill, in any number of ways. While Robert Ruark spent his time in New York working on *Horn of the Hunter*, his head filled with thoughts of the idyllic Africa he had experienced the year before, a dam was about to burst that would sweep away that Africa as if it had never been.

A safari is many things to different people, but above all it is a venture into a fantasy world. The fantasy might be "Eden regained," as some would have it after visiting the Ngorongoro Crater. Or it might be a return to a simpler life, without ringing telephones and impending deadlines. Whatever illusion the client desires, one of a professional hunter's major functions has always been to create it for him. In 1951, Robert Ruark left Kenya with a head full of illusions. Although he had seen Nairobi and its environs, and he had lived closely with the retinue of Africans staffing the safari, his actual view of what was happening in East Africa was anything but complete. Ruark and Harry Selby had had wide-ranging discussions around the campfire and while slogging mile after mile in the safari car, but Ruark's impressions of life in Africa were superficial at best. This once-over-lightly view, as he later termed it, showed through in the newspaper columns he wrote describing his experiences and comes through in *Horn of the Hunter*, less from what he wrote than from what he did not write. There is next to nothing in the book about the serious political problems that were already obvious in Kenya, even while Robert and Virginia Ruark were having lunch at the Norfolk with Donald Ker, or being measured for safari jackets at Ahamed Brothers, or having dinner with the American ambassador. *Horn of the Hunter* is a Genesis view of Eden, without the snakes.

This is not an indictment of Ruark. He did not set out to write a political tome. He and Virginia were on safari to have fun and repair their psyches, not to dig into the colony's politics or offend its inhabitants. Still, on his return to New York, the fact he made no secret that he was considering buying a farm in Kenya suggests he did not fully appreciate what was about to happen. But in that, he was not alone.

Several factors combined in 1952 to focus the world's attention on this small British colony on the far side of nowhere. Princess Elizabeth and her husband, the Duke of Edinburgh, visited the colony, following in the footsteps of her uncle, the Prince of Wales. In February, the royal couple was staying at Treetops, the famous game-viewing lodge, when word came that her father, King George VI, was dead. Jim Corbett, the famous tiger hunter who was acting as their escort, broke the sad news to the new queen.

Royalty of a different type was also preparing to descend on Kenya: Hollywood, having discovered Africa with a vengeance after the war, was preparing to make its latest blockbuster, *Mogambo*. The studio hired Kenya's foremost post-war rogue, Bunny Allen, to outfit the safari, and booked passage for Ava Gardner, the smoldering queen of Tinseltown. Every newspaper from the *Daily Mail* to *Variety* was struggling with the correct spelling of Serengeti.

The situation was a publicist's dream, if the publicist happened to be working for Jomo Kenyatta and his KAU, or for Fred Kubai and the shadowy movement known as the Mau Mau. The black Kenyan nationalist movements, both peaceful and otherwise, needed attention if they were to gain any kind of ascendancy, and there would never be a better opportunity than in mid-1952. It was as if the planets had all aligned in perfect formation and focused a beam of light on Kenya Colony.

The political situation was slowly coming to a boil. Jomo Kenyatta, with his blood-red ring and his menacing eyes, had become the focal point of settlers' fears of black nationalism, and each speech he made was studied closely by the colonial authorities. Behind the scenes, the Mau Mau were proceeding with their oathing ceremonies and drawing more and more Kikuyu into the organization, either as active participants or passive supporters. At the same time, the Kikuyu elements that opposed the Mau Mau, specifically the Christian Kikuyu and government supporters such as the powerful chiefs, were becoming more worried by what they saw happening. On August 22, 1952, a group of Kikuyu elders and representatives of Christian churches met in the town of Kiambu, near Nairobi, and adopted a six-point resolution condemning Mau Mau, rejecting violence, and swearing to oppose the movement. Two days later, a huge public gathering took place in Kiambu — a gathering historians now cite as one of the crucial dates in Kenya history.

As demonstrations go, it was one of the earliest organized "photo ops," an artificial event stage-managed by the government. It was intended to give Jomo Kenyatta and other Kikuyu leaders a public platform to condemn the Mau Mau. To ensure the event received wide coverage, there were movie cameras and sound equipment. Thirty thousand people gathered at the sports ground to hear what Kenyatta had to say. As well as the KAU leader, the group of speakers included Chief Waruhiu, a dignified man who had recently been inducted as a Member of the Order of the British Empire (MBE) by the Queen. Chief Waruhiu embodied both law-abiding support for the government and strong, peace-loving Christian beliefs. Waruhiu introduced Kenyatta to the crowd, and Kenyatta, flamboyant as always, mounted the stage with his elephant-head ebony walking stick and proceeded to denounce Mau Mau in ringing terms. "All people should search for Mau Mau and kill it," he thundered. "Let Mau Mau perish forever!" Even today, opinions are divided on whether Kenyatta was cleverly playing both sides against the middle or was merely caught in the middle himself. His speech was brilliant — so much so that, according to Robert Edgerton, the Central Committee of the KAU later warned him to tone it down. It was one thing to appear to denounce Mau Mau, but quite another to do it so convincingly that it actually harmed the movement.

Kenyatta's speech was followed by similar denunciations by Harry Thuku, the Kikuyu activist who had sparked the riot in 1922, and various elders. The final speaker was Chief Koinange, an 84-year-old man who was already an adult when the Kikuyu fought the British at the turn of the century and who had seen every development in his country, both good and bad, since the arrival of Lord Delamere. Edgerton's account of what Koinange said that day suggests the old chief was one of the most cunning of the Kikuyu leaders, because he appeared to condemn the Mau Mau while in reality drawing attention to the genuine underlying problems facing the country. He recalled the coming of the white man, he described the years he had spent working alongside the settlers to develop the land, and he drew attention to the Kikuyu blood that had been shed in two world wars, supporting the British. In the most recent war, he pointed out, they had fought the Germans and the Italians. Now he looked around and saw these same Germans and Italians being welcomed to Kenya while the Kikuyu were denied the opportunity to own land. "They can live and own land in the highlands from which we are banned, because they are white and we are black," he said. "What are we to think?" Koinange's "stinging rebuke," according to Edgerton, turned the government-orchestrated gathering from an anti-Mau Mau demonstration to a Kikuyu call to arms. It may not have been reported that way in the next day's *East African Standard*, Edgerton says, but that is what it was. The rebuke was not lost on the British, he adds; they neither forgot the incident nor forgave Chief Koinange. When it comes to wiliness and diplomatic sleight-of-hand worthy of Prince Metternich, however, the British and the Kikuyu were well-matched. In this instance, the score was "advantage Koinange."

At the time, there were some four hundred Kikuyu in British jails on one charge or another related to the movement, and although the Mau Mau leaders were concerned that events not move too far or too fast, their control over the far-flung elements of their organization was spotty at best. Violence continued and gathered speed. On September 26, Mau Mau raiders attacked some European farms near Mount Kenya, killing several hundred sheep and cattle and destroying a power station. The white settlers were growing more and more uneasy. A member of the Legislative Council (Legco) stood up and listed, for public consumption, the score of Mau Mau atrocities to date: twenty-three Africans murdered, including two women and three children. As well, he added, there had been another dozen attempted murders and an equal number of assaults, two dozen incidents of arson, and two churches desecrated. As Robert Edgerton points out, while "all these acts may not have been committed by members of the Mau Mau, many whites believed they had been, and they clamored for government action." Any lingering doubts they may have had were dispelled abruptly a week later when, on October 3, a white woman was stabbed to death in her home near Thika, just outside Nairobi. On the fifth, a white couple was attacked with guns and knives, but fought off their attackers.

The situation was reaching boiling point. For the Mau Mau, it may have come too soon. Although they had been preparing steadily for a planned, organized, all-out assault on the colonial government, the movement's decentralized structure allowed a fair degree of independent action, and events began to move too quickly. Hotheads were straining at the leash, and the insurrection gained a momentum of its own. According to Edgerton, it reached a crisis point and precipitated the government into declaring a state of emergency before the Mau Mau were ready for it. The catalyst was the murder, on October 9, of the loyal Kikuyu leader, Senior Chief Waruhiu.

Chief Waruhiu was driving into Nairobi in a chauffeur-driven limousine when it was stopped by armed men dressed in police uniforms. When the chief identified himself, one of the Mau Mau shot him four times — once in the head, three times in the body. No one else was harmed. The attackers escaped.

Waruhiu was known as a very "European" Kikuyu, a devout Christian and loyal friend of the British. Chief Koinange, after his pointed speech at Kiambu, was now considered an enemy. He was arrested on suspicion of complicity in Waruhiu's murder, but there was not enough evidence to convict him.

Sir Evelyn Baring was then governor of Kenya Colony. He had arrived on September 30, landing right in the middle of a rapidly developing crisis. If lineage is a factor in effectiveness, the British could hardly have asked for a better man than Baring. He was the son of Lord Cromer, who had virtually ruled Egypt in the latter years of the 19th century, when Egypt had become of strategic importance because of the Suez Canal and Chinese Gordon was fighting slavers in the Sudan. Lord Cromer was the quintessential imperial administrator. His son had been raised to follow in his footsteps and had already served in South Africa and Rhodesia. Within days of Baring's arrival in Nairobi, the violence escalated. The new governor listened to the settlers, read the police reports, and cabled London for permission to declare a state of emergency. On October 14, permission was granted. Three battalions of the King's African Rifles were mobilized, and three more were ordered to Kenya from other parts of East Africa; the Kenya Police Reserve was put on alert, as was the all-white Kenya Regiment. The 1st Battalion, Lancashire Fusiliers, stationed in Egypt, was ordered to the colony. Altogether, this amassing of troops made a very creditable showing. Over the next few months, Baring's performance was not so good — he acquired a reputation for being indecisive, and the settlers turned against him — but it is unlikely anyone could have maintained good relations with such a fractious lot.

On October 20, the British struck with Operation Jock Scott, a sweep that netted 187 suspected Mau Mau leaders in spite of the authorities losing the element of surprise when word leaked out. Too many government clerks and police employees were Mau Mau sympathizers for an operation of such magnitude to proceed undetected. Regardless, all 187 men were arrested, including the top Mau Mau leaders — Fred Kubai, Bildad Kaggia, and, even if mistakenly, Jomo Kenyatta. On the surface, at least, the sweep was a success. As Edgerton points out, however, it may have actually accelerated the bloodshed by eliminating the more conservative leaders and leaving the movement in the hands of young hotheads. To the average settler, however, things were finally taking a proper turn: Jomo Kenyatta was in jail, and truckloads of Lancashire Fusiliers were cruising through Nairobi with fixed bayonets. It was an open challenge to the Mau Mau, and they responded decisively. While the state of emergency was going into effect, they ambushed another senior Kikuyu chief, Nderi, and murdered him and several followers. His mutilated body was discovered the following day.

With troops arriving from Egypt, Tanganyika, Uganda, and Mauritius, the British capped the reinforcement by sending H.M.S. *Kenya*, a cruiser, to take up station in Kilindini Harbor in Mombasa. Exactly what the cruiser might be expected to do against armed insurgents operating three hundred miles inland gave rise to all kinds of jokes, and even open derision in the press. "It's in case Kenyatta tries to escape in a *dhow*," one remarked. But the British had been playing this game for a long time, and they knew the importance of symbolism. It is not called "gunboat diplomacy" for nothing. The sight of the *Kenya* lying at anchor was comforting for the settlers and a powerful reminder to the Mau Mau of exactly what they were up against. For their part, the Mau Mau did not disband, nor did they roll over and play dead. They countered the British symbol with one of their own.

On October 28, Mau Mau terrorists broke into an isolated farmhouse near Fort Hall. They found the farmer, fifty-year old Eric Bowker, in his bath. They chopped him to bits with *pangas* and killed two black servants in the same manner. All three bodies were horribly mutilated. When the police arrived, they were greeted by a gruesome spectacle that haunted white Kenya for years to come.

By now, everyone's nerves were on edge, and tension was running high. A few days after Bowker's death, a group of Kikuyu men and women confronted a police patrol in Fort Hall. They were ordered to disperse, refused, and the police opened fire. Twenty-five blacks were killed and many more wounded. The white officer who gave the order to shoot maintained he had been acting in self defense. His reason was accepted, no action was taken against him, and there was not so much as an official enquiry.

If there had been any doubt about the gravity of the situation, there was none at all now. Hundreds of suspected Mau Mau were in jail, and armed British soldiers were patrolling the streets of Nairobi. The Mau Mau organization was busy stockpiling weapons and supplies, moving them in darkness to depots in the forests of the Aberdare Mountains and on the slopes of Mount Kenya. The insurgents acquired their weapons, and even their cartridges, one at a time, buying them from sympathetic police and soldiers or stealing them wherever they could. The police issued formal security instructions to white settlers, urging them to take strict precautions. Not surprisingly, the settlers took to carrying guns at all times. Dinner was eaten with a revolver beside your plate; if you took a bath, the gun was in the soap dish close at hand. Bars were fixed on windows, and doors acquired double and triple locks. All Kikuyu were suspect. The police issued strict instructions that farm staff and laborers were to be locked in at night. This gave rise to continuing arguments among Kenya settlers, especially those who had lived in the country for many years and to whom their Kikuyu headman or cook were like alter egos. They simply could not believe "their Kikuyu" could be disloyal, and that belief cost some of them their lives.

Officially, conditions under the state of emergency were akin to martial law. Arbitrary restrictions were imposed and ruthlessly enforced. The government declared prohibited zones in areas of Mau Mau activity, and was prepared to shoot transgressors on sight. It imposed censorship and extended the death penalty to a wide array of offenses beyond the usual ones of murder and rape. As the emergency wore on, the list of restrictions grew. An African could be hanged for being found in possession of a single cartridge. Similarly, a white Kenyan who had a gun stolen was liable to six months in prison, no matter what the theft's circumstances.

For students of post-World War Two insurgency, the British government's reaction to events in Kenya is instructive. It could serve as a counter-insurgency textbook and did, in fact, provide a model for a book on modern warfare by a French officer. Quite simply (regardless of your feelings about the role of H.M.S. *Kenya*) the British did everything right, and even former Mau Mau ruefully agree they were up against a ruthless, and very effective, operation. From 1945 to 1961, there were brushfire wars in many parts of the world. The major colonial powers, Britain and France, were on the receiving end, and while their occasional losing efforts achieved a higher profile, both the British and French Armies learned from their losses. The French lost the war in Indochina to the Viet Minh, but their soldiers absorbed the lessons and applied them later in Algeria, a war they won on the ground only to have the territory given away by the government in Paris. That led to an army revolt in 1961. The ringleaders were officers of the paratroop regiments, and many of them later attained notoriety as mercenary soldiers in various parts of Africa, including the Belgian Congo. One such was Colonel Roger Trinquier, who was dispatched to the Congo as an observer and later wrote a classic book called *Modern Warfare*. Trinquier analyzed organized insurrection, divided it into distinct stages, and outlined what government's response should be, every step of the way. Trinquier freely admitted the colonial government's actions in Kenya provided one of the models for his book.

The very first action that must be taken, Trinquier insisted, was to acknowledge the seriousness of the situation and over-respond in order to shock the populace. Kenya's colonial government may have been slow to act before Governor Baring's arrival, but once he was in Nairobi events unfolded with military precision and ruthless determination. Civil rights, for both whites and blacks, virtually ceased to exist.

Eric Bowker's death was not the first killing by the Mau Mau, but it is now considered the initial act of the Mau Mau Emergency because of its timing and the gruesome way in which the farmer was murdered. Ghastly mutilation became a hallmark of Mau Mau activity. A month later another white couple was attacked on their farm near Thomson's Falls. Commander Ian Meiklejohn, late of the Royal Navy, and his wife, a retired doctor, lived near the Kikuyu Reserve. Late one night five men broke into their house and attacked them with pangas. The couple was left for dead. The commander did die, but his wife survived in spite of terrible wounds. Not long afterwards another leading anti-Mau Mau Kikuyu, Tom Mbotela, was killed in Nairobi as he walked home from a public meeting.

By now events in Kenya were inspiring headlines all over the world. Although no more whites would be killed in 1952, the specter of Mau Mau, of bloody late-night attacks, of gruesome mutilation and horrifying oathings, were taking on a life of their own. And, just to keep the ball rolling, the Mau Mau leadership let it be known that it was planning "a flock of Christmas killings" just in case any of the settlers might be tempted to relax over the holidays.

\* \* \*

Robert Ruark was in New York in the fall of 1952. He had been working hard, completing *Horn of the Hunter* and writing his daily newspaper column, as well as articles for various magazines. The eighteen-month period between his return from safari in 1951 and his second trip to Africa in late 1952 was pivotal for him in more ways than one. First, his exposure to Kenya and Tanganyika had changed his outlook dramatically. He wrote repeatedly about the idyllic life in the bush compared with the steaming concrete jungle of Manhattan, and his discontent with big-city life became palpable in his syndicated column. More than that, however, he began to write about increasingly serious subjects.

Everything from youth culture to drugs, to politics, to international affairs began to crop up — so much so that some editors objected. Robert Ruark was supposed to be light-hearted, witty, and wise-cracking. He could write about any subject he wanted, so long as he was amusing, but his column began to display alarming signs that he was taking the world — and, worse, himself — seriously. Occasional such forays were acceptable, but not on a continuing basis. An editor on a paper in North Carolina finally wrote him a letter reminding him that he was not a political or social affairs columnist — they were paying other people to fill those slots — and unless Ruark returned to his funny ways, his days as a widely syndicated columnist were likely to be numbered.

This was a serious threat. According to Hugh Foster, in 1951 Ruark made $5,500 a month. The bulk of this came from his column, which was carried in almost two hundred newspapers and reached fifteen million readers. Ruark had earned little from *Grenadine Etching*, a fact he mentioned ruefully in a column or two. While *Horn of the Hunter* would eventually sell very well, books of that type would never replace his newspaper work financially, and Ruark knew it. His column was not just the foundation of his income, it was also his daily claim to fame, so any threat to it had to be regarded seriously. At the same time, however, his change of journalistic tone was a sign of something deeper. Africa had awakened him to the essential worthlessness of the life he was living, being a saloon animal by night and a wiseguy by day. He wanted to tackle more serious things, but he now found the newspaper editors and his employers at Scripps-Howard putting obstacles in his way.

In October, 1951, Ruark did what many safari clients have wanted to do over the years: He brought his professional hunter to New York to spend a few weeks as his guest in Manhattan. Harry Selby had exposed Ruark to life in the African bush; now Ruark would expose Selby to the realities of *his* jungle. Naturally, this was written about in his column (lightheartedly, fortunately) and served as a platform for Ruark to ruminate on the perils of modern urban life. "I have seen him swim crocodile infested rivers, but just wait until he tries to cross Park Avenue against a light. A rhino you can dodge, but the cabs go up on the sidewalk after you," he wrote. "And don't follow any strange women into thick bush, wounded or not, with or without cubs. In my jungle they all bite."

One column that appeared during this period is notable for its subject matter: In January, 1952, Ruark wrote a piece about Herman Talmadge, the Governor of Georgia, who had condemned racial integration in television programs — specifically a singing group on Arthur Godfrey's program consisting of two white and two black singers. Such behavior, Talmadge suggested, undermined the moral purity of the South. After stating he was writing more out of "awe for ignorance than of violent outrage," Ruark proceeded to castigate the governor and anyone like him who opposed desegregation. "I am not so distantly removed from the land of cotton that I fail to realize that the period of adjustment between black and white is still in progress and that many a year will pass before it is satisfactorily solved. In the meantime, I suppose I must apologize as a Southerner for Gov. Talmadge." This was not the only column Ruark wrote on the subject. Later accusations that he was a racist because of his feelings about the white settlers of Kenya are directly at odds with the sentiments he expressed in his newspaper column and in his "Old Man" columns for *Field & Stream*.

Later, Ruark wrote another newspaper column almost prescient in its insight into trends in modern life. Pressed by his editors to make his readers laugh, Ruark wrote about the decline of modern humor, brought about by a surfeit of what would today be called "political correctness." His humor was, at times, heavy-handed, and naturally there was a butt to every joke, but he was getting more angry letters and fewer laughs. "Mad they get, or hurty-feelinged they get, but laugh they don't," he wrote. "I have an uneasy feeling that one day everything will be sacrosanct, and he who jeers is going to get lynched."

Things were changing for Ruark, not least of all in what he wanted for himself. The significance of this period in his life is illustrated by the fact that, a dozen years later when he wrote his final novel, *The Honey Badger*, the story begins on a steaming night in August, 1952. Alec Barr is a victim of smoldering, middle-aged dissatisfaction — with his life, his wife, and his work. He walks out on her that night and embarks on an affair with the blonde actress, Barbara Bayne. Looking back, Ruark undoubtedly pinpointed this period as a turning point for him. Unfortunately, while his time in Africa had made him aware of the shortcomings of his situation, it had done little to make him want to do anything concrete to change it. Instead of trying to live differently in New York, Ruark continued to stay out late, drinking as heavily as ever. The safari may have been a valuable break in his pattern of self-destructiveness, but that is all it was: When it was over, he seemed determined to make up for lost time.

A second significant event occurred in the summer of 1952. The Ruarks took another vacation, this time in Spain. He was good friends with Andrew Heiskell, the publisher of *Life*. Heiskell and his wife, actress Madeleine Carroll, owned a villa in the small town of Palamós, about fifty miles east of Barcelona on the Mediterranean coast. In the years immediately after the second world war, Spain occupied a unique place in Europe. It was the last fascist stronghold, ruled since 1938 by Francisco Franco, but it was undamaged by the war itself and had been largely rebuilt after its own civil war. The period from 1938 to 1950 was known as the "years of hunger" in Spain. The country was an international pariah because of Franco, and there were shortages of goods due to trade sanctions; yet it was deliciously inexpensive to live or visit there, and it became a favorite destination. The hunger for Spain and Spanish life that Ernest Hemingway had done so much to foster in his books was reflected in the steady stream of visitors, especially from Great Britain and America.

At that time, Palamós was about as far away from Manhattan as it was possible to get and still live in a town. It was small and out-of-the-way, and under the overbearing Mediterranean sun it moved at a sleep-walker's pace. In 1951, Ruark had returned from Africa with a half-formed intention of buying a farm in Kenya. The eruption of political turmoil and Mau Mau violence in the months since had put an end to that idea, but Palamós offered the perfect alternative: a place to settle that was far from New York, where living costs were low and pressure non-existent, and the sun shone benevolently twelve months of the year. Ruark began to toy with the idea, for the first time, of leaving New York altogether. Unfortunately, New York provided a huge amount of material for his newspaper column, and in this department Palamós could not compete. As well, it was highly unlikely his editors would put up with a columnist who was permanently expatriate, corresponding from such a remote backwater. Still, Palamós was something to keep in mind.

The third pivotal event was a decision that probably seemed quite small at the time. Ruark approached *Field & Stream* with an idea for a monthly column about his experiences as a boy, growing up hunting and fishing in North Carolina. It would be called "The Old Man and the Boy." The editors liked the idea and agreed to pay Ruark the unheard-of sum of $1,500 a month. The series, which turned into one of the most enduring works of literature Ruark produced, began in February, 1953.

By October, 1952, Mau Mau terrorism had become front-page news throughout the English-speaking world. As publisher of *Life*, which was essentially a weekly newsmagazine, Andrew Heiskell knew the significance of what was happening in Kenya and decided to put the Mau Mau front and center. *Life*, of course, was part of Henry Luce's Time-Life publishing empire, and Luce was a virulent anti-communist. The suggestion that the Mau Mau might be a communist-inspired movement, or that it was receiving backing from Moscow or Peking, was enough to catch his interest and open his checkbook. Heiskell and Luce needed a big-name reporter to go to Kenya to cover the story, and the perfect man for the job was right at hand: Robert Ruark. He owned a famous byline, he had just returned from East Africa and written a book about it, he had experience under fire in the war, and he knew how to dig up a story.

In *The Honey Badger*, Ruark describes how the assignment came about for Alec Barr. Barr reconciles with his wife, Amelia, in late 1952, but they have a violent argument on Christmas Eve and Barr retreats, alone, to his New Jersey house for the holidays. His agent, Marc Mantell, calls to tell him about the job he is being offered. He says the magazine wants Barr to go to Kenya, ostensibly on safari, but in reality to "dig into and dig up" the story. Barr hurriedly books with his white hunter, to provide a cover, and wings off to Africa. In real life that is essentially what Ruark did, although there is a curious difference of opinion about the affair. Even today Harry Selby insists Ruark really did go out on safari, but happened to do some magazine pieces on the Mau Mau while he was there. In fact, it was a journalistic assignment with a hunting facade.

\* \* \*

Ruark left New York in early December aboard the S.S. *Vulcania*, a fast Italian ocean liner. It seems a quirky way to embark on an urgent assignment when trans-Atlantic air travel was well established, but perhaps Ruark needed a couple of weeks vacation before the reporting began in earnest. Or perhaps it was intended to show this was a recreational safari, not a venture into journalism. Either way, the sojourn aboard the *Vulcania* provided Ruark with time to think and material for his column. He announced his departure in typical fashion, referring to himself as "Papa" and stating flatly that he was "on the lam" for a while. "There comes a time in the City of New York when the sight of a Fifth Avenue bus, stinking and spouting clouds of gas fumes, suddenly becomes unbearably obnoxious...and too much for one set of city frazzled nerves to bear," Ruark said. "I am in the mood to play hooky for a little while." He was heading for Kenya, he added, where the Mau Mau were "eating the citizens more or less raw" and noted he was quite a likely morsel himself, but this was a vacation and he felt "real lazy."

Ruark landed in Kenya a month later, smack into the beginning of the worst wave of violence of the Mau Mau Emergency. He hooked up with his professional hunters, Harry Selby and Andrew Holmberg, and together they visited several farms in the highlands. Ruark began a series of dispatches back to Scripps-Howard. These newspaper columns were generally breathless accounts of life under siege — of guns under pillows, of trusted servants coming throught the door wild-eyed and wielding pangas, and of mutilated pets hung on fence posts to die. Perhaps he was shocked, seeing such things in the idyllic land he had fallen in love with eighteen months before, but some of Ruark's words were so vitriolic that anyone looking for evidence of racism would need look no further. Beyond the Mau Mau leaders, he wrote, "The remainder of the movement are ignorant, superstitious sheep, who will laugh if told to laugh, kill if told to kill. The simplicity of the native African still has to be seen on the native heath to be believed." After the initial flurry of investigating, Ruark and company headed off into the Northern Frontier District to begin his actual safari.

Kenya was now in an uproar, although the flock of Christmas killings that had been promised never happened as such. The Mau

174

Mau had planned a mass butchering of loyal Kikuyu while they attended church on Christmas Eve, but the operation was cancelled because the leaders feared it would provoke a more serious white reaction than they really wanted. One unit, however, failed to get the message and went ahead with its plan. Eleven people died. Ruark reported this as the Mau Mau promising twelve deaths and delivering eleven, "with a couple more thrown in later for good measure." These two were white farmers, Richard Bingley and C.H. Ferguson, killed on New Year's Day, 1953. Over the next two weeks, thirty-five more Africans were slaughtered.

On January 24, an attack occurred that is the definitive Mau Mau action of the entire emergency: the murder of Roger Ruck, his wife, Esme, and their six-year-old son, Michael. Ruck was a tall, athletic man, well liked by everyone; Esme Ruck was a doctor, renowned for giving free medical treatment to Africans. They lived on a farm, not far from the one where Eric Bowker had been murdered three months earlier. The bloody attack began with the Mau Mau luring Roger Ruck out of the house, where he was killed with pangas. Seeing what was happening, his wife tried to help him. They butchered her, too. Then the terrorists went into the house and began to loot. They stole a shotgun and some cartridges. One started to play the piano and left the ivory keys smeared with his bloody fingerprints. Six-year-old Michael was in his bedroom. Frightened, he called out. One of the family servants, who was in on the attack, killed the boy with a panga, and his body was partly skinned. The man later confessed to the killing; he turned out to be the same servant who had carried Michael home a few days earlier, cradling him in his arms after he had fallen off his pony.

From a sensationalist media point of view, the Ruck killings had everything, and not surprisingly the press had a field day. They ran photographs of the bloody house and of Michael's room with his teddy bear and his toy train scattered and blood-stained. The active involvement of the family's trusted Kikuyu servants added an extra dimension of horror. From a purely objective view, it was a brilliant stroke of psychological warfare on the part of the Mau Mau. "This contradiction in behavior terrified the settlers," writes Robert Edgerton. "If Mau Mau could compel trusted servants to kill like this, then no one was safe. It is little wonder that white Kenyans were distraught. Something inexplicable and terrible was happening in Kenya."

The day after the murder of the Ruck family, fifteen hundred white settlers marched on Government House in Nairobi, demanding action. Sir Evelyn Baring ignored them — what could be done was being done, after all — but the very next day responsibility for the security forces was taken out of the hands of the police and turned over to a British Army major-general, W.R.N. Hinde, a veteran of the war in the Western Desert who was brought in from Cyrenaica to take command.

Many of the young professional hunters had already been pressed into service, most of them as members of the Kenya Police Reserve. The KPR has been described as an "anti-terrorist" unit of jungle fighters, which probably overstates the case but was in part due to Ruark's writings. Of particular interest to Ruark was an informal camp set up on a farm in the highlands. Known as *Campi a Simba*, or Lion Camp, it was staffed by young farmers, professional hunters filling in time between safaris, and various other settlers. Harry Selby took Ruark to visit the camp, and it was a nugget of pure gold that he later worked into the novel *Something of Value*. The activities of the men of *Campi a Simba*, in interrogation and, bluntly, torture of prisoners and suspects, provides one of the most compelling scenes in the novel. Today, recollections about the camp and its members vary from cautious to frankly denigrating.

The task of protecting the remote farms of the white highlands was difficult at best. The security forces set up systems of signals with lanterns that were visible from one settlement to the next and kept squads of police and soldiers ready to react to any emergency, but to a great extent, inevitably, most of the burden of a family's security fell upon its own members, and everyone who was old enough to lift a gun went armed. It became a regulation that black servants be locked in for the night, partly for their own security, partly because the so-called "loyal" Kikuyu servants had either abetted or taken active part in most of the successful attacks to date. The Ruck family murders in January underscored the problem. Even though genuinely loyal Kikuyu were being massacred in far greater numbers than Europeans, mistrust of all blacks became a fact of life. And the murders caused many Kikuyu to support the Mau Mau, actively or passively, out of fear.

Ruark reported on this phenomenon at length, noting one professional hunter who discovered to his horror that his trusted gunbearer of many years was a senior Mau Mau oath administrator. He also reported on the film crew of *Mogambo*, whose lorry drivers turned out to be terrorists and were carted away, leaving filming at a standstill.

For their part, the settlers were far from being helpless, terrified victims. Many were war veterans, almost all had extensive experience in the bush, and a great many had lived in Kenya for years. They owned guns, and they knew how to use them. One celebrated incident, which Ruark reported at the time and then used in his novel, involved two women who lived alone on a farm in the highlands. Kitty Hesselberger and Dorothy Raynes-Simson were sitting by the fire one evening with their two boxer dogs and a cocker spaniel. Two Mau Mau burst in through a door that had been mysteriously unlocked, and what ensued was a melee of gunfire and snarling dogs. When it was over, one Mau Mau lay dead in the living room, the cook was dead in the hall, and another terrorist on the lawn. The signal lantern continued to burn, indicating to distant patrols that the women were all right. To summon help, one of the two casually shot out the lantern. The raiders had been assisted by the two houseboys and the cook, giving rise to one of the great lines of the Mau Mau Emergency: "Why does it always have to be the cook?" Kitty asked bitterly. Apparently he had been a very good cook. This incident was also worked into *Something of Value*. The women were renamed as Marian Sorrell and Sally Henderson, and the dogs became Dobermanns; otherwise it is reported faithfully.

Life on a remote farm, out of sight of neighbors and far from help, was a nerve-wracking experience. Living tactically, as it is called, is fun for a while and soon becomes second nature, but the thought that any strange noise, any flickering light, any dog's bark, can mean impending doom eventually wears you down. Cherry Lander was an English widow who came to Kenya in 1946 and bought a farm near Mount Elgon, in western Kenya. She lived there by herself, raising coffee and various other crops. In 1957, she wrote a book about her experiences called My *Kenya Acres*:

*"For the umpteenth time I put my book down and listened, my hand on my gun. It wouldn't be so bad if I put up a fight for it — even killed some of them — but to be taken unawares was what I dreaded. That creaking door was a great help, as it was impossible to open it silently. Their usual trick was to get the houseboy to go in first. Then the victim, looking up from what she is doing, sees who it is and settles down again, while on stealthy bare feet others swiftly enter the room, armed with razor-sharp pangas. These broad blades, two feet long, would sever a head from a body with one flick of a supple black wrist."*

Mrs. Lander lived in a district far from the center of Mau Mau activity, but it had a substantial Kikuyu population, and by November, 1952 there were already armed gangs operating nearby. She was under no illusions about her chances. Her nearest neighbor was a mile away, over the brow of a hill; there was no hope of help if anything went wrong. Her only chance was to stay in a constant state of armed readiness. Sometimes she got the jitters in the evenings. Every lizard that fell from the roof was suspect, and each time the dogs barked she wondered what was alarming them. She gave up listening to the radio because it disturbed her other, more serious, listening. She let the dogs out by a different door each night, to avoid establishing a pattern of activity, and never allowed herself to be silhouetted against the light. Provided she was always on the alert, she wrote simply, "It seemed there was a good chance."

*"It was a simple choice: stick it, or go. I decided to stick it, for the simple reason that in no other way could I keep the think I loved best in the world — my farm. For I had at last found a way of life that suited me."*

\* \* \*

Cherry Lander was the kind of Kenyan settler who appealed to Robert Ruark. His article appeared in *Life* on February 16, 1953. He was on the cover, standing in the midst of a group of prisoners and wearing "a bloody great revolver." The headline read "Robert Ruark Among the Mau Mau," and the article was titled "Your Guns Go With You." Altogether, it was a big splash for Ruark the reporter, and in *The Honey Badger* he allows Alec Barr to bask in the glory. The Mau Mau gave Ruark a tremendous source of material, and the sensational events taking place in East Africa made the world's media ready to lap it up. Over the next few months, Ruark wrote pieces for *Collier's* and *The Saturday Evening Post*, among others.

By the end of February, 1953, Ruark was on safari in the NFD and the body count stood at nine Europeans, three Asians, and 177 Africans dead. In an attempt to gain more weapons, the Mau Mau began a series of raids on police posts. Sometimes these were successful; other times the raiders were driven off and pursued by military units, and there were running battles (and sometimes hand-to-hand combat) in the forests lasting two or three days.

It would be easy to go back now and point out the inconsistencies, inaccuracies, and factual gaps in Ruark's journalism from this period, but it is understandable these crept in when you consider how terrifying and confused the situation was in Kenya. More than once Ruark vilified Jomo Kenyatta in print as the leader of the Mau Mau and instigator of the terror. Fear of communism was widespread at the time, and it was the suggestion that the Mau Mau movement was communist-inspired that caught the interest of Andrew Heiskell and Henry Luce in the first place. Throughout his articles Ruark constantly referred back to communist links, even though these were tenuous as best. He also tended to glorify the settlers. This also was understandable, given the friendships he had among the professional hunters and their farming families, but from the beginning he sided with the Europeans, defending "their" land against the Mau Mau. The Mau Mau came across not as a legitimate political movement but as a mixture of barbarism, communism, witchcraft, and treachery.

Robert Edgerton maintains that the British authorities and the colonial government misrepresented the Mau Mau with a campaign of propaganda. He accuses Ruark of helping to further this facade of communist-inspired terror, when in fact Mau Mau was a legitimate nationalist cause. He also adds that while the press insisted the Mau Mau were receiving aid from any number of sources, including the Soviet Union, Red China, and India, in fact they received little outside material assistance. They had no external source of weapons; what they had they stole, and only a few at a time. "Except for encouraging radio broadcasts from Cairo and New Delhi," Edgerton writes, "they were on their own."

Certainly, Ruark did omit some facts that should have been reported, assuming he knew about them, and it is impossible to believe he did not. On March 26, for example, a small group of Mau Mau attacked the police post in the town of Naivasha. They shot a sentry, broke in, killed one policeman, drove off the others, released 173 prisoners, and ransacked the armory. They stole eighteen submachine guns, twenty-nine rifles, and a load of ammunition, then escaped in a stolen vehicle.

That same night, in the town of Lari, an event took place that came to symbolize the internal black-against-black violence of Mau Mau. Lari was a farming settlement a few miles from Nairobi, populated by a mixture of both loyal and pro-Mau Mau Kikuyu. Around ten in the evening, up to three thousand Mau Mau (estimates vary) attacked the separated farmsteads. Many people were burned to death in their huts; others were killed with pangas when they tried to escape. Members of the loyal Home Guard counter-attacked. By morning, ninety-seven people were dead, two hundred huts were burned, and a thousand cattle mutilated. Those were the official figures, released by the government when it brought in the press to witness the carnage. According to Edgerton, however, up to another four hundred Mau Mau supporters were killed in retribution the same night by the army and loyal Kikuyu. Either way, the Lari Massacre took its place among the major events of the Mau Mau Emergency.

On his arrival in Kenya, Maj.-Gen. Hinde had conducted a tour of the affected areas. He found a surprisingly high degree of complacency in Nairobi, but loud fury among the settlers in the highlands. Their anger was directed partly at the Mau Mau and partly at the government for its perceived ineffectiveness. Hinde estimated there were about 12,000 Mau Mau activists holed up in the forested enclaves of the Aberdares and Mount Kenya. Edgerton's sources say there were 15,000. They were in various stages of training, and their armament also varied. Some had modern military weapons, others had looted shotguns, and still others carried only pangas and bows and arrows. As noted earlier, the insurrection's swift progression from isolated incidents to full-scale military action had caught the Mau Mau wrong-footed and not fully prepared in either training or equipment.

Because the Mau Mau were concentrated in one area, however, and because the movement largely excluded tribes other than the Kikuyu, it was possible for the government forces to isolate the Mau Mau and impose measures, such as prohibited zones, that severely inhibited their movements and freedom of action. Once this had been accomplished, the war settled down to a series of isolated actions tracking down Mau Mau units in the thick, wet, gloomy forests and deep ravines that criss-crossed the mountains. The Mau Mau (also nicknamed "Mickey Mice") were generally referred to as "gangsters." Accordingly, the British created a small unit of "pseudo-gangsters," white men who blacked their bodies and, accompanied by former Mau Mau who had been "turned," ventured into the mountains on long fighting patrols designed either to suborn the terrorists into surrendering or to ambush those who did not. Tony Archer, later a noted professional hunter and still a resident of Kenya, was little more than a teenager when he became a pseudo-gangster and took part in the operations against the Mau Mau in the forests.

Not surprisingly, the exploits of these men, while not widely reported outside Kenya, became legendary among the settlers. There were even a few hilarious incidents. While the Mau Mau might have no qualms about slaughtering and mutilating women and children on the one hand, once turned and part of an anti-Mau Mau unit they became good friends and cheerful companions of the white pseudo-gangsters — one more contradiction that is typically African. In one incident, a young pseudo-gangster was in a Mau Mau camp, attempting, with some former gangsters, to persuade the bunch to surrender. Naturally he stayed well in the background, trying to be unobtrusive, because no amount of black dye makes a white man genuinely African. Unfortunately, he was overcome by a need to urinate. This presented a dilemma: An African would have casually turned away, done what needed to be done, and thought nothing of it. The problem was, certain parts of him were not blackened and so could not be exposed without considerable risk. Yet retreating behind a bush would have been out of character for an African. He held out as long as possible, then, in order to avoid urinating down his leg — which would have raised a few eyebrows — he turned away, shielding himself as much as possible, did the necessary deed, and returned to the group. After they came down the mountain he was charged under military law with having, by his actions, endangered his unit. He was found guilty.

Perhaps the worst punishment, however, was the fact that to this day he is known throughout Kenya as "Whizzer."

\* \* \*

The Mau Mau Emergency had become, for the British and the Kenya colonists, a full-scale military operation. In May, a new commanding officer, General Sir George Erskine, arrived to take command from Maj.-Gen. Hinde, along with two more infantry battalions of the British Army. General Erskine had authority from the prime minister, Winston Churchill, to implement martial law at any time should he consider it necessary. This implied threat gave Erskine the leverage to run the anti-Mau Mau operation as he saw fit, with no civilian-government dithering or interference. Early on, Erskine met with representatives of the Kenya settlers, including Michael Blundell, a man who was to play a prominent role in Kenya affairs from that time until independence in 1963. General Erskine was anything but impressed with the settlers. In a letter to his wife later that year, he wrote that black Kenyans had confidence in the British Army but that "they hate the police and absolutely loathe the settlers. It is difficult to realize how much the settler is loathed and the settler does not realize it himself." It was a telling observation.

The antagonism that had existed for decades between the settlers and the colonial administration, and between the settlers and the Colonial Office in London, was to grow deeper as the Emergency dragged on. What the settlers saw was government inaction, or insufficient action, combined with a lack of understanding of life in Kenya and the temperament of the Africans; the government saw intransigent troublemakers who seemed willing to shoot anything that moved. Eventually rifts occurred among the settlers, between hard-liners and men like Michael Blundell, who began to advocate a peaceful accommodation, if not with the bloodstained Mau Mau hordes themselves, then at least with mainstream black organizations like the KAU. When Kenya did finally achieve independence, there was a widespread feeling of betrayal among the settlers, who saw themselves as being sold out by London for the sake of world opinion and a peaceful life.

If the black population of Kenya was divided in its attitude to the government, so was the European element. The Mau Mau Emergency was not simply a case of black versus white, or even Kikuyu versus settler. The complexities of the situation made any easy settlement impossible.

For his part, Robert Ruark very quickly identified with the settlers' cause. In his writing — newspapers, magazines, and ultimately novels — he glorified the accomplishments and the character of the Kenya settlers. In so doing he was being rather selective in the traits he chose to portray and those he chose to ignore. Nowhere does he mention the overt racism that was frequently displayed by recent immigrants from post-war Europe, choosing instead to magnify people like Henry McKenzie, the father of Peter McKenzie, in *Something of Value*. Henry was so close to the Kikuyu that he was almost an honorary member of the tribe, and he was an accomplished witchdoctor into the bargain. He spoke the language, had lived the life, and even thought the thoughts. His real-life counterpart might have been Dr. Louis Leakey, the anthropologist who wrote extensively about Kikuyu culture. There is no question such men existed, but they were not typical of Kenya settlers; to suggest otherwise (as Ruark seems to do) is simply wishful thinking.

Ruark wound up his safari and left East Africa in April, 1953. The colony was virtually in a state of war in many ways — people wore guns as casually as Doc Holliday in Tombstone — and security was a nerve-wracking, never-ending necessity. But in other ways, curious ways, life continued and even picked up. Tourism did not drop off substantially (there were 26,000 visitors in 1953, compared with 33,000 the year before), and the government encouraged the safari companies to continue operations in order to present a normal face to the world. Later that year, in fact, Ernest Hemingway arrived with his fourth wife, Mary, to begin his second, rather bizarre, safari. Their visit was encouraged by the colonial government to show that life in Kenya was returning to normal.

Shortly before Ruark left, Jomo Kenyatta was sentenced to ten years in prison for running an illegal organization — the only charge they could really make stick — and Ruark reacted with a scathing newspaper column in which he condemned Kenyatta as the instigator of the Mau Mau terror and suggested the death penalty was too good for him. He castigated Kenyatta's character, impugned his motives, and called him a murderer and a tool of the Russians.

The Mau Mau Emergency ground on. Officially it would last another four years, during which time the British would smash the insurrection, at least militarily. Unfortunately for the settlers, the damage done to their society and the changes set in motion by the Mau Mau were impossible to stop. Ruark's views on what happened in Kenya would mellow slightly — at least he began to say in print that there were two sides to consider. In a 1955 article in *Look*, he wrote, "When the Mau Mau invaded the Africa I knew, I experienced an anger that, I suspect, was first based on selfishness, because my Paradise was spoiled. Now the killing was useless — on both sides — since it served no purpose."

Robert Ruark left the colony with his earlier illusions gone. The dream of buying a farm and settling in Kenya was completely out of the question now, even though a few settlers were leaving in a panic and prime land could be had for a song. Both the dream and the prospect of turning his life around had been stolen by the Mau Mau. In its place, however, they handed him the raw material for the major novel that would transform his life. Any writer would say that was a fair deal.

\* \* \*

# MAU MAU:
# *Something of Value*

In the forty-five years since *Something of Value* was published, Kenya became an independent nation and has undergone a steady change that turned it into a vastly different country than it was in 1953, or at independence in 1963, or, for that matter, as recently as 1993. Predictably, history's view of the events of the Mau Mau Emergency, which lasted officially from late 1952 to 1960, has altered dramatically as well.

Like a pendulum, the world's view and historians' assessments have swung wildly between two extremes. On the one hand, there is the settlers' view of the Mau Mau as a gang of bestial thugs and cut-throats, urged on by Moscow and fueled by bloodlust; on the other, there is the left-wing (for want of a better term) and generally academic view of the Mau Mau as a legitimate independence movement that was victimized by the British and inaccurately portrayed in the media. Likewise, perceptions and opinions on *Something of Value* as a novel, and as a reflection of life in East Africa in the early 1950s, have changed over the years as well.

A rule of thumb in journalism states that if you write a story and everyone involved accuses you of bias, then probably you have presented a reasonably accurate, balanced, factual picture. As general rules go, it is not a bad one. To a great extent that sums up the reactions to *Something of Value*, from all sides, from the time it was first released, right up until today. This is not to say it is not a widely admired novel, because it is. It is only to say that the different political factions all seem to view it as unduly partial to the other side. To Robert Ruark the journalist, that alone would be a source of rueful satisfaction.

\* \* \*

Robert Ruark returned from his second safari in 1953 and immediately began working on the novel. Published in 1955, it became an instant best-seller. It was a Book-of-the-Month Club selection, which guaranteed tremendous sales. It was also widely anticipated, and although there was an embargo on its sales, bookstores in New York broke the embargo left and right and the books flew out the door.

The novel was unquestionably Ruark's most controversial work. For the time, it was unbelievably gory, with graphic descriptions of killings, mutilations, Kikuyu oathing ceremonies, bastardized oathing ceremonies employed by the Mau Mau that became progressively more ghastly and revolting, and torture employed by the settlers to gain information. By comparison, the murders carried out on both sides, also described in considerable detail, almost pale. There are stories of dogs and cats with their stomachs slit open, hung up on gate posts while still alive, to greet their returning owners. There are mutilations of farm animals and torture of prisoners.

Not surprisingly, the gore took center stage when the book was reviewed, and also not surprisingly, many reviewers seemed unable to see past the blood and the horrors to what lay in the depths of the story itself. The fact is, Ruark described nothing whatever that did not actually happen. The book is factual to a fault. In the introduction to the book, his defense that it was not written "for the pre-bedtime amusement of small children," did not change the critics' view that it was unnecessarily graphic, bloody, and loathsome.

\* \* \*

The plot is classic and symmetrical. The story begins in 1942 with two boys, one white, one black. They are childhood friends. Together they have grown up on a farm in the highlands outside Nairobi. The boy, Peter McKenzie, is destined to be a professional hunter, and it is generally acknowledged that he was modeled on Harry Selby. The black boy, Kimani, is a Kikuyu, the son of McKenzie's father's headman, Karanja. His destiny is less certain; he may become Peter's gunbearer, or a farmer like his father, or who knows? That he is black, and Kikuyu, limits him in the Kenya of the time. On a safari with Peter and his future brother-in-law, Jeff, Kimani is insubordinate and Jeff strikes him — a terrible insult to a Kikuyu, which will bring an evil spirit. This comes to pass in the eyes of the Kikuyu and events gradually unfold with a tragic inevitability. Kimani tries to kill Jeff to ward off the evil, but the attempt fails; Kimani flees and disappears. As the reader discovers later, he drifts into the arms of one of the Moscow-inspired freedom groups, and commits a crime for the express purpose of being sent to prison, where he learns the craft of terrorism from other incarcerated "freedom fighters" who used British jails as universities. By 1952, when the Emergency erupts, Kimani is a confirmed Mau Mau.

By this time, Peter McKenzie is a successful white hunter. He gets married and while on his honeymoon, a Mau Mau gang led by Kimani attacks Jeff's farm, killing Jeff and his children, and leaving Peter's sister for dead. Unbeknownst to anyone, she is pregnant and later delivers a baby boy. Peter then devotes his life to fighting the Mau Mau and almost destroys himself in the process. His marriage falls apart under the strain, and he watches as everything he values disintegrates. Meanwhile, Kimani becomes a top Mau Mau, a completely dehumanized thug divorced from the ancient, honorable values of the Kikuyu. Peter finally tracks him down on Mount Kenya, kills him, and comes down off the mountain with Kimani's illegitimate son, who is still an infant. He returns to his family farm with the idea that the two small boys, Kimani's son and Peter's sister's son, one black, one white, should be raised together.

In the course of the novel, Ruark lays out vast amounts of information about Kikuyu life, customs, and superstitions. He is anything but unsympathetic, as the title clearly implies. It is allegedly taken (doubt was later raised on this point) from a Basuto proverb that states: "If a man does away with his traditional way of living and throws away his good customs, he had better first make certain that he has something of value to replace them."

Ruark's premise was that the Kikuyu had lost their traditional values and had not found a set of suitable replacements. Whether this was the fault of the British colonialists, or the Kikuyu themselves being seduced by missionary teachings, or by formal education, or by the Western material world, is not really important. The novel is a penetrating and succinct analysis of the essential conflict that existed between Kenya's white civilization and its black population. The conflict had less to do with land than with a way of life. As they did everywhere else, the white settlers, the colonial administration, and the missionaries and teachers, fundamentally changed the way the black people lived without seeming to take into account that they were meddling with an ancient culture that was a product of centuries of social evolution. Overlaying a mission-school education, forcing women to cover their breasts, preaching against multiple marriage, attempting to halt female circumcision, and enforcing a plethora of petty rules and regulations that prevented black people from pursuing their traditional way of life — all of these things were bound to cause confusion, chaos, and as it ultimately turned out, conflict and bloodshed. Land may have been at the root of the trouble, but even had there been sufficient land to satisfy everyone, there would still have been serious problems eventually.

Ruark's portraits of Karanja and the Kikuyu are almost loving. Even as he degenerates into the worst kind of amoral thug, Kimani is not painted as inherently evil. He is a product of a seriously flawed system, as well as a victim of events beyond his control. This does not justify his brutality, which he pays for in the end. No one would accuse Ruark of being a bleeding-heart liberal, but Kimani starts out as an admirable boy, and when he dies he is not totally unadmirable by any means.

The book's other major characters likewise have their good points and flaws. Jeff, who sets off the tragic train of events by striking Kimani, is a good example of a particular type of colonial white man who sees black people as one-dimensional beings, best managed much as one would manage a draught horse, with a combination of stick and carrot and no attempt to understand their point of view. Yet Jeff is also a fun-loving, charming character, wounded in the war and invalided home. He is Peter's boyhood hero as well as the catalyst of the destruction of Peter's world.

Henry McKenzie, Peter's father, is almost the prototypical Kenya colonial farmer that Ruark came to idealize, if not idolize. Henry is a man embraced by the land and is so close to the Kikuyu as to be almost one of them. In fact, at one point Henry utilizes his knowledge of Kikuyu magic to combat the Mau Mau. He is hard-working and devoted to his family, his farm, and his Kikuyu friends, especially his headman and alter-ego, Karanja. In his younger, elephant-hunting days, Karanja had been Henry's gunbearer and constant companion. In old age, they are closer than brothers. Had more colonials been like Henry McKenzie, and fewer like his son-in-law Jeff, perhaps the Mau Mau movement would never have been born.

\* \* \*

*Something of Value* was published to a decidedly mixed reception in America, Britain, and Kenya.

Reviewers were critical of the blood but enthralled by the story and the writing. Regardless of what they thought, however, the book-buying public was in no doubt. The book became a best-seller and established Robert Ruark as a major novelist. The transformation from wiseguy columnist and lightweight comic novelist that began with *Horn of the Hunter* was completed with *Something of Value*. From that point on, Ruark was a writer to be taken seriously.

In Kenya, the book's reception among the colonials it portrayed was curious. No one denied Ruark had told the truth about life in the colony, as well as about the Mau Mau. If anything, they felt, he had told it too well. Then, as now, Kenya's white population was a small, insular community where everyone knew everyone else. Because of the book's specific subject matter, many of its characters were, naturally, portraits of real people. Peter McKenzie based on Selby is one example, but there are other, more specific ones, as well. The two women who ran their remote farm by themselves, and fought off a Mau Mau attack one night, were real people who did exactly what Ruark described, although he changed the names in the book. The farmer who ran the anti-terrorist *Campi a Simba* on his property in the highlands was also real. Harry Selby took Ruark to the camp to meet the anti-Mau Mau forces when Ruark returned to Kenya on his second safari.

Under these circumstances, it is understandable the people Ruark knew in Kenya would pore over the book to see if they appeared in its pages and if Ruark had painted them sympathetically. This attitude is perfectly normal and occurs with any novel. The criticisms of *Something of Value* did not stem from people feeling slighted or misrepresented, however; they came from two entirely different sources.

The first concerned Kenya's resident novelist and chronicler, Elspeth Huxley, who had published her own novel about the Mau Mau, *A Thing to Love*, the year before Ruark's book appeared. Elspeth Huxley ranks with Karen Blixen as a Kenya writer with an international reputation, and she has written both fiction and non-fiction books about her adopted country. English by birth, she emigrated to Kenya with her parents in 1913 and grew up on a farm in the highlands near Thika. She was educated in England, but returned to Kenya in 1931. Over the years she spent long periods in both countries, giving her both an insider's view of Kenya and an outsider's perspective. She was Lord Delamere's biographer (*White Man's Country*) and wrote acclaimed books about life in Kenya, including *The Flame Trees of Thika*, *The Sorcerer's Apprentice*, and *Out in the Midday Sun*. *A Thing to Love*, her novel about the Mau Mau, appeared in 1954 and is not considered one of her best works. The book contains a predictable mixture of white people and black, with good and bad on both sides. There are heroes and villains, but most of the characters are somewhere in between. There is a love affair, and there are atrocities.

It would be difficult for anyone to write a book about the Mau Mau and not include all of the above. After all, Kenya was a small stage with a limited cast, and any attempt at portraying reality would be bound to have similar people, settings, and circumstances. Immediately upon publication of *Something of Value*, critics in Kenya began to compare it with Huxley's novel, and there were even whisperings that Ruark had, if not actually plagiarized, then at least drawn heavily on Huxley's book for characters and situations.

Aside from the obvious parallels, however, there are actually very few similarities between the novels. Logistically, it would have been impossible for Ruark to steal Huxley's material even had he wished to, since too little time was available between the appearance of the two novels for Ruark to have obtained a copy of A *Thing to Love*, stolen material, and grafted it into a book that is as well planned and constructed as *Something of Value*. And also, aside from the obvious aspects, the two novels are about as different as it is possible to get and still write about the same subject.

Elspeth Huxley was writing about a land and people she knew intimately and from long association. She was an insider. She knew firsthand many of the contradictions and complexities and ambiguities of life in Kenya — nuances which Ruark did not fully appreciate at that time, having been exposed to Kenya life for all of three years — and this tortuous view shows through in Huxley's book. For want of a better term, there is a listless, resigned quality about A *Thing to Love*, as if Huxley saw what was happening in Kenya with all the inexorable slow-motion doom of a waking dream. It is despairing, if not actually desperate, and its characters are trapped in a situation not of their making, but which will destroy them inevitably nonetheless. There is also a quality about the book found in many novels originating in England in the early 1950s — a reflection of the drab, lifeless, disillusioned, almost hopeless society postwar England became with its socialist governments and the disintegration of its empire. It is perhaps unfair to call Huxley's novel lifeless, but there is a definite sense that its characters are simply going through the motions.

*Something of Value*, on the other hand, is anything *but* lifeless. It is exuberant to a fault, whether it involves black terrorists mutilating pet dogs or white hunters mutilating black prisoners. There may be no hope, but it is certainly not hopeless.

Robert Ruark freely conceded, publicly and in print, that he had studied Elspeth Huxley's writings as part of his voracious consumption of anything and everything he could get on Kenya over the years, from Speke and Burton, to Baker and Blixen. Huxley's books — all her books — graced his bookshelves in Palamós, but so did many others. He may have cheerfully admitted that he "stole relentlessly" from other writers, but the admission is the kind of self-deprecating, apocryphal statement any writer would make. Ruark certainly read everything, and made use of it as background, but he did not plagiarize.

Still, the innuendoes began in Kenya in 1955 and continue to this day.

In a society as insular as Kenya's white community, which is both protective and jealous at the same time, it is natural that many would champion their home-grown novelist against the intrusions of the big-city American. That attitude undoubtedly played a part as well.

The other criticism of *Something of Value*, according to Harry Selby, was that Ruark betrayed his white contacts by portraying them too accurately — which is to say, warts and all — and even presented the Mau Mau and the Kikuyu in a too-sympathetic light. This is puzzling, given that black historians say the book fails to show the genuinely dark — that is, racist — side of white Kenya society. If the novel does have a serious failing, that is it. There were many white supremacists in Kenya, of the extreme right-wing Afrikaner stamp still found in parts of South Africa today. None of Ruark's characters come close to portraying that kind of ingrained racism, and in a sense he idealizes the Kenya settlers, showing their best side while ignoring their worst. As a Southerner, Ruark undoubtedly knew anti-black racism when he saw it. Whether he simply chose to ignore it, or it did not fit into his premise for the novel, or — and this is most likely — the constraints of plot did not allow the introduction of a completely different and complex thread, is impossible to say. In his defense, to a great extent he idealizes traditional Kikuyu culture as well. And, it should be remembered, he was writing a novel, not a definitive history of black-white relations in Africa.

Looking at *Something of Value* today, forty-five years after it was first published (and with the benefit of hindsight, if not historical revision-ism), one can see the overall even-handedness of Ruark's treatment and view it dispassionately as evidence of good journalism. In the Kenya of 1955, with terror outside every door, blood running freely, and daily stories of fresh atrocities, any idea that Ruark was siding with the enemy would have been grounds for castigation. But that is the dif-ference between literature and propaganda. Robert Ruark may not have been Tolstoy, but he was not Dr. Goebbels, either. While his sym-pathies as a man lay with the Kenya settlers, his instincts as a journal-ist were simply too strong for him not to tell the whole story.

* * *

Criticism by Kenya's white community may be slightly puzzling, but condemnation by blacks, both Mau Mau and pro-black historians, is perfectly understandable. It was immediate and long-lasting.

Historian Robert J. Edgerton, in his history *Mau Mau: An African Crucible*, published in 1989, refers to *Something of Value* as a "caricature of white heroism and black savagery" that reinforced government propaganda and portrayed the Mau Mau as something it was not. Edgerton's premise is best summed up by the subtitle on the cover, which says it is "The extraordinary story behind the bloody liberation of Kenya in the 1950s and the British deception that hid the truth from the world." Edgerton is also the author of *Like Lions They Fought*, a history of the Zulu Wars in South Africa. He writes from a particular point of view, which seems to be that African blacks can do no wrong, and African whites can do no right. Like many people who adopt a cause, he goes to greater extremes in his advocacy than would most of the actual participants. His book is, however, a good look at how the Mau Mau are viewed from the other side.

It is understandable Edgerton would feel the need to criticize *Something of Value*, because many non-Kenyans learned what they knew of the Mau Mau from its pages. Not only was it a best-seller, two years later it was made into a movie starring Rock Hudson and Sidney Poitier. The novel remained in print, in softcover at least, until 1980, which is astonishing longevity for a book by an author who had not only been dead for fifteen years, but was also largely discredited among mainstream readers.

When I first visited Kenya in 1972, I found *Something of Value* displayed prominently in bookshops in Nairobi — a fact I found more than a little surprising, given its subject matter and the political leanings of Jomo Kenyatta's government. Even today you will find the book on shelves in any literate household from the Cape to the end of the English-speaking African world. Historians like Edgerton may hate it, but it is still the extant picture of the Mau Mau uprising for significant numbers of people.

In the years since it appeared, other books have been written about

Kenya life, including some by combatants on both sides, and any number of memoirs have been published by professional hunters writing about their adventures in the field. These memoirs share one trait: a general reluctance, by those who were most directly involved in the combat operations against the Mau Mau, to go public with their memories. Some professional hunters today, who were then little more than teenagers, still refuse to speak for publication about the activities in which they were involved. Harry Selby says that even living in Botswana, two thousand miles from Kenya, he would not be comfortable revealing some of the things that happened, and his former partner, professional hunter Andrew Holmberg, insists that in writing his memoirs he will not discuss the Mau Mau Emergency, nor the events of that time. This leaves a curious gap in these autobiographies and memoirs, but it is understandable and, from a social point of view, perhaps even laudable. What happened, happened. Nothing can undo it, but that is no reason to put it all on display.

Tony Archer, a professional hunter who was one of the "pseudo-gangsters" — white men who blackened their bodies and participated in operations against the Mau Mau in their forested mountain strongholds, working with former Mau Mau who had been turned — talks about those times with some reluctance. This reticence has to do, not with fear of reprisal, so much as with Jomo Kenyatta's famous speech at the time of independence, in which he urged his countrymen, and the remaining white settlers, to allow the old wounds to heal over — to seek neither retribution nor revenge, but to live and work together in peace. Many greeted the speech at the time with derision and bitterness, but Archer believes Kenyatta meant what he said and that enough people accepted his words that it staved off the kind of post-independence bloodbath many people, including Robert Ruark in some of his more bellicose moments, predicted for the former colony.

Today, fifty years after the beginning of the Emergency, those who saw it firsthand are growing old. Most have died. Sometimes, Archer says, he will attend a social gathering and meet a black man of his own age who was a Mau Mau in his youth. They do not fall into each other's arms like old comrades, but nor do they reach for a gun. There is a feeling of having lived through a bad time, a feeling both know and share, that outsiders can never fully appreciate. Like old soldiers from opposing armies, they have more in common with each other than they do with the civilians from either side who did not see the things they saw.

Robert Ruark foresaw much of this in *Something of Value*. He even predicted it, indirectly, at the end of the novel when Peter McKenzie comes down off the mountain with Kimani's infant son and takes him home to be raised with his newly born nephew. Peter knows that if there is to be any hope of a decent future for Kenya, the two sides will have to learn to live together. Most important, they will have to do things differently than they did in the past. Seen from the vantage point of fifty years on, with the immediacy of the atrocities gone, *Something of Value* more than lives up to its name.

* * *

*Chapter Nine*

# HOME
# NO MORE

Robert Ruark stayed in Kenya covering the Mau Mau Emergency for about two months before returning to New York with his head filled with the sights, sounds, and smells of the violent upheaval in the colony. Undoubtedly, the seeds of *Something of Value* were already in his mind. Unfortunately, he returned to a life that was even more pressure-filled than before.

As well as his daily column for Scripps-Howard, he now had a deal not only to produce the "Old Man" series for *Field & Stream* every month, but also a half-dozen feature articles for that magazine every year, on top of the regular freelance writing he was already pursuing. This work load was undoubtedly lucrative, but it was also extremely demanding even for a writer of Ruark's energy. After the leisurely pace of Kenya's NFD, even on a cover safari for a journalistic assignment, Manhattan seemed like a madhouse.

Robert and Virginia Ruark were never known for their frugality, and the money flowed out as fast as it flowed in — and sometimes faster. No matter how hard Ruark ran, his financial situation was like a treadmill that kept picking up speed. Like most high-income people, he began to worry about his tax situation. To people at that time, income taxes seemed like an abnormal burden, and Ruark began to look for ways of minimizing this. Not surprisingly, memories of his trip to Spain the year before gave rise to the idea of living abroad, not only for its less frenetic pace, but also for the tax advantages it would afford. The Ruarks had been talking about moving to Europe from the moment they returned from Spain, and word of their intentions got around. In March, *Time* reported that Ruark was planning to leave New York and settle in Europe, probably in Rome, for the tax advantages.

There was another problem as well: Ruark's health. As early as December, 1951, his doctor had warned him to stop drinking, or there was a real possibility of his developing cirrhosis of the liver. Ruark reportedly responded by going to "Twenty-One" and downing the first of what would become a decade-long succession of farewell scotches. He fell off the wagon almost immediately. In the spring of 1953, the warning was repeated, more forcefully this time, but it was not really needed — Ruark knew very well what was happening to him. He even said so in print. He had somehow found the time to write a sequel to his first novel, *Grenadine Etching*, called *Grenadine's Spawn* (many years later he referred to it as a "very unfunny sequel"). It was "respectfully dedicated to the author's liver, without whose constant encouragement he would feel no choler and would also be dead." In June, 1953, he reviewed his situation: "In the past seven years I have written five books, about 200 magazine articles, and something like 2,000 columns. I have travelled over a million miles by air alone, and sat up too late too many nights while drinking entirely too much social whiskey. This has given me a dreadful liver and a tendency to quiver in crowds. So this is a left-handed way of announcing that I am going to cut down..."

Ruark "cut down" by renegotiating his contract with Scripps-Howard. Henceforth he would write only three newspaper columns a week instead of five, and his contract was transferred to the United Features payroll. He remained a United Features columnist for the next eleven years. To escape what he saw as the destructive influence of Manhattan, Robert and Virginia Ruark left for Europe in May, taking their household goods and their dogs, a boxer and a poodle. They rented Andrew Heiskell's villa in Palamós for the summer while they looked for a permanent home. Ruark then proceeded to illustrate that Hemingway's observation — "you take yourself with you wherever you go" — was all too true. If anything, his arduous pace picked up once he arrived in Europe, and over the next few months he would dateline his columns and articles from London, Madrid, Paris, Munich, Oran, French Morocco, and even Sidi-bel-Abbès, Algerian headquarters of the French Foreign Legion.

Around this time he met an upper-class Spaniard, Ricardo Sicré, who would become a close friend. Sicré was a wealthy man with high connections in the Franco government. According to Hugh Foster, Sicré was also a friend of Ernest Hemingway and introduced the two writers during the Fiesta of San Fermin, in Pamplona, in July, 1953. If there is any truth to this, it is not supported elsewhere. Ricardo Sicré is not mentioned in Carlos Baker's biography of Hemingway, and it seems highly unlikely the fervently republican author would have a friend so highly placed in the Franco regime. As well, that year Hemingway was outspokenly anxious about his personal safety returning to Spain for the first time since the end of the Spanish Civil War. He was then en route to Africa to begin his second safari. Ruark did write a newspaper column about attending a bullfight with Hemingway in Pamplona, and in later years referred to getting "notably drunk" with Hemingway that summer.

In Palamós, Ruark found a villa for sale that suited his purposes perfectly. Ricardo Sicré helped him with the financing, and he settled into the house that would be his permanent home for the rest of his life. Apparently, however, while Ruark's devotion to work did not suffer, his attention to detail did. His agent, Harold Matson, complained that his articles were not as professional as they should be — excessively long, or with overlapping subjects when magazines were expecting exclusivity. Ruark responded by hiring an ex-British Army sergeant, Alan Ritchie, to become his combination secretary and major domo. Ritchie moved into the house in Palamós and instantly became a fixture in Ruark's life. Ruark's affectionate portrait of Ritchie's fictional counterpart in *The Honey Badger*, Luke Germani, is an indication of just how important Ritchie became to him.

Ritchie's purpose in life, essentially, was to run the house, ensure there were adequate supplies of all the necessities (from Gordon's gin to carbon paper), do the cooking, act as a sounding board or as Ruark's conscience, collect the mail, answer the telephone, and clean-copy Ruark's prose before it was sent off to the Matson agency in New York. In other words, he had responsibility for doing everything in Ruark's life that was either an irritation or that might have distracted Ruark from the activity that paid the bills: sitting down at his typewriter and putting fingers to keys. From that day on, Ruark could travel the world, with or without Virginia, and know the house would be well looked after and waiting for him, in perfect order. As a novelist, hiring Alan Ritchie might have been the best thing he ever did.

* * *

By the fall of 1953, Ruark was well settled in Spain and leading a very relaxed life, if you believe the things he wrote in his column. Late that year, in an article in *Reader's Digest*, he explained exactly why he had left New York and the rat race. He referred to the chains that had bound him and said that when lying on the beach in Palamós, he was "fettered by no chains not of my own making." A *Newsweek* article in December, talking about Ruark, remarked wryly that the same was true of his life in New York — the chains were *all* of his own making. As well, it said, Ruark's New York lifestyle had been "a boulevardier's dream, though...not the dream of most newspapermen."

Ruark had become not only a man who wrote, but a man about whom others wrote — a personality, a celebrity — with all the negatives that implies. He both enjoyed and rued the attention. Many years later, in an autobiographical sketch, he stated that as a reporter he was so shy he had to steel himself to face a stranger for an interview. This is completely at odds with his reputation for being a braggart who loudly insisted he knew everything about everything, but the two traits are not incompatible. Many shy people compensate by being overly outgoing, all the while cringing inside. As well, alcohol can be a great social lubricant and shock absorber for the psyche, and Ruark used it freely.

Ruark was riding high professionally and making extraordinarily good money. *Horn of the Hunter* had been published in July, received excellent reviews, sold out the first printing very quickly, and was in its second printing within months. True to form, however, he was living beyond his means. Hugh Foster reported that Matson wrote to Ruark in Spain in the fall of 1953 to warn that his finances were "in chaos," with the Internal Revenue Service demanding payment of $5,600 in back taxes for 1952 and Ruark's bank account already $6,000 in the red because of all his travel. His reaction was to plan an even longer trip — four months in Australia, the South Pacific, and the Far East — that would provide fresh material for his column. As well, he was now deep into planning *Carrion Men*, the original working title for *Something of Value*. While he packed his portable typewriter and headed for points east, Virginia Ruark went home to her family in Chevy Chase for the holidays. Ruark celebrated the New Year with a column in which he reviewed his non-stop travel, beginning with the Mau Mau in Kenya on New Year's Day, 1953, and ending with him "plumb wore out" on New Year's Day, 1954.

\* \* \*

In Kenya, the second full year of the Mau Mau Emergency began with the continuation of what had become a full-scale military campaign. General Erskine now had three battalions of British troops to augment six battalions of KAR, as well as the Kenya Regiment, the Kenya Police, and the African loyalist Home Guard. He had artillery and several Royal Air Force units for reconnaisance and bombing missions. The main military targets were still the mountainous forests of Mount Kenya and the Aberdares, and the aircraft engaged in both strafing and bombing. These were not lighthearted sorties. Erskine had at his disposal nine four-engine Lincoln bombers, capable of dropping thousand-pound bombs, to go with his Harvard light bombers; even the Cessnas and Pipers of the Kenya Police Air Wing were equipped to drop small bombs, and the planes flew constant missions against the Mau Mau. The army was skeptical about just how effective the air war really was, but later interrogation of Mau Mau prisoners showed that, while the bombing and strafing may not have caused many casualties, they did force the Mau Mau to move their camps constantly, and this took a serious toll on morale. By the end of the Emergency, the Royal Air Force had dropped an astounding fifty thousand tons of bombs and expended more than two million rounds of machine-gun ammunition in strafing runs in the mountains.

On the ground, late 1953 saw several pitched battles between the Mau Mau and units of the Home Guard. By October, General Erskine had more than 10,000 British troops under his command, including a battalion of the Black Watch, fresh from Korea. The insurgents were careful to avoid getting into a serious shooting war with the British Army battalions, many of whose professional, experienced soldiers had acquired their combat skills in the jungles of Malaya. Generally, the Mau Mau would break off an engagement with the Home Guard and disappear back into the forests before the regulars arrived on the scene.

The year ended with a series of battles in which General Erskine tried to surround Mau Mau units south of Nyeri. These engagements involved artillery, mortars, machine guns, and rifles on the British side; the Mau Mau returned fire with rifles and light machine guns. At times, the battles degenerated into hand-to-hand combat.

According to Robert Edgerton, Mau Mau losses by the end of 1953 amounted to "3,064 confirmed killed, 1,000 captured, and an unknown number of wounded. In addition, almost 100,000 Mau Mau supporters had been arrested and 64,000 of these had been brought to trial." For their part, on Christmas Eve the Mau Mau killed Major Archibald Wavell, a company commander in the Black Watch, in a battle near Thika. Major Wavell was the son of Field Marshal Wavell, one of the greatest British soldiers of the second world war. As well, the Mau Mau struck for the first time in Tanganyika, wiping out a loyalist Kikuyu family. The British responded by rounding up 650 Mau Mau suspects and returning them to Kenya for trial.

Although the major military actions were taking place in the mountains, the crowded black districts of Nairobi remained the nerve center of Mau Mau activity. It was in Nairobi that the Mau Mau War Council met, and it was there supplies and money were gathered to support the movement. By early 1954, Mau Mau activity in Nairobi had become so widespread and brazen that a battalion of the Royal Inniskilling Fusiliers was sent to patrol the city with fixed bayonets. The terror that had gripped the white community with the first killings and mutilations of 1952 and '53 continued as well: In April, 1954, the four-year-old son of a Royal Air Force officer was decapitated with a panga as he was riding his tricycle outside the family's home in Nairobi. His parents were inside cooking breakfast at the time.

General Erskine realized that, try as he might, he could not defeat the

Mau Mau by attacking them in the mountains alone. To kill that particular snake he needed to cut off the head, and the head was in Nairobi. He began to plan a massive military and police operation against the Mau Mau strongholds in the city. It was codenamed "Anvil."

Later students of counter-insurgency methods point to Anvil as one of the great operations of its type — a model for wars to come. It was a sweep intended to clear the town of Mau Mau sympathizers once and for all. Troops surrounding the city would be the anvil; police going from house to house, from hiding hole to hiding hole, were the hammer. The theory of such an operation is simple, but the execution is not, mainly because of the need to maintain complete secrecy while preparing a massive effort. Without the element of surprise, the main targets will fly the coop ahead of the police. The British established the main detention center at an old military camp in Langata, a few miles outside Nairobi beside the Nairobi Game Park. Two more camps were set up in eastern Kenya. On the night of April 23, 1954, General Erskine surrounded the city with 25,000 troops. The citizens awoke on the 24th to find themselves in a huge trap. Police units moved in and swept one area after another, screening and arresting suspected Mau Mau. If a door would not open, they broke it down. Anyone who was in the least suspicious was sent to Langata. In the first forty-eight hours, 8,300 people were detained; by the end of a month, the number had risen to 24,000. As well, the British gathered up almost ten thousand women and children and shipped them out of Nairobi, back to the Kikuyu Reserve. They joined thousands who had already been evicted from squatter camps and slums in smaller towns and from the farms in the white highlands.

One Kenyan who was arrested and roughed up by the police was Tom Mboya, a radical young Luo activist who would later become a prominent politician and Robert Ruark's particular bête noir in Kenya. At one point Ruark asked Mboya how it felt "not to be Kwame Nkrumah's bumboy anymore" — forgetting, Ruark insisted disingenuously, the original British meaning of the term. The memory of this exchange was so delicious that Ruark bestowed the incident on Alec Barr. For his part, after publication of Something of Value, Mboya travelled to Europe and the United States, campaigning against continued white rule and the idea of white supremacy, which he said the book promoted.

Operation Anvil was undoubtedly brutal, but it was an overwhelming success. A few Mau Mau leaders escaped the net, but most were in custody, and the Mau Mau hold on Nairobi was broken. "The effect (of this) on the men and women fighting in the forest would soon become devastating," Edgerton noted.

Having cut the head off the snake, General Erskine turned on the remaining supply lines along which food and ammunition moved from the Kikuyu settlements to the insurgents in the forests. He ordered the construction of an immense moat — a fifty-mile-long ditch, ten feet deep and sixteen feet wide. This barrier was strung with barbed wire and planted with sharpened bamboo stakes and booby traps, and police posts were located every half mile. Its purpose was to cut the flow of supplies into the forests and prevent the Mau Mau from emerging to attack villages and police posts. General Erskine's moat was an eerie echo of the double lines of barbed wire and blockhouses with which the British had crisscrossed the South African veldt during the Boer War fifty years earlier. Three years later, the French Army copied Operation Anvil almost to the letter when it broke the Algerian insurgents in the Battle of Algiers. Clearly, General Erskine's time studying counterinsurgency methods in India, Egypt, and other parts of the crumbling empire had taught him a great deal.

While the British were winning the military battles with the Mau Mau on most fronts, the Emergency was causing a serious upheaval in the colony's social structure. There was the obvious impact of relocating tens of thousands of Kikuyu back to the reserves from the cities and off the farms, and of gathering the Kikuyu from their traditional small holdings into villages that were more easily defended. There had also developed a deep mistrust between black and white Kenyans that would never really disappear thereafter, and rifts appeared within the ranks of the whites as well. Early on, there were suggestions that Jomo Kenyatta should be released as a way to bring about peace and reconciliation. This idea was promoted by none other than Ewart Grogan, Kenya's most influential settler, a man who had become famous early in the century for walking from the Cape to Cairo to win the hand of a lady. Grogan's proposal was shouted down. By now, relations among the colonial government, the settlers, and the military were openly hostile. General Erskine remarked at one point that Kenya was "a sunny land for shady people" and stated flatly that he hoped never to see another Kenya settler in his life.

\* \* \*

Robert Ruark arrived back in Nairobi in April, at the end of his long swing through the Far East, just in time to witness Operation Anvil. Virginia Ruark had joined him in Australia. Ruark had already spent some time in Indonesia, and the couple went on to New Zealand, where Ruark went on a fishing trip, then took in Singapore, Ceylon, and India. In India, Ruark went tiger hunting for the first time. Both the tiger hunt and the fishing showed up in *Field & Stream* later that year. Ruark also wrote an article for *The Saturday Evening Post*, in October, 1954, titled "The Tiger Doesn't Stand A Chance." The title pretty well sums up the message of the article. Ruark professed to find tiger hunting absurdly easy, shooting from a *machan* at night over baits. He pointed out that the tiger had been little hunted since before the second world war, that the tiger crop in central India had become both "bumper and bumptious," and that a hunter wanting a rug for the den "may order up a tiger as coolly as he'd buy a rug from a department store." Ruark killed two tigers that trip and wounded a third that appeared to be dead, but later escaped because he was merely creased and temporarily unconscious. Ruark did not put in a finishing shot because he did not want to damage the skin unnecessarily. The story, he said, preceded him to Kenya and was a "source of shame." And well it should have been, considering the prominence he had given to Harry Selby's motto, "It's the dead ones that kill you," in *Horn of the Hunter*, stressing the importance of always putting in a finishing shot. But if you hunt long enough, these things happen. Ruark reported it faithfully, if ruefully, and took full responsibility. Such frankness was one of his most endearing traits in his early hunting writing.

By the time he landed in Nairobi, he had been on the road for the better part of four months. This was his new "relaxed" schedule. The day Operation Anvil was launched, Ruark wrote a bitter newspaper column about events in Kenya that today would be reviled as racist, but was aimed more at "primitive savagery" than at Africans merely because of the color of their skin. The influence of some of the more radical settler elements was beginning to show up in Ruark's writings. Oddly enough, the hyperbole and overstatement of his newspaper columns of 1953 and '54 do not occur in *Something of Value*, which is very even-handed (and, in fact, incurred the wrath of some of those same settlers for that very reason). Ruark had a tendency to go off half-cocked in his newspaper writing, jumping to conclusions and not digging beneath the surface. Even so, the Operation Anvil column is outrageous: "If (the settlers) had been allowed to pursue a completely ruthless extermination policy in the beginning — repaying one murder with a hundred deaths, using wholesale torture to extract information and killing the innocent with the guilty, they might have wiped out the early nucleus and prevented its spread..." Ruark virtually recommended that such a policy would have been the proper response. "The horror and evil that spread never will be completely sponged away by time, and I am very much afraid that beautiful, turbulent Kenya...can never again be tranquilly described as 'white man's country'." Kenya and the "whole surging seething mass of Africa," he wrote, would be left to the "stewardship of savages."

This column is a weird combination of bitter invective, bordering on racism, and thoughtful analysis calling for a compromise "painful on both sides." Ruark's sympathies were clearly with the settlers, who had come to Kenya, cleared the land, established the farms, fought the elements and the animals and the tribes, and were now in danger of losing everything. But he also recognized that the Kikuyu and other black Kenyans had rights as well. Whatever happened, he knew, life in Kenya could not, and would not, go back to what it had been.

By this time Ruark had friends among the settler community as well as professional hunters like Harry Selby. The previous year, he met a young woman named Eva Monley, the adopted daughter of a farm family named Nightingale. Born in Germany, Eva and her mother had emigrated to Tanganyika in 1932, but were not welcome among the colony's German community because they were part Jewish. They continued on to Nairobi, where Jews were more than welcome — Abraham Block and his family had helped found the city, and the Blocks were both loved and respected — and settled there. They became close friends with the Nightingales, who were farmers, and Eva's mother asked them to formally adopt her daughter. This they did. Ironically, when war came their German background counted against them, and Eva's mother was interned as an enemy alien. Because she was legally part of the Nightingale family, however, Eva was left alone. When Ruark met her, Eva Monley was working in the film industry as one of the crew of *Mogambo*. She and Ruark became close friends, a relationship that lasted until the day he died.

Naturally, she introduced the American writer to her adopted family and their circle of friends in the highlands, and they played a significant role in his life in Kenya for the next several years. He used the Nightingales as models for Brian Dermott's family in *Uhuru*.

Having witnessed the latest events in the Mau Mau saga, Robert and Virginia Ruark continued on to Spain, arriving in Palamós in May. Ruark wrote to Harold Matson that the two of them had come down with a "bug," from which it took several weeks to recover, and that, as he got older, travelling was taking an increasing toll on his constitution. Realistically, he admitted his drinking was not helping the situation, and accordingly he and Virginia had decided to "take the veil" for the summer. Ruark was now almost forty years old, and both his health and age began to preoccupy him. He wrote about both, in letters to his agent and to his editor at Doubleday, and for public consumption in his column. In one instance, he described coming across his old naval uniforms and trying them on, finding they still fit well, and used the incident as a peg to reflect on the twelve years since he had ordered them and prepared to go off to war. This incident showed up later near the beginning of *The Honey Badger*. For Ruark, as for many men and women, his looming fortieth birthday caused considerable introspection.

Once he was feeling better and his alcohol intake had been cut down, he returned to work in earnest on his new novel, and his editor was pleased to hear that he hoped to have the manuscript ready by August. The plan was to put the book on the publisher's winter list. Ruark's literary star was clearly ascending. *Horn of the Hunter*, he was told, had now sold 18,500 copies and was expected to sell even more during the months before Christmas. Coming out with a major African novel hard on the heels of this non-fiction best-seller would be, they were all confident, a smash hit.

Unfortunately, it did not work out that way. August came and went, then September, then October, and still the novel was not finished. For the first time, Ruark ran into the difficulty of producing a major effort like a novel, while continuing to earn a living with other writing and, at the same time, coping with the demands of house and spouse. The villa in Palamós required renovating, which Virginia undertook; still, it was impossible to work in a house under renovation and not be distracted. As well, when the bills for the work began to pour in, Ruark was faced with a rapidly depleting bank account.

Writing a novel is a massive undertaking, requiring the writer to live within his creation, thinking his characters' thoughts, following their actions, and allowing them to develop and grow on their own. As Ruark pointed out years later, "In the working life of a professional author, when he is lucky, the fictional characters take over and become fleshly people, with solid dimensions and minds of their own. They do things the author never intended. They say things the author never dreamed of. The happy author is thus reduced to the minor role of coachman, using no whip, driving only slightly with a very slack rein." It is never that easy, of course, and such a happy state of affairs does not occur readily, especially when carpenters are hammering on the roof, stonemasons are making deliveries at the back door, and the little woman is knocking with timid insistence, asking if she can interrupt "just for a moment, sweetie — I need to know which pattern you like."

Successful author though he was, Ruark's main income came from his column and magazine writing, and the need to take time from the novel to write them was a worse distraction than the renovations. According to Hugh Foster, Ruark wrote checks on his New York account totalling $20,000 in the three months between May and August 3, when he sent Harold Matson a progress report on the book. It was coming along well, he said, but more slowly than expected. It would likely run to at least five hundred pages, and maybe even six hundred (it ended up at 566). He said he doubted he could make the new deadline of September 15 and blamed at least two months of delays on the work being done on the house. Ruark then warned Matson that he could not promise the manuscript, realistically, before November, and he was writing to his editor at Doubleday, Lee Barker, to inform him of that. Having dealt with the logistics of the book, Ruark then gave a literary assessment of what he had accomplished so far. "I think that this book to date is as honest a piece of construction as Herman (Wouk, another Matson client) did in *Caine Mutiny* in which the characters are built by what they do and say completely on stage."

Money was a problem that steadfastly refused to go away. Ruark tried to solve it by writing magazine articles in bursts of feverish activity, throwing the pieces together and sometimes allowing subjects to overlap in submissions to competing magazines. As well, Matson reportedly complained more than once that Ruark was not even submitting properly typed copy. Since the Matson agency prided itself on the professional quality of its submissions to editors (and demanded professional sums of money in return), this was not to be taken lightly. Ruark responded to the first charge, somewhat testily, that the trips he took were expensive, and he could not limit himself to just one article for one magazine from a long and costly venture to some remote area.

The final straw, apparently, was a renewed demand for money from his parents in North Carolina. Ruark responded with a long, detailed, bitter letter upbraiding his father and mother for their feckless ways, for his father's alcoholism and his mother's drug addiction. He pointed out that he had bought his grandfather's old house in Southport specifically for them to live in, and that the purchase had plunged him deep into debt from which he had only just emerged. There is an air of over-reaction about this letter, like the exasperation that sometimes appeared in his columns. He ended it with what amounted to an order to his father to stop being childish, and rather self-righteously noted that he, Robert, had "never allowed himself to be a child."

Somehow, some way, *Something of Value* was finally finished, and Ruark booked passage to New York for himself and Virginia. He intended to deliver the manuscript personally, stay in New York for about a week, then go on an extended shooting vacation with friends around the country. From there they would go to Haiti and Cuba for a couple of weeks and return to New York toward the end of January. As it turned out, Virginia went home for a while to visit her parents, and Ruark ended up in a hospital in Houston for an operation for varicose veins. He took this opportunity for a complete check-up, which he gleefully reported showed him completely free of "cancer, clap, and most important, liver."

The combination of completing a major novel and having his health at least under control gave Ruark a feeling of "palpable freedom," according to Hugh Foster. "His financial and family concerns, though worrisome, (were) virtually forgotten." In a letter Ruark wrote to his friend Ben Wright, he said that for the first time in his life "nobody but me knows when, where or why I am going to do anything and after a lifetime of being told to come and go it is a wonderful feeling."

The idea that the seemingly footloose Ruark was actually living in chains would have been surprising news to the average reader of *Field & Stream*, working on an assembly line by day and reading, by night, Ruark's accounts of trout fishing in New Zealand, of tiger hunting in India, or of chasing Mau Mau terrorists on the slopes of Mount Kenya. This theme of shedding chains is repeated over and over in Ruark's life — when he first was given the freedom of a syndicated column and settled in New York, and again when he left New York and moved to Palamós, and yet again when he completed *Something of Value* and began anticipating the financial security a major best-seller would bring. The *Newsweek* columnist who had remarked the previous year that Ruark's chains were all of his own making, wherever he lived, had hit the nail on the head. Years later, Ruark rather ruefully agreed when he made this a major theme of *The Honey Badger* and reflected on the strange conflict of emotions a writer calls upon in order to do his best work. In what amounts to a caustic piece of self-analysis, Ruark realizes (through the fictional Alec Barr) that he needs to feel chains in order to do his best work "despite." And so his life was one long flight from the imagined chains, and one long return to them, like a small boy running away from home.

* * *

*Something of Value* was officially released on April 6, 1955, to a blizzard of extreme reviews, both good and bad, legal hysteria over possible libel actions, and instant best-seller status. It was made the Book-of-the-Month Club selection that month, and in its assessment the club said the novel "made Hemingway look like a tenderfoot." Ruark commented that the remark would irritate Hemingway, but might finally free him of his inferiority complex "about the great man." Unfortunately, it did not.

The reviews concentrated on the blood and gore in the book. Those who loved the novel reflected that it was accurate in its depiction of events and, in the words of *The New York Times*, showed it was written by a man "deeply shaken by the enormity of change." Other terms included "high voltage shocker," "pile driver of a book," and "most sensational novel of the year." But it also had its detractors. *Harper's* and *The Atlantic Monthly* both condemned it, the latter challenging Ruark's use of Swahili, which the reviewer insisted he could not have had time to learn in his brief visits to Africa. The legal problems were irritating, based on various lawyers' reservations about what might and might not be libelous. Ruark pointed out somewhat acidly that no one was likely to "declare himself a murderer" in order to identify with a character in the book, and so he was not about to spend the next year wet-nursing lawyers or chasing quit-claims. While the reviewers and attorneys wrung their hands over the perceived problems or shortcomings of *Something of Value*, the public responded by sweeping it off the shelves as fast as they could be restocked.

The reaction in Kenya was mixed. Tony Seth-Smith, a professional hunter who at the time was a young man, taking part in the military operations against the Mau Mau, says the novel depicted the Emergency "as it actually was. Ruark compressed events, but all the things he talked about and the stories he told were true.

"Everything we did at the time reads differently now, though," he reflected. "For example, we wanted to identify people we had shot. We would simply cut the hands off and take them back with us for fingerprinting, and the hyenas would eat the bodies. It was callous by today's standards. But look at the Mau Mau: I remember one incident where they captured a British soldier, tortured him, killed him, and then skinned him. One of the Mau Mau went around for a time, wearing the skin."

Most of the objections from Kenya dwelt on Ruark's perceived sympathy for the Kikuyu, rather than an outcry from people who thought they had been unfairly portrayed. But then, as Ruark shrewdly noted, who would proclaim himself a murderer in order to claim damages, particularly in a country where he might have his head chopped as a result?

By the time the book actually went on sale, Ruark was back in Palamós, hard at work as a journalist. He had neglected his newspaper column as work on the novel became more intense, and the editors showed their displeasure by relegating the column to the travel pages, or else not running it at all. The syndicated column was still his bread-and-butter — and, just as important, kept him in the public eye — and he needed to mend fences. Harold Matson and Ruark's editor at Doubleday, Lee Barker, kept him informed by mail as *Something of Value* racked up one triumph after another. Matson sold the paperback rights to Pocket Books for $100,000, until then the highest price ever paid for a novel, and Metro-Goldwyn-Mayer bought the movie rights. Ruark's financial return from the novel was large and immediate. Hugh Foster says he eventually made more than a half-million dollars altogether, the equivalent of several million dollars in today's (1999) terms. But not everything was rosy. Ruark's relationship with Doubleday began to deteriorate over a number of issues, and he was having problems with United Features as well. These were the usual writerly things: not enough money, too much interference, over-eager editors sabotaging his copy. Ruark began to look around for a new publisher and a new syndicate to sell his column. For the time being, however, both issues blew over.

Financial success did no more to tone down Ruark's destructive lifestyle than had the move to Europe. Both Robert and Virginia were drinking heavily, and he was smoking three packs of cigarettes a day. On a visit to London in June, Ruark collapsed in a Rolls-Royce showroom and was taken to hospital. Three doctors gave three different diagnoses, from epilepsy to thrombophlebitis to overindulgence in alcohol and nicotine. Ruark returned to Palamós to recover. He did, however, find time that summer to buy the Rolls-Royce he had been looking at, and purchased a license plate with the designation "R2R." It was a happy coincidence this rolling status symbol had the same initials he had, and he eagerly pointed out that the "R1R" plate belonged to Queen Elizabeth. Ruark ended the year by booking passage to Australia on an ocean liner. He shipped out for Sydney just before Christmas and celebrated his fortieth birthday on December 29, 1955.

Turning forty was no pleasure for Robert Ruark. In a column filed from Australia in January, he reflected on this most dreaded of milestones; to read his words, you would think he was now a hundred years old and tottering daily from bed to bath chair, dribbling food into his frosty beard. There is no doubt, however, that he felt older than he was. Chronologically he may have been forty — really the prime of life — but in terms of mileage on his frame he was more like sixty, and a not particularly healthy sixty at that. Steadfastly, though, he refused to obey his doctor's orders and slow down, or even moderate his almost manic liquor intake.

Through 1956, he continued to rack up the miles and work hard. He began compiling the first volume of his anthology of *Field & Stream* articles, *The Old Man and the Boy*. His exasperation with Doubleday had finally reached breaking point, and after six books he found a new publisher. *Old Man* would be his first effort for Henry Holt & Co., and his editor there was an outdoor writer by the name of Bill Buckley. As Ruark worked on the anthology, sifting through his columns, choosing the best and discarding others, occasionally combining those dealing with similar themes, he was struck by the sincerity and quality of the work he had done for *Field & Stream* over the past three years. Ruark may have been an egotist (what writer is not?) but he was a good judge of writing and his own harshest critic; even so, he remarked, what he had set out to do with the "Old Man" series had succeeded far beyond his expectations, and he thought he would "never again be able to write so well."

Meanwhile, Hollywood was busy shooting *Something of Value*, starring Rock Hudson and Sidney Poitier, two of the best (and most box-office friendly) actors of the time. Ruark was riding high, and he celebrated at the end of 1956 by heading, once again, for Kenya.

\* \* \*

Militarily, the Mau Mau were being steadily worn down. General Erskine had followed up the success of Operation Anvil with two major sweeps through the forests, intended to drive out the Mau Mau as a line of beaters drives pheasants to the waiting guns. Although the sweeps did bag some insurgents, both dead and captured, their main effect was to force the gangs to move their camps and go deeper into hiding. In early 1955, General Erskine completed his two-year stint and was replaced by General Sir Gerald Lathbury.

Erskine's two years would have to be considered a success. When he arrived the Mau Mau were killing an estimated one hundred people a month; when he departed, they were down to twenty a month. From fifteen thousand insurgents in the forests, poised to strike at settlements and police posts, the Mau Mau now numbered about five thousand, many of whom were forced to use clubs and bows and arrows because of a shortage of guns and ammunition. If the Mau Mau were losing the military war, however, they were winning the propaganda war, in part because the cost of the campaign was rising and the British government and taxpayers were objecting strenuously. Britain at this time was no longer a wealthy country, and Kenya was not a priceless jewel of empire to be saved at all costs. In fact, it was becoming a money sink. Even the prime minister, Winston Churchill, no shrinking violet and a rabid defender of the Empire, was urging the colonists to reach some sort of accord with the Mau Mau and their supporters.

The two military sweeps of the forests had shown the deficiencies of conventional armies in combating guerrilla groups, especially those who, after years of hiding out, were as much at home in the bush as a fish is in the sea, and the new general changed tactics. He initiated the "pseudo-gang," in effect one of the first "anti-guerrilla guerrilla" forces. Led by black-stained white men wearing Afro wigs, bands of reformed Mau Mau and loyal Kikuyu took to the mountain trails, tracking the Mau Mau gangs to their lairs, ambushing them, and raiding their camps. They fought silently, with knives, crossbows, and lengths of piano wire, throttling and decapitating their victims. One of the pseudo-gangsters was Tony Archer, later a well-known professional hunter in Botswana and East Africa.

*Campi a Simba* was still in operation, providing an anti-Mau Mau home away from home for professional hunters in the off season. One of the residents then was John Dugmore, later a professional hunter with

216

Ker & Downey. In 1952, Dugmore, then twenty-three years old, volunteered for the all-white Kenya Regiment and spent the next two years "chasing the Mau Mau on horseback." Because he had spent many years near Thomson's Falls hunting in the forests, Dugmore was an expert tracker and woodsman — just the kind of man they wanted at *Campi a Simba*. He was assisting the game warden, Roger Hurt (father of professional hunter Robin Hurt), when he met Ruark for the first time. "I remember that Robert Ruark dropped into the camp with Harry Selby," said Dugmore, "And later he went on to Nyeri where he hung out in the Outspan Hotel. That was a favorite watering hole for guys coming in from the mountains where they had been chasing Mau Mau. That is where he got much of his information for *Something of Value* — there, and at the Long Bar in the New Stanley." Both Dugmore and Tony Seth-Smith recall Ruark's almost supernatural ability to drink all day, all the while talking and listening, and later to be able to remember stories down to the last detail in spite of consuming an enormous quantity of booze. "Ruark was quite humble in his way," Seth-Smith said. "Not like old Hemingway. Bob really loved hunting, and he talked with us about it just like everyone else did. He could remember the stories we told him and reproduce them word for word."

Later, when Metro-Goldwyn-Mayer was in Kenya filming *Something of Value*, John Dugmore met Rock Hudson and introduced him to the joys of shooting a .470 Nitro Express. "That was on Chris Aschan's farm, where they were filming," he said. Like threads through a tapestry, the names from that era keep appearing and reappearing. John Dugmore himself became one of the best known professional hunters of the late twentieth century. He and his cousin, Bill Ryan, began hunting professionally at the urging of Andrew Holmberg. After leaving the Kenya Regiment, Dugmore went to work as a storeman for Ker & Downey, to learn the business. He was recommended for his full professional hunter's license by Roger Hurt, spent a year working as second hunter to K&D's big names, and then moved on to taking out his own safaris. He moved to Botswana in 1970, ending up as a hunter with Safari South (along with Harry Selby, Tony Henley, Lionel Palmer, and Soren Lindstrom, among others.) Today he lives in Maun, in semi-retirement, where he runs several businesses, including a photographic safari operation.

Although Dugmore's memories of Ruark are necessarily colored by time and dominated by long evenings, bars, and bottles, he says Ruark's influence was immense and has lasted long after his death. "Every American client I ever took out had read Robert Ruark," he said. "Every one. And today, people still know him, still read him." Adds Tony Seth-Smith, "Bob Ruark put Kenya on the map."

* * *

Ruark spent two months in Africa at the end of 1956 and returned to Palamós suffering from a particularly virulent bout of malaria. In the spring, he set sail once again for New York, this time bringing his Rolls-Royce with him. The world-travelling, lion-bearding, rich-and-famous author was coming home to rub their noses in it. There would be a special screening of *Something of Value*, and Ruark planned to drive down to North Carolina to visit the folks at home. Although he did not say it in so many words, he was staging for himself the equivalent of a Roman triumph, and the Rolls was the victorious general's war chariot. Blockbuster novel, big-budget movie, Hollywood stars, the stars over Africa — Bob Ruark had it all, and by God he was going to show everyone.

Several of his business acquaintances warned him against bringing the Rolls. Why give the critics ammunition to blast him for living abroad and not paying U.S. taxes? But it was too late. "The car is already on the ship," Ruark said. And it gave him the chance for one bit of good-humored one-upmanship. The head of the Scripps-Howard news service, Roy Howard, was in the habit of taking his columnists to lunch when they visited New York, riding in his chauffeur-driven limousine. On the day he was scheduled to meet with Ruark, Howard walked out of his office and across the sidewalk toward the car. Ruark appeared, took his arm, and guided him instead to the Rolls-Royce, which was parked a car-length behind. Everyone got a good laugh out of it. But by and large, it was all downhill from there.

Ruark spent some time in New York, dazzling the locals. The *Daily News* ran a profile on the now larger-than-life book author, which wavered between slavering admiration and sarcastic put-down; finally, the writer settled grudgingly on admiration. Ruark then set out for

Wilmington, North Carolina, and a reunion with his younger self. The previous year Wilmington had made national headlines when its newspaper refused to run a picture of a black man on its front page. From afar, Ruark had taken his home town to task, writing at length about the good relations that had existed between the races when he was a boy — about Aunt Laura and Uncle Cornelius and Aunt Lily, ex-slaves who had helped to raise him and were respected members of the community. This was not the first time, nor would it be the last, that the Southern-born national syndicated columnist would speak out publicly against segregation and racial hatred. The anti-black views that critics perceived in his columns about Kenya, and later about other parts of emerging Africa, were not directed on the basis of race, but on the ex-colonies' ability to govern themselves and function as modern countries in a rapidly changing world. As it turned out, even Ruark's forebodings, dire as they were, paled against the actual events that consumed much of Africa in the four decades after his death.

At any rate, for the first time in many years, he was going back home to visit the small towns where he had spent his boyhood, and that he was now in the process of making famous through "The Old Man and the Boy" in *Field & Stream*. If he expected streets strewn with palm fronds as he approached, however, he was gravely disappointed. For one thing, Virginia Ruark chose to visit her own family in Washington rather than go down to Carolina with him, and Ruark drove into town alone. The reception was cordial and friendly, but not unlike what the residents might have done for one of their own who was now an accountant in Greensboro, for example, or a native son practicing law in Washington. In other words, the denizens of his home town treated Robert Ruark, Novelist, as if he were merely little Bobby Ruark come home to visit. This was not what Ruark had anticipated. But worse was to come.

Some years later, in a magazine article about his own life, he treated the whole episode with tongue in cheek, poking fun at his own expectations:

*Well, sir, the Rolls and I swept triumphantly into the seaboard town in which I was unable to get a job even as a copyboy on the local paper, and my triumphs rode ahead of me, like a police escort. (Perhaps it was a police escort. At that moment I wouldn't have put it past me to have hired one.)*

But the genuine hurt he felt showed through even as he lampooned himself with wry comments. There was no civic reception, no public adulation. Some friends threw a cocktail party, but invited only one other couple. There was a small dinner party, modest to a fault. Finally, Ruark overheard a conversation between two Southern belles, "Miss Sarah Sue Somebody talking to Miss Dimity Ann Somebody Else." Their soft voices floated "like melted marshmallow from behind an oleander bush." One said to the other that she just did not believe a word of it, to which the other asked, "What don't you believe a word of, sugah?" The first answered that she did not care how good they said Bobby was doing, what with his picture on the magazine cover between Prince Philip and President Eisenhower, and his being a big book author and living in Spain and all. "He can't be doin' as good as everybody says, or he wouldn't have come back home after all these years *in that old beat-up Pierce Arrow!*" Deflated, Ruark climbed into his Rolls-Royce and drove back north, heading for New York, and Spain, and his home in Palamós — one place on earth where he was grimly confident of being treated like a somebody. Wilmington, North Carolina, was no longer his home.

\* \* \*

*The Old Man and the Boy* was published in 1957, and Robert Ruark then turned his attention to his next big book. Established now as a major novelist, he wanted to follow up *Something of Value* with a book equally weighty and significant. He had already begun a novel, tentatively titled *Poor No More*. According to Hugh Foster, the title was given to Ruark by a friend in Houston, and originally the plot was based in Texas. His reception at home in North Carolina, however, and the sometimes ambivalent attitude of people in New York, had ignited a smoldering anger in Ruark that not only his friends noticed, but also reporters sent to interview him. One noted that he was "shaking his clenched fist at the world." Ruark relocated *Poor No More* to the Carolinas and proceeded to use the printed word as a club to wreak revenge on the people who had slighted him.

If ever Ruark wrote a book "totemizing money," a criticism later directed at *The Honey Badger*, it was *Poor No More*. The hero is Craig Price, a Southern boy from a poverty-stricken background who claws his way to the top of the business world. Along the way he coldly marries for money, betrays the one woman who really loves him, and eventually ends up as an outright crook. Much of the early action takes place in Ruark's scarcely disguised home town, and Craig Price follows in Ruark's footsteps from childhood through university. When the book was published in 1959, Ruark told Harry Selby, "This is my autobiography." At the time, he may even have meant it.

By the time *Poor No More* appeared in bookstores, however, Ruark had already followed up *Something of Value* with a solid, hardcover success — albeit an unexpected one. *The Old Man and the Boy*, which was the antithesis of *Poor No More* in every way, had sold twenty thousand copies by the end of 1957, outselling *Horn of the Hunter* in the first few months by a substantial margin. By January, 1958, sales had reached thirty-six thousand. The reviewers loved it — how could they not? — and the American government was so taken with Ruark's vision of small-town, small-boy life, it decided to distribute the book through its foreign service to show what America was like. Meanwhile, the movie *Something of Value* had opened to generally positive reviews. If Rock Hudson had been "wooden," Sidney Poitier was "brilliant," and the film conveyed the message that violence on either side was not the answer to Kenya's problems. Ruark complained that the final script was not the story as he had written it, but it was a minor cavil. No novelist of the twentieth century, from Hemingway on down, was completely happy with the way Hollywood treated his creations.

*Poor No More* opened with a disclaimer, of sorts: "It is customary to say that the characters in this book bear no resemblance to anyone, living or dead. This would certainly be a lie, but working out just who is who is bound to be difficult," Ruark wrote, knowing full well there would be little difficulty for anyone from his home town, and knowing equally well that everyone would buy the book and pore over it, sorting out who was who. To make the task easier, he even put in people with their real names when they were being portrayed sympathetically. The aforementioned Aunt Laura, Uncle Cornelius, and Aunt Lily appeared right at the beginning. Even the Wilmington, Brunswick and Southport railroad (WB&S), which served Wilmington and Southport and whose initials were corrupted as "Willing but Slow," was in the book by name, proof that Ruark's fictional New Truro was, in reality, Southport. Ruark included enough real names to ensure that everyone knew whom he was talking about, and enough fictional ones to ensure there would be no lawsuits. As a piece of literary revenge, *Poor No More* was about as subtle as a brick through the courthouse window.

In its final published form the novel runs more than eight hundred pages, long by any standard except Marcel Proust, and the writing of it did not come easy. In fact, it was a re-run of the pattern Ruark had fallen into with *Something of Value*: one missed deadline after another in delivering the manuscript to Bill Buckley at Henry Holt, with the newspaper column neglected to the increasing irritation of newspaper editors. The column became repetitive and was generally not up to Ruark's usual high standard. Ruark defended himself on the novel's delay, insisting it was better to take the time necessary to produce a good book rather than rushing and producing a bad one.

In September, 1958, he escaped to Alaska for a vacation and hunting trip. This was one of the very few real hunting expeditions Ruark ever undertook, for magazine purposes, that was not in Africa. Although he hunted and fished there, as well as in India, New Zealand, and Australia at various times, those articles never contained the magic spark of his African pieces. Ruark had a mystical affinity for Africa; the Dark Continent fascinated and rejuvenated him, and he returned the compliment by bringing it alive in the printed word and giving it immortality. Ruark liked Alaska, enjoyed his time with the Alaskans, and wrote a couple of competent articles about the adventure. He also suffered another collapse, similar to the celebrated Rolls-Royce showroom incident in London, and ended up in hospital in San Francisco. From there he limped home to Palamós to recuperate. When he arrived, he found a letter from Harold Matson advising him that the partial manuscript of *Poor No More* indicated the book was going to be a "helluva novel," but suggesting massive rewrites and revisions. Ruark's poor health, combined with the daunting prospect of starting almost from the beginning with a book he had thought was virtually finished, caused him to flee once more to Kenya for rest and rejuvenation.

Harry Selby says that in the later years he would meet Ruark at Embakasi Airport in Nairobi and see the author descend slowly from the airplane onto the tarmac, looking grey and ill. After a week in Africa he would be noticeably better, Selby says, and after a month or two he would be back to the chipper, laughing, enthusiastic man who had made their first safari together "such a joy." Africa worked on Ruark like a tonic, and it was a tonic he found himself dipping into more and more often as the years passed. After 1955, he visited Africa once and sometimes twice a year, becoming more the old hand each time out, a regular at the Long Bar in the New Stanley, and a fixture in the dining room of the Muthaiga Club — the haven that was founded by the early settler, Berkeley Cole, "so I can at least get my drinks the way I like them," and which by that time had become the gathering place for the elite of Kenya Colony (as it is to this day).

As Ruark became an old hand, he also became good friends with many of the settlers and professional hunters. He was no longer a sometime client; he was now part of the family. In 1957, Selby followed Ruark's urging and left Ker & Downey Safaris. He went into partnership with Andrew Holmberg to form Selby & Holmberg, capitalizing on the fame he had achieved, partly due to his prowess as a professional hunter, but augmented considerably by the publicity Ruark gave him. *Horn of the Hunter* had made Harry Selby one of the most sought-after hunting guides in East Africa, constantly in demand, especially by wealthy Americans. Why should someone else profit by this, Ruark reasoned, when Selby could go on his own and make the money himself? Selby & Holmberg hired many top names away from Ker & Downey, including John Sutton, Reggie Destro, and Mike Rowbotham. Naturally, Ruark used the firm for almost all of his Kenya safaris until he left the colony for the final time in 1962.

Another famous American who was a fixture in Kenya at that time was the actor William Holden. Holden first visited Kenya in the mid-1950s and was so taken with the place that he came back, year after year, until he was almost a resident. On his arrival in Nairobi in January, 1959, Ruark ran into Holden, and the two proceeded to "tie one on" at the Norfolk Hotel, according to a letter Virginia Ruark wrote to Alan

Ritchie at the time. The Ruarks then left on safari; they were in Africa for two months. Meanwhile, William Holden went on safari with an oilman named Ray Ryan. Their professionals were from K&D — Terry Mathews and Tony Archer. During the course of the safari, Ryan was slightly injured when his rifle recoiled and the scope hit him in the eye. To recuperate, Ryan and Holden were taken to the Mawingo Hotel, an estate on the equator that looked out onto the peaks of Mount Kenya.

The Mawingo was a former coffee plantation, fitted out like a luxury hotel on the French Riviera. It had been purchased in the early fifties by Jack Block, of Block Hotels, who also owned the Norfolk, the New Stanley, and a chunk of K&D. Ryan was so impressed with the Mawingo's spectacular setting that he said he would like to buy it. Jack Block said he could have it for fifty thousand pounds — an enormous sum in Kenya at that time — and everyone was taken aback when Ryan replied instantly, "Done!" Ryan bought the Mawingo Hotel on the spot, and then proceeded to pour money into developing what became the showpiece of the colony: The Mount Kenya Safari Club. Over the next few years, the club was host to everyone who was anyone, from Winston Churchill to John Wayne to Prince Bernhard of the Netherlands. One of the regular visitors, of course, was Robert Ruark.

Technically, at this time, the Mau Mau Emergency was still in effect. In reality, the insurrection had long since ended, but the government did not declare it over officially until 1960. As long as the Emergency was in effect, so were the arbitrary laws that supported it, and the civil rights suspended under its provisions stayed suspended. The last British troops left Kenya on November 2, 1956. The official government figures for Mau Mau killed by the police and army was 11,503, but Robert Edgerton says, "There can be little doubt that this figure is a substantial, and intentional, underestimate." He says many more died of their wounds in the mountains, and the bodies were never found — eaten by hyenas and other scavengers that leave no trace. As well, he insists, prisoners who died during interrogation were buried in unmarked graves and not included in the overall numbers. Edgerton's conclusion from the published figures is that the ratio of dead to wounded Mau Mau was seven to one, evidence that the emphasis among the security forces was on

killing the insurgents, not wounding or capturing them alive. Exactly
why this should surprise him, or be taken as an indication of General
Erskine's inhumanity, is puzzling. For their part, Edgerton reports the
Mau Mau killed 590 members of the security forces, of whom only sixty-
three were white, as well as 1,819 loyalist Kikuyus, and twenty-six Asian
civilians. Although the primary target of the Mau Mau gangs was supposedly the white settlers and farmers in the highlands, only thirty-two
were killed during the entire Emergency. "Over the same period of time,
more white Kenyans were killed in traffic accidents in Nairobi alone
than were killed by the Mau Mau rebels," he wrote.

The number of dead and wounded on both sides has been argued for
more than forty years and will never be known with absolute certainty.
There is no doubt whatever, though, that the Mau Mau dead outnumbered the white-settler dead by a huge margin. Entire declared wars have
been fought with fewer casualties than the Kikuyu suffered over the four
years of fighting in the Mau Mau Emergency, from 1952 until 1956.

Gradually, peace returned to Kenya. Women started going to parties
again without a revolver on their hip. The security precautions of the
Mau Mau years — the burning lanterns at night, the prearranged signals
— were relaxed. Never, however, would the sparkling little colony
return to the carefree days the settlers had known before the Emergency.
Locks on doors and windows, the security bars and tiger screens, had
come to stay — and remain to this day. As well, relations between the
races in Kenya were permanently scarred. Certainly there had been
racism and injustice before, but there had also been mutual trust and
respect, at least among individuals. The suspicion and fear born during
the Mau Mau Emergency became a permanent part of Kenya life.

In a series of newspaper columns written during the safari and filed
from various points in Kenya, Ruark reflected on the changes he saw
occurring around him. He was not optimistic about the direction in
which Africa was heading. At home he might revile the governor of
Arkansas, and the Southern rednecks who tried to stall the coming of
racial integration, but in Africa he was outspokenly critical of the ability of black Africans to run a country, or even a modern farm. Kenya, he
said, was "nervous and edgy," with the black majority now demanding

more than mere equality with the white population. Africa's two hundred million inhabitants were "no more ready for democracy than they are to build guided missiles." He predicted that, come independence, the unsophisticated many would be exploited by the sophisticated few, and all of them would fall prey to the communists, who would find easy pickings among the newly independent states. Again Ruark sided with the settlers who had fought the hard battles to create something out of nothing in much of Africa. The history of colonial Africa was not nearly so bad as the exploitation of the American Indian, Ruark contended. Where the white man had exploited the native North American, "poisoned his blankets and gave him diphtheria, fed him bad booze and stole his land," the Kenya colonists had "attempted to dissuade people from eating each other" and "tried to introduce improvements in hygiene, agriculture, land preservation and the maintenance of the integrity of certain wild tribes which do not readily adapt to trousers."

Ruark was indisputably correct on many of the points he made. Some years later the Rhodesian whites used the same reasoning to defend their record, having stopped the Ndebele and the Shona from killing each other and by so doing having ensured they themselves would eventually lose control to the black majority. As arguments go it may well be true, but that does not make continued minority rule right or just, and Ruark knew it. His main point was that there were good aspects to colonialism as well as bad. Emerging Africa should remember this, he suggested, and preserve the good aspects as it pursued independence and political power. There had to be a place in "Africa for the Africans" that recognized the rights of those Africans who happened to be white, or yellow, or brown. Ruark's obvious bitterness stemmed from his doubts that such a state of affairs could actually come to pass in an atmosphere increasingly poisoned with hatred, resentment, and mistrust.

\* \* \*

Ruark returned to Palamós in March, 1959, revitalized and ready to renew his attack on his partially written novel, *Poor No More*. By late July, the rewrites and revisions were complete. He headed for New York with the manuscript in his briefcase and handed it over to Harold Matson in August. Ruark then continued on to Texas for a vacation while the book was set in type and Holt prepared for publication. It appeared in October, just in time for Christmas.

Ruark now had three serious books in print, and a fourth just coming out. His rather precarious health aside, to all appearances he was in great shape, financially and professionally. As usual, though, while the money was certainly coming in by the bucket, it was leaving by the barrel. The nagging financial worries that dogged Ruark throughout his professional life, no matter how successful he became, continued to bedevil him. As well, certain unpleasant character traits were becoming more and more dominant.

Robert Ruark was a charming man, shy with strangers, but open and witty and amusing with people he knew. With women, especially, he could be charming beyond belief, and his seductions were legendary. As he got older and became recognized as an authority on Africa and on certain aspects of big game hunting, it was as if he began to believe his own press clippings. His shyness was replaced by arrogance, and he became more and more of a braggart. As Hugh Foster notes, "No one could tell Bob anything he didn't already know." Combined with the combativeness stemming from his reception from the folks at home, the bragging and arrogance became overwhelming.

Although he was still producing his syndicated column for United Features, his relationship with that organization was deteriorating. Both his writing style and choice of subjects had suffered while writing *Poor No More*, which once again raised the ire of the newspaper editors who bought the column. Ruark accused the editors at United Features of "gutting" his column. His old friend Roy Howard tried to smooth things over, attributing the specific problems to one editor in particular and assuring Ruark it would not happen again, but other executives felt the real problem was the fact Ruark now believed his work was above criticism.

This unlovely side of Robert Ruark is illustrated by an incident described by Hugh Foster. When *Poor No More* was published in October, 1959, Ruark attended a private party thrown by Henry Holt at the Elysée Hotel. Foster says Ruark walked from the Holt offices back to the hotel that afternoon "carrying a copy of the book held to his chest with the photograph of his face on the back cover in plain view." No one on the sidewalk recognized him, apparently. The exercise in self-aggrandizement fell flat. Critically, at least, the book fell even flatter.

The reviews were anything but positive. Almost no one liked the novel. *Newsweek* was the harshest of the important publications, saying "the generally boorish pronouncements for which the columnist-author Ruark is paid $110,000 a year lose much of their charm and relevance in the pages of a novel." It was Ruark's first serious encounter with hostility toward a book that stemmed not from the relative merits of the book itself but from the reviewers' dislike of him personally, of his political leanings, or of the views he expressed in his newspaper column. Reading *Poor No More*, it is hard to see exactly what some of the critics were referring to, just as later criticisms of *Uhuru* and *The Honey Badger* seem completely divorced from what Ruark actually wrote. It was as if the reviewers had been saving up their dislike and disapproval of him personally, and the novel gave them both the opportunity and the excuse to rake him over the coals. He could have written *War and Peace*, it sometimes seemed, and he would still have been castigated as a racist, bloodthirsty boor.

In spite of the nasty reviews — or perhaps because of them — *Poor No More* quickly became a best-seller, but even so it was eminently forgettable. Another "thick slice of slickness," to quote Alec Barr, that made little more than a ripple in the greater literary scheme of things. Ruark's purpose in writing it, however, was more than achieved: He had taken a roundhouse right at the folks back home and connected square on the jaw. As he expected, the book was widely purchased, handed around, and pored over by the people he knew in Wilmington and Southport. "Friends and family tried to identify their roles in the book and after a time concluded that they would not speak to Bob again," Foster recorded.

The novel created a permanent breach between the novelist and the people who saw themselves crucified in its pages. Ruark obviously liked the novel at the time he published it, for the simple reason that no writer publishes something he does not like, but his view of it changed as the years went by. When it came out, he certainly saw it as autobiographical, as Selby insists, but that view did not last. The bravado that later caused him to remark, "I don't know anyone except bartenders, fisher-men, and professional hunters," was the same sentiment that caused him to identify with Craig Price. Price is a hard-boiled, ruthless man who will stop at nothing to get to the top. This may have been part of the persona Ruark presented to the world, but it was not the persona he pre-sented to himself.

In a later evaluation of his success as a novelist, Ruark concluded that in *Something of Value*, by the grace of God, he made no major mistakes, but when he "tackled another one about the home country, *Poor No More*, (he) made every mistake there was, doubled and redoubled." If nothing else, however, the novel served to get a lot of things off Ruark's chest. Every novelist has to write at least one autobiographical work. For most it is the first effort, and the majority never go beyond that first one because they have nothing else to write. In Ruark's case, the huge catharsis and cleansing of old hurts and resentments occurred with his second, and once it was out of the way he could continue with the work he was really put on earth to do: writing about Africa.

In *Poor No More*, however, there was one very cogent insight that almost (but not quite) redeems the book. By the end, Craig Price has clawed, fought, stolen, defrauded, and betrayed his way to a state of inverse grace in which he has no more friends, no woman to love, and no business empire. He does, on the other hand, have a million dollars squirrelled away in a Swiss bank account. He drives, alone, one step ahead of the law, reflecting on his curious state. *"How very rich he'd be, Craig suddenly thought, if he owned anything except the million dollars wait-ing for him in Switzerland."*

* * *

*Chapter Ten*

# MILES AND MILES OF BLOODY AFRICA

In the eight years since he made his first safari, Ruark had hunted with Harry Selby again and again, returning to Africa at least once a year, and often staying for several months. Together they had hunted throughout East Africa, from Somaliland in the north to the Mozambique border in the south, and as far west as the Mountains of the Moon. When he was not actually on safari, Ruark would visit friends in Nairobi or on farms in the Aberdares, or stay with friendly game wardens in their own private Edens. He had become close friends with Brian Burrows, the manager of the New Stanley Hotel, and often camped out in Burrows's penthouse suite when he was in town. From reading, from talking with people, and just through extensive "exposure to the scene," Ruark had learned an awful lot about Africa, and much of what he knew he had poured into two books, dozens of magazine articles, and hundreds of newspaper columns.

What he had seen during those eight years had both fascinated him and troubled him deeply. The bloodshed of the Mau Mau years had been bad enough, but by 1960 Africa was passing through an era of political change and instability far beyond what any but the most pessimistic observers had foreseen. After India gained its independence in 1947, it was a foregone conclusion that other British colonies would follow suit, and many of them were in Africa. Britain ruled a dozen separate colonies on the Dark Continent, many of them potentially wealthy or strategically valuable both to the West and to the expansionist Soviet

Union. As Britain, France, Belgium, and Portugal struggled, each in its own way, to deal with the independence movements that sprang up in their colonies, and with the pressure applied through the United Nations and other diplomatic channels, the superpowers of the time — the United States and the Soviet Union — pursued their own interests and prepared to turn Africa into an ideological battleground.

Kenya and the Mau Mau aside, of the colonial powers Britain was the one most prepared to give its colonies their independence. France, having lost Indochina to the Viet Minh at Dienbienphu in 1954, turned its attention to Algeria and fought a long war to keep it part of France. Belgium, pressured to give up the Congo, watched as the colony descended into chaos. Portugal declared that Mozambique, Angola, and the Cape Verde Islands were provinces of Portugal, and that it would never pull out. The Suez Crisis of 1956 provided the moral turning point. Britain and France invaded Egypt in an attempt to take back control of the Suez Canal, expecting the United States to (at least tacitly) back the move in order to protect its own interests in the Middle East. Instead, President Eisenhower strongly condemned the military action. As Egyptian units pulled back into Cairo, pursued by British and French paratroops, international pressure mounted on the two colonial powers. They were forced to halt their advance and, ultimately, to withdraw. Nasser, the Egyptian president, had won by losing. Suez was a turning point because Britain and France had been humiliated; the world had repudiated imperial military action, and it gave the African independence movements, from Cairo to the Cape, a new confidence.

The first to go was Ghana, formerly the Gold Coast, which became independent in 1957. It is generally considered the first of Britain's African colonies to achieve independence, although the Sudan, jointly ruled by Britain and Egypt for more than fifty years and technically not a colony, became a country on January 1, 1956. Ghana's first president was Kwame Nkrumah, an American-educated politician and darling of the liberal left, who became something of a moral leader of black Africa. Between 1956 and 1960, almost all of France's colonies in black Africa became independent. By 1960, conditions in the Belgian Congo were red-hot, and there was racial unrest in South Africa. Kenya, in its post-

Mau Mau years, was moving toward independence as well.

From New York and Palamós, Robert Ruark watched the events unfolding and decided it was time to make a major journalistic safari in Africa — a serious attempt to visit the dark corners and to understand what was really happening, to go far beyond the "once over lightly journalism" he had been practicing sporadically between hunting trips. Hugh Foster says it was an effort to resurrect a career that was flagging as "his column popularity declined and his writing skills weakened," but the facts do not support that conclusion. *Poor No More* may have received mixed reviews, but it was not poorly written by any means. It could have been better, but that does not mean it was bad. If, as a novel, it appears to be the weak link in Ruark's chain of work, it is only because the other links are so strong. A more plausible explanation is the simplest one: Ruark was, by training and inclination, a reporter, and the events shaking Africa in 1959 comprised the hottest story around. Not only that, he was the acknowledged expert on the subject. Where else would he go but Africa?

As well, in the back of his mind he already had the basic idea for his next novel. *Something of Value* cried out for a sequel, and what Ruark had seen in Kenya since 1955 gave him the basis for a major work on emerging Africa. The British prime minister, Harold Macmillan, had spoken of "the winds of change" that were sweeping across the continent. Robert Ruark would stand with those winds on his face and turn them into literature.

A major journey of exploration such as Ruark envisioned, the modern-day equivalent of Sir Richard Burton's quest for the Nile, would be neither easy nor inexpensive. As well, Ruark had to have the blessing of Scripps-Howard and United Features, because if he was in Africa for five or six months, it meant his column would be Africa — all Africa — for virtually that entire period. There was no way he could carry out such a mission while trying, at the same time, to sprinkle his column with variety by writing on subjects like hemlines, women's hair, and the domination of American children by television.

The other issue, as always, was money. Ruark had a very large income, but he was not independently wealthy. Such a venture would be very, very expensive. Although Ruark knew his way around some parts of

Africa and certainly felt at home there, it was a highly dangerous place to be. It would be foolhardy for him to try to cover it on his own, and he knew it. For one thing, it was simply too big. For another, he did not speak all the languages, and the fact that he was a known journalist would shut some doors to him. Finally, there was the question of personal safety. He needed someone with him who knew the place intimately. On this ultimate safari after the biggest game of all, Ruark needed the best white hunter he could find. The obvious choice was Harry Selby, but hiring a Harry Selby virtually full-time for six months would cost a not-so-small fortune.

Ruark went to Roy Howard with his idea, and Howard jumped at it. Ruark was at his best, his liveliest, his most passionate and controversial, when writing about Africa, and this was reflected in reader polls. Howard was not at all averse to a full six months of in-depth coverage of Africa, as long as it was written in vintage Ruark. And he was prepared to unlock the vault to fund it. Armed with that most vital item of a foreign correspondent's equipment — a lavish expense account — Ruark alerted Selby by cable and boarded a plane for Nairobi.

* * *

Ruark arrived in December, 1959. The Kenyan capital was then — and is now — the major communications center of sub-Saharan Africa outside of Johannesburg. Newspapers and wire services with only one correspondent for the whole continent stationed them in Nairobi because it had passable telephone service and reliable flights in and out. In that era, television was not yet a force in news gathering, and satelite television was not even a dream. Radio was strictly local except for short-wave like the BBC World Service and Radio Moscow. Urgent stories were filed by cable or telex. Longer magazine articles went by post, mailed from out-of-the-way places; the careful correspondent would later mail the top carbon from the next outpost, and keep the second carbon on file for insurance.

News gathering was done in person, on foot as often as not. You landed in a strange place, found a hotel, and ventured out into the streets to see what was happening. Sometimes you watched from the safety of your hotel window, and seasoned hands always asked for a room on the third or fourth floor. The view is better. So is the security.

When Ruark arrived, there were so many conflicting currents at work in Africa that it would take an entire book even to skim the surface. It was a huge continent, with two hundred million people divided by tribe, geography, history, and culture. Attempting to cover even a portion of it, and provide readers back home with a coherent picture of what was happening as the various colonies lurched toward independence, was a truly daunting prospect. What had seemed like a great idea at home in Palamós, on the beach looking out at the Mediterranean, became an impossible task when seen up close, with Roy Howard waiting at the other end of the line for the dispatches to flow in.

Ruark was not physically well when he landed in Nairobi, either. His chronic health problems, the ailments that always seemed to bedevil him in Europe and America, had reduced him almost to invalid status. He and Selby set out from Nairobi by Land-Rover to drive to Somalia, a round trip of several thousand miles over either bad roads or no roads at all. They reached Mogadishu, the uninspiring Somali capital with its heat, sand, camels, goats, and flies, spent a couple of days, then headed back for Nairobi. Ruark was not impressed by Somalia, nor was he encouraged. He foresaw only disaster for the Somalis when the Italian and British colonial masters departed, as they would later that year. Worse, he realized the immensity of the task he had set for himself. In a letter to Virginia, mailed on his return to Nairobi, he said, "I don't know if I can do it. It's a job for a several man team. There's so many places and so much going on that I frankly don't know where to turn." He even suggested that unless he saw something on which he could focus as a theme, he might give up and go home.

Meanwhile, he stuck it out. He flew to Addis Ababa, capital of Ethiopia, and was given an audience with Emperor Haile Selassie. Ethiopia was not part of emerging Africa — it had been an independent country longer than the United States, and its civilization dated to the time of Christ — but it was about to be threatened by the emergence of newly independent countries all around it: Somalia to the east, Sudan to the west, Kenya to the south. The Sudan, independent for only four years, was already deep into a civil war between the black people of the south and the Arabic north. This war would continue from 1956 until 1972, pause briefly, then resume and continue until this day. It soon spilled over into the surrounding countries as refugees sought safety and the guerrillas a haven and base of operations. Then there was Somalia. The Somalis are fierce, warlike people. Their neighbors are frightened to death of them (they were the chief perpetrators of the elephant and rhino poaching that became rampant in the 1970s and '80s), and as soon as independence loomed, they announced their intention of carving off part of Ethiopia. The Ethiopians were no slouches when it came to war, but Haile Selassie had seen enough bloodshed during the Italian occupation of his country before the second world war. Overt American support for the Somali claim, Ruark said, would drive Ethiopia into the arms of the Russians. It was the beginning of a long chess game, involving Ethiopia, Somalia, the U.S., and the U.S.S.R., that continued for twenty years.

Russian encroachment in Africa was one of the themes Ruark dwelt upon in his columns, along with his view that no African country was even remotely prepared to govern itself after the colonialists left, nor to get along with its neighbors. In general terms, Ruark saw Africa as a tribal bloodbath just waiting to happen, with the Russians and Americans providing the firepower that would take hundreds of thousands of lives, rather than the mere thousands who would die if the wars were fought with old-fashioned bows and spears. It was not an optimistic outlook; unfortunately, it proved to be more accurate than not.

In February, Ruark made his first visit to Leopoldville (later Kinshasa), the capital of the Belgian Congo. He went on his own, without Selby for once, and returned for a second look in May. The Congo was scheduled to become independent on July 1, and the politicians were frantically jockeying for position. Names like Joseph Kasavubu, Patrice Lumumba, and General Joseph Mobutu would soon become familiar to anyone who read a newspaper. Ruark looked into the abyss and did not like what he saw. He predicted chaos for the Congo. It had no institutions, no political traditions, no stability. The province of Katanga, which was rich in minerals and bordered on the British colony of Northern Rhodesia (now Zambia), was poised to secede. Katanga's president, Moise Tshombe, was supported by the Belgian mining giant, the *Union Minière*.

Civil war broke out as the government in Leopoldville attempted to force Katanga back into the fold. What ensued was a melee of warring factions, foreign mercenaries, assassinations, and United Nations military intervention. This translated ultimately into the horror stories of white hostages, raped nuns, mutilated priests, and tribal bloodbaths that were splashed over front pages around the world.

In April, South Africa made headlines when police opened fire on demonstrators in the black township of Sharpeville, killing sixty-seven people and wounding several hundred more. Ruark and Selby headed for Johannesburg. Again Ruark did not like what he saw, but for vastly different reasons. Instead of warring black tribes, he saw a "fascist" state in which the white minority kept the black majority in virtual slavery. He was openly fearful that his telephone was tapped. He wrote that South Africa "lacks only an official Gestapo to be a complete police state." Ruark should have looked more closely; they did have one. Because his health was so poor, Ruark did not venture up into Southern Rhodesia, the self-governing colony that would unilaterally declare its independence in 1965 under Prime Minister Ian Smith. Instead, he dispatched Harry Selby to Salisbury (later Harare) to get the lay of the land. After a few days, Selby reported back to Ruark, and the two of them fled South Africa for Nairobi, which more and more looked like home and mother, as Ruark put it, "if you had a home, and liked your mother."

Once safely ensconced in Brian Burrows's penthouse suite at the New Stanley, with unfettered access to telephone, typewriter, cable office, and the hotel's excellent Grill, Ruark was free to write what he really thought about events in the stronghold of apartheid south of the Limpopo. Again, his condemnation of the South African government for its official racist policies are a better indication of Ruark's real beliefs about race than his anti-independence columns from Somalia, the Congo, or rural Kenya. Ironically, his later support for "fortress Kenya" to keep the colony as "white man's country" was exactly what the Afrikaners were trying to do in South Africa, and a few years later, the Rhodesians. Ruark rightly saw that as unjust and ultimately unsustainable — but then, he had no personal stake in the problems of white farmers in the Transvaal, or on the high veldt of the Orange Free State.

He did have, on the other hand, a very real, very personal, stake in what happened in the Aberdares.

Kenya was then in the last throes of its approach to independence. Jomo Kenyatta was still in prison, serving the final years of his seven-year sentence for running an illegal organization. A conference was taking place in London — the Lancaster House conference — involving the settlers, the British government, and the Asian and black populations of Kenya. What was happening was widely perceived in Kenya as a betrayal of the white settlers, and Ruark glumly adopted that viewpoint. The conservative prime minister of Great Britain, Harold Macmillan, the man who coined the phrase "winds of change," was resigned to the fact that all of Britain's colonies in Africa would become independent; he was determined that if it had to happen, it may as well happen soon. Anti-colonial sentiment was strong in the United States and growing in Europe, and even in Britain there was only negligible support for the Kenya settlers. A few conservative members of parliament owned property in Kenya, but aside from them the general attitude was that the Kenya settlers were nothing but an irritation who should be left to fend for themselves. The costly military intervention of the Mau Mau Emergency had not sat well with a country that was deep in debt and whose balance of payments problems, by 1960, had forced the government to implement a severe austerity program. A colony that contributed little and cost a great deal, both financially and politically, was unlikely to get much sympathy from a motherland that was fast becoming a second-class power, and more dependent on the goodwill of the United States.

Altogether, the African continent was in political turmoil from one end to the other — in "ferment" as Ruark later described it. During his five months there, he travelled thousands of miles by jeep, airplane, and any other mode of transportation that came to hand — from foot to camel-back. His description of the odyssey, fictionalized for Alec Barr, captures the surreal, kaleidoscopic effect of seeing so much in so short a time, one country after another, one hotel after another, packing and unpacking, seeing one customs officer after another go through your bag looking for contraband, and having newly liberated black prostitutes demand money simply because they were black. In The Honey Badger,

Barr's eighteen-month assignment in Africa was the way Ruark perhaps wished it could have been. Barr saw everyone and everything; he spent time with Dr. Schweitzer and Tom Mboya and Haile Selassie, and he saw the inside of the Mogadishu Jail. By the end he was exhausted but not unhappy, with a new non-fiction book wrapped up and the idea for a fictional series firmly in his head. Barr was deeply tanned and lean, and the grey hair on his temples was a distinguished contrast to his faded safari jacket.

For Ruark, the truth was just the opposite. Five months of living like a gypsy, of driving himself by day and drinking by night, had caused his already fragile health to collapse. On his return to Nairobi from the Congo in early May, he suffered what he later called "a nervous breakdown due to overwork, nervous tension, whiskey, too much travel and the usual." If anything, he understated the case. He was admitted to Nairobi Hospital for a week of drying out, then caught a plane for Spain.

Hugh Foster says Ruark's health problems can really be reduced to one thing: alcohol. In letters to Harold Matson and Roy Howard, Ruark alluded to other factors — overwork, tension, travel, obscure Congolese illnesses, stress, and even pneumonia. But the fact was, Ruark had become an out-and-out drunk. In Brian Burrows's penthouse at the New Stanley, he had suffered a severe blackout; Ruark referred to them as "cutouts," and they had been occurring with increasing regularity. Burrows said he had crawled around on the floor "on all fours, acting like a dog." There were three such blackouts toward the end of the African trip. The friend who drove Ruark to Embakasi Airport said he was suffering from one of the most severe cases of *delirium tremens* he had ever seen.

There are contradictions in the various accounts of what happened. For one thing, it is unlikely Ruark would still have been suffering from DT's if he had just been released from a week in hospital, during which he had at least started to dry out. And even in those free-wheeling days, it is unlikely he would have been allowed on an airplane in that condition. It is obvious, however, that his drinking had now reached crisis proportions. More than his liver was at risk; blackouts and DT's are symptoms of serious alcoholism affecting the brain. While he tried to place at least part of the blame on other factors, Ruark was too intelligent to lie to himself. He knew the root cause of his problem; after all, he had seen the effects of alcohol and drug abuse on his parents. In London for his annual checkup, the doctors confirmed his diagnosis, and warned him that his drinking was seriously affecting his liver. Unless he stopped, he could look forward to the certainty — not merely the possibility — of cirrhosis. Back in Spain, he wrote again to Matson and Howard, advising them he was going on the wagon, "including wine, beer and vermouth," for the next six months.

The summer of 1960 marked a serious change for the better in Robert Ruark. It was long overdue, and unfortunately only temporary, but he had acknowledged his physical problems and seemed to be making an attempt to deal with them. He was only forty-four years old, and he should have been in the prime of life, professionally and physically. Yet he was literally facing death, and soon, if he did not alter his self-destructive ways. First and foremost, he had to quit drinking for good. If the first step to a cure is recognizing the disease, then Ruark was well on his way. In letters to his close friends and associates, and even to his parents, he confessed that he knew alcohol was his mortal enemy, and he even went so far as to claim "I was so close to death this time that I don't ever want to drink again." In order to be close to his doctors and save on hotel bills, the Ruarks rented a flat in London, and he spent the summer drinking mineral water and watching events in Africa unfold from afar.

* * *

In the spring of 1960, Robert Ruark was little more than an invalid by any standard. Although he stopped drinking and managed to stay on the wagon for nine full months, he did little else to speed his recovery. In fact, if the pace of his existence was the root cause of his problems, he may have actually aggravated them. From May, 1960 until July, 1962, Ruark lived as if he was in a race with death. In that twenty-six month period he wrote a major novel, watched his marriage break down, went on several major safaris, and managed to get himself chewed by a wounded leopard in India. It is a wonder he survived, given the frantic, driven pace he set. During that time, as well, Congolese paratroops took Stanleyville, a young American reporter, Harry Taylor, was killed in Kasai Province of the Congo, a white Kenyan named Peter Poole was hanged in Nairobi for murdering a black man, and Ernest Hemingway shot himself in Ketchum, Idaho. All these events had a serious impact on Ruark, but they helped to shape his next novel, *Uhuru*, the major accomplishment from this period of his life.

Ruark had returned home from Africa with the idea for this book firmly in his mind. It would be a novel about emerging Africa, the new Africa he had witnessed being born, a sequel to *Something of Value* that would look beyond the past. Ruark had learned much about Africa in his nine years as a regular visitor and in the five-month journalistic safari. He was confident he could pour this knowledge and understanding — this *feel* for his subject — into the definitive novel about a huge and frightening continent that was, in its own way, slouching toward Bethlehem to be born.

It was all there, everything he needed: The solid facts of history, the contacts among the actual people, both white and black, and his eyewitness memories of tragedy and blood. As well, Ruark owned a tangible emotion about his subject. By this time, he loved Africa the way a man loves a woman, and Africa could betray such a love in the most feminine of ways. If all this was not the raw material from which to build a great work of literature, then Ruark did not know what was. Unfortunately, merely having the raw materials at hand was no guarantee that intent would turn effortlessly into art. Anything but. The smooth vision he had in his mind turned into a very rocky road of writing. He encountered more difficulty writing *Uhuru* than any other book he ever attempted.

When he arrived back in Palamós, Ruark wrote to Harold Matson that he was planning a series of four novels, all with African settings and all tied together. In addition to *Something of Value*, there would be a sequel, tentatively titled *Burnt Offering*, about the current situation of countries emerging to independence through fire and blood. This pair would be bracketed by two more: the first, *A Long View from a Tall Hill*, would cover Africa from the turn of the century to the rise of the Mau Mau in 1952, while the fourth, *Act of God*, would be what Ruark called a "post-freedom thing," taking place sometime in the future. It was a great, all-encompassing plan. The first step to realizing it was to write *Burnt Offering*, and Ruark set a deadline for himself of spring, 1961. As events proved almost immediately, he had set himself an impossible task.

Pablo Picasso once said "A clear vision — that is the thing." Robert Ruark may have had a very clear vision of what he wanted to accomplish with *Burnt Offering*, but his vision of how to get there was anything but. The main problem was that his raw material was the events occurring in Africa, and that was a very fluid, very unpredictable situation. No one, Ruark included, knew what was going to happen in Kenya from month to month, much less the ultimate outcome for the colony. Unlike journalism, which is a breathless account of what has just happened, a novel is a distillation — an in-depth examination of events with the perspective that time allows. Ruark was trying to build a novel from current events, while anticipating what would happen tomorrow. It almost never works, and *Burnt Offering* was no exception. He worked away at it throughout the summer of 1960, getting basically nowhere. He went fishing with his friend Ricardo Sicré, entertained other friends at his home in Palamós, stayed on the wagon, and sat down at his typewriter each day, with little to show for it when the sun went down.

Looking for a reason, Ruark naturally began to worry that not drinking was affecting his creativity. He was a writer who not only was able to function while he was drinking, to actually put words on paper while he was drunk, but one who could do it well. Other writers, including Faulkner, Hemingway, and Fitzgerald, drank heavily, but usually after the day's serious work was done, and as a way of unwinding. Ruark wrote while he was drinking, as often as not, so it is not surprising, finding his work not going well while he was on the wagon, that he seized on sobriety as the culprit for non-production. He did not really want to be on the wagon in the first place, and he fretted that perhaps he needed alcohol to lubricate the wheels of imagination. Still, he stayed sober and pounded away at his typewriter, hoping desperately for either inspiration or an event that would pull everything into focus.

In August, Ruark invited Harold Matson to Palamós to see what he had accomplished so far. What ensued was a scene Ruark later used in *The Honey Badger*, in which Matson read his manuscript, then described it as "an elaborate treatment," a framework for a novel Ruark might write "when he really got down to it." In other words, what he had accomplished so far was lifeless, if not formless. All Ruark's knowledge of Africa, and all his good intentions, could not compensate for his lack of a coherent vision of who was who in the book, what was what, and why the events were taking place. In an attempt to find the answers, Ruark left for Kenya once again.

Political conditions in Kenya were already perilous. All the conflict-ing forces — black nationalists, white settlers, British colonial-office rep-resentatives, Asians, Communists, and loudmouthed Belgian refugees — presented a steaming pot that did not require much stirring. The Lan-caster House Conference in London had ended with a startling result in early 1960: After five weeks of debate, the colonial secretary, Ian Macleod, announced that Kenya would become a parliamentary democ-racy with a universal franchise. A white Kenya moderate, Michael Blundell, was at the conference as leader of the New Kenya Party. He accepted the decision reluctantly, but left London believing Britain would not grant the colony full independence for at least ten years. This, he felt, was enough time to prepare the population (estimated at 60,000 whites and six million blacks) for the effects of full majority (i.e., black) rule. Blundell might have accepted it, but there was a white element that did not: On his arrival at Embakasi Airport, he was cheered by a crowd of blacks, while a white settler threw thirty pieces of silver at his feet. The divisions within the colony were becoming deeper, wider, more confusing, and more bitter by the hour.

The Belgian Congo became independent on July 1. Almost immedi-ately the Congolese Army mutinied against its white officers, the coun-try descended into civil war, and more than thirteen thousand Belgian settlers fled in panic, leaving everything behind. More than two thou-sand of these refugees made it to Kenya, penniless and bitter, and soon the sound of Belgian accents in the hotel bars, raised in condemnation of black nationalism, was common throughout the colony. White Kenyans welcomed these "reinforcements," but black Kenyans resented them and urged them to keep right on going. One trainload of Belgians arrived in Nairobi on July 14 to be met by a mob of a thousand blacks rioting in protest. As the situation in Kenya grew uglier, the settlers demanded the colonial government form a European "defence force," and local politicians reported that white Kenyans were stockpiling weapons and supplies. Britain responded by airlifting a battalion of troops to Nairobi and sending an aircraft carrier with six hundred Royal Marines.

At this point Mau Mau activity broke out once again, small in scale and limited in area, but enough to send some settlers over the edge. The threat of a return to conditions of the Emergency sent property values tumbling, and "For Sale" signs went up on houses and farms all over the colony. Prices on the Nairobi stock exchange tumbled by fifty per cent and capital poured out of the colony as settlers tried to get their savings out. A new governor, Sir Patrick Renison, had been appointed to replace Baring. He tried to restore both civil order and settler confidence by refusing demands for the release of Jomo Kenyatta. Sir Patrick was a colonial civil servant of long standing, but a man who knew little about Kenya or the Mau Mau. For the latter he relied on a government report on the origins of Mau Mau prepared by an official named Frank Corfield. The Corfield Report was thorough in some ways, superficial in others. Robert Edgerton dismisses it as a document that relied exclusively on government and Kikuyu loyalist sources. Robert Ruark, on the other hand, cited the Corfield Report more than once to support his views on the roots of Mau Mau and his increasingly dire predictions about impending chaos in the colony. Considering Frank Corfield prepared his report at a time of political upheaval, with Jomo Kenyatta and many acknowledged Mau Mau leaders still in prison, and with many central figures having a vested interest in presenting only one point of view, the chances of his preparing a document that would withstand the test of time, hindsight, and emerging information was as unlikely as Ruark's attempt to write a coherent novel based on the same events.

Conditions in Kenya were, to put it mildly, confused and fearful. In August, 1960, while Ruark was still in Palamós, a small drama rich in symbolism ground to its tragic close. A year earlier, a young white Kenyan named Peter Poole, a former member of the Kenya Police Reserve, shot and killed a black African for abusing Poole's dog. The KPR had been heavily involved in many operations against the Mau Mau, and was made up mostly of farmers, settlers, and professional hunters, so Poole was well-known among the more extreme elements.

He was tried for murder, convicted, and sentenced to hang. Whether he would in fact become the first white man in the colony's history to be executed for the murder of a black man became the pivotal issue of a summer that had no shortage of issues.

Looking back, it is easy to say what the government should have done. Poole was clearly guilty. The question was, should he die for the crime? Was the shooting premeditated, thereby warranting capital punishment? Ruark's later assessment was that Poole signed his own death warrant because he saw the African kicking the dog and went into his house to get his gun. Had the gun already been in his possession, Ruark felt, Poole could have argued the shooting was a reflex action; given the temper of the times and the events of the preceding eight years of the Mau Mau Emergency, he would probably have been given a stiff prison sentence instead. Poole having been condemned, the issue then became whether the British Government would ask the Queen to commute the death sentence. The risks were obvious both ways. There was no easy way out. There was no solution that would not enrage one faction or the other.

If Poole did not hang, it would be a clear statement that a white life was more valuable than a black one. If Poole died, it was an equally clear statement that Kenya was no longer a white-run colony. As white extremists made veiled threats and black politicians delivered thundering condemnations, tension mounted. Settlers took their guns and drifted into town to be close to the event. There was talk of storming the prison to free Poole. In the end, Ian Macleod, the colonial secretary, declined to ask the Queen to commute the sentence, and Peter Poole was hanged in Nairobi Jail. A crowd of three hundred whites hung about glumly outside the gates. When word emerged that the execution had been carried out, they drifted off in groups to drink away the day and reflect on the end of the colony as they knew it. But there was no violence.

The event gave Ruark what he was looking for: an incident upon which to base the plot of *Burnt Offering*. He arrived in Nairobi shortly after the hanging and set about gathering information. Then occurred one of the pivotal events of this period in his life. In the Congo, Kasai Province was threatening to secede, backed by Moise Tshombe in the also-rebellious province of Katanga. Federal Congolese troops were sent

245

in by Patrice Lumumba to occupy Kasai and heavy fighting ensued on the border between the two provinces. On September 6, a Scripps-Howard reporter by the name of Harry Taylor was shot and killed while covering the fighting. Ruark, who knew Taylor and was very fond of him, was devastated by the event. To him Taylor's death symbolized everything that was pointlessly bloody and tragic about Africa. He wrote a newspaper column on September 15 that Hugh Foster calls "the most vicious and altogether savage" of his twenty years as a columnist. Most people today would add "racist" to the description. It was a blanket condemnation of black liberation in Africa, and its central theme was a personal attack on Patrice Lumumba, the Congolese premier. In trying to force Katanga and Kasai back into the federal fold, Lumumba was playing all sides against the middle. To Ruark, Lumumba personified everything that was wrong, corrupt, and perverse about black African politicians. His attack was also directed at black troops who still filed their teeth (as many did then, and some still do) and went about armed with machine guns, looting in the name of "the true God of all Black Africa, the God of Give Me, the God of Take." The column was undoubtedly hyperbolic and would almost certainly never be published in the mainstream press today, but anyone judging it objectively would have to say, with the benefit of forty years of hindsight, that Ruark's assessment was dead on.

Taylor's death provided Ruark with more than the subject matter for one enraged piece of journalism. In its curious juxtaposition to the death of Poole, another young white man who died in Africa, it gave Ruark a peg for ruminating on the importance of blood and death. Four years later he incorporated it into *The Honey Badger*. The young reporter became Larry Orde, a foreign correspondent sent out to assist Alec Barr in his assignment of covering all of Africa for the magazines. It also provided Ruark, through Barr's fictional article, an opportunity to reflect on life as a foreign correspondent, and on mortality and disillusionment.

While Ruark was in Kenya in late 1960, his friend Eva Monley helped him a great deal as he dug around for facts and reaction to Poole's death and the ongoing political developments. Miss Monley then gave him the final, vital element he needed to give *Burnt Offering* the depth it needed. She took him to see the Nightingale family, who had raised her, and who owned a farm near Kinangop. The Nightingales were a different element altogether from the white hunters and extremist elements Ruark knew so well. They were moderate Kenya whites who recognized that black people had rights and a place in an independent Kenya — that, in fact, Kenya was their country. Yet they felt they too belonged in Kenya, had rights there, and would stay regardless what happened. This was the moderate element of which Michael Blundell was leader. They believed bloodshed could be avoided, that Kenya need not become another Belgian Congo, and the way to do this was for moderate blacks and whites to work together to defeat the extremist elements on both sides.

Ruark spent some weeks at the Nightingale farm, talking with the family members and black workers who lived there, including some ex-Mau Mau. By the end of his stay he had found a new direction for *Burnt Offering*. Ruark and Eva Monley held a small private ceremony in which he burned the original manuscript and prepared to start on the novel all over again.

* * *

November is the time of the small rains in East Africa. This is the shorter rainy season, a time of fine weather punctuated by sudden downpours. In high-altitude cities like Nairobi and Kampala, the small rains are a blessing that brings green grass and washes the streets clean, leaving the air sparkling crisp in the sunshine. Sometimes, though, the clouds roll in for days at a time and the rain falls in sheets. Trees drip sullenly, and dirt tracks turn into quagmires that swallow vehicles with a happy gulp. The small rains in Kenya can be as depressing as any monsoon out of Somerset Maugham.

Before returning to Spain, Ruark took a couple of weeks off for an impromptu safari with professional hunter Ken Jesperson. It was the kind of safari that happens rarely these days — two guys, a couple of trackers, and a truck full of camping equipment, heading off in whatever direction offers the best chance of adventure. Because of the heavy rains, Ruark and Jesperson did not have many options. Roads were washed out or impassable, and few of the hunting blocks were even accessible, much less in any condition to be hunted.

Ruark was insistent, however, and eventually they booked a picturesque little block down toward Amboseli, and pulled out of Nairobi with their lorry leaving a bow-wave in the driving rain. As safaris go, not much happened. They were not really after anything except a break from sodden, sullen Nairobi. What they found, for a few days at least, was a peaceful, sunny little slice of paradise. They lived quietly, drinking little (according to Ruark), shooting only for camp meat, and going to bed early. By day they cruised around just to see what they could see. They looked at the animals. The animals looked back at them. Everyone was happy.

All of this Ruark reported in an article titled "A Leopard in the Rain," which appeared in *Field & Stream* the following July. He set up the piece as an object lesson in the importance of all-out effort, of never taking no for an answer, of persevering against all odds. Theirs was not an epic quest in the sense of *Moby Dick*. But the trip itself supported the contention that, as Ruark said, very few leopards get shot in saloons, and if you want to get something, you head out after it regardless of the conditions. An astounding piece of insight? Hardly. But the article was Robert Ruark at his best, capturing Africa at *its* best. As the title indicates, the only animal of note they bagged was a leopard, taken just as the rains swept over their little oasis and put an end to the safari. The real message of the piece, reading it almost forty years later, is even more gentle than the one Ruark intended: That the value of a safari lies not in what you shoot, but in what you do. What counts is the journey, not the destination.

\* \* \*

Back in Palamós by December, Ruark was rested, eager to get to work, "full of his subject," as he wrote to Harold Matson, and aiming to complete the manuscript by April, 1961. To do so, he added, he would be writing at "white heat." All through Christmas he labored away at his typewriter, and the pages piled up. Even as the novel was taking shape, however, many of his old problems returned to haunt him. He was still on the wagon — barely. He was writing his column — just. His health was under control — sort of. Virginia went home to the States to spend the holidays with her family near Washington, leaving him in Palamós. Even with Alan Ritchie for company it was a lonely time, and although

Ruark claimed to love solitude and being on his own, he did not deal well with the loneliness only Christmas can bring.

The long period of abstinence had effectively ended in Africa after about nine months, when he began having wine with meals again, then a sherry or two before dinner, and from there a gradual return to his old ways. There were several reasons for this. According to Harry Selby, this long period on the wagon was the only time in their decade-long friendship that he ever saw Ruark despondent or depressed. Rather than raising his spirits, strict sobriety depressed Ruark. This is contrary to what happens with most alcoholics, who go through an endless round of alcohol-induced happiness alternating with hung-over depression, then renewed drinking to counter the depression. The drinking naturally affects sleep patterns and induces insomnia, and sleep deprivation adds to the depression. This is the cycle that needs to be broken. After the first few days of not drinking, the heavy drinker finds himself sleeping better and awakening each morning feeling considerably improved both physically and mentally. Once this reverse cycle begins, it feeds on itself. The trick, of course, is the first few hours, the first day, the first week. It is obviously more complicated than it sounds, and is never easy.

Ruark acknowledged this pattern in *The Honey Badger*. Alec Barr, though not an alcoholic, purposefully abstains from drinking when he is seriously "stuck into" a book, and Ruark describes in considerable detail the beneficial effects this regimen has for his protagonist. For his part, however, Ruark never stopped wanting a drink. He was not cheered up by sobriety and feared that the lack of alcohol was adversely affecting his imagination and his literary skills. In late 1960, when his doctor in London wrote to him advancing the opinion that Ruark's blackouts in Kenya earlier that year had been due not to booze but to a "glandular fever," it was a license to reach for the Scotch bottle. Privately he may have insisted that he was still restricting himself to a little "dietary wine," but the truth was he quickly slid back into all his old habits.

Once again the demands of writing a novel damaged his column, and now the cumulative effects started to show. Newspapers began running it sporadically or dropped it altogether. Since United Features' revenue was based on usage, and Ruark's own remuneration was based on

United Features' revenue, his income began to suffer along with his reputation. By then Ruark thought of himself (and wanted to be thought of) as a novelist first and foremost, and a serious novelist at that — not merely a producer of slick popular fiction. Trying to be both a national syndicated columnist of the first order and a serious novelist was too much for anyone, even for a writer of Ruark's indisputable energy. Something had to suffer, and in the end everything did. The column declined in quality, circulation, and readership, and the novel went unfinished, missing deadline after deadline. For his part, Ruark continued to drive himself hard. And he continued to drink.

As he labored in Palamós, conditions in much of Africa went from bad to worse. The Congo, especially, was in the headlines day after day. The bodies were piling up as mutinous troops, tribal warriors, and out-and-out thugs fought private wars that soon ceased to have much meaning. Few people understood who was fighting whom, much less over what. The fighting also spilled over into neighboring territories as Congolese troops raided across borders. The main conflict inside the country still pitted the mineral-rich province of Katanga against the central government in Leopoldville. Finally Patrice Lumumba was assassinated, setting the stage for the army chief, Joseph Mobutu, who eventually seized complete control and proceeded to bleed the country dry for the next thirty-five years. Lumumba's death, however, gave Ruark an opportunity for a journalistic epitaph that set a new standard in vitriol. Lumumba may have symbolized everything Ruark disliked about emerging Africans, but he did not embody it: There were plenty more to take over after he departed the scene.

In January, Ruark sent Matson a big chunk of the new manuscript. He evinced great optimism about the direction it was taking and said he was still aiming to have it completed by spring. Matson handed the manuscript over to the editors at Henry Holt & Co. for their opinion. Almost incidentally, amidst all this literary labor, Holt had put together a sequel to the highly successful anthology, *The Old Man and the Boy*. This second volume of *Field & Stream* columns was called *The Old Man's Boy Grows Older*, and it was published in March, 1961.

Two months later Ruark informed Matson that his new novel was finished. He had scrapped the title, *Burnt Offering*, in favor of the Swahili word *Uhuru* — Freedom — that was sweeping East Africa. Like most great titles, in hindsight it is hard to see what else he could have called the book. In early May Ruark boarded a plane in Barcelona and prepared, as had become his custom, to hand over the finished manuscript in person.

Unfortunately, he did not receive a hero's welcome. The editors at Holt were less than enthusiastic about what they had seen. In their opinion, the manuscript required extensive rewriting before it could be published. It was too long. It was too expository. It had to be cut, and most of what was left would need thorough revisions. This criticism was not what Ruark had expected or wanted to hear. Harold Matson, seeing what was happening, began to consider looking for a new publisher. This search led him to McGraw-Hill. Ruark, meanwhile, rather grudgingly accepted Holt's request for revisions — their contractual demand, actually — and decamped to Florida to spend several weeks going over the manuscript, assisted by one of his former secretaries from the New York days. In June he came back to New York, handed over the revised manuscript, and caught a plane for points east: Spain first, then Nairobi. He was planning to meet Harry Selby to set off on a safari into the Northern Frontier District, the desert region of northern Kenya that was known for its warlike tribes and its big tuskers. A new remote area had just been opened for safaris, limited to foot, camel, and horse-back — no safari cars — and the two friends wanted to be the first to see it with gun in hand. Professional hunter John Sutton — "Little John" of Ruark's writings — noted tersely in his diary for Saturday, June 24, 1961: "Ruark arrives 8:15."

* * *

On July 1, 1961, the new area opened up for hunting. On that same morning, ten thousand miles away in Ketchum, Idaho, Ernest Hemingway held the muzzles of his Boss game gun to his forehead and tripped the trigger. Ruark was in Kenya when he received the news, just back from a quick flying trip to the Masai Mara before heading north into the NFD. There are conflicting accounts of how he was given the news, and also his reaction to it. According to Ruark's published accounts, he climbed out of an airplane and was handed a newspaper story. According to Harry Selby, they were at the Mount Kenya Safari Club having a drink. Then there is the reaction: Ruark claims to have been shocked and saddened; Selby insists he was almost elated, shouting, "You know what this means? It means I'm the herd bull now!" Regardless of Ruark's initial reaction, however, what he subsequently wrote in his newspaper column and in magazine articles, and later in *The Honey Badger*, was sincere and eloquent. He may have seen Hemingway as a rival, but he never denigrated Hemingway's writing or his place in the modern world of literature, and his tributes to "the master" were heart-felt.

\* \* \*

*Chapter Eleven*

# RUARK & HEMINGWAY

Throughout his serious writing career, Robert Ruark found himself being compared with Ernest Hemingway. The early references were mostly flattering; in later years, they were denigrating. And so Ruark's attitude toward Hemingway varied from ambiguous to venomous. While he always professed to revere "the master's" writing, he eventually came almost to hate what he represented, because the long Hemingway shadow was always falling in the way of Ruark's own ambition.

This was more than mere rivalry between two writers. And even the most rabid Ruark admirer would admit that, in terms of literature, he was not and never could be a rival for Hemingway, whose impact on prose changed the English language. The problem for Ruark was that everything Hemingway touched became, in the public mind, his intellectual property. This created an immense obstacle for any writer coming later who wanted to write about the same subjects.

To understand this, it is necessary to appreciate the stature that Ernest Hemingway enjoyed in the 1950s, not just in the United States, but all over the English-speaking world and much of the rest of the world as well. He was a genuine personality, a man whose life was just as much a public property as his work. Hemingway's name was in the gossip columns, and his picture appeared regularly on magazine covers. Even when he published a book that was mediocre, or that received negative reviews, his critics gained stature just from being his enemies. Today, with celebrity measured in fifteen-minute segments according to

Andy Warhol's formula, Hemingway's overpowering presence, combined with his longevity — almost forty years in the limelight — is difficult to comprehend.

Looking back, however, it is easy to see why Hemingway became what he was: He possessed both a profound talent for writing and a powerful, magnetic personality. He made people want to be with him, to emulate him, compete with him, or beat him. People not only wanted to read what he wrote, they wanted to read what others wrote about him. Other writers attained literary success, and other personalities became great celebrities, but no one combined the two the way Hemingway did. He may or may not have been the greatest prose stylist of his time, but he was unquestionably the most influential writer in terms of shaping the lives, as well as the styles, of writers who came after him. An entire generation of novelists grew up determined to beat Hemingway, and more than a few destroyed themselves in the process. A considerable number simply drank themselves into oblivion, either by trying to emulate Hemingway in that department, or by drowning their sorrows in the knowledge that they could never be him.

Ernest Hemingway was one of the generation of writers that came out of the literary incubator that was Paris in the 1920s. It was an era that spawned (or tolerated or indulged, depending on your point of view) many experimental writing styles, from James Joyce to Gertrude Stein. After the florid, verbose, obscure styles of many of the Victorians, this new generation of writers wanted to break away and create something new. Most did not last: Gertrude Stein, for example, is both unread and unreadable — an academic footnote to literature; James Joyce is more revered than read, except among a small few; Ezra Pound is respected more for his influence on poetry than for the actual poems he wrote. Hemingway's only serious rival as a novelist, F. Scott Fitzgerald, left one major work, *The Great Gatsby*. Only Ernest Hemingway, who chose clarity as his goal over opacity, and who pursued economy of words rather than expansive, repetitive prose, comes out of the century with his reputation intact.

Hemingway's style was essentially journalistic. He conveyed basic emotions by describing specific details so truly that the larger picture would take shape of its own accord in the reader's mind. The key to doing this was to experience the emotions and recognize them for what they were. Equally important, as he pointed out more than once, was knowing what to leave out. In his search for material he lived a voracious life, travelling and experiencing everything he could. While other writers lounged around cafes in Paris, he was glacier skiing in the Austrian Alps; while they drank late into the night, he was in Pamplona studying the cape work of the matadors. Fitzgerald might be passed out in a saloon, but Hemingway was in the foothills of the Pyrenees with his fly rod, with a bottle of wine chilling in a mountain stream.

Given his personality, it was only natural that the things he did would be of just as much interest as the things he wrote; from there, it was a short step for people to try to gain some of the same *cachet* by following in his footsteps. The ranks of Hemingway imitators began to grow almost from the time he achieved his first literary success in the 1920s. During an early visit to Pamplona for the Fiesta of San Fermín, Hemingway and his wife, Hadley, were the only foreigners in attendance; today, eighty years after that first glimpse and almost forty years after his death, the running of the bulls in Pamplona is Spain's largest single tourist attraction — all due to Hemingway.

Ernest Hemingway broke ranks with the other writers of his time, and with the Victorians before him, by writing about very basic things — supposedly unintellectual pursuits like hunting and fishing. Hunting, fishing, and bullfighting are all concerned with life and death, and with a man's or an animal's behavior in the face of death, all of which fascinated Hemingway. In his early short stories he wrote about hunting and fishing; in 1929, he published a full-length nonfiction book, *Death in the Afternoon*, which dealt at length with the arcane pastime of bullfighting in Spain. In the mid-1930s, he wrote *Green Hills of Africa*, a book about a big-game hunting safari. Such was his reputation and influence, once he had written about a subject it became, in the minds of the public and the critics, his own personal property for all time. Every writer since who has attempted to write about these subjects has found himself running headlong into the Hemingway mystique. First the writer's work is compared with Hemingway's, usually to its detriment, then the writer himself is accused of trying to emulate Hemingway. It is a trap that refuses to go away.

* * *

In 1953, Robert Ruark published his first serious book, *Horn of the Hunter*. In a review in *Newsweek*, a critic mentioned Ruark's status as a columnist, called the book "independently deserving" as an account of an African safari, and then rather shrewdly concluded that Ruark's ambitions went beyond recognition as a columnist. He now had his sights set on "a mark (established) by a hairy-chested fisherman and hunter now resident in Cuba and named Ernest Hemingway." The reviewer then went on about the mysticism Ruark and Hemingway had discovered in big game hunting, as well as in bullfighting. If the *corrida* was a passion Ruark "shared" with Hemingway, as was alleged, it was one he had kept well hidden until this point.

Although Ruark later professed to be irritated with the constant comparisons, there is no question that he brought them upon himself. First, in *Horn of the Hunter*, he recalls seeing Hemingway before the war, in the Floridita Cafe in Havana. He tells how he was there for two weeks and saw Hemingway almost every day, sitting in a corner reading *El Diario*, and how he, Ruark, was "too shy or too proud" to go over and introduce himself, or to have Constante (the proprietor) introduce them. He even mentions he had been told he looked like Hemingway in his younger days — at least he had a moustache, just as Hemingway had one when he was young. Consciously or unconsciously, Ruark invited — indeed, almost begged for — the comparison which the reviewer duly made. At the time, Ruark was no doubt flattered and gratified. Once out of the bottle, however, this particular *gini* could never be made to climb back in; he grew bigger with every subsequent safari and book, and was always there, looking over Ruark's shoulder.

*Horn of the Hunter* was published in mid-1953; in August of that year, Ruark wrote a column in which he told of meeting Hemingway in Pamplona a month earlier, during the fiesta. According to the column, the pair attended a bullfight together, in which the star performer was Antonio Ordóñez. Many years later, Ruark referred to the meeting as the time he and Hemingway "got notably drunk together." From that time on, he said, "we corresponded occasionally." According to Ruark, "We were friends; I greatly admired some of his work. But we were not close friends."

Hemingway's life has been exhaustively documented; books were written about him while he was alive, and many more after he was dead. There are complete biographies as well as biographical works covering specific periods of his life, such as the years in Paris. His major biographer, Professor Carlos Baker, also published his collected letters and included correspondence with people both famous and obscure. Nowhere in this vast documentation of the life and times of Ernest Hemingway have I found even the slightest reference to Robert Ruark — no mention of meeting him, no letter from or to "the poor man's Hemingway." Nothing.

This is more than passing strange, because had any such correspondence existed, it would have come to light. By the time Ruark was allegedly corresponding with him, Hemingway was the recipient of the Nobel Prize for Literature. His letters had been collectors' items for some years, and people who received letters from him had been tucking them away for literary posterity, if not financial gain. Given his respect for Hemingway, Ruark would never have destroyed, discarded, or otherwise disposed of any letter he received from him. Ruark's remaining correspondence, down to and including electricity bills for his house in Spain, are stored at the University of North Carolina in Chapel Hill. These have been sifted through and pored over. As well, Ruark's remaining artifacts that were of any worth have been disposed of by his heirs. Again, no Hemingway letter has surfaced.

This is not conclusive proof of anything. Perhaps Ruark and Hemingway did cross paths in Pamplona, and perhaps they even sat together at the bull ring, either by accident or design. At this late date, no one will ever know for certain.

\* \* \*

Robert Ruark wrote about Ernest Hemingway many times over the years, first in his newspaper column and later in retrospective magazine articles. One of the earliest pieces is a column he wrote shortly after Hemingway published his first post-war novel, *Across the River and into the Trees,* in 1950. The novel is short — almost a novella, really — and tells the story of an American infantry colonel, Richard Cantwell, who is dying of heart disease and spends his last days in Venice with his teenaged Italian sweetheart. Passed over for promotion, Colonel Cantwell is bitter about the treatment he received from the army after the war. For much of the novel, he lectures the girl on life. Without going into detail about personalities, suffice to say the characters in the novel were based upon real-life models, including the British general, Eric Dorman-Smith (Hemingway's old friend "Chink" from his Paris days) and the American soldier, Buck Lanham. The novel was not about war so much as it was about old soldiers. Considering that Hemingway was a war correspondent in Europe and did not actually serve in any military unit during the conflict, and so was unqualified to write a war novel "from within," it is understandable that he would write what he did. He could not tell "how it was" — which was his stock in trade — because he did not really know, first-hand, how it was, and he was honest enough to acknowledge that. No war correspondent, no matter how diligent and self-sacrificing, understands what it is really like to serve in the military in war. This was one area where Ruark did know, and Hemingway did not. But then Hemingway wisely chose to write his war novel on a different subject.

Regardless of the motivation, *Across the River and into the Trees* met with a resounding chorus of boos. On balance, it is one of Hemingway's weakest efforts, and Robert Ruark, in his column, became one of the chorus:

> *I am afraid Papa is getting old. This new one is garrulous as an old man is garrulous, and irritable as an old man is irritable, and kind of patchy in over all hide as a saddle long worn will wear the hair away. His mood is petulant, his plot an incident, and the purpose of his narrative a lecture.*

While Ruark softened his criticism somewhat by praising Hemingway's previous work and noting that "he never wrote a cheap word in the twenty odd years I have worshipped him, while never knowing him," Ruark's words look, half a century later, both patronizing and presumptuous. The column was written in the Winchell-esque gossipy, slangy style he affected for his newspaper pieces and comes across, finally, as simply uncalled-for. It is ironic, too, that in later years Ruark would rant and rave about literary critics and their cheap shots, since he was never loth to use his column for the same purpose.

Three years later — after Ruark's first safari, the alleged meeting in Pamplona, and the publication of *Horn of the Hunter* — Hemingway published *The Old Man and the Sea* and in 1954 was awarded the Nobel Prize for Literature. Ruark reacted with a column that was more congratulation than anything and began by knocking both Sinclair Lewis (for his "drab dramatization of the drab...done drabbily fine") and William Faulkner, America's other recent Nobel laureate. "(Faulkner) has given us the same kind of prose that James Joyce produced, which is to say it is largely incomprehensible to the people who do not .speak unknown tongues." Hemingway, on the other hand, Ruark had always been able to understand "even in his poorer efforts."

Ruark rather shrewdly noted at the time what others have only grasped since, that the Nobel Prize was probably given to Hemingway not just for the one fishing novella, wonderful as it was, but for "a couple of plane crashes" when it should have been given "earlier on other merit." Hemingway had just returned from his second, rather bizarre African safari, during which he had endured some serious physical damage in two airplane crashes. He was reported dead, and the newspapers were carrying his obituaries, when he emerged from the bush, alive if not well. Hemingway, who had been more or less in steady competition with William Faulkner (in his own mind, if not in Faulkner's) for almost thirty years, received the Nobel Prize five years after Faulkner did.

"What Papa got the prize for, it seems to me, was more for being Hemingway than for any particular thing he wrote," Ruark said. "One of his short stories is called *The Undefeated*, and that is Papa all the way. He doesn't quit, and doesn't care what the fellows say in the store."

There was no doubt, he added, "no doubt whatsoever" that Hemingway had had "more lasting effect on prose as she is writ today than anybody who came down the literary pike in the last fifty years. His disdain for cheapness of composition alone would make him worthy of an award."

Ruark then ended the column with a collection of cheaply composed bullfighting analogies about Hemingway being awarded both ears and the tail.

\* \* \*

Over the next half-dozen years, the circumstances for both men changed considerably. After *The Old Man and the Sea*, Hemingway deteriorated both physically and psychologically. By the late 1950s, he was a shell of what he had been. His last major project was a series for *Life* Magazine, which later became the book *The Dangerous Summer*. It was about the rivalry between two matadors, Antonio Ordóñez and Luis Miguel Dominguín, in the 1959 bullfight season. The magazine pieces were widely perceived as a disaster, and the book, when it was eventually cut to size and published in 1985, was not a great deal better.

During the same period, Robert Ruark went from strength to strength. He travelled the world, made at least one safari in Africa every year, wrote one big novel after another, and became recognized as an authority on African affairs. With every novel that was published, however, the comparisons with Hemingway became more vitriolic. The critics did not approve of Ruark's novels, by and large. *Something of Value* and *Uhuru*, his two novels about emerging Africa, did not strike the right political chord with most literary critics. They did not fit the accepted liberal view in America about the oppressed African blacks and their struggle for freedom. The story of the Mau Mau, graphically presented in *Something of Value*, was too bloody and shocking; *Uhuru* contained a lower level of gore, but also struck an ambivalent pose in terms of right and wrong. The view of Kenya, as seen from Manhattan literary salons, was one of clearly delineated principles, not the shades of grey that Ruark recognized more and more in the course of working for a decade, seeing Africa up close.

By 1961, the sneering epithet, "poor man's Hemingway," had become an irritating cross for Ruark to bear, and he seemed to be fighting a running battle with the critics. He complained that he would like to see, just once, a review based on the actual novel, not on the reviewer's views on shooting for sport, or on his opinion of Ruark's "last column on Adlai Stevenson." His resentment of any comparison with Hemingway had become almost palpable.

In a feature written for *True* Magazine in September, 1963, Ruark reflected on his own life as a writer and took the opportunity for a final view of Hemingway, and of what he became later in his life when "the myth obscured the man." Ruark was both harsh and blunt.

"That bullfight thing he did for *Life* was excruciatingly embarrassing for anyone who had known the man and loved the work," he wrote. "It was, at best, a pitiful parody of the style which had made Hemingway famous." He said he was a "reasonably good friend and great admirer" who had never called him "Papa, or Ernie, or Hem." (In fact, Ruark often referred to him as "Papa" in print.) They were both embarrassed, he said, by the title "poor man's Hemingway," which someone had hung on him "possibly because we resembled each other physically, and certainly because my life had followed a similar pattern." Ruark then continued:

> It used to bother me — at least, annoy me — until one day, well taken in wine, Hemingway said: "Look, kid. Screw 'em all. You've been a better reporter, been in better wars, seen more bullfights, shot more big game, know more about Africa, lived longer in Spain, seen more of the world...."

The passage went on in the same vein, with Hemingway allegedly telling Ruark all the areas in which he had outdone "the master." It finished, rather lamely, with the comment that Ruark would "probably write more books, although I doubt if any will be as good as my best or as bad as my worst." If Ernest Hemingway ever actually said that to Robert Ruark, there is no known documentary evidence, and anyone who believes that Ernest Hemingway would actually say that to anyone, regardless of his wine intake, would believe almost anything. A better reporter? Better wars? More bullfights? Even if it were true — and that is debatable — it would take a man who had been seriously keeping score to utter such a thing, and the man who had been keeping score was not Ernest Hemingway, it was Robert Ruark.

\* \* \*

Ruark was in Africa when word arrived, in early July, 1961, that Ernest Hemingway had shot himself. There are conflicting reports about where and how he heard the news, and radically different versions of his reaction to it. Ruark's thoughts as he expressed them to his friends, and those he committed to paper for publication, were not necessarily identical. To deal with the less worthy first, Harry Selby recalled many years later that he and Ruark were with a group of people at the Mount Kenya Safari Club — "Bill Holden was there; it was the night they decided to buy the place" — when they heard the news. Ruark's reaction, according to Selby, was almost jubilant. "You know what this means?" he shouted. "It means I'm the herd bull now." If by that Ruark meant that he would now be recognized as the pre-eminent writer on Africa, free of Hemingway's looming presence, he was dead wrong.

By contrast, in print for all to see, Ruark reported that he was handed a newspaper with the news of the suicide when he stepped out of a plane at a remote airstrip in Kenya. "Your friend Hemingway just shot himself," he says he was told. Regardless of how he heard, however, he wrote several tributes for publication, first in the New York *World Telegram and Sun* and later in *Field & Stream*. All were devoid of any resentment. They were written quietly, sincerely, and with a great sensitivity completely unlike the usual slang-ridden, wise-guy language of his newspaper column. He made the point that, at heart, Hemingway was a very simple man who enjoyed doing simple things, like fishing and drinking wine, but doing them as well as he could. Also, he pointed out, Hemingway was not a phony. He did the things he did because those were the things he liked doing.

Ruark added, from the vantage point of personal knowledge, that there was a considerable element of ham actor in Hemingway, just as there is in any writer, because "A writing man must of bitter necessity be acutely conscious of himself in relation to the things in the world in which he moves. Any author is all 'me,' or he wouldn't be an author," Ruark wrote. And when he did so, he was describing himself as much as Hemingway.

\* \* \*

Ruark's most penetrating analysis occurs in *The Honey Badger*. The hero, Alec Barr, is portrayed as a friend, although Hemingway does not make an actual appearance. Like Ruark, Barr is afflicted by constant comparisons with Hemingway; at one point, his lover, Barbara Bayne, needles him with not being "the *real* tough writer." Later, Barr discusses Hemingway's death with his secretary, Luke, and later still his writing with another lover, Jill Richard.

Sitting by the fire in her London townhouse, Alec and Jill are discussing Africa, a subject on which both Barr and Ruark were recognized authorities. The inevitable comparison arises, and Jill remarks that Hemingway caught some of Barr's complex feelings for Africa in his two short stories, *The Snows of Kilimanjaro* and *The Short Happy Life of Francis Macomber*. Barr agrees, to a point, but suggests that he got it "superficially." Hemingway, he says, was never in Africa long enough at one stretch and was always on "some sort of houseparty, with a new woman and a reputation for he-mannishness to maintain."

This is a very good point. It is a measure of Hemingway's overpowering personality that his name is irrevocably connected with Africa, yet he spent relatively little time there, and only a fraction of his work is either connected with Africa or has an African setting. He was there on safari in 1933, with his second wife, Pauline Pfeiffer. Out of that three-month trip came *Green Hills of Africa* and those two short stories. A third short story, *An African Story*, appears within the novel *The Garden of Eden*, which was published in 1986. Although *Green Hills* is not among Hemingway's best work, the two short stories most definitely are. *Macomber* has been described as "the perfect short story," while the more complex *Snows of Kilimanjaro* almost defines the contradictory nature of the continent, the irresistible yet often fatal nature of its attraction, and the forces that drive men to become what they are, and what they are not. Given the brevity of his experience in Africa at the time, it is remarkable Hemingway could have absorbed all this and then turned it into literature in the way he did. Ruark spent considerably more time in Africa over a twelve-year period, saw far more of the continent, and certainly knew more about its history and culture, but he never wrote anything that was even remotely comparable.

For all that, however, as Alec Barr points out to Jill Richard, Hemingway was not an authority on Africa and should not be considered one. The major strike against him was the fact that he never hunted elephant, "any more than he was ever really in a war." Hunting elephant was not merely a matter of shooting a large animal. To Ruark, by that time, elephant hunting was the dividing line between those who knew and those who did not. There are two kinds of war, he says: those for "volunteer ambulance drivers on a joke front and famous war correspondents who roar in for the kill after the real fighting's over," and the other kind, where "you smell bad and don't have any whiskey and may or may not trip over your own guts, physical and mental." Barr softens the criticism with a self-deprecating assessment of his own war — "I heard shots fired in anger, but fled in fear and won no medals" — which understates his actual war record by a considerable margin.

On Ruark's first safari, he told his outfitters he had no interest in hunting elephant, since anything that God took so long to make he did not want to be involved in pulling down. Later he did hunt elephant, of course, and killed several bulls, including two with tusks of more than a hundred pounds. Even in the early 1960s, that was a rare feat. It is interesting to note that *An African Story*, good though it is in some ways, deals with elephant hunting — something Hemingway had never done — and the man who prided himself on telling of things as they were failed precisely because he did not really know what it entailed.

There is a widespread tendency today to make elephants into something they are not; while elephants are undoubtedly intelligent creatures with great longevity and a complicated social structure, they are not demigods. What's more, people who live in close proximity to elephants, who have their crops trampled and their huts pulled apart and a brother or an aunt destroyed by a furious elephant, regard them with fear and hatred more than awe. Being chased by an elephant, either a lone bull or a breeding herd of ill-tempered females bent on your destruction, gives a person a different view of this "masterpiece of God's creation." Elephants are huge and powerful, sometimes intelligent, sometimes bad-tempered, and almost always destructive. In the old days, elephants were free to roam the length and breadth of Africa, and their activities helped to regenerate areas through which they passed, pulling down trees and uprooting bushes, creating new little ecosystems. Today, when they are confined to small areas, they relentlessly destroy their environment and ultimately themselves, as well as almost everything else that lives there, directly or indirectly.

Elephants can be a powerful metaphor for many things. The old elephant of Illaut, which Ruark and Harry Selby shot on one of his last safaris, is immortalized in *The Honey Badger* and used as a metaphor for the passing of the Africa he loved; equally, it is a metaphor for Ernest Hemingway. "I did for the old elephant what Hemingway did for himself," Barr says.

Perhaps by the time he wrote *The Honey Badger* Ruark's resentment had softened, or he no longer had the same sense of being in competition. Whatever the reason, Barr's views are considerably more temperate, and light-years more insightful, than those expressed by Ruark in his newspaper column. First of all, he notes that Hemingway invented a whole new world and then died for it. He compares him with the war correspondent Ernie Pyle, who was killed on the island of Ie Shima near the end of the war in the Pacific; although Pyle was killed by a Japanese soldier and Hemingway died by his own hand, there was very little difference in method, Barr says.

"We all come from other places, other times," he tells Luke. "Some people belong to a particular epoch, an era, like a war. Some people can only find themselves in the time of their involuntary choosing. Some never find themselves at all.

"(Both Hemingway and Pyle) gave themselves wholly to a time. They both more or less died...for their *age*, for their *time*."

Hemingway, he said, had hung around too long, like the old elephant at the waterhole at Illaut. Although the passage is a eulogy for Hemingway, it can just as easily be read as a eulogy for Ruark. He too only found himself in a particular place, during a particular epoch — Africa in the post-war, pre-independence era — and both writers were facing the prospect of becoming superannuated in a changing world.

In the end, through Alec Barr, Robert Ruark expresses a considerable amount of sympathy for Ernest Hemingway, perhaps because he found himself facing exactly the same fate.

❊ ❊ ❊

*Chapter Twelve*

# EXPLORATION
# & FAREWELL

Ruark and Selby set off north, eventually reaching the new, virgin hunting territory they would be the first to explore. This part of Kenya is a stark contrast both to the lush plains of the Masai Mara and to the bright lights of Nairobi. It is a desert, populated by warlike tribes who live hard lives. The Turkana and the Samburu spend their days herding goats and raiding back and forth. Throughout history they have fought the Karamojong in Uganda to the west, the Ethiopians from the north, and the Somalis from the east. When not fighting intruders, they fight among themselves. Foremost among the animals that populated the NFD were herds of elephant, mostly gone now because of poaching. In Ruark's day, however, it was famous for big tuskers. Very few people had even seen most of the NFD. Large sections of it were closed to hunting, and even to routine travel, because of tribal raiding and the depredations of gangs of armed *shiftas*. Today (1999) the NFD is again closed to almost all traffic, for these same reasons.

This was not the first time Ruark had undertaken a journey of exploration disguised as a safari. The previous year, he and Selby had mounted a major expedition into the Karamoja of northeastern Uganda. Together with professional hunters John Sutton and Don Bousfield, and accompanied by two other American couples, they hunted a region that had been closed to sporting safaris for half a century. The Karamoja is remote and rugged; whereas most of Uganda is tropical and green, the Karamoja is a land of bare rocks and far horizons, populated by a tribe — the

Karamojong — noted for being unfriendly. The name, of course, is familiar to all hunters because it was the nickname of Walter Dalrymple Maitland Bell. Karamoja Bell was one of the most famous elephant hunters, a Scot who ranged through Uganda up into the Lado Enclave of the southern Sudan in his quest for big ivory. Bell is particularly noted for preferring a smallbore rifle rather than a big elephant gun, and for shooting for the brain with pinpoint accuracy. Ruark's safari into the Karamoja had special significance because he had bought Bell's own rifle, a bolt-action .275 Rigby, in London. He described the rifle and the safari in some detail in an article in *Field & Stream* titled "Sentimental Safari," which appeared in August, 1961.

Aside from the rifle, the article is noteworthy for its tone. Ruark's descriptions of his safaris had begun a subtle transition in the late 1950s. Instead of dwelling on the hunting aspects, the killing, or the size of the trophies, he now emphasized the almost therapeutic value of safaris, the joy of just seeing new country or of showing country he knew intimately to people who had never seen it. In a 1958 piece in *Field & Stream*, "The Babysitting Was Just Fine Last Year," he talked about conducting a trip for three youngsters, the children of Ricardo Sicré and Harold Matson. In "Sentimental Safari," his American friends were seeing Africa for the first time, and Ruark set himself up less as a fellow client than as an unofficial extra professional hunter. In this sense, he was undergoing a transformation from the "Boy" of his stories to the "Old Man." He was now Bwana Bob, the old Africa hand, who could have taken out safaris himself were it not for the technicality of not having a professional's license. Although this tendency became more pronounced later, and rubbed many people the wrong way (even today, professional hunters insist he overstepped himself and was not nearly so knowledgeable as he made out), in his writing he came across as more appreciative of the finer aspects of safaris and less of the bloodshed.

One of the best articles he ever wrote was one about trophy hunting in which he looked at the philosophical aspects of the chase. Ever since Hemingway made the pursuit of greater kudu, in *Green Hills of Africa*, a metaphor for obsession (and for all the worst competitive aspects of trophy hunting), the all-consuming desire for horns an extra inch longer has been one of the sicknesses of hunting. Ruark pointed out that, as often as not, the biggest heads are killed by accident, by meat hunters looking for a steak or by natives defending their mealie crop. Rarely, he said, were the number-one heads shot by serious men who set out to do it. He cited several examples to prove his point, including one Kenya bongo, killed by a farmer, that was good enough for number two in the all-time records. Whether this ironic tendency is a little joke enjoyed by the gods of hunting, or just coincidence, Ruark wrote that the most important element of trophy hunting is not the horns you bring back, but the work you put into it.

*If you have learned nothing else from hunting, you have learned patience and stubbornness and concentration on what you really want at the expense of what is there to shoot. You have learned that man can as easily be debased as ennobled by a sport...*

In 1959, Ruark's friend Bob Lee was in Kenya hunting bongo, the elusive, reclusive spiral-horned antelope of the high Aberdares. Lee is a wealthy businessman today, but in the late 1950s he was a young man in love with hunting who was busy pursuing every animal on the African continent. He was also a noted Manhattan playboy, for lack of a better term. Around 1960 he started his own safari business in Nairobi, was the first outfitter to open up the Portuguese colonies of Mozambique and Angola, and took Ruark to Mozambique on the first major commercial safari a few years later. In 1959, though, the two were acquaintances who shared many of the same interests (wine, women, and bongo, mainly) and rubbed shoulders in some of the more exotic watering holes of the world. Lee tells the story of hunting bongo with Fred Bartlett, the famous PH, of "lucking into" a trophy animal and coming back down off the mountain, out of the cold and dripping bamboo forests, with a serious desire for a hot shower, clean sheets, and a good meal at the New Stanley Grill. Ruark happened to be in town at the time and undertook to organize a party to celebrate Lee's bongo. In the hotel's wine cellar he unearthed a cache of Chambolle-Musigny, Lee's favorite wine, and Jack Block, the hotel's owner, unleashed his chef on the backstrap of the bongo. The party that followed was small in numbers — just eight or nine friends — but large in quality. Having the best chef in Africa prepare one of the rarest cuts of meat, and washing it down with one of the finer French wines, is not an everyday occurrence.

In the case of the bongo, both males and females carry horns, and both are legitimate trophies. Lee, however, wanted a bull bongo, and since the animal he took was a large cow, he returned to the Aberdares the following year and the year after, trying to get a bull. He never succeeded. As Ruark wrote, however, "None of it is any good unless you work for it, and if the work is hard enough you do not really have to possess the trophy to own it." For that insight alone, Ruark deserves to be regarded as one of the finest hunting writers of all time.

Ruark also began to write specifically about game conservation. The prospects for Africa's game herds when countries like Tanganyika achieved independence were becoming a concern for the professional hunters and game wardens Ruark knew so well. Black Africans are not noted for their devotion to conservation or preservation of wild species, and more than one politician had stated bluntly that there could be no modern future for Africa until the hunters and the animals they hunted had been gotten rid of. To black socialist politicians with degrees from the London School of Economics, hunting was an anachronism and hunters were enemies of the state. The lions and the herds of wildebeest would go, to be replaced by communal farms in the best left-wing theoretical mold. Such a prospect moved Ruark to write about the animals, not as game but as a great natural resource Africans should cherish and protect. Once again, Ruark's vision of the future was disturbingly, tragically accurate.

* * *

The safari into the NFD in July, 1961, was for Ruark more than simply a hunting trip after a big elephant. After the fact, he wrote that he had intended to use it as an opportunity to write an epitaph for the Africa he had known and loved, that was in the process of disintegrating. That may well have been. Ernest Hemingway's death gave him an even more personal and immediate event upon which to hang a metaphorical eulogy. Ruark and Selby did find the elephant they were looking for, at a waterhole near the village of Illaut. He was an old, old elephant, eking out a sad existence by himself, waiting for death — from starvation or, as Ruark suggested, from "purest boredom." The hunters were told of his existence by a young Samburu girl, and when Ruark shot him they paid her a reward. Ruark wrote an account of how her relatives, or at least those claiming to be close family friends, tried to defraud her out of the money, and the story works well as a microcosm of life in Africa — or anywhere else, for that matter, where people have older brothers and close family friends.

The old elephant of Illaut provided Ruark with everything he was looking for: a symbol of a passing age that became a metaphor for Africa, for Hemingway, and even for himself. His account of the elephant's life and death appeared first in a newspaper column, then in several magazine articles, and finally — in its most eloquent and refined version — in *The Honey Badger*. One line from an earlier version is memorable, however: "When the green hills of Africa go brown and change afflicts the land, and the old good things are no longer as they were, there are worse memorials to a great life than a book or a tusk."

\* \* \*

The death of Hemingway and of the ancient elephant, and the impending death of Kenya Colony as Ruark had known it, marked the end of one chapter in his life. In New York another chapter was also drawing to a close.

Harold Matson's negotiations with Holt and McGraw-Hill had reached a conclusion. After receiving a long and detailed letter from the editors at Holt about the changes they required in *Uhuru* before they would consider publishing it, Matson recommended that Ruark accept the alternative offer from McGraw-Hill. Oddly enough, the editors at McGraw-Hill had many of the same reservations — especially regarding the novel's inordinate length — but they were lavish in their praise of Ruark both as a novelist and as an authority on Africa, and on the impact they foresaw for *Uhuru* as one of the "most important" novels of the latter part of the twentieth century. They wanted Ruark to cut about four hundred pages from the manuscript, however, and they knew the work would take time. They were prepared to wait and planned to publish the book in 1962. The delay, they said, would not lessen its value by any means. In fact, they pointed out, trying to have the novel coincide with current events actually diminished it. Matson wrote to Ruark in Africa, apprising him of the negotiations and recommending he accept McGraw-Hill's offer, which was actually a multi-book deal that would allow him to construct the series of novels he had in mind. Ruark cabled his acceptance, finished his safari, returned to Spain to finish the revisions, and then went on to New York.

Ruark's visit to New York in September was very stressful both professionally and personally. Aside from ending a long-standing relationship with one publisher (Holt) and the elation of beginning a new one with McGraw-Hill, Ruark also resigned from *Field & Stream*. The "Old Man" series had run its course; in fact, in recent years that theme had been dropped as Ruark wrote more and more about his current-day adventures. Hugh Foster says that, ultimately, the decision to leave Holt was more commercial than artistic: McGraw-Hill demanded virtually the same revisions to *Uhuru*, but was prepared to offer a great deal more money to get them and to bag Ruark as an author for future books. According to Foster, the deal was worth a quarter-million dollars guaranteed for a five-book package, and Ruark would be able to borrow against the contract in the meantime. This, as it turned out, was a two-edged sword. Although the financial security allowed Ruark to slacken off on his magazine work, taking advantage of the loan facility bound him ever more tightly to McGraw-Hill regardless of what happened.

Ruark's own expenses, always high, were about to get higher. In North Carolina, his parents were deteriorating physically and mentally. They had moved into the old Adkins house in Southport and received an allowance Matson sent once a month, but there was never enough money to satisfy their alcohol and drug addictions, to say nothing of the frequent hospital confinements and long-distance ambulance rides brought on by their illnesses, both real and imagined. They took to borrowing money from anyone and everyone, and never, ever, paid anything back. This tendency did not damage their reputations so much as that of their rich and famous son, who was seen by the residents of Southport and Wilmington as not fulfilling his filial obligations. Naturally, Ruark was enraged at receiving letters demanding repayments of his parents' debts and being accused of leaving them to rot while he jet-setted the world. He was "bleeding himself white" supporting them, he rather hyperbolically described it. The problem was dealt with in typical Ruark fashion: He increased their monthly allowance to $500 but informed them there would be no further increase or extraordinary payments, and he followed this up with advertisements in the local newspapers advising that he would not be responsible for his parents' debts. This was a shocking step to take in the old-fashioned world of small-town North Carolina, and several acquaintances wrote to him, accusing him of shirking his responsibility to his parents. When Matson received a letter from the elder Ruark's doctor advising him the old man was dying of lung disease, Ruark wrote a letter to his parents bluntly telling them they would have to get by on what he sent and nothing more. "I have discharged my responsibility as son and sucker," he wrote.

\* \* \*

The deal with McGraw-Hill was signed, the first checks were cashed, and *Uhuru* was scheduled for publication in June, 1962. The Book-of-the-Month Club chose the book as its main selection for July, and Harold Matson began scouting out a paperback contract. Even as the money and acclaim piled up, however, Ruark was facing some severe personal problems. He was back on the bottle in a big way, as was Virginia, and her alcoholism was becoming serious.

Kenya was now well on the road to independence. The British colonial office was hoping to have a constitution hammered out by July of 1962, with elections later that year and nationhood by the beginning of 1963. For Kenya's 60,000 whites, the future was forbidding. Property values in the colony were depressed, and the majority of settlers had most of their assets tied up in their farms. Even if they could find a buyer, however, the government was making it extremely difficult for them to get their money out of the country. They were damned if they tried to leave and damned if they chose to stay. Ruark wrote a series of columns about the plight of the settlers and the colony's prospects after independence. Needless to say, he was sympathetic to the former and not optimistic about the latter.

Having delivered the final manuscript of *Uhuru*, the Ruarks' plans for 1962 were, first, a hunting trip in India, then on to Nairobi and down to Mozambique on a safari organized by their friend Bob Lee. What actually happened, however, was considerably different.

The main purpose of the trip to India was to hunt leopard, an animal with which Ruark fell in love in his later years in Africa. For Hemingway it had been the greater kudu; for Ruark, in *Horn of the Hunter*, it had been the Cape buffalo. As he spent more and more time in Africa, however, the clever and reclusive nocturnal cat had become his personal favorite. He killed many of them, almost all by the traditional method of baiting. Leopards like to feed at night, emerging very late in the afternoon as the sun goes down. Hunters hang a dead animal in a tree, hoping a leopard will come to feed. Leopards prefer their meat almost rotten, so a carcass in a tree will last several days. The hunters wait in a blind for hours, absolutely motionless, hoping a leopard will show itself while there is still shooting light. Even this description makes it all seem much easier than it is. Sitting motionless in a blind for several hours, with tsetse flies and mosquitoes, is far from easy, and there is never a guarantee the leopard will show, much less that the hunter will get a shot.

Ruark had become a leopard specialist, according to his own writing, and he boasted in print about his ability to pick a likely tree, hang a bait, and attract a big cat. He even went so far as to advise Harry Selby on the proper method of hanging a carcass, which did not go over well. At any rate, in India he would hunt his favorite animal, using different methods on new ground.

India did not have the same strict hunting regulations as Kenya or North America. There the leopard was vermin, to be found and dispatched in the most effective way possible. For a nocturnal animal that usually means jack-lighting — the practice, abhorred in most of North America, of hunting in the dark with a spotlight, which you shine in the animal's eyes. The animal freezes, you aim between the eyes, and that's that. As a North Carolina boy schooled in hunting ethics by the Old Man, Ruark was not a jack-lighter, but when in Rome you do as the Romans do. As his later accounts suggested, what went on in India in the name of hunting in the twenty years immediately after independence was not ethical by modern sport-hunting standards, but when dealing with carnivores like tigers and leopards, which lift cattle and eat human beings, ethics are not an issue. The line becomes considerably blurred, even when the game involves young healthy animals that eat antelope shot by fee-paying tourists with rifles.

Ruark was driving along a dirt track at night with an English hunter, Hugh Allen, when they spotted a large female leopard. Allen caught it in the headlights, and Ruark promptly drilled it with his .30-06, which just as promptly jammed. It did not seem to matter at the time: The leopard was down and motionless with a large hole in her. Having learned the hard way always to put in a finishing shot, Ruark took a shotgun and gave the leopard two blasts of buckshot. According to him, the rifle jammed because of faulty Indian ammunition. The buckshot he used was also of Indian origin, and later examination showed it had barely penetrated the leopard's hide. All of this was unknown at the time, but it accounts for the strange sequence of events. The seemingly dead leopard was in the bushes, and Ruark and Allen were struggling to unjam the rifle, when the leopard emerged at high speed, snarling and very much alive. Ruark raised his arm to guard his face, and the leopard sunk her fangs into it while furiously scrabbling at his belly with her hind claws. Ruark's description of the action was simple and direct:

*As a hunter of big-toothed stuff, I have often wondered about the sensation of close work with a wounded, angry animal. There are no sensations, not even of fear. It is all reactions...*

Allen eventually managed to choke the animal with the barrels of the shotgun, leaving the two hunters to bind each other's wounds and make an excruciatingly painful return to their camp eighteen miles away, where Virginia Ruark was waiting. Among the supplies, Ruark says, were a vital bottle of Dettol, and an equally vital bottle of gin.

His wounds, however, were no joke. The next day his arm was swollen and red, with the skin lacerated and stretched as tightly as a fresh blood sausage. A Swedish missionary pumped him full of penicillin and antitetanus, and he and Virginia caught a plane for Nairobi, where the doctors had ample first-hand experience dealing with the results of leopard hunts gone wrong. Ruark was immediately admitted to Nairobi Hospital and stayed there for the better part of a week. Virginia, who was never a really enthusiastic hunter, had had enough. Rather than wait for him to recover and continue on to Mozambique, she returned to the United States to spend some time with her family. She was also ill at the time, and as soon as she got home she saw a doctor, who diagnosed a variety of ailments related to nerves. The real problem, however, was alcohol.

For his part Ruark got himself out of the hospital, repaired his nerves (if not his liver) with several days of "wild partying," then continued on to Mozambique. People who saw him at the beginning of the safari there, in the hotel at Beira, describe a man who was near the end of his rope — whether from the after-effects of the leopard attack or the cumulative effects of overwork and alcoholism.

It would be a mistake to underestimate the psychological scars of the leopard attack. A serious brush with death of that nature has lasting effects, and Ruark could well have been killed had it not been for his own instincts and the actions of Hugh Allen. The word "trauma" is overused in modern life, but the overwhelming adrenalin rush of such an incident seems to bring on a strange psychological state that takes weeks, if not months, to overcome. Ruark's natural reliance on gin would not help, either. Sometimes, the victim never completely recovers. There are instances of professional hunters surviving serious animal attacks, but being unable to hunt that particular animal afterward. The same is true in bullfighting. A matador is trained from childhood to face bulls in the ring, and he accepts the possibility of being gored with a matter-of-fact fatalism. Each cornada, however, tears away a little more of the psychological fabric that allows him to go on doing it, fight after fight. One day, a matador wakes up to find his courage gone, if not his valor.

It would be remarkable if something similar did not happen to Ruark — if the attack did not leave deep psychological scars. During the final few years of his life, several traits emerged which made him difficult, if not unpleasant, to be around. Most people attribute this to a combination of ego and alcoholism, but that seems unfair. As became his practice, he bestowed the leopard incident on his alter-ego, Alec Barr. He gave him the scars on his forearm and the scars on his stomach where the hind claws ripped, and he also gave him the scars on his psyche that prevented him from really thinking about the attack, keeping it locked away in a hidden vault like a rare and deadly gem.

\* \* \*

# WINDS OF CHANGE:

# *Uhuru*

In his acceptance speech for the 1949 Nobel Prize for Literature, William Faulkner spoke of the great truths that are essential in an enduring work of art. He referred to these themes as "the verities and truths of the heart, the old universal truths lacking which any story is ephemeral and doomed."

Robert Ruark needed such truths to provide a foundation for *Uhuru*. It was this search that caused him so much difficulty in writing the novel, and which took so long (and so many missed deadlines) to resolve. In the end, *Uhuru* dwells on the nature of justice in a country with a system in which true justice is so difficult to define. The result was Ruark's most complex novel, not in its structure (that honor belongs to *The Honey Badger*) so much as in its characters' motivations and inner conflicts. It is an interweaving of many threads that becomes a tapestry depicting the traumatic transition of Kenya — and, by extension, all of Africa — from a tightly run colony to an independent, quasi-democratic country. There are many conflicts in the book, although the basic one is between black people and white people. The conclusion Ruark finally reaches is that, in spite of this, there are no real blacks and whites, but only many different shades of gray.

Each of Ruark's other major novels can be classified relatively easily. *Something of Value* is a classic adventure story with a symmetrical structure. There is a hero, a villain, and a large cast of supporting characters. The Mau Mau cause may or may not be justified, but their methods can never be excused. *Poor No More* is an autobiographical novel whose universal theme (in the Faulknerian sense) is betrayal and the cost of ruthlessness and greed. *The Honey Badger* is an examination of the price of art to the artist himself. In terms of their themes, truths, and values, any of these could have been written by novelists from Tolstoy on down. *Uhuru* is not so easy to classify, mainly because it has a hero with many faults, an anti-hero with many good qualities, villains of several degrees of evil, and many protagonists who are neither wholly good nor wholly evil. If there is a real villain in the book, however, it is not a person, but rather the system that evolved in Kenya over the course of sixty years and created tragic, irreconcilable differences among its people. No matter how the book ends, justice will not be served because it cannot be.

* * *

When Ruark first conceived his great novel of emerging Africa, it was projected as a direct sequel to *Something of Value*. Unfortunately, he found himself restricted by the characters he had already created in the earlier book. The McKenzie family had been drawn with a fine hand, and there was no room for later alterations to fit the demands of the new plot. Consequently, Ruark had to abandon his original idea. The Nightingale family provided him with a cast of models, as well as the basic philosophies of the moderate white element in Kenya, so he created new characters to fit the plot based upon some of them.

Many readers open *Uhuru* expecting to find a professional hunter as the hero. They do find a PH — Brian Dermott — but he is not the hero nor even the major character. What's more, because he was partly drawn from Peter McKenzie, who in turn was based on Harry Selby, there are similarities among the three, but in Dermott's case disturbing differences as well. Anyone approaching *Uhuru* with preconceived notions about plot and characters will have some difficulty fitting Dermott into his expectations. This, I believe, accounts for the ambivalence toward *Uhuru* that has existed since its publication and which is even more pronounced today. Ruark's admirers are now mainly hunters and people with a strong interest in Africa and animals, and Brian Dermott does not fit their idealized image of the professional hunter. He is not larger than life. He has serious failings that outweigh his virtues, and his role is to provide the pivot point that forces the real hero, the Kikuyu lawyer/politician Stephen Ndegwa, to choose between doing what is right for his country and doing what is beneficial for himself.

The novel opens in the summer of 1960. Kenya is approaching independence, and Jomo Kenyatta is still in prison. Various black political parties are jockeying for position. Their leaders are busy forming alliances and just as readily abandoning them, hoping to win power when the British pull out. The white settlers are watching events with serious trepidation. The more extreme element is talking about a pre-emptive strike — unilateral independence in the Rhodesian mold — or armed resistance to black rule, or at the very least, preparation to resist if necessary. Moderate whites are looking for a way to save what they can by cooperating with moderate blacks in forming a country which is tolerant of racial differences.

The first part of the novel focuses on the hanging, in August 1960, of the young white Kenya police reservist, Peter Poole, for the murder of a black man in Nairobi. Until then, no white had ever been executed for killing a black. In fact, in Kenya executions of white people were almost unknown, even for murdering another white. There were demonstrably different standards of sentencing, depending on the killer's race. There was no question Poole was guilty. The only contentious issue was whether the killing had been premeditated. If not, it was believed, there were grounds for requesting the British government to commute the sentence to a long imprisonment. The Poole case, in the novel as in real life, was symbolic for both sides and placed the British government in an impossible position. If Poole died, it faced the possibility of armed revolt by the white settlers; if Poole was reprieved, it would poison relations between Britain and whichever black party achieved power after independence. There was no possible compromise.

Of course, by this time, sympathy for the Kenya settlers in Britain was minimal. The colonial office viewed them as a bunch of drunken, wife-swapping troublemakers, who were forever demanding this and complaining about that, and generally obstructing attempts by London to govern the colony in the best interests of the entire population, not just one segment. This view of the settlers was promoted by the anti-colonial media and drew on fifty years of Kenya's reputation as the adultery and alcohol capital of the empire. Whether the judgement was fair is irrelevant. The result was the increasing isolation of Kenya's sixty thousand white settlers, who felt betrayed by the British government and friendless in an anti-imperial world.

The story begins with Brian Dermott driving into Nairobi to meet two new clients arriving at Embakasi Airport. Very quickly we learn that Dermott is an alcoholic, who is subject to strange fits when he drinks and has been on the wagon for six months. His doctor has told him he must give up drinking or face an early death. This is almost exactly Ruark's own situation when he was writing the novel, and he imposes his condition on Dermott, detail for detail. Dermott is part of a family of land-owning white settlers with a farm near Mount Kenya. He is divorced, and his ex-wife, Valerie, lives in London. She is Kenyan by birth, but the Mau Mau Emergency proved she was not Kenyan by inclination, and she has fled to the safety of "home."

Dermott's clients are a wealthy American, Paul Drake, and his sister, Katie Crane. Katie is also a divorced alcoholic on the wagon. A suicide attempt failed, and her brother has brought her on safari in the hope of rekindling her enthusiasm for life. Dermott and Katie are two sides of the same coin — damaged people at odds with their world. The safari leaves town, has a very successful beginning, and Dermott suggests the clients take a day to relax while he drives back into Nairobi. He wants to be present for the hanging of Peter Poole and whatever that event brings — or does not. Back in Nairobi Dermott has one drink, then another, and is soon off the wagon. His partner, Don Bruce, another professional hunter and ex-Mau Mau fighter, asks Dermott if he would buy his farm. Bruce has learned his infant son has been tagged for human sacrifice by the black underworld carrying on with the remnants of Mau Mau, and he wants to get his family out of the country.

At dinner that night, Dermott becomes drunk and belligerent, deliberately insulting black people who are dining in the Grill Room at the New Stanley Hotel — an enclave that was previously "whites only." Among the diners are three black political leaders: Matthew Kamau, Abraham Matisia, and Stephen Ndegwa. Kamau and Ndegwa are leaders of rival parties, in an uneasy alliance; Matisia is Kamau's enforcer, a smoothly evil, educated African, greedy for everything the white man has that he does not. Kamau is an ascetic, mission-educated Kikuyu who takes the high road uttering fine words while Matisia does the dirty work he acknowledges but would rather not know about. Ndegwa is a lawyer, a pragmatic Kikuyu who straddles the cultural divide, keeping his traditional Kikuyu wives in their *shambas* on the Reserve while having a westernized, *café crème* wife in a modern house in the suburbs. He has a law partner, a wealthy Asian named Vidhya Mukerjee, who gives him access to the third pillar of Kenyan society.

These are the main characters who make the plot work. Ruark draws in all the various types who then inhabited Kenya: Asians, Belgian refugees, extremist whites, cynical, educated blacks, traditional Kikuyus, politicians, recently arrived Englishmen anxious to tell the settlers what they should do, and moderate settlers fearful of the future but determined to stay in the land they created. Because of the number of characters and subplots, it is difficult to give a brief synopsis of the story, following every thread through which Ruark creates his portrait of Kenya.

Dermott fights the bottle and watches his country deteriorate. He proves to have a strong streak of intolerance, both of black politicians and people like his English brother-in-law, George Locke. Locke is a physician who now lives on the family farm and has all kinds of "progressive" ideas about how the farm, and the fledgling country, should be run, just as he prescribes how Dermott should quell his drinking. Dermott eventually falls in love with Katie Crane, but Katie is killed by Matisia's terrorists when they kidnap a small Kikuyu boy for sacrifice in an oathing ceremony, part of their program to sabotage the moderate elements who would defuse their plans for the country. In revenge, Dermott shoots and kills Matthew Kamau on Delamere Avenue outside the New Stanley Hotel. He is arrested for murder.

Stephen Ndegwa, meanwhile, has been drawn into a plan by the moderates, led by Dermott's Aunt Charlotte, for a land-sharing, profit-sharing scheme they hope will satisfy the requirements of both whites and blacks in an independent Kenya. The plan is sabotaged by Matisia's men, but a Belgian woman, Matisia's mistress, passes information to Ndegwa about the machinations of Kamau and Matisia. The lawyer is thus put in a position to destroy his political rivals and place himself in line for political power. After Kamau's murder, however, Brian Dermott's brother approaches Ndegwa and asks him to defend Dermott when he goes on trial. Because of what happened to Katie Crane, and because of Dermott's mental state, Ndegwa knows he can save him from the hangman's noose, if not from prison. He also knows, however, that doing so will destroy his own political career. Philip Dermott tells him that if Brian Dermott hangs, as Peter Poole did, the extremist settler elements are ready and willing to turn Kenya into a charnel house that would make the Mau Mau pale by comparison. Thus Ndegwa must choose between his own career and the well-being of his country. He chooses to defend Dermott, and the book ends.

Along the way, Ruark's extensive knowledge of Kenya produces excellent hunting scenes from the Drake safari — especially of leopard hunting, by then Ruark's favorite big-game pursuit — and detailed portraits of traditional Kikuyu life seen through the eyes of Stephen Ndegwa and his tribal wives. Ndegwa has an older wife who sees the country, its politics, and its people one way, and a younger wife who sees them another. Through their conversations, Ruark conveys the many facets of Kenyan culture without lecturing or resorting to unduly long stretches of description or background. Don Bruce and his infant son, who is marked for sacrifice, allow Ruark to expound upon witchcraft, oath-giving, and the traditional African fears that dominate life even as black children attend mission schools and the country prepares to govern itself.

\* \* \*

*Uhuru* was published on June 25, 1962. It was chosen as the Book-of-the-Month Club selection and very quickly climbed onto the *New*

*York Times* best-seller list. The novel was already in the top ten when it was banned in South Africa, which helped propel it into fourth place. Events in Africa were unfolding by the day, in waves. Having Africa constantly in the headlines naturally focused attention on the book. Critics read it and wrote about it, while countries like Kenya and South Africa, where racial tension and the prospect of tribal warfare were not just material for novels, searched it for threats of sedition. South Africa was then a tightly controlled racist society, with a propensity to ban books and motion pictures on almost any pretext. It would have been surprising if *Uhuru* had *not* been banned; still, the news was taken as evidence that it must contain more than a little threatening truth, and this helped sales considerably.

Critics trotted out most of the clichés reserved for blockbuster novels of the time. Terms like "proud and prophetic" and "explosive and sprawling" are critical codewords for a particular type of novel — and generally not the kind that endures beyond next year's Christmas list. Ruark had enemies and detractors among the New York and London critics. Many of them disliked him for his strong views and belligerent manners. Others objected to his political opinions, especially concerning the capabilities of black Africans. Although the term "politically correct" was not yet in general use, it might have been invented just to describe what Robert Ruark was not. Late in life, Ruark said he would like to see even one of his novels reviewed on its own merits and not in terms of a critic's views on blood sports, but obviously *Uhuru* was not to be the one.

One critic referred to the novel as a "deluge of profanity and human degradation that only Robert Ruark can concoct," which is a very strange and unfair criticism when you consider the recent activities of the Mau Mau and the atrocities in the Congo and elsewhere that had become daily fare for newspaper front pages. Ruark did not invent anything that had not actually occurred, and reading the novel today in light of forty years of subsequent bloodshed, torture, and death in many parts of Africa, it actually seems understated. The Mau Mau oathings Ruark describes in both of his major African novels were real, not fictional. Witchcraft was integral to African tribal life then and still is

today. Of course, in the intervening forty years the limits of accept-
ability in both print and film have expanded considerably, and what
was shocking in 1962 would not rate a passing glance in 2000. Still,
the level of personal animosity coloring the book reviews is surprising.

For Ruark the author, the reviews may have been painful, but for
Ruark the businessman, who saw sales rising even as the reviews
became more damning — or because of them — the results were gratifying. People bought the book and read the book, and Ruark pock-
eted the better part of half a million dollars from his guarantee from
McGraw-Hill, from the paperback rights sold to Fawcett/Crest, and
from the Book-of-the-Month deal. *Uhuru* went into print, and stayed
in print (in paperback at least), for many years. Today it shows up on
bookshelves throughout Africa. If anything, it is more common to
find *Uhuru* in a library in a remote corner of the continent than to
find *Something of Value*, although both have become mainstays of
modern Africana.

The decolonialization of Africa produced some literature, but less
than might have been expected given its explosive nature and the
lurid events occurring in countries like the Congo. In Kenya, there
was Elspeth Huxley, writing from the moderate, dispossessed colonial's point of view. In France there was Jean Lartéguy, an ex-army
officer who wrote from the French Army's viewpoint about the loss
of Indochina and Algeria (*The Centurions* and *The Praetorians*) and
then about the Congo mercenaries (*The Hounds of Hell*), many of
whom were French professional soldiers or Foreign Legion veterans.
Even so, Lartéguy was writing less about colonialism than about the
evolution, and move to the left, of French society as its empire collapsed. Nicholas Monsarrat wrote two notable novels about emerging Africa (*The Tribe That Lost Its Head* and *Richer Than All His Tribe*)
which were published in the 1960s and describe the coming of independence in a fictional country, a large island similar to Madagascar
but which Monsarrat placed off the west coast of Africa. Like most
stories set in fictional countries, however, both novels are more like
fables than serious social commentary grounded in harsh reality.
Also, because the country and its tribes are fictional, the novels do

not carry the genuine anthropological or social impact of a novel like *Uhuru*, which utilizes the real culture and customs of the Kikuyu as an integral part of the book.

On the continent itself, South Africa would have been the natural place for a novelist to emerge to document these earth-shaking changes. South Africa had a long history of literature springing from Afrikaner society, writing about the "white tribe of Africa," its mysticism and its Old Testament values, its two-century quest for freedom, and its ingrained religious and racial conflicts. At the time, Stuart Cloete was the pre-eminent South African novelist, and he was also a writer of world renown. Like most Afrikaners, however, Cloete was more concerned with the struggle and the future of his people than with the travails of emerging black countries to the north. While South Africa continued to produce novels and plays that gained (and still have) global stature, such as Alan Paton's *Cry, the Beloved Country*, almost all dealt with apartheid and its evils in a particularly South African context.

It is for these reasons, as much as for the novel's considerable merits, that *Uhuru* gained and retained such a prominent place in postcolonial literature. The new black governments of Africa, the liberal lecturers at the London School of Economics, and the African specialists in the State Department may not have liked Ruark's message, but they could not deny its truthfulness.

* * *

Anyone reading Robert Ruark's syndicated newspaper columns from 1960 to 1962 will be struck by the contrast between their strident disapproval, and even rage at what was being allowed to happen in Africa, and the sympathetic insight of *Uhuru*. Dreadful events occur in *Uhuru*, but there is a level of understanding for most of the characters and for the situation in which they find themselves. Even Abraham Matisia, the sadistic mastermind who engineers murder and human sacrifice on Matthew Kamau's behalf, is not completely despicable. Newspapers and daily journalism — especially commentary on current events, the essence of column writing — are extremely shallow by comparison with novels, but that hardly accounts for the different tone of Ruark's writing in the two forms. It is almost as if, knowing the novel was being written for posterity, Ruark did not allow his personal feelings to eclipse his belief in what was right and what was wrong. He might allow himself to vent his rage in a newspaper column against a man like Patrice Lumumba, whom he held responsible for Harry Taylor's death, but he did not allow that animosity to dictate Matthew Kamau's character.

There are many small truths in *Uhuru*. Early in the book, Don Bruce says to Brian Dermott, "I don't think I'll be able to live under these apes. I don't think that violence is going to be the thing that drives the white man out of Africa, Brian. I think it'll be constantly living with this bloody arrogant incompetence that'll send us screaming mad." Forty years of subsequent experience, from Nigeria to Somalia, from Cape Town to the Sudan, have proven how prescient that was. But a page later Dermott reflects on the people around him in the Grill at the New Stanley: "All I can spot on this dance floor is the kind of Kenya cowboy that got us into this mess in the first place, and it doesn't do my disposition very much good to reflect that I'm one of them." That is about as even-handed as literature gets.

Ruark recognized and wrote many small truths, but it is doubtful he managed to find one that Faulkner would acknowledge as the basis for an enduring work of literature. Although all the characters contribute to the plot, and each reflects on his personal situation or the problems facing the country, Stephen Ndegwa's logical self-analysis provides the closest thing to a concentrated message. Ndegwa would be a hero in any book, yet he is not without faults by any means. If Brian Dermott is a tortured alcoholic who eventually becomes almost deranged, Ndegwa is an intelligent, educated, thoughtful, and honorable man whose sins are laziness and cynicism. In the end, faced with the difficult choice he must make, he concludes that he is at least partly responsible for Kamau's and Matisia's actions because he recognized them at the time for what they were, but took no steps to curb them. That being the case, it is only right he should pay for his neglect with the destruction of his own political ambitions, and atone for his failings by saving Kenya through the defense of Brian Dermott.

*Uhuru* does not have a happy ending, but it does have a hopeful one. In emerging Africa there were certainly men like Stephen Ndegwa, just as there were men like Kamau and, unfortunately, all too many like Abraham Matisia. For most of the next half century, in most black African countries, the Matisias rose to the top of the heap. The Ndegwas were either pushed aside, destroyed, or forced to flee.

On the settler side, Brian Dermott was typical of a particular type of settler, the anachronistic professional hunter who valued the land the way it was, the animals the way they were, and the tribes in their old ways — not wearing trousers and attending mission schools. Many of those people left Kenya at the time of independence. Some went to South Africa, whose apartheid regime welcomed white reinforcements. The moderates like Charlotte Stuart and the rest of Dermott's family mostly stayed put and tried to run their farms under the new regimes. Some succeeded, but the tide of history was against them. All of these things are accurate and true, but they do not add up to the great "verities of the heart" to which Faulkner referred. Perhaps the fact that Ruark was unable to find any such verities around which to build his novel says everything necessary about the society he was depicting. On the other hand, that Ndegwa is cast as the hero of the novel reflects one piece of truth Ruark acknowledged: Kenya's future lay in the course of action that was chosen by its black population. There was little the white settlers could do, one way or the other, to alter it.

＊ ＊ ＊

· *Chapter Thirteen*

# BWANA BOB

As a boy, Robert Ruark had what he called the "going-to-sleep dream."

"You might say that *Field & Stream* was my early Bible," he wrote in *Horn of the Hunter*. "I worshipped before men like Archibald Rutledge a far piece ahead of Ernest Hemingway or Thomas Wolfe. I had good dogs as a kid, and a great many marvelous things happened to me in the woods. For a long time I had a small boy's dream of writing a story about my dogs and my quail — and of course, me — and seeing it printed in a magazine with a cover by Lynn Bogue Hunt."

It was a dream shared by many small boys in America in the days when the Big Three —*Field & Stream, Outdoor Life*, and *Sports Afield* — were truly the *Big Three*, and the writers whose work appeared in them were household names. Ruark was one of the very few for whom the dream came true.

Before 1950, with one or two exceptions like the venerable *American Rifleman*, there were no specialty magazines as there are today. The Big Three dominated the hunting and fishing world, covering every aspect of shooting and field sports from rabbit hunting in Michigan to trolling for sharks off Tahiti. If you wanted to learn about sighting a rifle, you read Jack O'Connor in *Outdoor Life*; if you wanted to know about putting out duck decoys, there was Ray Holland (Ruark's own hero) in *Field & Stream*; if it was fishing for marlin, there was Zane Grey, also in *Field & Stream*. Serious outdoorsmen subscribed to at least one of these publications. If you found a snug room with a fireplace, a deer head on the wall, and a rack of oiled guns, chances were there was a comfortable chair nearby with a stack of outdoor magazines beside it. And if a small boy's father or grandfather did not buy them, there were sure to be a few down at the barber shop.

The Big Three were fiercely competitive, far more so than today. The editors pored over each issue as it came out, looking to see what the others had that they had missed or trying to find new ideas for features and columns. Several generations of wildlife artists got their start painting game scenes for the covers and illustrating the features and short stories that were found in their pages. The best artists were in great demand, as were the better freelance writers. Russell Annabel, for example, worked for all three over the years but eventually became associated mostly with *Sports Afield.* The editor at the time, Ted Kesting, went out of his way to lock up Annabel for the magazine because it was said that having his name on the cover would sell an extra hundred thousand copies at the newsstand. All the big magazines had their own "name" writer. *Sports Afield* had Annabel, *Outdoor Life* had Jack O'Connor, and from 1953 onward, *Field & Stream* had Robert Ruark.

A name like Annabel on the cover might sell more of one particular issue, but knowing a Jack O'Connor would be in every month caused people to become regular readers, those priceless beings who pick up the magazine and plunk down their money, month after month, without even glancing at the table of contents. It is going too far to say these writers were celebrities, but they were not anonymous by any means. Readers paid attention to by-lines.

Until he returned from safari in 1951, Ruark had not done much in the way of "outdoor writing," as it is known. He was a newspaper columnist first and a magazine writer second, but his magazine work had been almost entirely general-interest pieces for magazines like *The Saturday Evening Post* and *Collier's.* As he roamed the world looking for material for his column, he would find larger stories that could be treated in greater depth, and these he turned into magazine articles. Outdoor writing, on the other hand, required more concentrated research. Since even then an outdoor article was usually first-person — an account of a hunting or fishing trip made by the author — it could not really be done on a casual basis. Once Ruark had been to Africa, however, he had a fund of information on which to draw. As he became more interested and made more trips to Africa as well as hunting and fishing expeditions to places like India, Alaska, and New Zealand, that reservoir of material filled up faster than he could empty it.

David Petzal, long-time executive editor of *Field & Stream*, arrived at the magazine a few years after Ruark had departed, but recalls the aura Ruark left behind. Particularly, there was the awe at the rate the magazine paid him for "The Old Man and the Boy" — $1,500 a month, a sum that was unheard of in 1953, and even today is in the higher realms of rates paid for articles by such magazines. That Ruark could command such an astronomical sum, for a column that was purchased sight-unseen month after month, says a great deal about his reputation and the effect having his name on the masthead would have for the magazine. Whether Ruark could command that money today — whether, in fact, he could even find a market today — is another question.

The 1950s and '60s have been described, with some justification, as the golden age of outdoor magazines, and no doubt it was a very different time. It was the last flowering of the pre-television era, and although there was barely a fraction of the publications there are today, a magazine's circulation and influence was much greater. If people depended on newspapers for news and comment, they looked to magazines for entertainment, intellectual stimulation, and enlightenment. Magazines still had some pretensions to culture, including publishing short stories and serialized novels, two art forms that have all but died in that format.

Mainstream general-interest periodicals like *The Saturday Evening Post* regularly published short fiction, even including stories that were shooting and hunting related, such as the series of J.M. Pyne stories by Lucian Cary. Cary was an excellent writer of both short fiction and non-fiction articles who did a great deal of work for the *Post*. Some, but not all, of his stories were gun related. In the J.M. Pyne series, the hero is a barrel maker, loosely modeled on Harry Pope. Obviously, in those days hunting was still a widely accepted pastime, and guns and shooting were considered suitable material for general-interest publications. Cary died a penniless alcoholic in a seedy hotel in Manhattan. In his day, however, he commanded big money writing for the *Post*, and Jack O'Connor, a man not given to praising rivals lightly, had a high regard for Lucian Cary as a writer.

\* \* \*

The Big Three almost always had at least one fiction piece per issue, and both articles and columns were "softer" and less technical than they are today. As competition from television heated up, and readers' tastes changed, there was a general transition to the "how-to" article, which stressed equipment, techniques, and methods. There was more emphasis on *how* to do something and less on why it was fun to do.

Robert Ruark's "Old Man and the Boy" columns struck a balance somewhere in between. Almost all of them had a philosophical message, but each contained titbits of useful information as well, or at least something to think about. And there was not one that was not lively, entertaining, and well written. Robert Ruark was paid big, but he earned it.

By today's standards, however, Ruark was almost an amateur when it came to hunting, and an occasionally incompetent one at that. Although his name is associated today primarily with big game hunting, especially in Africa, he points out repeatedly that he was not a rifleman. When he went on safari in 1951, he wrote, he had never before fired a rifle at an animal (all his southern deer hunting had been done with a shotgun), and on his second safari eighteen months later, he said he had not touched a rifle in all the time he was home. David Petzal says one of the favorite stories making the rounds at *Field & Stream* in his early years there was how the shooting editor, Warren Page, would take Ruark to the Campfire Club, the famous shooting range outside New York City, to sight in his rifles before he left on a safari. "Most of the time Page had to do it for him," Petzal says, "because Ruark would be too drunk to do it himself."

Jack O'Connor, *Outdoor Life's* shooting editor throughout this period, held Ruark in rather low regard. In *The Last Book — Confessions of a Gun Editor*, he refers to Ruark as "a one-timer who returned to write a book about African safaris," and later as someone who was "shy on ballistic sophistication." There is certainly no argument there. Ruark shot a lot of game, and did so with many different rifles, but his knowledge of bullet weights and trajectories and velocities was limited at best — which is no crime unless you put it in print for all to read, including someone who might take your advice and, as a result, get stomped by a Cape buffalo. Although O'Connor was on solid ground in his criticism, Ruark was also a big draw for O'Connor's major competition, and that rivalry probably played a part. As well, O'Connor was a man of not inconsequential ego, and Ruark's posturing later in his career could not have sat well, especially when he started to pontificate on rifles and cartridges.

In his early articles Ruark tended to make light of his lack of experience and in-depth knowledge of rifles and relates anecdotes in which he makes one mistake after another. The .220 Swift incident involving the hyena, for example was not really a mistake on his part, except for taking the rifle to Africa in the first place. In *Horn of the Hunter* he also tells about shooting his Westley Richards .470 Nitro Express and having the rifle double and knock him off his feet. He had tried to emulate Harry Selby by holding two spare cartridges between the fingers of his right hand when he shot, not making the connection that Selby was left-handed and that he, Ruark, should have held them in his *left* hand. Somehow one of the spare cartridges got tangled up in the trigger guard and pressed the second trigger. I have read and re-read that passage, and attempted (with an unloaded gun) to repeat the maneuver, and I am damned if I can see how it happened, but it makes a good story.

Aside from the Swift, Ruark's arsenal on that first safari was eminently sensible: a Remington .30-06, a Winchester Model 70 .375 H&H, and the Westley Richards, as well as a couple of shotguns — a Churchill 12-bore, and a Sauer 16, both side-by-sides.

Ruark's hero-worship of professional hunters led him into several gaffes of a ballistic nature, or at least outlandish claims on behalf of various professionals. At one point, he insisted that Harry Selby had shot, flying, two swooping yellow-billed kites with the right and left barrels of a Rigby .450 No. 2. I, for one, reserve the right to take that with a grain of salt. First of all, Rigby never made a .450 No. 2, but that is quibbling. And, it should be noted, he was in good company in attributing such feats to his heroes: Ernest Hemingway did exactly the same thing, twenty years earlier, in his dispatches from East Africa that were printed in *Esquire*. According to Hemingway, Baron Bror von Blixen regularly shot partridges in flight, also with a .450 No. 2.

During a trip to Australia in 1950, Ruark visited a sheep station in the Outback and went along on some kangaroo-hunting expeditions. Kangaroos were then, as they are now, a tremendous pest ranchers tried to control by shooting. According to Ruark, the kangaroos were coursing along at forty miles an hour with the hunters' vehicle in hot pursuit, dodging trees and stump holes. "To hit a running roo from a speeding car, at a distance of several hundred yards, calls for a brand of marksmanship I do not possess," he said, "but the professional exterminators can pop them over at 500 to 1,000 yards with remarkable consistency." As if this were not sufficient hogwash, Ruark went on to explain how he hit one kangaroo with "five big bullets," the first of which hit "front and center," after which the kangaroo hopped up, sped away, and fled at a dead run for an hour, while Ruark hit him four more times. Any one of the bullets would have "killed an ordinary beast, but they seemed only a minor annoyance to the kangaroo." If Jack O'Connor read that passage, which was in Ruark's newspaper column in 1950 (admittedly before he had done much rifle shooting), it was no wonder he gritted his teeth and said the things he did about Ruark.

This passage raises another nitpicking point as well. In *Horn of the Hunter*, Ruark insists he had never before fired a rifle at a game animal, yet here he was, eighteen months earlier, shooting at kangaroos. It shows the danger of taking everything he wrote as literal truth. He was not above using hyperbole to clinch an argument. It also should be remembered that in some ways writers were granted considerable leeway in those days. Russell Annabel is a perfect example. It is generally conceded now that many, if not most, of the stories he wrote about hunting in Alaska were pure fiction, drawn from his imagination; they were not non-fiction accounts of actual events, as they were presented and accepted by the reading public. One of the minor mysteries of the trade is how Annabel acquired the knowledge of hunting and the outdoors that he did, how he got away with writing fiction for so long, and why he was finally forced to leave Alaska. He emigrated to Mexico, where he spent the last years of his life — writing, predictably, about hair-raising adventures hunting jaguars.

Annabel was a strange case. He populated his stories with characters drawn directly from Jack London — for example, the Malemute Kid, a London hero, pops up in many of Annabel's tales. Yet people thought he was writing the literal truth, and even today you can cause violent arguments by suggesting Annabel was less than kosher. Perhaps the simplest answer is the best: Annabel was a hell of a writer, his readers loved him, and they just did not care if he was telling the truth. For the record, Ernest Hemingway described Russell Annabel as "the finest outdoor writer" he had ever read.

Ruark never manufactured stories outright, but if he wanted to stretch the truth here and there, no one minded. In the case of "The Old Man and the Boy," people thought every story was an account of an incident from his boyhood, and even now some people insist the stories are straight, unembellished autobiography. The fact is, they were apocryphal in some instances and did not tell the entire truth in others. Overall, however, they were typical of the articles appearing in the Big Three in the 1950s, when fiction and truth mixed freely and no one cared a great deal as long as magazines flew off the shelves.

* * *

If there was one area of shooting on which Ruark could be considered an authority, it was shotguns and wingshooting, but to my knowledge he never wrote very much about them in technical terms. As he became more of a big-game hunter, however, he began to wax eloquent about new rifles he had purchased and their capabilities. The most glaring example, perhaps, was when he purchased a .244 H&H and proceeded to make extravagant claims for it.

By the end of his career, after he had basically written himself out on "The Old Man and the Boy" and was a novelist first and foremost, Ruark became sports editor of *Playboy*. Imagine, if you will, exactly what such a job might entail. In those days *Playboy* was continually breaking new ground in one direction, all the while trying to give itself journalistic legitimacy by publishing articles on such subjects as stereo systems, Ferraris, jazz pianists, and the like. Ruark, who had refused to write for *Playboy* earlier in his career when they tried to commission a piece — he referred to it as "a jerk-off sheet" — was now more than happy to accept the money Hugh Hefner offered him. By then, Ruark was the very embodiment of the globe-trotting, big-time, big-game hunter, and through his novels a mainstream celebrity as well — perfect for the image *Playboy* was trying to project. In 1964, when Ruark was on safari in Mozambique, the magazine commissioned him to do an article for which they paid the handsome sum of $5,000. Ruark pulled out his portable typewriter, set up a temporary office in camp, and proceeded to produce one of the best overview articles on modern safaris that has ever been written — "Far-Out Safari". This article was reprinted many years later in the limited edition of Michael McIntosh's anthology *Robert Ruark's Africa*, and again in James Casada's anthology *The Lost Classics of Robert Ruark*. As McIntosh noted in his introduction, in spite of the "insufferably hip" title, the article could only have been written by a man who had done it all and seen it all.

By this time Ruark had discarded the double-*terai* hat that he had affected in his early African days and now wore an army beret, which was popular with professional hunters. In "Far-Out Safari," Ruark waxed eloquent for six or seven long paragraphs on rifles and bullets, especially a "Holland & Holland tailor-made .244" that he said had "changed my entire concept of weaponry." He went on to describe how he had used the rifle to drop everything up to a Cape buffalo "with a bullet no bigger than a sharpened point of a pencil." The .244, he said, "is good enough for anything except elephant and rhino." All you had to do was "hold tight." He recounted a story of one of his professional hunter friends shooting an animal with the rifle at some outlandish distance — six hundred yards or more — without having to allow for bullet drop, so flat did it shoot. Which, of course, is totally ridiculous.

For big rifles, he insisted, the solid bullet was "part of the buggy-whip age" and proceeded to praise the Winchester Silvertip as "the best bullet ever mass-produced." Overall, reading Ruark on ballistics and rifle technicana is enough to send a shooting editor to the funny farm, and to have most professional hunters climbing the walls. Granted, there are disagreements as to what constitutes "enough gun" for a given animal (and Ruark was the very one who made that phrase part of the modern lexicon), but he should have realized his own limitations and not gone beating the drum for such horrendous ballistic disasters as the .244 Belted Rimless Magnum (H&H). Considering he had lambasted the .220 Swift for its inadequacies in 1952, how could he praise the .244 — just an overgrown Swift with a belt and a slightly bigger bullet — in 1964?

Although the article is full of useful information and carries the unmistakable mark of extensive first-hand knowledge, such sweeping pronouncements on suitable rifles for dangerous game should be avoided. They have a way of coming back to haunt the writer. Overall, Ruark's pronouncements on suitable rifles were actually better in his early days, before he thought he was an expert.

Fortunately, such forays into the murky world of ballistics were relatively rare, and truth to tell, touting the .244 H&H in the pages of *Playboy* was unlikely to cause too many problems. Most of these articles date from the period in Ruark's life when, everyone agreed, he knew everything about everything, and no one could tell him anything he did not already know.

\* \* \*

While writing for *Field & Stream*, Robert Ruark went to Africa at least once a year and stayed for weeks or months at a time. He also travelled to other parts of the world: to Alaska for brown bear, to New Zealand for fishing, and several times to India, where he killed tigers, leopards, and other game, and was badly mauled by a wounded leopard. Occasionally, Ruark even wrote about hunting and fishing in the United States, including a few pieces on quail hunting in the South (involving his friend, financier Bernard Baruch) and hunting white-tailed deer. All of these adventures showed up in print, and all were competently written, but none displayed the magic touch Ruark possessed when he wrote about Africa. It was if there was a supernatural link between him and his adopted country, Kenya.

One article in particular springs to mind. "A Leopard in the Rain" appeared in *Field & Stream* in July, 1961 and, like "Far-Out Safari," was included in the limited edition of McIntosh's anthology, as well as in Casada's anthology. This story alone is worth the price of either book. As a piece of outdoor writing it brings tears to the eyes. The action takes place during the rainy season in Kenya; Ruark is there working on a novel (*Uhuru*) and finds himself with time on his hands. He enlists Ken Jesperson, a professional hunter, and together they go off looking for a place to hunt that has not been shut down by the rains. They end up down near Amboseli, spend an idyllic week or so just prowling around, finally get a leopard as the rains catch up to them, and make it back into Nairobi one step ahead of drowning. As a description of Africa and safari life the way it should be experienced, this article is second to none. There is serious hunting, but no obsession, no competition, no real deadlines. Ruark's love of Africa shines through in every beautifully crafted word.

This ability to plunk the reader down in a distant place was a talent Ruark and only a few others had. He could not always make it happen, but when he did, he produced a diamond. Gene Hill, one of the best outdoor writers of all time, said he admired Ruark for his blend of humor, truth, and teaching — that he was "a master at introducing us to his friends, his home country, and a strong sense of ethics...He showed us how to be serious but not overly so, to regard our time with guns and dogs and rods and the people that come with them as a period of grace that enriches us in a very special way."

❋ ❋ ❋

## OTHER DAYS:
# The Old Man and the Boy & The Old Man's Boy Grows Older

If Robert Ruark had never written any outdoor literature except *The Old Man and the Boy*, he would still be one of the greatest hunting and fishing writers of the twentieth century. As a series of magazine articles, they drew millions of readers to *Field & Stream* every month for almost nine years. More hunters and fishermen knew about Robert Ruark from those columns than from any of his other writings in the field. To a great degree, they were the cornerstone upon which he built his reputation in what is, admittedly, a somewhat arcane corner of literature. Arcane it may be, but men who love hunting stories cherish them forever.

"The Old Man and the Boy" began as a magazine series in February, 1953 and ran continuously for 106 episodes, the last one appearing in November, 1961. By that time, the theme of the series had evolved and broadened to include Ruark's adult activities, and along the way the name was changed to reflect that. To a great extent, many of the later pieces are not really distinct from other outdoor writing of the time, except, of course, that Ruark's writing was itself always a cut above. Ruark at his worst was still better than most.

The premise of the *Old Man* stories is deceptively simple: They are the adventures of a young boy with his grandfather in and around a small town on the North Carolina coast in the 1920s. The small boy, of course, is Bobby Ruark; the Old Man is an amalgam of his two grandfathers, Hanson Kelly Ruark and Captain Edward Hall Adkins. In the series, the Old Man is occasionally referred to as "Ned Adkins," but the semifictional character incorporates the good qualities (and none of the bad) of both men. From Hanson Ruark comes the Old Man's erudition and devotion to reading; from the real Ned Adkins comes his seafaring background, his love of hunting and fishing, his real-life wife, Charlotte (Miss Lottie), and his house in Southport, just down the Cape Fear River from Ruark's home in Wilmington. The earliest story takes place when Bobby is about eight years old and receives his first shotgun; in the last column (in terms of his age, but not the last of the series) he is fifteen, the Old Man has died of cancer, and Bob is about to leave for college.

In between, the pair hunt and fish, loaf around, build a cabin, go duck hunting in Louisiana, shoot pool, and travel to Maryland to hunt pheasant; Bobby gets his first shotgun and learns about safe gun handling; he shoots his first quail, and his first deer. He fishes for blues, at night, with the surf rolling. But there is more than hunting and fishing; he writes about Thanksgiving and Christmas, complete with rum-soaked fruitcake and all the smells, magnified by time and memory, of a small boy's Christmas in a house with a woodstove. A great deal of eating gets done, formal and informal, and a little drinking here and there. Bob learns about reading, particularly about reading great literature, and loses himself in Chaucer and Shakespeare. He receives a puppy, and is then taught how to train a bird dog. Throughout it all, the Old Man is the teacher, the boy the (usually) willing student.

As literary themes go, this is not original, but then nothing is. If writers only tackled purely original subjects, literature would have died with Shakespeare. But Robert Ruark's recollections of his boyhood in North Carolina (biographically inexact as they are) have an ingredient, a quality, that sets them apart from, and mostly above, other stories of the type that have been written over the years. It is this quality that has kept them fresh and re-readable almost half a century after they were written. It is also this quality that has kept the

306

demand brisk and the hard-bound anthology continuously in print for more than forty years — ironic when you consider that the magazine column was a sideline, a hobby almost, for Ruark the novelist, and the anthology was compiled almost as an afterthought. Literary hits come in strange ways.

Although all the stories are written from the vantage point of a child and the events are seen through a child's eyes, this innocent view is tempered by Ruark's adult experience. He is able to couch the words in a child's terms, yet the thoughts are not always a child's thoughts. Sometimes it is Ruark the boy describing events, other times Ruark the man. The tales he tells are sometimes adventures, sometimes parables, sometimes modern-day fables. Almost all have a moral, but usually the moral is a very practical one — how not to shoot yourself or anyone else accidentally, for example, as opposed to preaching that honesty is the best policy.

Unlike many stories with similar themes, Ruark never preaches, and is never mealy-mouthed or moralistic or holier-than-thou. He is always enthusiastic, as if he can't wait to get back out there in the wind and rain to be made happily, gloriously miserable once more. Most of all, Ruark is never, ever maudlin. Even in the episode where the Old Man confides to the boy that he is dying ("But Not On Opening Day") and later when he dies ("All He Left Me Was The World"), there is never any obvious heart-tugging from the Corey Ford school of tear-jerkers. Ruark seemingly never felt sorry for himself in his life — not for public consumption, anyway.

Another quality of the writing is its deceptive, artless simplicity. Reading the stories, you would think Ruark was sitting right there with you, talking. He never over-writes, he never strays into excessive description or purple prose or the attempts at profundity that litter so much of the short fiction from that era. Ruark came from the Hemingway school of emotion, where whatever evokes the writer's emotion is isolated and described simply and well, to evoke the same emotion in the reader. Ruark does that to perfection, time after time. This may be due in part to Ruark's own professionalism, because each episode started as a magazine column, with strict limitations on word count. No matter how enchanting the story, it had to fit into the space available. The discipline this imposes, which actually was the basis for Hemingway's own terse style and economy of words, is very good for a writer. When you have room for only a few words, they have to be the right words.

* * *

Examining these stories as a magazine series is different than discussing the two anthologies as separate, self-contained books. The first anthology, *The Old Man and the Boy*, was published in 1957, shortly after *Something of Value*, when Ruark's career as a novelist was very much on the rise. At that time, the column had been running for four years, or about forty-eight episodes. When the book was compiled, of course, there were fewer episodes available, and almost all of them went into the first volume; sometimes two or more stories were blended into one, because of similar themes or because one was the beginning and the next month's installment the conclusion. So the first book was really what had been written up until that point, gathered in one place.

The second anthology, *The Old Man's Boy Grows Older*, was published in 1961 with another four years and another forty-eight episodes from which to draw, along with what had not been used the first time around. By then, the column's direction had changed somewhat. As Ruark's store of boyhood memories ran thin, he began to interject tales from his adulthood. For a while, the column title was retained, although each article was given an individual heading; then the *Old Man* designation was dropped altogether. The second anthology appeared just about the time Ruark and *Field & Stream* concluded that the series had run its course.

There are thirty articles in the second anthology, which, allowing for instances of several being combined into one, means that most of the series is included in those two books. Readers today sometimes make the assumption that both volumes were compiled after all the episodes of the column were written, and that the first volume contains the best pieces, the second only those that failed to make the cut for the first. This is not true at all; the first contains the best pieces available at the time, and likewise the second for those that appeared in the ensuing four years. This still left a residue of four-dozen articles out of 106 for latter-day anthologists to pick over and include in collections, several of which have appeared since Ruark's death (see Chapter 16, "A Tusk and a Book").

For this reason, anyone attempting a review of *The Old Man and the Boy* needs to differentiate between the column, taken as a whole over almost nine years, and the separate anthologies. Each has its strengths and weaknesses.

The first anthology has a freshness, almost a naiveté, to it. It is the first rush of memories, with Ruark taking the best themes and strongest recollections and turning them into anecdotes and fables about his youth. The second volume has a distinctly different flavor. It is more mature, more thoughtful, more polished, but more disparate. If volume one is a *Beaujolais nouveau*, volume two is a *Grand Echezaux* — darker, more complex, more reflective.

* * *

Volume one was dedicated to the memory of Ruark's two grandfathers, as well as to his father, Robert Chester Ruark, Sr., and "all the honorary uncles, black and white, who took me to raise." In an author's note, Ruark wrote: "Anybody who reads this book is bound to realize that I had a real fine time as a kid." And that was it: Without further ado, with no preface or introduction, Ruark swept into his first tale of quail, "It Takes a Gentleman to Approach Another Gentleman." And he began it with one of his most famous lines, "The Old Man knows pretty near close to everything. And mostly he ain't painful with it." From this, many people have concluded that the series is almost pure autobiography, but that is not the case. While it is certainly autobiographical, the events have been carefully cleansed of any negative reality. Following the dictum that if you can't say anything nice don't say anything at all, Ruark deliberately fails to mention, except in passing, his parents. Once or twice they appear, such as in his recollections of Christmas, but only as walk-on figures or shadows behind the door. Even in "Life Among the Giants," an amalgam piece in which he talks at length about the grownups he knew in the town, his grandfather is front and center, but his parents are conspicuous by their absence.

As with Alec Barr in *The Honey Badger*, the Boy is Bobby Ruark partly as he was and partly as he wished he had been. Whereas the real Bobby Ruark's childhood contained serious, continuing conflict because of his bookishness, his tendency to be a loner, and his mother's and father's vicissitudes and questionable standing in the community, the Boy is well-read but outgoing, able to hold his own with a baseball bat or a fishing rod. Friendships with other children are mentioned sparingly. Sometimes they are good, but generally children his own age are dismissed as louts. Mostly, however, they simply are not mentioned. Other kids were not welcome in Bobby Ruark's paradise in which he, a Boy, moved as a man among men, and was not a plump, bookish dreamer.

In the course of the series, Ruark manages to pack an awful lot of truth, some trivial and some profound, into stories that are deceptively sweet. Reviewers, and those who write dust-jacket copy, have latched onto this quality and presented *The Old Man and the Boy* using such clichéd terms as "heartwarming," "wit and wisdom," and "homespun;" occasionally they employ the execrable "yesteryear" and "trials and tribulations." To hear them tell it, *The Old Man and the Boy* is the embodiment of the Norman Rockwell myth of small-town American life. But if Robert Ruark wrote the stories carefully omitting certain aspects of his childhood, it was not with the intention that readers would absorb only the "warm and touching" aspects of what he wrote; there is a harder edge that lies beneath the surface of many of the stories.

This edge is apparent more in the second volume because it reflects Ruark's views of life from the vantage point of successful adulthood, as well as his growing disillusionment. In many ways, the author's foreword to the second volume, "A Word from the Boy," is one of the best pieces in it. Here Ruark explains how the column first came about and what was involved in conceiving it, delving into his memory, and writing it, month by month, for eight years, to unearth the material he needed:

"I was moved to think again, for the first time in many a year, of just how hell-conscious a small boy can be, and of that frightening span of two or three years when I was sure I was going to hell for telling a lie or for cutting Sunday school or for saying damn, and of how I was sore stricken with the enormity of eternity." Such thoughts usually occurred to young Ruark in a cypress swamp toward sundown. Even in adulthood, he wrote, when he found himself in a darkly mysterious swamp surrounded by Spanish moss, "I feel something of the old fear of the wrath of God, and a chilly finger runs up and down my spine."

In one story titled "Nobility is Wrecking the Country," Ruark recalls his university graduation day, in which he and a couple of friends got drunk while waiting to be called up on stage to receive their diplomas. They had a jar of "home-brewed happiness" under their chairs and a long plastic tube through which to drink it. As Ruark sat there getting more and more juiced, he thought about the length of the oratory and "how much more fun a colored camp meeting was." His reflections led to some thoughts about what the Old Man might have said to the graduating class. They ranged from admonitions on literature ("Stay away from Horatio Alger books. You can't build a life hoping to find a pocketbook on the street.") to drinking ("You either come to hunt or you come to drink. Drinking's for when the work's done.") to religion ("Whether you call him God, Allah, Jehovah or Mug-Mug doesn't make much difference as long as you believe in him.") to women ("As for women, I don't know. They got a sort of contrary, different chemistry of brain and action from men, which makes them unruly and subject to strange fits. My only advice on women is to stay out of the house when they're cleaning and don't say yes too often.")

Perhaps the sagest observation the Old Man ever made, however, was a simple statement: "There are all sorts of ways to get to be a man — and none of 'em easy."

Although the series is undoubtedly and unapologetically nostalgic, Ruark cannot resist deflating nostalgia as an art form and debunking the old "when I was a boy" school of writing that attempted to show that kids back then had it better (or worse), were more resourceful (or less lazy), or had to walk further to school, climbing higher hills through deeper snow. Much of this reflection, Ruark wrote, was magnified by the years. If anyone asked him, he confesses, he would testify on a stack of bibles that he had to walk twenty miles to school, even though the school was just around the corner in Wilmington, and since early childhood he had always owned a bicycle.

From beginning to end, *The Old Man and the Boy* resists any urge to pontificate or lecture, and the morals of the stories are never overbearing. The Old Man is sometimes cranky, but never self-righteous, pompous, or unctuous — all of which traits pervade other "coming of age" parables. Perhaps most of all, Ruark never takes himself too seriously. In the end, life is there to be enjoyed; otherwise, what's the point?

\* \* \*

*The Old Man and the Boy* has been in print since 1957, a span of more than forty years, which is a remarkable accomplishment for any hardcover book. *The Old Man's Boy Grows Older* has been in and out of print. It does not have the automatic name-recognition factor of the other book, and the volumes are not sold as a set. Consequently, it is sometimes hard to obtain, and first editions sell at a premium in the secondary book market. Unlike Ruark's major novels, which received either mixed or outright negative reviews in the mainstream press, *The Old Man and the Boy* has been generally highly regarded by everyone. Whether Ruark would consider it one of his most serious works of literature is open to debate, but there is no question the rest of the world does, if longevity is any measure. If Robert Ruark is still being read when the twenty-first century becomes the twenty-second, chances are the book will be *The Old Man and the Boy*. Readers could do much worse.

\* \* \*

*Chapter Fourteen*

# THE LION
# AT TWILIGHT

On the evening of July 10, 1962, Robert Ruark boarded a South African Airways flight in Nairobi and left Kenya for the last time. He fled the country one step ahead of the law. Although he did not know it then, he would never see Kenya again. Three months later, the colonial government declared him a prohibited immigrant, and he could not have returned to East Africa even if he had wanted to. Although he would travel to Mozambique on safari at least twice more before he died, Ruark's career in Africa was effectively over.

The events surrounding his departure are clear-cut. *Uhuru* was published on June 25, and in it Ruark included the name of Chief James Gichuru as a prominent Mau Mau. Chief Gichuru was minister of finance in the transitional Kenya government and a close associate of Jomo Kenyatta, who was tagged to lead Kenya after independence. Knowing Ruark was in the colony, Chief Gichuru sued him for libel, and the documents were delivered to Ruark's hotel. Chief Gichuru had indeed been detained and questioned during the Emergency, and had even admitted undergoing two oathing ceremonies in order to save his own life, but he was not and had never been an actual member of the Mau Mau. Ruark had made a mistake, and he knew it. The suit demanded a public apology and five hundred thousand Kenya shillings (about one hundred thousand dollars) in damages. Harry Selby helped Ruark hide out until the flight left from Embakasi that evening, then drove him to the airport. Ruark boarded the plane and Selby never saw him again.

The official reason given for Ruark being declared a prohibited immigrant was not the lawsuit so much as a combination of factors, including the descriptions of the political situation and personalities in *Uhuru* and various articles Ruark had published about the political situation and Kenya's approaching independence. It was a tense time in Kenya. The British government had established a large army base at Kahawa and stationed 2,500 British troops there as a precaution. The run-up to independence was going to be difficult enough without people like Ruark stirring things up.

Ruark later wrote a magazine article about his last safari, his ultimate look at the country that had become his second home. The article was published first in *The Saturday Evening Post* and later reprinted in *Use Enough Gun*. It was a poignant swan song for his time in East Africa and made a fitting finale for his last (albeit posthumous) hunting book. When you consider the volumes he wrote and the influence he had, it was an amazingly short period. From his first, idyllic safari with Selby in 1951 until his final departure was only eleven years.

\* \* \*

Robert Ruark now had less than three years to live. In some ways his last years were his most successful, while in others they constituted little more than an epilogue to a career that had become centered on Africa. On the positive side, Ruark was a famous man and (on paper at least) a wealthy man; on the negative, his health was failing quickly before an onslaught of alcohol, his marriage was on the rocks, and without Africa his life lacked much of the purpose he had found there. The continent was decolonizing, and Ruark's warnings and misgivings about the process, and about the ability of the emerging countries to govern themselves, were becoming repetitive and increasingly irrelevant in a world that knew where it wanted to go regardless of the consequences. By 1963, the rush to independence had become a flood, and new flags were being hoisted in bunches in front of the United Nations in New York. Robert Ruark, the Cassandra of emerging Africa, was already being elbowed aside.

One immediate casualty of his being declared a prohibited immigrant was his planned tetralogy about Kenya. Two volumes remained to be written, and while he might have been able to write *A Long View from a*

*Tall Hill*, covering the period 1900 to 1952, from academic research and his memories, there was no way he could ever write *Act of God*, the final novel about post-independent Kenya, without seeing it for himself. Not knowing the postponement would be permanent, Ruark put the project away and began work on his final novel, *The Honey Badger*. It was to be his last testament, an epitaph for himself and for what he had tried to be. Meanwhile, he had some major problems to face — marital, familial, financial, and not least of all, his health.

Actually, his alcoholism and marital problems were tied closely together because Virginia Ruark had become almost as bad an alcoholic as he was. Bizarrely, drinking became an issue between them, with each accusing the other of being a drunk and trading self-righteous lectures. Whether it was cause, effect, or both, Ruark was also carrying on his extramarital love affairs more and more openly. None of the women was a household name — no starlets, no opera divas — and there is little point in either belaboring them or naming names. Suffice to say, however, his flaunting of his infidelities was part of the reason for Virginia's rapidly worsening psychological condition. All through the summer of 1962, the couple stayed in Palamós, drinking and quarreling.

On August 25, Robert Ruark Sr. died of lung disease in Southport, North Carolina. He had been in the hospital, terminally ill, for many months. Ruark's mother died not long after, and their deaths severed any remaining links with his boyhood home, although he had long since ceased to think of North Carolina as home anyway. His home was now in Palamós.

In September he left for New York for a trip that was supposed to be one month but stretched to two, and then three. He wrote to Virginia in Spain to tell her he was considering a divorce. There were various reasons for it: Her drinking, his footloose ways, her constant suspicion and accusations (both well grounded, it should be noted), and his chronic inability to function as a conventional stay-at-home husband. The breakdown of his marriage of long standing, with its legal and financial ramifications as well as the tearful recriminations, did nothing for Ruark's mental well-being. It did, however, provide him with useful research material for *The Honey Badger*.

While he was in America (and his wife was in Spain, attempting spo-radically to stay off the booze) Ruark visited some friends in Virginia, where he fell from a horse and fractured his pelvis. In the hospital he was given a complete physical, which showed him to have, as he put it, "the veins of an eighty-year-old man, a bad liver, and a bad aorta." The last was the result of liver dysfunction, resulting in calcium buildup. As well, X-rays showed his testicles to be "calcified," according to a friend who saw the slides, but exactly what that portended has never really been explained. If he was suffering from any ailments in that depart-ment, he never acknowledged it, then or later. By November he was back in London, publicly keeping company with other women and insisting a divorce from Virginia was the only solution to their situation. Meanwhile, the Ruarks maintained a rather vitriolic correspondence, trading accusations.

The effects of drinking on Virginia Ruark were similar in some ways to her husband, but different in others. While he was a cheerful drinker of unbelievable capacity (Tony Henley said that, by the end, he drank straight gin over ice out of a one-pint beer mug), Virginia tended to become drunk quickly. Even when not drinking, she had periods in which she wandered vaguely, as if her mind was elsewhere. Ruark referred to these periods as her "fits," compared them to his own "cutouts," and bluntly ascribed them to alcohol. Virginia looked for other explanations, but it was obvious alcohol was at the root of her psychological problems, even if you concede his infidelity was the cause of her drinking.

In a long letter to his wife, quoted at length by Hugh Foster, Ruark acknowledged his responsibility in the failing marriage. The real fault lay, he said, in his not ending the marriage sooner — fifteen years earlier, when both he and Virginia were young enough to start over.

"I was never intended to be a husband in the sense that women want a husband, in terms of total possession," he wrote. "I am a rover, I am a loner, and I am selfish. If I am faithful to anything it is a typewriter, with-out which I am nothing at all.

"Perhaps if there had been no sportswriting, no war, and then no col-umn, I might have conformed more. If there had been no Africa, no Spain, no novels...I don't know."

* * *

In January, 1963, the divorce became final. Although there were some last-minute legal disputes over the financial settlement, Robert and Virginia Ruark eventually managed to reach a more or less amicable agreement. She received a hundred thousand dollars and a quarter of his future income; he kept the house in Palamós. By February, he had begun work on *The Honey Badger* and was hoping to have a first draft by the middle of the year.

Kenya, meanwhile, was moving quickly to full independence. A constitutional change in 1960 had replaced the old system of multiracial representation in the legislature with full majority government; in 1961, Jomo Kenyatta was freed from prison after nine years and assumed the leadership of the Kenya African National Union (KANU). In May, 1963, KANU swept the first election and assumed power when the colony became internally self-governing. On December 12, 1963, Kenya formally achieved full independence from Great Britain, and Jomo Kenyatta became its first prime minister.

In his column, Ruark commented on the results of the election, explaining for his readers the tribal makeup and rivalries of each of the political parties in the contest, as well as the background of their leaders. He concluded that if Kenya escaped chaos, "the age of miracles is very much upon us." Already, however, Ruark was becoming remote from East Africa, and his warnings about the future were receiving less and less attention. When he could not see for himself what was happening and dig for the material behind the headlines, his columns smacked of distance — what an old working-journalist friend of mine described as the professional failing of editorial writers "who come down out of the hills after the battle to shoot the wounded."

Work on *The Honey Badger* was progressing slowly, for a variety of reasons — not least of all the fact that Ruark was taking advantage of his now full and public freedom to lead a carefree bachelor life compounded of wine, women and, presumably, song. According to Hugh Foster, at least one woman with whom he had carried on an affair for many years expected she would become the next Mrs. Robert Ruark, and flew to Spain for the happy event. She was disabused of the notion when she knocked on the door in Palamós and Ruark answered it with a "*Playboy Bunny* type" on each arm. If Ruark's testicles were indeed "calcified," as the previous year's X-rays suggested, it was not from disuse — or at least, he was not letting their condition interfere.

There was a deeper problem with the writing of the new novel, however — a truly ironic one considering its subject matter, and an issue that takes up a good many pages of the finished work. All his professional life Ruark had depended heavily on Virginia as a sounding board and a critic. According to Harry Selby, every idea he had was tried out on Virginia first, and if she did not like it, it was not used. Now, divorced and physically separated, he found himself without her literary judgement, and he was lost. Foster says the pair corresponded through early 1963, relatively amicably, and that he sent her letters about both the new novel and his magazine work. But it was not the same.

Other problems also began to pile up. Virginia wrote back complaining about lack of money, and Ruark was forced to borrow from McGraw-Hill against future royalties under the terms of their multi-book contract. He did this to pay Virginia the initial instalment on the lump-sum settlement. Ruark then received word that he was in dire financial straits himself, and that the publisher was cutting off any future funds because he had failed to deliver the manuscript, as promised, on June 1. At home in Southport, his mother (who was nearing the end herself) was requiring more and more money to pay the medical bills, and there were increasing demands from Ruark's Aunt Mae, who was looking after her. Not surprisingly, all of these pressures appear prominently in *The Honey Badger*. To a writer, nothing is ever truly bad if it provides literary material.

By now, *Uhuru* had been out for almost a year, and there was talk of making it into a motion picture. Ruark intended to co-produce it — "just putting up the property," as he described it — and took a break from his labors to fly to Mozambique to scout possible locations since it was a foregone conclusion it could never be filmed in Kenya. He returned to Spain in August to find fresh money problems awaiting him. Again he promised the manuscript to Harold Matson, assuring him he would have it to him by the middle of November. He did get a portion of the book to his agent early that month, but the novel was far from finished.

Other professional problems were arising. The quality of his syndi-cated column was really suffering, as much from his isolation in Spain as from his neglect. Just as it had with *Uhuru*, the strain of writing a novel took his attention away from the daily grind of producing a column that was supposed to be timely, insightful, witty, and non-repetitious. As 1963 wore on, editors across the United States began to complain more and more about Ruark reworking the same themes, and worse, doing it badly. Where was "the old Ruark," they asked United Features. Ruark's boss there, Larry Rutman, complained to Harold Matson, who passed his concerns on to Ruark. The problem, Rutman said, stemmed from the fact that Ruark had ceased to be the columnist he had been — which he himself had defined as "a reporter with a point of view." The point of view was important, but so was the reporting aspect — either comment-ing on very recent events or digging up new material to shed light on those events. Ruark was doing none of the above. Many times he was commenting on events that had long since faded from the news pages, and readers were not interested in a tired rehash of something that was already half-forgotten.

When he lived in New York, Ruark had constant access to the newswires carrying stories about events as they broke. In Palamós he did not. Limited to what he read in the newspapers and magazines, without timely information or being able to watch news stories as they unfolded (as he had so often in Africa), it was inevitable that his column would become stale even without the distracting demands of novel writing. As the clamor from editors became louder, United Features threatened to cut his salary, and even to cancel his contract altogether. In spite of his income from books (and the money seemed to flow out faster than it flowed in), his newspaper work was still a financial mainstay. Worrying about his column became one more source of pressure in a life that did not need any more than it already had.

In the end the dispute was settled, albeit uneasily. Ruark's annual income was reduced by ten thousand dollars, but United Features agreed to continue the column for another three years.

For some time, Ruark had been fascinated by motion pictures. His friend Eva Monley worked in the industry, so he was exposed to the production side as well as seeing the business personally through the sale to Hollywood of *Something of Value*. Ruark was under no illusions about the artistic value of motion pictures and script-writing, but he was very much aware of the money to be made there. His idea of co-producing *Uhuru* was based as much on ensuring that a large chunk of the profits go to him as on any idea of artistic control. As it turned out, the project never came to anything. Ruark's other involvement was a short feature film, released in 1962 around the same time *Uhuru* was published, called *Robert Ruark's Africa*. It was filmed in Kenya and involved some of Ruark's professional-hunter friends, including John Sutton. Viewed today, the film is rather amateurish — some of the staged scenes almost painfully so — but it is interesting for Ruark's narration. It shows up occasionally on late-night television in scratchy black-and-white prints.

At various times Ruark approached Matson about seeking script-writing jobs in Hollywood, but Matson talked him out of it on the grounds that he was a novelist — several cuts above a script-writer in prestige — and that was where he would make his real money. And if there was any doubt about the effect of Tinseltown on serious writers, especially those with drinking problems and large egos, one had only to remember F. Scott Fitzgerald. Still, as Ruark's money worries plagued him, the prospect of a lush job as a script-doctor in Hollywood appealed to him more and more. In an interview in 1964, he even suggested he had firm plans to do so. But nothing ever came of it.

\* \* \*

Within a month of official independence, it appeared East Africa would do exactly as Ruark had so often predicted and blow sky high. In early 1964, soldiers of the fledgling national armies of Kenya, Uganda, and Tanganyika mutinied. Shots were fired, politicians fled, newspapers blared headlines, and Britain diverted warships to the East African coast to rescue fleeing settlers. It was all as Ruark had foreseen — except it ended almost as quickly as it flared up. British troops at Kahawa, near Nairobi, swiftly reasserted control, while Royal Marines took Dar-es-Salaam, arrested the ringleaders, and propped up Julius Nyerere's government. Ruark watched it all unfold with a certain grim satisfaction. He had predicted an explosion in the Congo, and it happened within two weeks of his estimate. Although he admitted he had not expected trouble in East Africa to be so widespread so quickly, it was more or less in line with his expectations. In print for all to see, he suggested that with British military assistance the trouble would be contained, in the short term. However, he said, eventually the Somalis would rise up and claim the whole northeastern part of Kenya, the Wakamba in the south would try to take over Masai tribal lands, various ancient tribal rivalries would reassert themselves, the army would demand more money, and in the end, "What will happen is a war." As it turned out, Ruark was wrong, but at various times over the next few years, East Africa gave every appearance that he might well be right.

Through the winter of 1963-64 he worked on the manuscript of *The Honey Badger*. There were serious problems with the section he sent Harold Matson in November, and he reworked it extensively, removing some 30,000 words in "the notably mushy spots." He had the almost-complete manuscript with him when he arrived in New York in February. To his relief, the editors at McGraw-Hill decided he had made enough progress to allow him to start drawing money again. That did not mean they thought the book was ready to go to press, however. They wanted changes, and they wanted to meet with Ruark to discuss them. Since Ruark was planning to visit friends in Houston after paying a visit to his old acquaintance, President Lyndon Johnson, at the White House, the publisher suggested they meet with him there. Ruark flew down in March. It was during this visit that Ruark conducted the long taped interview Hugh Foster quotes at length in his biography.

Now, with little more than a year left to live, more serious cracks appeared in Ruark's psyche. According to Foster he was lonely and unhappy, desperate to remarry in order to have someone near him. He proposed to an old girlfriend, then recanted and ended their relationship. He proposed to an ex-secretary, only to be reminded she was already married. One by one, it seemed, he ran down the list of who was available and might be willing to marry him. He asked Eva Monley, his old friend and safari companion, and she gently told him that if he was still available in ten years, to give her a call. Back in Palamós, he embarked on a regime of alcohol consumption that suggested he was deliberately drinking himself to death.

As always, money problems lurked like a wolf at the door. His mother had been made a ward of the state and been committed to the state hospital in Dixhill, North Carolina, but Ruark was still responsible for many of her hospital bills, from expensive pychiatric evaluations to rebuilding a broken hip. As if that were not enough, McGraw-Hill pointed out that the money he was now drawing was, in fact, an advance against the next African book — not *The Honey Badger* — and that manuscript was due, according to the contract, by the end of 1965. Before one novel was even published, he was under pressure to produce the next.

Ruark relieved the pressure in two ways. First, he drank. He drank copiously, beginning early in the morning and continuing right through the day. The regime of abstinence he imposes on Alec Barr, when his fictional counterpart is working, had no place at Palamós. The attitude Harry Selby found toward the end — where no one could tell him anything he did not already know — evinced itself more and more if anyone suggested he should stop drinking, or at the very least, drink less. His friends came to one of two conclusions: Either Ruark felt he was immune to the adverse effects of alcohol, or he was drinking himself to death. Under the circumstances, there was really no third option. Considering he was just forty-eight years old at the time, successful, occasionally broke but far from poor, it is difficult to comprehend that he would not see he had a lot to live for, assuming there was no hidden cause such as an undisclosed, terminal illness.

Ruark had often listed his goals and ambitions in life, and he had achieved most if not all of them. Certainly he was barred from Kenya, the land he loved so much, and cut off from his friends who lived there, but he could still travel freely in other parts of Africa and nothing, not even being a prohibited immigrant in emerging Africa, lasts forever. And even if it did, there were other vistas in the great wide world. Ruark's behavior late in his life has never really been explained, and while his old friends, notably Eva Monley and Harry Selby, insist there was no suggestion of a terminal illness as a reason for deliberately choosing death by liver failure, it still seems like a possibility. And it certainly fits the facts, especially since that was the fate he decreed for Alec Barr. It is worth noting, also, that when he receives the bad news, Barr elects to keep it secret as long as possible, at least from his professional colleagues and the public at large. He does not want stories purchased "out of pity."

Ruark's second method of relieving stress had always been to flee to Africa on safari, and in the summer of 1964 he did just that. He travelled to Mozambique on what turned out to be his last safari, accompanied by two old friends from North America. They settled into the camp on the Save River. While he was there, Ruark received word that *Playboy* wanted him to write an article about modern-day safaris, and was offering a five-thousand-dollar fee. It was an enormous amount then for a magazine article, although in line with what Ruark normally received from *The Saturday Evening Post* or *Reader's Digest*. Ruark's disdain for "the jerk-off sheet" disappeared at the prospect of a large chunk of ready cash, and he hauled out his portable typewriter and set up shop on the Save River while Walker Stone and Ben Wright continued hunting. The result was a masterpiece of magazine writing, "Far-Out Safari." As Michael McIntosh comments, the title may be "insufferably hip," but the content is the modern safari through the eyes of a man "who has seen it all" and who also was one of the most effortlessly gifted magazine writers who ever lived.

The safari lasted several weeks. The two friends returned to America, to be replaced by Eva Monley, who flew in from Honolulu where she was involved in making a picture. She and Ruark stayed on in the camp for a couple of weeks more, then parted. Miss Monley left for home while Ruark flew to Southern Rhodesia. The situation there was becoming more tense as the white Rhodesians, a quarter of a million in number, resisted the idea of majority rule. Prime Minister Ian Smith was moving steadily toward the unilateral declaration of independence that would come later, in 1965. It was, by that time, the hottest story in Africa, and a natural for Ruark to cover.

On his return to Spain, Ruark found things going from bad to worse, professionally and financially. He was advised that Virginia was very ill. After making some changes to *The Honey Badger*, he flew to New York. According to Virginia, they had dinner together and he proposed that they remarry. She, too, turned him down, and he flew back to Spain. When he arrived, he found a cable informing him that Roy Howard, his old friend, was dead. What's more, there was a letter from United Features advising him that his contract had been cancelled. His column had been arriving late, or not at all, and United Features had had enough. It was not even signed by the managing editor: Ruark had been fired, in effect, by an accountant in the audit department.

Ruark immediately contacted Harold Matson and asked him to look for an alternative syndicate for the column. He also approached Scripps-Howard with the idea of a contract for newspaper articles to be purchased individually. The simple truth was, however, Robert Ruark's career as a newspaperman was over. He had few readers left, the editors were exasperated with poor quality and missed deadlines, and the syndicate was fed up with dealing with Ruark's ego, on the one hand, and his failure to perform on the other. There was no interest in any further journalistic efforts he might make. That he was appointed Sports Editor of *Playboy* a short time later — a job for which he was richly qualified in so many ways — did not make up for the loss of income, nor for the blow to his self-esteem.

Still, his career as a novelist was intact. *The Honey Badger* was almost finished. In January, 1965, he flew to New York to deliver the final manuscript and to spend some time with his ex-wife. Virginia's illness had grown progressively worse. At Christmas, at home with her family near Washington, she had begun coughing blood and was diagnosed with lung cancer. It was well advanced, and a rushed operation to remove the tumor was only partly successful. She was receiving radiation treatments when Ruark arrived for his visit, and even in her own far-gone condition, she wrote, she was shocked at how terrible her ex-husband looked.

With *The Honey Badger* safely at the publisher, it might have been expected the pressure would be off, but instead it just seemed to grow worse. Ruark's finances were a disaster. He was now in debt to McGraw-Hill to the tune of $150,000 in loans taken out against future royalties — an enormous sum. He was behind in his alimony payments and asked for extra time to pay. Instead of returning to Palamós to start work on the next (!) novel, he began to travel here and there, never staying long in one place, drinking heavily and spending a lot of time talking about the past. Another writer had tried to adapt *Uhuru* for a motion picture, but Ruark did not like the script; he tried to do a screenplay himself, but it was even worse — long, with unmanageable soliloquies.

On the positive side, *Playboy* agreed to serialize portions of *The Honey Badger*, to coincide with its publication in the summer of 1965, and paid Ruark a handsome, and very welcome, advance. As well, his old friend Walker Stone at Scripps-Howard Newspapers agreed to take Ruark on as an occasional correspondent, filing stories from wherever he happened to find them, on condition that the arrangement last only one year and that he be paid by the piece. In effect, he became a stringer for the organization. No one, it seemed, had any faith left in Ruark's ability to meet a deadline or to fulfil professional obligations. What Stone was offering was little more than a gesture of pity, extended to what Ruark once had been, on the basis of friendship.

Over the course of a decade, Ruark had worn out his welcome with several publishers, and McGraw-Hill was no exception. The company had been anxious to lure Ruark away from Henry Holt when he was finishing *Uhuru* and had offered him a fat, multi-book package with generous money provisions; now it came back to haunt them. Ruark had signed the contract and taken the money, and then taken more, drawing on the loan provisions they had offered, but he had failed to meet one deadline after another. Now he was deep in debt to the company, behind in delivering his novels, and had no source of steady money to pay the bills while he wrote the next one.

In fact, the contract he signed was a huge mistake, not just on McGraw-Hill's part, but on Ruark's and Harold Matson's part as well. Ruark was an extremely energetic writer who could produce reams of copy in a very short time, working at what he called "white heat," exercising admirable discipline (and sometimes unbelievable stamina) in sitting down at the typewriter, hour after hour, and "churning it out." Not only that, the copy he churned out had always been extremely good. As a writer, Ruark at his worst was still better than most. The problem with the McGraw-Hill contract was that it allowed Ruark to draw virtually unlimited advances without having, really, to meet deadlines. By the time McGraw-Hill had had enough, Ruark was in hock up to his neck, was behind with his alimony (a serious legal obligation had Virginia chosen to enforce it), had large, continuing expenses from his extravagant lifestyle, and had no way to pay the bills for the six to nine months of effort necessary to produce the next novel.

When he agreed to the contract, Ruark had absolute confidence in his own ability to shoulder the arduous workload. Presumably Matson did as well. But an agent has many responsibilities, one of which is to keep a client from getting himself into an impossible situation from which there is no escape. In that sense, Matson failed Ruark, although it would be unfair to lay much of the blame on him. If Ruark insisted on something, he would get his way. It was as simple as that. At any rate, by early 1965 Ruark was facing financial and professional ruin. There is no other way to describe it.

In May, 1965, Ruark wrote one last column for United Features, saying goodbye to "an old friend," in a rambling reminiscence of his time as a top-flight syndicated columnist and newspaperman. He recalled when he could "eat airline food and use gin as a substitute for sleep." He told his readers he was returning to his roots, working as a glorified copy boy for Scripps-Howard, filing stories when he felt like it, doing the things he had started off doing back in the 1930s. It was the last journalistic flicker of the old Ruark — humorous, irreverent, gently self-deprecating. He had been a columnist for only twenty years — little more than half a working career — yet it seemed like several lifetimes. And now it was over, in spite of Ruark's brave words about being a roving correspondent and doing those things that "got me syndicated" in the first place. It was too late. If anyone read his words and cared, there is no evidence of it. He had written his own epitaph.

* * *

At dinner in London with Eva Monley, Ruark looked a wreck. He drank heavily and popped pills.

"There was something going on inside him and he knew it, but he hid whatever it might have been," she told Hugh Foster. "I don't know why he kept drinking once he knew it would kill him. He just seemed very sad and tired at the end. Just all wore out."

That interview was in 1989. Ten years later, she told me much the same thing, but insisted she did not believe he was suffering from any terminal illness other than the self-inflicted one of imminent liver failure.

Drinking aside, however, Ruark was certainly exhibiting symptoms of something worse. He behaved like a man who knew his days were numbered. He had lost thirty pounds in less than six months and was vomiting blood. Still, he maintained a frantic, desperate pace. He travelled to Italy, then back to London, then back to Spain. There he received a letter from Matson telling him, yet again, about his worsening financial straits. The old family house in Southport, which Ruark had repurchased fifteen years earlier, was now up for sale since his mother had been committed to the state hospital. There was a possible buyer, and the prospect of money forthcoming cheered him up a little. He wrote back to Matson and referred to "this bug" that refused to leave him, that made him weak, caused him to lose weight, to cough, to vomit blood, to bleed from his rectum. Many of these symptoms are consistent with cirrhosis of the liver, which he undoubtedly had, but they are also consistent with various forms of cancer.

Ruark's friends, looking back, say they do not believe he had cancer. Perhaps they really do not. But it is difficult, looking for an explanation for his relentlessly self-destructive behavior, to come to any other conclusion.

On June 29, 1965, Ruark was in Barcelona when he suffered a severe rectal hemorrhage. Although he agreed to fly to London as soon as possible to see his doctor there, he refused medical assistance from a Spanish doctor in the meantime. In London his lawyer, Paul Gitlin, met him at Heathrow with an ambulance. Ruark looked dreadful when he emerged from the aircraft. He was wrapped in a blanket. His face was white. He did not seem to know where he was and required help down the steps from two flight attendants. Ruark, a man who had always been burly and tending to overweight, was now so thin he could be lifted onto a stretcher like a child. The ambulance took him into London to his flat on Park Street, where his doctor was waiting. The building had a tiny elevator of the type common in Europe, crowded even with three people in it. The ambulance attendants had to prop Ruark up on the stretcher. As the elevator jerked into motion he began to hemorrhage again, to the point where, Gitlin later told Foster, the floor was slippery with blood. As they moved him down the hall, Ruark "exploded with blood," and was in a critical state, lying on the floor, when the physician examined him.

The doctor ordered him to be taken to Middlesex Hospital and telephoned ahead to arrange for immediate blood transfusions. There, Ruark continued to hemorrhage, losing blood as fast as it could be pumped into him. All through the night the doctors worked on him, attempting to stanch the flow of blood, and in the early morning of June 30 they performed an emergency operation on his liver. When the surgeon opened him up, the liver was beyond repair — so diseased that according to Foster, "it almost came apart in the surgeon's hands." All they could do was sew up the incision and hope for the best. Ruark lasted through the day and into the evening. As midnight approached, he fell into a coma, and in the early hours of July 1, 1965, Robert Ruark died.

\* \* \*

The Spanish motorway from the gunmaking town of Eibar, on the chilly Bay of Biscay, to the resort town of Palamós, on the sunny Mediterranean, sweeps for five hundred miles through one mountain range after another, across a high plateau, through the bull-raising country of Navarre, and down into Catalonia.

Late June in Eibar is the time of the Fiesta of San Juan, country cousin to the Fiesta of San Fermin in nearby Pamplona. If Pamplona with its running of the bulls has the literary tradition, Eibar tries to make up for it with enthusiasm. It was still dark, not yet six in the morning, when I picked my way through the broken bottles on the sidewalk and past the last of the revellers to my rented car. The Renault had a wonderful new smell to it, and the green lights of the dashboard glowed brightly as I crawled through the narrow streets, up to the first of the mountain tunnels that led, eventually, to Palamós.

The sun was just rising as I came down through a pass and saw Pamplona spread out off to my left. All around me were the hills and the wheat fields, the wheat growing up and down the hills today just as it had eighty years ago when Ernest Hemingway saw them first and described them best. I had seen those wheat fields in my mind a thousand times before I ever saw them with my eyes, and there they were, exactly as he said. And, because of that, I knew all of Navarre would be just as he said, as well.

Robert Ruark wrote that Hemingway had taught him, through his writing, that if you lovingly burnish one fingernail to a high sheen, you can show the entire arm without mentioning it. Ruark had been through here many times. I wonder if Hemingway's wheat fields did for him what they did for me.

They brought Ruark's body home from London to be buried in Palamós. It was supposed to be cremated, apparently, but the Spanish authorities would not allow the ashes into the country. So Ruark's friend, Ricardo Sicré, negotiated a deal to bring the body back in a coffin. Then he had to negotiate further to get it out of the airport, and it required a third round of negotiations to get it into the municipal cemetery in Palamós. Robert Ruark was not a Roman Catholic, and so most of the cemetery was off limits for him. Even in death, it seems, he had difficulty finding a place where he belonged.

In the end, of course, he belonged in Palamós more than anywhere else. Certainly more than North Carolina or New York. Ruark lived in Spain for twelve years, which is a good long time in the life of a man. Long enough to know your neighbors, to watch people arrive and move away, to see new houses built and old landmarks torn down. Ruark did not become a Spaniard, but Spain certainly became his home, and he knew the country and loved it. Strangely enough, though, he never wrote about it. In *The Honey Badger*, a Spanish aristocrat asks Alec Barr why, since he knew bulls and bullfighting so well, he had never written about them. Barr replies that, in truth, all there was to say about the bulls had already been written, by Hemingway first, and later by Barnaby Conrad and others. Late in life, as he attempted to trump Hemingway, Ruark remarked that he had lived longer in Spain. Perhaps. But Hemingway lived here first, and wrote about it first, and owned it first, and would own it last. Ruark was shrewd to save Spain for himself and not write about it and invite further comparisons with Hemingway. There were too many of those as it was.

This motorway, now, this is a grand thing if you want to cover country. Four lanes, widening to six near the cities — Pamplona, Zaragoza.

The old bullfighters would have loved this. Instead of racketing over dusty mountain roads traveling from one bull ring to the next, they could have piled into a fast car and been to their next date in a few hours, rather than two days, or three. This motorway would have been a new thing to Hemingway, but it would not have ruined Pamplona for him. Pamplona was already ruined, even as he wrote *Death in the Afternoon* in the late twenties. They had torn out the center of the town he knew and put in a wide thoroughfare leading to the bull ring, and built apartment blocks so you could not see the mountains. There they are, those apartment blocks — and many more of them now than there were then. From the motorway, sweeping past, you can still see the mountains, though. The running of the bulls is now Spain's largest annual tourist attraction, according to the guidebooks. When Hemingway came first, he and Hadley were the only non-Spaniards in Pamplona. Then he wrote *The Sun Also Rises*, and that was pretty much the end of that. Hemingway destroyed the Pamplona he loved as surely as if he put a torch to the old wooden buildings that lined the route to the bull pens. Destroyed it and made it immortal, all in one stroke. Now that's power.

East of Pamplona the motorway crosses a high plateau, driving on for miles with a line of brown hills in the distance. This is bull-raising country and if there was any doubt, there is a huge black silhouette of a bull on a hilltop off in the distance. Across the plain there are black dots, grazing.

According to Eva Monley, Ruark was known to the townspeople of Palamós as "Don Roberto." When his coffin arrived there, it was placed in the library of his house, and on the day of the funeral it was carried through the town by hand, with a long line of mourners. This sounds suspiciously like Ruark's own description of Ned Adkins's funeral in Southport, thirty-five years earlier, in the *Old Man* stories.

As you approach Barcelona, the landscape changes. The hills come closer, and the earth turns reddish, and there are dark evergreens marching up and down. The motorways around Barcelona are a jungle, never mind the fact that now the signs are all in Catalan as well as Spanish. Palamós is sixty miles farther along the coast toward the French frontier, but the fact that the name shows up on road signs as soon as you get past

Barcelona tells you it is no longer the sleepy little coastal town Ruark fell in love with. The signs guide you in, off the motorway onto a secondary highway, and from that onto another that snakes along the coast, connecting all the little towns that have grown out and into each other until it is hard to tell, now, where one ends and the next one begins. Like all the Costa Brava, Palamós has become a hot and hazy, slightly lurid, holiday spot of beaches and cheap seaside hotels. The old town is engulfed by the new town, and gives every appearance of not liking it one little bit.

You can still find the old section, if you look. The streets are narrow and converge at odd angles. But there is nowhere, really, that you can get a look at the town as a whole, and so you feel your way around like a rat in a maze. The municipal cemetery sits on a patch of elevated ground — you could not call it a hill — surrounded by a high wall that shuts out the noise of the housing development on one side, and the camp ground on the other, with its temporary caravans and campers. There are a couple of hotels nearby as well, with rows of tour buses lined up along the sides. Overall, Palamós is an unlikely candidate if you are looking for a town in which to get away from it all. But it was considerably different when Ruark settled here.

The cemetery is an ancient oasis in the midst of all this tourist turmoil, a place where the residents can hide, finally and for all time, from the visitors that descend on Palamós from the sunless north. Inside the gate, the noise falls away to silence. The keeper's small house and a couple of giant palm trees stand guard and a pathway leads down between high rows of vaults on both sides. Here and there are small plots with trees and shrubs and individual headstones, but mostly the denizens are packed together in death just as Europeans so often live in voluble togetherness in life, living in apartments and flats and never dreaming, as North Americans do, of home ownership. At the far end of the cemetery it opens out into a kind of park, and there, off to one side, is Robert Ruark's tomb. It is a flat marble edifice with a small bronze plaque, flanked by shrubs — so totally different from the rest of the cemetery that, at first, you think it must be some kind of monument.

Virginia Ruark died of lung cancer about six months after her husband. Alan Ritchie, Ruark's "secretary cum slave," stayed on in

Palamós, and died in 1982. He is buried a few yards away. His is a simpler grave, with a tiny white marble cross that reads "Alan M. Ritchie 1919 - 1982" The top has broken off the cross, and sits, propped up, against one side. The grave has not been weeded recently. Master and man, together for all eternity, but with the proper differentiation upon which Alec Barr insisted when he equipped Luke Germani with a less ornate desk and a smaller office. Is there no end to the echoes?

It is very quiet where Robert Ruark lies. The high wall shuts out all the sounds of Palamós, and there is only a rustling of leaves as the shrubs murmur among themselves.

The bronze plaque is sparing in its praise. *Robert Ruark, Escritor. Nacio en Carolina del Norte el 29 de Diciembre de 1915. Fallecio en Londres el 1 de Julio de 1965. Gran Amigo de España. E.P.D.* Robert Ruark, Writer. A great friend of Spain. E.P.D.

Ernest Hemingway found himself referred to, publicly in print, as a "Friend of Spain," and mentioned it in Esquire, in early 1934. "Now I do not know just what constitutes a Friend of Spain," he wrote, "But when they call you that it is time to lay off." By the 1950s, Spain was in need of all the friends it could get, and it found a good one in Robert Ruark, although whether the notation was an official comment or just the feelings of Ricardo Sicré and the people of Palamós is hard to say. For its part, Spain was a *Gran Amigo de Ruark*, and it seems comfortable for him there in the cemetery, in the Spanish earth. I know what Hemingway meant, though. And after seeing the grave, there is nothing of Ruark left to find in Palamós. It is as different now from what it was as Kenya is different from what it was. There is no going back and no way to recapture it, except through books. Walking out of the cemetery, away from Ruark's shady Protestant plot with its simple plaque and two little bushes, past the ornate vaults of the Catholics with their gold-framed photographs and gilded flower pots, out past the tall palm trees to the shiny Renault, champing at its 200-horsepower bit to get back on the motorway, it all seemed like the end of a very long road that led here.

\* \* \*

Back in Eibar, near midnight, I found my friend Paul leaning on the long bar of the Cafe Arkupe. A line of bulls' heads, with and without ears, ran along the wall overhead. Paul was standing under a fierce-looking Miura chatting with the proprietor, Gabriel Sanchez, the old matador. While Paul addressed his glass of *tinto* and a plate of olives, Gabriel was talking bullfighting, speculating on the bulls we would see the next day when they ran through the streets. The *aficionados* of Eibar were at the Arkupe, three deep along the bar and spilling out into the street. The fiesta was gathering steam for a third night. Paul looked at me. "Good trip?" "All right," I said. "Find what you were looking for?" "Pretty much." Gabriel placed a glass in front of me. Gabriel Sanchez is in his seventies. He lost a testicle in the bull ring and walks with a pronounced limp and works twelve-hour days running his cafe and is the president of the Eibar *afición*. Smiling at him as I raised the glass, I thought of Tony Henley, an old bullfighter of a different type. He had liked Ruark very much.

"Bob was a very pleasant fellow," Tony told me one time, "Very amusing. He left the party much too early."

"*Salud*," I said.

* * *

## SELF PORTRAIT:
# The Honey Badger

If there was a tragedy in Robert Ruark's literary life, it was the fact that he died a few months before the publication of his last and greatest novel, *The Honey Badger*. Had he lived even six months or a year longer, the book would not have been tagged a "posthumous" novel — almost always the kiss of death. Nor would the critics have felt so completely unconstrained in savaging it. As it was, with Ruark safely dead and no one to defend the book, everyone from the *New York Times* to *Newsweek* had a field day. *Newsweek* called it "a legacy of weakness," while the *New York Times* described it as "a luxuriously bad novel," among other things.

These comments are puzzling to anyone who has read the book and paid attention to the words Ruark wrote. The reviews leave the impression that they had less to do with the novel than with getting back at a man who could not only write rings around all of the critics, but who also espoused unfashionable causes, unfashionable pastimes, and had the disquieting habit of telling the truth as he saw it. It is well known, also, that by this time, Robert Ruark had very few friends among the literary establishment.

In September, 1963, *True* magazine published an autobiographical article by Ruark, titled "The Man I Know Best." It was a deeply introspective piece in which he said he would like to see, someday, "Ruark the man separated from Ruark the columnist and Ruark the magazine writer from Ruark the novelist in at least one review of a book. I am tired," he wrote, "of having books evaluated in terms of whether or not the reviewer objects to the last column I wrote on Adlai Stevenson, or whether the reviewer disapproves of shooting for sport." He then acknowledged that he was asking a lot of reviewers, who were "a poozly lot at best." There was a great deal of prescience in those observations, considering the reception *The Honey Badger* received two years later.

Even today, it is still not completely accepted as part of the serious Ruark pantheon. Various recent critics, writing about his position in the firmament of outdoor writers, dismiss *The Honey Badger*. One called it "unreadable." Another suggested it was "unworthy" of the author of *Horn of the Hunter*. Yet there are also admirers of Ruark who consider it to be his finest work overall, a mature piece of literature by a complex man who had so completely mastered the art of writing that he made it look effortless.

When you strip away the ad-copy hype that litters the dust jacket of *The Honey Badger*, when you remove the innuendo that is usually attached to it (that it was written by a worn-out alcoholic), and when you actually read the book, what you are left with is the best portrait yet of what it actually means to be a writer.

Without a doubt, *The Honey Badger* is Robert Ruark's autobiography in everything but name, although there are many who contest that statement. There are those, Harry Selby among them, who insist that *Poor No More* was his autobiography, and that Ruark explicitly said so, more than once. That may well have been true in 1959, when *Poor No More* was published, but *The Honey Badger* appeared six years later. A great deal had happened in those six years, and Selby admits he never spoke to Ruark after 1962. What may have been the heart-felt truth for Ruark in 1959 could certainly have been revised by 1965. There are obvious autobiographical aspects to *Poor No More*, and many of the incidents early in the book are drawn from Ruark's younger life. But it is not an autobiography, fictional or otherwise. *The Honey Badger*, on the other hand, is based on Ruark's life from beginning to end. Upon publication, there was a brief flurry of controversy over just how autobiographical the book actually was, partly because it contained what were considered some highly unflattering portraits based on real people. Ruark's ex-wife, Virginia, wrote a scathing note about the book in the flyleaf of a copy she gave to a member of her family, in which she denounced the work as "a cruel book (that will) possibly hurt many people."

At the time, there was a half-hearted effort made to distance the book from real-life people, and there were even a few newspaper articles that purported to prove that the hero of the novel, Alec Barr, was not based on Robert Ruark at all, but rather on an obscure magazine writer of the time. To anyone who has read the novel seriously, and has any knowledge whatever about Ruark's life, such claims are simply fatuous. Alec Barr is Robert Ruark, and Robert Ruark is Alec Barr, psychologically at least. Certainly some differences exist, but these serve only to underscore that essential point. The two are inseparable.

*The Honey Badger* is the story of a man who "comes hungry out of Kingtown, South Carolina," learns the newspaper business in Washington, marries a girl from Chevy Chase, and ends up a successful novelist living in a penthouse on Manhattan's upper east side. The events described take place mainly between August, 1952, and the summer of 1962. Alec Barr has all the trappings of success, but he is missing its essence. He is not completely happy with his life or his marriage, and is naggingly dissatisfied with his work. He is certain he has bigger, more serious novels yet to be written, but he feels trapped by the various demands that are made upon him. The one thing he craves above all else (or so he believes) is to be truly in love — to find someone he would care about even more than he does about his work. But that is something he is unable to find. The one thing that commands his complete fidelity is his typewriter, the Iron Maiden, the "mistress he keeps in the back room." Much as he may think he wants other things outside of writing, his only irrevocable loyalty is to his work.

Structurally, the novel is the most complex Ruark ever attempted, and the fact that he was able to pull it off given his own physical and mental condition during the last two years of his life is conclusive proof that, if nothing else, he was a superb craftsman and a true professional. As well, such complexity is the result, largely, of instinct — of a storyteller setting out to tell a tale and doing so in his own way, not knowing really why, just knowing that it works. It would be impossible to plan a novel like *The Honey Badger* and work from a structural diagram. The writer would certainly start out with the broad structure in his mind, but the intricate weave of forward and back that makes up the novel could only come about as the writer wrote, and the characters assumed minds of their own.

*The Honey Badger* is a novel of layered flashbacks, flashbacks within flashbacks, and flash-forwards. It opens on a steaming hot night in Manhattan in August, 1952, with Barr walking out on his wife, Amelia, as they are preparing to go to a dinner party. Three months later they attempt to reconcile, but during that period Barr has an affair with an actress with whom he had struck up an acquaintance a few months earlier. In the meantime, separate flashbacks have covered Barr's wartime career in the Navy, his newspaper apprenticeship in Washington, his wife's life in Washington during the war, and Barr's childhood, university, and the beginnings of his climb to success in New York. It also covers, concurrently, Amelia's reaction to the break-up and how she deals with it. There is then a brief, present-day interlude, during which the Barrs' marriage again falters, the Mau Mau Emergency erupts in Kenya, and Barr departs to cover it for *Life* magazine.

The second part of the novel opens six years later, and the intervening time is covered, sporadically, in small flashbacks as the book moves to its conclusion.

Such a structure, while enormously difficult to orchestrate from a writer's point of view, keeping all the dates synchronized, offers several advantages. For one, it allows Alec Barr always to be the focal point, even when, as in sections about Amelia, he is not even present. It ensures that no walk-on character will steal the show, and it also eliminates any requirement to develop characters beyond a certain depth, or to intertwine their lives and activities beyond what is required to tell Barr's story. Whether Ruark intentionally made everything else in the novel merely a frame for a portrait of Alec Barr, or whether he just knew instinctively how to do so, it certainly works. And in storytelling, that is what counts.

\* \* \*

When basing a character on himself, a writer generally does two things: First and most obviously, he attributes characteristics and qualities that are identical to his own, good and bad. Less obviously, where a character differs from his model, he is given both virtues and vices the writer would like to have had himself. In other words, an autobiographical character like Alec Barr is a combination of what Ruark was and what he would like to have been. In Ernest Hemingway's *Islands in the Stream*, for example, the hero, Thomas Hudson, is closely modeled on Hemingway. But while he has many of Hemingway's characteristics, he also has several that were distinct improvements on the original. He drinks moderately, or at least is able to when he wants; he has also learned "the usages of divorce," and how not to quarrel with women, and how not to get married. In many ways Hudson is what Hemingway would like to have been. The same can be said of Alec Barr and Robert Ruark.

While the similarities between Barr and Ruark are seemingly endless, there are some differences. Physical appearance is one of them. Alec Barr is tall and lean, while Ruark tended to be overweight. Barr is ash-blond and "clean-shaven, always." Ruark was dark and had a moustache his entire adult life. And where on Ruark the finest suit of clothes looked like they had been "flung at him in a fit of rage," on Barr clothes "hang elegantly from his ropy frame." Writers view their creations as real people and give them qualities and even material possessions almost as one would give a gift to a loved one, and in this respect Ruark was generous to Barr. One thing Ruark allowed him, which he himself did not possess, was a certain disdain for money; toward the end Barr becomes a millionaire, "a fact which failed to impress him." Conversely, financial success impressed Ruark mightily, especially his own. Where Ruark hungered after and then flaunted his Rolls-Royce, Barr showed no interest in such a status symbol.

Naturally there are other differences between Ruark and Barr, yet despite the fact that most of them are minor, people sometimes cite them as evidence that the two cannot be one and the same. What they overlook, of course, is the fact that a man's life is not the plot of a book. It is too messy and has too many loose ends to translate directly into a tightly crafted plot. To make a viable plot, some things are left out and others are either altered or moved forward or back. For example, Ruark was born in 1915; as close as one can figure, Barr was born in 1911. The few years difference here was done purely because of the demands of plot. Ruark went to college when he was just fifteen, while Alec was a more mature nineteen. This allows him to be "barely on the right side of thirty" at the time of Pearl Harbor to qualify for the rank of Lieutenant. (j.g.) rather than Ensign in the Navy. It also allows him a credible level of professional achievement before the war begins.

On the other side of the ledger, the evidence is conclusive. Alec Barr was born in South Carolina rather than North Carolina, an inexplicable difference, but his childhood was Ruark's own. His mother and father, as well as his paternal grandparents, are all drawn from real life. The portrayal of Alec Barr's mother, Emma, is as scathing as Ruark's description of his own mother in magazine articles and interviews late in his life. In fact, many of the same phrases keep cropping up, such as "a driving woman." Emma Barr is a domineering woman, a hypochondriac, a morphine addict; like Charlotte Ruark, she has a history of repeated miscarriages. Although Ruark was an only child, Barr ends up with a younger brother, Martin, who is a wastrel and is referred to, but never appears in, the novel. James Barr, his father, is a weak, ineffectual man, dominated by his wife. Late in life, both parents are in and out of institutions, supported by remittances from their successful son in New York. In real life, the Ruark parents' affairs were financed by son Robert and managed by his Aunt Mae; Barr's parents are looked after by his Aunt Sal.

The vagaries of the Barr parents, with their escalating demands for money to pay hospital bills (mostly unnecessary) and frantic late-night ambulance rides, as well as their chronic bad debts, is a recurring theme in the book, just as that situation was a real problem for Robert Ruark late in his life.

Young Alec learns to read early, is a loner, and spends a great deal of time off in the woods with a shotgun or a book. With the Great Depression of 1929, his father loses his job, and the family home becomes a boarding house and quasi-bordello. Alec flees to university as soon as he can, returns home to visit only sporadically, and eventually shuns his home town altogether — again, just like Ruark.

Oddly enough, given his birthplace and the residency requirements of state universities, Alec goes to college in Chapel Hill, North Carolina, Ruark's own *alma mater* and an institution he both resented and revered the rest of his life. Dirt poor, Alec is forced to hold down two jobs to support himself, all the while begging the Student Loan Fund for another infusion and spending the rest of his time studying. He falls in love with a young woman who is majoring in journalism and find himself drawn into the class of a journalism professor, Skipper Henry. From there, Barr settles on writing as a career, and his subsequent progress is so closely drawn from Ruark's life that it can hardly be called fiction. From Barr's first job on the one-horse weekly in Center City in the Piedmont (Hamlet, North Carolina, in Ruark's actual case), to shipping out on the tramp steamer S.S. *Sundance*, to going to work in Washington — all are Ruark. Only the odd jobs, dead ends, and false starts — such as Ruark's career as an accountant with the WPA — are left out as distractions, and young Barr works his way up from detail boy to copy boy to reporter just as Ruark eventually did.

From his spartan boarding house to the menu at Papa Livera's Italian restaurant, to the people he worked with at the Washington *Daily News*, the details of Barr's life in Washington could be drawn from Ruark's resumé. For example, when Barr is hired by the *News*, his boss is John Barry, who jokes about the similarity of their names; when Ruark worked for the *News*, the managing editor was John O'Rourke. The authenticity of the detail in Ruark's loving depiction of the newspaper business is apparent from the beginning. It stems from the fact that Ruark was drawing on memory, not on imagination or third-party research. Like Hemingway's descriptions of deep-sea fishing in *Islands in the Stream*, drawn from experience, Ruark's newspaperman's Washington has the unmistakable ring of truth.

*The Honey Badger's* authenticity based on memory is reminiscent of the better pieces in Ruark's memoir of childhood, *The Old Man and the Boy*. Later in his life, commenting about the *Old Man* series, Ruark talks about unlocking his memory and exploring areas of his childhood he had not thought about in years. He talks about the effect of certain aromas, like Christmas, and evergreens, and wood fires, and the delicious smells of cooking that flooded the house. He never cites Marcel Proust, either as forerunner or mentor, but both *The Old Man and the Boy* and *The Honey Badger* contain passages that directly follow Proust's style in *Remembrance of Things Past*. In all likelihood, Proust would have been too highbrow for Ruark to mention, given his he-man persona, but that would not be the case for Alec Barr, who might well have included Proust on the extensive bookshelves in his Manhattan penthouse office.

* * *

After 1945, an entire generation of writers built their reputations on war novels or memoirs. Ruark was the exception: Although he was an officer in the U.S. Navy for the entire conflict, and served in some hair-raising theatres such as the North Atlantic convoys, he never wrote a novel drawing on his experiences. The closest he came was putting Alec Barr into a naval officer's uniform and giving him most of the same experiences he himself had, starting with the North Atlantic run as part of the Armed Guard, a naval service posted to the merchant marine to shoot at submarines and prevent "a wholesale diversion of our ships to Russia if Ivan signs a separate peace." Ruark served in the North Atlantic and in some of the hottest (gunfire-wise) parts of the Mediterranean before he was posted to the Pacific and ended the war in a series of staff jobs.

These experiences are mentioned briefly in *Horn of the Hunter*, but only in *The Honey Badger* do they play a major role in shaping the protagonist. For his part, Alec Barr plays down any idea of personal heroism. Although Barr did not have all the same experiences Ruark did, he had none that Ruark did not, with the exception of making it to Murmansk on one run. Like Ruark, Barr has a boxing match on the number-three hatch with an insubordinate seaman from New Jersey named Zabinski. And speaking of boxing, Alec Barr once gets into a fistfight with a professional baseball player, just as Ruark had his own inflated encounter with pitcher Louis Norman (Buck) Newsom of the Detroit Tigers.

After 1945, Ruark moved to New York. Similarly, Alec Barr migrates to New York. Ruark went on safari in 1951. Barr, by implication, goes hunting in Africa as well. One deviation from fact is that Ruark gives his hero considerably more experience hunting Africa than he himself had had by 1952. Both cover the Mau Mau Emergency for the magazines, but it is important for dramatic reasons that Barr be asked to go on the basis of his considerable experience there. So when the book opens in 1952 Barr already has a house full of hunting trophies and shelves of books on Africa, as well as the extensive scars from a wounded leopard, something which did not happen to Ruark until his trip to India in 1962. The Mau Mau Emergency accords Ruark and Barr a certain notoriety, which leads each to be considered an authority on Africa. In Barr's case, as in Ruark's, this has a significant impact on his career and his marriage.

An especially important parallel is the fact that, like Robert Ruark, Alec Barr is sterile. They have childless marriages, and in each case it is their fault, not the fault of their wives. Although Ruark never wrote about this in his own case, it plays a prominent part in *The Honey Badger* by implication; it is mentioned near the beginning of the book and then crops up several times later. In one of the most poignant scenes, Amelia Barr raises the possibility of adopting a child, sparking a tirade from Alec and the usual tears and recriminations; in the end, Amelia is sobbing in the bedroom while Alec tries to read the paper. For some reason, he finds Art Buchwald to be not as funny as usual.

One of the most basic instincts in human life is the desire to have children, and beyond the simple biological urge to procreate, it is generally conceded that having children is the average person's only real hope for immortality. For a writer, a book confers immortality, because as long as that book sits in the Library of Congress, and as long as your name is in the card file, you are immortal. Books are to an author what children are to a woman. Understand this and you go a long way toward understanding both Robert Ruark and Alec Barr. While Alec may have been able to overcome the psychological effects of sterility by substituting books for children, the same outlet was not available to Amelia — nor, for that matter, to Virginia Ruark. In the end, Alec felt sorry for Amelia, but there was nothing he could do about it. And adopting a child, he was convinced, was not the answer.

* * *

There is one vital area where Ruark made Barr different from himself, and that is in his affairs with women. On the surface, the book is about a series of extramarital affairs, but in reality Alec Barr was more faithful to his wife than most men, given the opportunity. He was not promiscuous, he was not a notorious womanizer, he was not a gratuitous flirt, he did not set out to seduce every woman he met — none of which could be said about Ruark. Did Ruark consciously create Barr to be different than himself in this way, or is this how he actually saw himself? No one will ever know. Certainly Barr has a few high-profile flings, the affair with actress Barbara Bayne being the focal point of the first half of the book. By and large, however, he leads a writer's typically drudge-like existence: up in the morning, work, eat, try to sleep, get up, start over. For long periods, he is at least sexually a faithful husband. Unfortunately, Amelia is convinced otherwise; she is perpetually suspicious of his absences, certain that he is carrying on constant love affairs.

This suspicion is central to the conflict in their marriage. Ruark rather plaintively points out that Barr is not a philanderer ("I'm not that good, Sweetie, I'm really not," he says to Amelia at one point) and that his occasional falls from grace are due to circumstance more than deliberate intent —which is true of most married men, but was most certainly not true of Ruark himself. Devotees of pop psychology might argue that Ruark's constant pursuit of women was an attempt to prove his manhood in spite of his sterility, and possibly there is an element of truth in that. If so, it was a quality he mercifully withheld from Alec Barr.

Ruark's dependence on alcohol, which was almost total and a governing factor in his life, is another area where their paths diverge. In *The Honey Badger*, just about everyone does a great deal of drinking, but Alec Barr is not an alcoholic. In fact, when he gets down to serious novel-writing, he purposefully goes on the wagon for months at a time. As a young reporter in Washington, he tells his future father-in-law, "I can work, or I can drink, but I can't work *and* drink." Many

346

years later, living in New York and writing seriously, he finds that the two most emphatically do not mix. Again, this is the exact opposite of Ruark, who, it could almost be said, could not work *without* drinking. Certainly he worked while he was drinking, and worked marvelously well. Harry Selby said of him, "Liquor was essential to him. He needed it. Drinking lit him up and fired his imagination." For whatever reason, however, Ruark did give Alec Barr this trait — just as Hemingway made his alter ego, Thomas Hudson, a man who occasionally drank too much but always had it under control. When Alec Barr does drink, it is sometimes romanticized, but never glorified; he does not revel or take refuge in alcoholism as did Malcolm Lowry, Dylan Thomas, Faulkner, Fitzgerald, or James Dickey (author of *Deliverance*). Considering literary fashions of the mid-20th century, he could certainly have gotten away with it, and it would have provided a blanket explanation for many of Barr's shortcomings. Perhaps Ruark saw that as taking the easy way out. The real explanation of Barr's faults lay in the strange genes that make a man a writer, something that Ruark did not pretend to understand, much as he wanted to. In the end, *The Honey Badger*, taken as a whole, is as close to an answer as anyone is likely to get.

\* \* \*

For most of the major characters in *The Honey Badger*, there are obvious real-life models. There is Ruark's immediate family in Wilmington, North Carolina. At Chapel Hill, there is Skipper Henry and the lissome co-ed, Fran Mayfield; both are based on real characters (Skipper Coffin, the journalism professor, and Nan Norman, his unrequited sweetheart), as is Mrs. MacPhail, Ruark's fraternity housemother. The story of how Ruark was drawn to the journalism course by an attractive female student is "absolutely true," says Eva Monley. "Bob told me that story many times." Then there is Jimmy James, Barr's best friend, classmate, and roommate in Washington, and the man who introduces Barr to Amelia, his ex-girlfriend and lover. In real life, it was Ruark's best friend, Jim Queen. Like Queen, Jim James is killed in the war.

In New York, the most important person in Alec Barr's professional life is his agent and close friend, Marc Mantell, who is modelled on Harold Matson. The Mantell Agency and The Matson Agency are one and the same, both occupying offices in Rockefeller Plaza. In *The Honey Badger*, Ruark name-drops shamelessly on Alec Barr's behalf: Toots Shor, Joe DiMaggio, Angelo Dundee, the denizens of The Twenty-One Club. These are all real friends and acquaintances from Ruark's life as sportswriter, syndicated columnist, and man-about-town, and he bestows their friendship on Barr almost like a benediction.

Needless to say, Amelia Barr is very much Virginia Webb, which makes her parents, Walker and Betsy MacMillan, Virginia's own. The entire Webb family can be forgiven if they found the portrait of themselves to be less than flattering. Alec's recollections of being broke and hungry in Washington, faced with the overladen table of the MacMillan family Sunday dinners, and the feeling of wanting the domestic stability they represented but feeling trapped by it at the same time, all have a ring of horrifying truth to them. The Webbs may have been very nice people, but even nice people have their dark side, and Ruark painted it with a vividly vindictive flair.

Unlike Ruark, Alec Barr is not an expatriate. He lives in a penthouse in New York, but has a country house in New Jersey, where he spends much of his serious writing time. The Jersey house is modeled directly on Ruark's *hacienda* in Palamós, and the major domo, ex-Navy petty officer Luca Germani, is Alan Ritchie, the ex-British Army sergeant who ran the house in Palamós and who is buried in the municipal cemetery there, a few yards from Ruark's own grave. In Africa, professional hunter Mike Denton (a minor character) is modeled at least partly on Harry Selby, while Barr's closest friend is Brian Burrows, manager of the New Stanley Hotel. He is none other than the real-life Brian Burrows, real-life manager of the New Stanley Hotel for many years and a good friend of Robert Ruark.

Given so many obvious models, it is logical that people close to Ruark should look for the counterparts of the few major characters who were not blatant. Who, for example, was Barbara Bayne? Who was Ben Lea? Who were Jill Richard and Dinah Lawrence? In all likelihood there were no specific models for the women in Barr's life, except for Dinah Lawrence, and even she was probably an amalgam of several people, not just one. Friends and acquaintances of writers always look for themselves in books, inevitably with one of two outcomes: If they do not find themselves, they are disappointed; if they do find themselves, they are shocked, dismayed, insulted, outraged, and, often, litigious. This is why authors are at such pains to put disclaimers in the front of their books, to obtain written quit-claims, and to affect surprise and pain that anyone should be offended. This was a serious problem for Ruark in his home town after the publication of *Poor No More*, in which all his former acquaintances saw themselves painted in various unflattering hues. Since he was dead, it was less of a problem with *The Honey Badger*, but both his publisher and his heirs were concerned about the possibility of a libel suit that would drain an already depleted Ruark treasury. This accounts for the denials that took place, distancing the book from its autobiographical nature. It was in everyone's best interests. There was little enough left to go around as it was, without handing most of the money over to the lawyers.

\* \* \*

Acknowledging the autobiographical basis of *The Honey Badger* is important to appreciating and understanding the book, not for the facts it presents, but as a foundation for accepting that, if Alec Barr is Robert Ruark, then his thoughts are Ruark's thoughts, and his principles Ruark's principles. If that is the case, and I believe it is, then Alec Barr's view of life and how it should be lived, with all its stresses and contradictions, are all Ruark. Having made Alec Barr a surrogate for himself, Robert Ruark was free to express, through Barr's words, his own deepest feelings.

There are specific instances throughout the book, but two especially stand out. One is a conversation Barr has with Luke Germani when he receives the news that Ernest Hemingway has committed suicide. Alec Barr is friends with Hemingway, something to which Ruark alluded in his own case. According to Ruark, they met in Pamplona in 1953, attended a bullfight, and got drunk together. Supposedly, Hemingway imparted many words of wisdom, both then and in later conversations when Ruark had a growing record of literary achievement. If any solid evidence of this relationship exists, however, I have been unable to find it. Ruark's name is mentioned nowhere in any of the Hemingway biographies, nor is there any correspondence between the two included in his collected letters. Hemingway's visit to Pamplona in 1953 has been documented, in detail, but Robert Ruark's name is nowhere to be found. Considering that Ruark himself was a man of some celebrity at that time, it is hard to believe it would not be mentioned somewhere, by someone.

At any rate, there was a rivalry between the two throughout Ruark's professional life, at least in the minds of the reviewers and in Ruark's as well, although probably not in Hemingway's. Being a pale imitation of Hemingway was an accusation that dogged Ruark for many years and that he deeply resented. He reacted by consciously trying to outdo Hemingway in some ways, and to a great degree he succeeded. By the end of his life, Ruark was a genuine authority on Africa and African big game hunting, something Hemingway never was (but never really purported to be, either). Ruark himself heard the news of Hemingway's death while he was in Africa, on a safari with Harry Selby. He immediately wrote a couple of journalistic tributes about Hemingway and his place in the literary world. These, however, were reaction pieces, while the conversation between Luke and Alec is Ruark's thoughtful assessment of what Hemingway was and why he had died, written several years later when his thoughts had distilled and gained perspective. It is summed up by Alec's comment: "I never called him Papa. I always thought of him as Mr. Hemingway." Ruark might have resented Hemingway as a rival in some ways, but he did not let the public image obscure the real man, and he never questioned the respect Hemingway deserved as a writer.

The second example of Barr speaking for Ruark occurs during Alec's eighteen-month odyssey through Africa. Convinced that Africa is too big an assignment for one man, the magazine for which he is working dispatches an assistant to help him. This young reporter, Larry Orde, promptly gets himself shot during a gunfight in the Kasai province of the Belgian Congo. Larry Orde was modeled on a real person, Scripps-Howard reporter Harry Taylor, who was killed in the Congo. Robert Ruark knew Taylor, and his death affected him quite deeply. The obituary Barr wrote for Orde is included in *The Honey Badger* as a comment on the nature of Africa and its eternal demand for blood. Barr's reflections on Orde, on reporting, and on Africa generally, are as close to a philosophical statement as Ruark allows himself to get. As a reflection of everything Ruark had learned about journalism, however, it is a masterpiece.

In fact, *The Honey Badger* is itself an excellent primer on writing and journalism, and many of the nuts-and-bolts aspects of the business. For example, in the first meeting between Barr and his future agent, Marc Mantell, the older man draws a diagram of the structure of a proper magazine article, to show the would-be magazine writer where he was going wrong in the structure of pieces that he had been unable to sell. Ruark's description of that classic construction could be used in a journalism class today, and would probably be more useful than any number of creative writing courses. If there was one type of writing of which Ruark was the undisputed master, it was magazine articles. Interestingly enough, Ruark drew just such a diagram himself, showing the structure of a novel, and gave it to his friend Leida Farrant just before his death.

\* \* \*

Alec Barr has many weaknesses that Ruark makes apparent in the book, and which are sometimes pointed out to him by his wife and his friends. He also has many strengths. In other words, he is a very believable human being, not some sort of mythical hero. To a great extent, he is a man who just wants to be left alone to do his work, which is all-important. At the same time, he feels trapped by the work as much as by the demands of his life in New York and his marriage, and he longs to break out of it, to fall in love, to have some fun, to be free of his wife, his parents and his "dreary Aunt Sal."

While the book is primarily a portrait of Alec Barr, the other major characters are given considerable depth, especially Amelia. On first reading, *The Honey Badger* appears to be a book about a man who has several extramarital affairs — or as an acquaintance of mine summed it up after skimming the book quickly, "It's about a guy who cheats on his wife. And you love it!"

This is a superficial summary of a book that is anything but superficial. Certainly Alec Barr cheats on his wife, but he is not a serial womanizer in the modern sense, and at various times Amelia Barr does her own share of cheating (such as when Alec is in the North Atlantic during the war and she is stuck, alone and lonely, in Washington). Read the book once and Amelia comes across as the villain; read it twice or three times and you begin to see a different side to her. She is actually a very sympathetic person — beautiful, intelligent, well-read. If she was a harridan, or a lush, or a shrew, or a cretin, Alec himself would be a far less complex person; the fact that he is dissatisfied with his life with a woman that most people would be more than happy to be married to merely adds to the depth of his contradictions.

Because of its structure and its wealth of detail, *The Honey Badger* is like an iceberg: Much of its substance is hidden beneath the surface. In other ways, it is like a hologram. Looked at from different angles, it reveals different shapes and shades and colors. When I first read it as a teenager, I saw one story; reading it years later as a married man, I saw another, and years later still, as a writer, something different yet again. With each reading, the characters acquired more depth. People that, at first glance, might have appeared to be caricatures, or villains, are shown to have good qualities as well. For example, there is Amelia's lifelong friend, the homosexual Francis Hopkins. Francis appears at various times throughout the book as Amelia's confidante and advisor, travel companion, and stand-in at dinner parties Alec refuses to attend. He is variously described in negative terms; the word "faggot," which Ruark employs liberally, is politically highly incorrect today, to say nothing of "fairy" and "pansy;" even in 1965 they would have been considered insensitive at best — something Alec is occasionally accused of, and that he sometimes ruefully admits. The portrait of Francis is not unremittingly negative, however. By the end of the book there is even a glimmer of understanding, and repeated readings reveal Francis in a more and more sympathetic light.

Because of what he wrote about emerging Africa in his newspaper column, Ruark was occasionally accused of racism (a blatant libel), and his portrayal of Francis, among other things, could lead to the assumption that he also hated homosexuals, especially overt ones. What is not commonly known is that Truman Capote, that most overt of homosexual writers, was a good personal friend of Ruark and regularly stayed at the Ruark house in Palamós. What Ruark disliked was not homosexuals themselves; it was any overweening display of homosexuality.

This general softening of characters as their true personalities are revealed extends also to the other women in Barr's life, especially the actress Barbara Bayne, who may be the love of his life, if there is such a thing. The failures of these love affairs are shown to be, with a relentless honesty, at least as much his fault as the fault of the women involved, all of whom are desperately in love with Alec at some point, yet are unable to come between him and his work.

\* \* \*

In *The Honey Badger*, Ruark created a real world, occupied by real people. They are not cardboard cutouts, nor are they caricatures. None of them is universally good, nor universally bad. There are no heroes, and no villains either. As a novelist he retained the one essential quality of a good journalist, and that is the ability to see both sides and to present them fairly and evenhandedly.

This quality emerged first with *Something of Value*. Although Peter McKenzie is the hero, he is far from totally heroic; and while Kimani is the villain, he is a villain not of his own making, nor totally villainous either. When that novel appeared, Ruark was seriously criticized by some of the settlers in Kenya for precisely that reason: He presented both sides, and the novel is sympathetic to everyone, to a degree, both black and white, who are caught up in a situation of historical magnitude, that was not of their making. Horrible things happened on both sides. By the time he wrote *Uhuru*, perhaps the best novel ever written about the conflicts involved in the decolonization of Africa, there were almost no blacks and whites anymore, only shades of grey. There are some unremittingly bad people in that book, but it has less to do with their skin color than with their nature and upbringing, and the really good people come in all colors.

In its own way, *The Honey Badger* is just as journalistically sound as those two great African novels, although it deals with one man's life and times rather than those of a country or a people.

Professional hunters, those anachronisms of the twentieth century that Ruark idolized, are central characters in the African novels, but play only bit parts in *The Honey Badger*. Hunting is not central to the novel, although it is certainly an important element, as is Africa. Robert Ruark loved Africa as a man might desperately love a faithless woman, or a woman adore a favorite child gone bad. Only in *The Honey Badger* does he really express that love. Through Alec Barr's words, you see Ruark's feelings for "the country, the people, the animals — *the country*." He muses about it in front of a fireplace in London with Jill Richard, then goes off to Africa on his long assignment. In the end, he chooses an extra few months of bugs and dust and horror, rather than a lifetime with her (although he does not know it at the time). For her part, realizing she would always play second fiddle to Barr's work, Jill Richard marries someone else. After he comes to terms with the hurt of the rejection, on the surface at least, Alec Barr realizes his greatest emotion is relief. Everything is "suddenly simpler." Now I can go home, he says, "and write my book."

\* \* \*

Barr does go home, to find that Amelia has divorced him because she is tired of being married to a will o' the wisp. At the age of forty-eight, he finds himself alone. Eventually the big book does get written, and he achieves solid financial success as well. He marries a woman much younger than himself. At his moment of greatest literary triumph, he finds that he is suffering from prostate cancer — or so it is assumed, since he never says explicitly where the cancer is except in the vicinity of the lower bowel. The immediate effect of the illness and its treatment is to render Alec Barr impotent. He is given ten years to live at the outside — ten years of progressive torture. Barr reacts the way most men would want to react, bearing up manfully on the outside in spite of being a squirming mass of fears and regrets underneath.

At this point, Ruark introduces a story that is his masterpiece of introspection on life and death: the ancient elephant of Illaut. It is a metaphor for Alec Barr, and it is also a metaphor for the Africa Ruark loved. This passage in *The Honey Badger* is, by itself, worth the price of admission. Ruark wrote about that same elephant three times for publication. The first two were in magazine articles; the last was this section of the novel. By the time the account reached this stage he had refined it to the point where every word was perfect.

\* \* \*

A honey badger, as is pointed out in the dust jacket copy, is a small African animal, a relative of the wolverine that, among other unlovable traits, tends to go for the groin when cornered, rather than for the throat. It is suggested that, as a title, it is a metaphor for modern American women and their desire to emasculate men, figuratively at least. Ruark may well have intended that meaning in part, but taking it as the whole story diminishes the novel's significance considerably. In my opinion, there is a broader meaning to the honey badger. It is not so much a metaphor for women as it is a metaphor for life. There is an actual honey badger in the novel that kills, wantonly, a large flock of tame exotic fowl at a game warden's headquarters in Tanganyika. An animal that kills for the fun of it, because it enjoys the taste of blood, might seem to be an unqualified villain, but even here Ruark's sense of fairness comes through. The animal, dreadful as it may be, was just "acting according to its lights," and while the game warden traps and kills the honey badger all the same, he does it quickly and without malice.

At the end, emasculated himself, Alec Barr and Amelia reconcile yet again, this time with the first real hope that they will be able to live together without the jealousy and conflict that sex inspires. The idea that she will no longer have any cause for suspicion, and therefore no conflict, is an intriguing one. For his part, Alec Barr looks at the time he has left and thinks "Ten years. I can do five books in ten years. That's a fair shake."

\* \* \*

*The Honey Badger*, as it was published, was a "big novel" in the fashion of the day — almost 600 pages long. Robert Ruark worked on the manuscript all through 1964 and into 1965. Its original form was much longer than even the final published version. At one point, he wrote his agent, he had cut 30,000 words from the most obviously "mushy" parts, and he continued to refine the book through the manuscript stage and even with the galley proofs, which he proof-read not so much to correct typographical errors as to polish the words even further. Considering the subject matter, it would be fascinating for anyone interested in Ruark's life to see those 30,000 words. The final manuscript that was clean-copied by Alan Ritchie was bound into two volumes of about 500 pages each, double-spaced. Even after it reached this stage, however, Ruark continued to edit it. He made many excisions on the manuscript, removing whole passages and changing individual words and sentences. When he then followed his normal practice of making two copies of the original, one for his agent, Harold Matson, and one for Virginia Webb, these changes were reproduced on the photocopies. Even these late alterations produce some fascinating insights into the characters in the novel.

For example, Ben Lea, a minor figure who is Barr's best friend in New York outside of Marc Mantell, is a senior man in an advertising agency whose function in life consists mainly of schmoozing and boozing, living off a fat expense account and pursuing classy women. He is fat and his hair is thinning, but he is still an "exceptional lover" who has been married five times. In the manuscript, Ruark mentions that, at one point, "Three of the city's reigning glamor women had worn simultaneous black eyes, announcing that Ben Lea had been feeling pretty testy that week." This line was expunged from the book before it went to press, probably in the galley stage. If Lea had been based on a real person, and was identifiable, such a line would have been acutely embarrassing, if not actionable. Worse, from a literary point of view, it would have colored Ben Lea in a decidedly negative light; even in 1965, giving a woman a black eye was not acceptable, and having three girlfriends simultaneously running around with black eyes would have painted Lea as a monster. Whatever the reason, literary or litigious, by the time the book went into print Ben Lea came across as a sparkling, lovable rogue, but no worse. This is important for one reason: At various points in the book, Lea sits down with Alec Barr — over lunch or in front of the fire in a hunting camp — and reads him the riot act about his life and his marriage. Invariably, Barr admits the truth in what Lea says, even if he does not immediately follow the advice.

In another section of the manuscript, Barbara Bayne jokingly insists that she is, in fact, a lesbian. This line is removed, but there is some suggestion that in the original manuscript Ruark painted her as a lesbian, or at least a bisexual, but this aspect of her was gradually removed as the novel was reworked and polished. Sexual preferences aside, Barbara plays a major role in the novel and her character in its final form is considerably more admirable than Ruark had, in all probability, originally intended. Barbara and Alec have a stormy relationship, with violent arguments, but no actual violence. In some of these arguments, Barbara is described as a lesbian, a whore, a cheat, or all three.

This brings up an interesting aspect of writing, especially when it is applied to an author writing about himself and filling his book with real people under false names. That is, in spite of what the author may have originally intended, characters change; they develop personalities of their own, and they say and do things the author never consciously planned. Sometimes, a writer may put in a character, intending to depict him in a highly unflattering light, then finds that the character develops in an entirely different direction. By the same token, a writer sometimes finds himself incapable of writing something he knows to be untrue, unfair, or unjust. If Barbara Bayne was based on a real person, Ruark may have gradually removed the untrue references as he refined the character. In other words, the *real* Barbara Bayne, whoever she was, may have emerged in spite of Ruark's original intentions. Certainly by the end of the book she is one of the most likable and sympathetic characters, outside of Alec Barr himself.

* * *

If Alec Barr was Robert Ruark, then Alec's wife, Amelia, was Virginia Webb Ruark. Like Barr and Ruark, the parallels between the real person and the fictional character are extremely close. Amelia came from a well-to-do family in Washington, she was talented as an interior decorator, and at one point was determined to pursue a career in that field. Likewise Virginia. This fact that was not lost on Ruark's ex-wife when she read the book. Her reaction to the novel was immediate and unequivocal. In a note to her family, written on page one of the novel's *Book I / Amelia*, she wrote:

*Dear Ones —*

*This book has made me very sad for a man I loved. It has also disgusted me at truth and fiction being so mixed together. It is a cruel book (not too well-written) and will possibly hurt many people. Not me — I'm beyond that. I have cried and cursed but the one thing we must all remember is that it was written by a very sick and despondent man. I think not fully rational but completely aware the bells were tolling for him.*

*All my love — Ginny Ruark*

Virginia Ruark's harsh assessment of the book is puzzling in several ways. First of all, Amelia is a very sympathetic character throughout the book. She is beautiful, well-built, sexy, intelligent, and witty. She is self-contained, sophisticated, and talented as an interior decorator. She has good taste and knows how to employ it. She is neither a falling-down drunk nor a slut. Amelia MacMillan Barr comes from a good family, and if she has had a somewhat checkered love life, well, who hasn't? On the negative side of the ledger, Amelia is extremely jealous of her husband, especially during his absences due to the nature of his work. Writers travel. Usually they travel alone. Amelia is portrayed as a woman who feels shut out of his life because she does not participate in his work, and is haunted by the suspicion that during these absences Alec is having endless affairs with other women. She has a "positive genius" for hoarding Alec's sins of omission and commission and then laying them before him at some future date. Anyone who has ever been married to a woman has experienced exactly that same trait. It is as much a trademark of womanhood as the periodic indispositions that govern their adult lives. And there is nothing that anyone can do about it, least of all the women themselves, assuming they even recognize it, acknowledge it, and would want to change it.

What sets Amelia apart is that she does indeed recognize that tendency in herself and even suggests she would rather not be that way, but she cannot help herself. As for Alec, he admits that he "contributed more than his share of barbs, if a girl were in the thorn-gathering business." At one point he says wryly to himself, "I poisoned a pretty good well."

Like her husband, Amelia Barr is a complex and contradictory character, and it takes time to get to know her. Repeated readings of the book reveal more and more of her qualities. She emerges gradually, like a butterfly from a cocoon, and when she stands fully revealed she is, by all accounts, a woman who is at least as admirable as Virginia Ruark and, in many ways, more so. One way in which she is very much unlike Virginia, however, is in her involvement in her husband's work. According to Harry Selby, Robert Ruark depended heavily on Virginia throughout his career, to offer opinions on ideas, on work in progress, and on finished manuscripts. Alec Barr depends on Amelia, in this way, not at all; he shuts her out of his work completely, to Amelia's regret. Virginia Ruark, knowing how important she had been to her husband's writing, may have taken this personally. Alternatively, since the book was written in its entirety after their stormy separation and divorce, she may have simply resented the fact that he was able to work at all without her involvement, and have seen *The Honey Badger* as a negation of her own sizable contribution over the years.

Amelia's non-involvement is, however, merely on the surface. A major theme of the book is the fact that Alec Barr does depend on Amelia heavily, if indirectly. In fact, it emerges, he cannot write without her. She may not participate by debating ideas or reviewing the copy he writes, but she is vital nonetheless. If Virginia Ruark chose to view this as an insult rather than as a compliment, then she was seeing only the surface facts and not what lay underneath.

\* \* \*

*The Honey Badger* elicited a number of adverse reactions from critics, one of whom wrote scathingly that it "totemized money." This is the kind of criticism that could come only from someone secure in the knowledge that his next paycheck would arrive on Thursday, or that the university would honor his tenure. The truth is, money is a central, *central* concern to every freelance writer who ever lived, and Ruark's employment of it adds to the realism of the novel, rather than detracting from it.

A failing of many novels is that the grubby necessity of earning a living never seems to enter into the plot, and the characters float through life blissfully immune to what Ruark called "nagging money problems." For some reason, artists — and writers in particular — are expected to be disdainful of money, as if filthy lucre were somehow unbecoming to the higher calling of art. This is self-serving hogwash, usually employed by publishers and editors who seem to think writers exist, as Hunter S. Thompson once put it, on some sort of "divine dole." Robert Ruark did not, and Alec Barr does not. Both came from poor, if not poverty-stricken, backgrounds, both worked and lived through the Depression, and both had only their writing on which to depend for the next check that will pay for the penthouse, the country place in New Jersey, or the repairs to the Rolls-Royce.

Freelance writing is, by definition, a precarious way to make a living. There is no job security whatsoever. Money dribbles in, usually less than expected, and almost always late. Magazines go under owing writers thousands; publishers sell their paperback rights for a song. Writers live in fear of literary tastes changing, or of a debilitating illness that might keep them away from the typewriter for a week or a month. In Barr's case, add to this the necessity of paying the bills to live in a Manhattan penthouse, and it is no wonder that earning money is a preoccupation for him. Yet, to Alec Barr money is merely the means to an end — living and working the way he wants to — and not an end in itself. Unlike Ruark, he is not given to flaunting what wealth he has. Although the "nagging money problems" are a recurring theme throughout the book, usually when he has been playing truant from his typewriter and his agent confronts him with his overdrawn bank account and dearth of accounts receivable, Alec is never, in his adult life, poor. And toward the end of the novel, when he scores his greatest artistic (and financial) success and becomes a "millionaire in fact," it changes nothing about him except to allow him to relax a little and not worry about paying next month's bills.

The Great Depression and the reality of grinding poverty shaped a generation of writers. Its influence is found in John Steinbeck and Ernest Hemingway, so it is no wonder it also crops up in Ruark. Having lived through it, he was terrified of a recurrence — as is Alec Barr. "I couldn't stand being poor again," Barr reflects. "Not at my age." Acknowledging the necessity of making a living, of "scuffling in the commercial end of the trade," is a far, far cry from "totemizing money." In another moment of harsh self-assessment, Barr reflects that if he were to find himself incapable of working and earning the money, everyone from his wife to his agent to his parents to his Aunt Sal would regard it as a personal affront, of being deprived of a tangible asset like a mink coat or a movie sale. He sees himself as their meal ticket, even if they do not.

Ivan Turgenev once wrote that "the heart of another is a dark forest." No one really knows what is taking place in another person's innermost thoughts, even if he has been married to that person for fifty years. Writers are not known for unburdening themselves anywhere except on the printed page, and then usually through the mouth of a fictional third party, the better to deny anything that comes back to haunt.

This may or may not have been a factor when Robert Ruark wrote the more introspective passages of *The Honey Badger*. But Alec Barr's reflections on his life, his work, his wife, his family, and his background, and on the demands of the people that surround him, are an amplification of many of the views that Ruark expressed in interviews and magazine articles toward the end of his life. At the heart of the book is Alec Barr's inability, in his own mind at least, to produce a work of the quality to which he aspires, and of which he thinks himself capable. Although he writes and produces competently and regularly, and various novels get written, none of them measures up as a "big work" in his own mind. One he dismisses as "just one more thick slice of slickness" that makes Book-of-the-Month, etcetera, and brings in a ton of cash that just as quickly gets paid out, leaving barely a ripple to tell of its passing.

Alec Barr's life in New York, like Ruark's own, is a directionless existence. Without children, without a meaningful married life, he sits down at the typewriter each day, produces the copy that gets sold, brings in the money that gets spent, and starts all over again the next day. Ruark gives Barr a Pulitzer early in his career, but turns him into a "steady plodder" as a novelist. Barr's salvation is Africa, and especially the "big work" that he produces as a result of the eighteen-month safari late in the novel. This book is called *Dark Dawning* and is projected as the first in a series of novels, like *The Forsyte Saga*, that will depict all of East Africa from first colonization to the Winds of Change. It wins Barr a second Pulitzer and makes him a millionaire. And it is at that moment of triumph, when he is happily married for a second time, that he is confronted with prostate cancer and his impending death.

At the end of his life, Robert Ruark was planning his own *magnum opus*, a series of novels exactly like Alec Barr's *Dark Dawning*, that would tell the history of Africa. In Ruark's case, it would include *Something of Value* and *Uhuru*, plus a preceding work yet to be written (what is now called, in the movie business, a *pre-quel*) and a novel of post-independence Africa. Neither was ever written. What was written instead was *The Honey Badger*. Did Ruark know at the time that he would die before the work was completed? Did he have a terminal illness, like Barr's, that would end his life horribly if he did not drink himself to death in the meantime? Some acquaintances, such as Harry Selby, insist that that is impossible; others, like Eva Monley, profess not to know. It is difficult to believe, however, given the relentlessly autobiographical nature of his last novel, that he did not have some inkling that his time was fast running out.

Every serious writer wants to leave in written form what he has learned of life, or thinks he has learned. *The Honey Badger* is a study of Ruark the writer by Ruark the man, and of Ruark the man by Ruark the writer. It is sometimes rueful, sometimes wry, often introspective, and always philosophical, although not in an academic sense. By the end of the novel, Alec Barr has learned the difference between what is really important and what is not. As presented by Ruark, the smallest truths are often the biggest ones, and the novel ends with Barr fitting a pair of cufflinks into a shirt and preparing to go into New York City, to "go home" to Amelia, and to prepare to live out his last few years as best he can. He is looking forward to seeing Francis Hopkins again, and maybe even going to dinner with the Hazeltines — an excruciating ordeal that caused him to walk out on Amelia in the first pages of the book, but which now beckons as a vaguely comforting irritant as the novel comes full circle. It is this structure that has caused more than one reader to immediately turn back to page one and begin reading it all over again. In the end, Robert Ruark creates a cast of characters, headed by Alec Barr, that you want to get to know better.

✳ ✳ ✳

*Chapter Fifteen*

# Ruark
# & Selby

In the old days we probably would have met at the Long Bar of the New Stanley Hotel in Nairobi. That was the customary meeting place for professional hunters just in off safari, wanting to look around and catch up on the news. But the Long Bar is no longer there, gone in a flurry of renovations to the New Stanley, which in turn has been engulfed by a Kenya that is now just one more struggling black African country and no longer the romantic Mecca for hunters from around the world.

Today the big-time safari industry is spread far and wide, with enclaves from Ethiopia to Botswana, as the professionals look for the last remaining pockets, not just of big game, but of an Africa that bears at least some resemblance, however faint, to the Dark Continent that held such sway over men's imaginations.

The "Steers" fast-food restaurant in Maun is about as far a cry from the old Long Bar of hallowed memory as you are likely to find this side of the Kabuli Mosque. It is located in a tiny mall next to the Spar supermarket, along with a travel agency and a curio shop. Steers is the kind of bright, polished, slightly upscale burger joint where the menu combinations are displayed in large glossy photographs and the staff members are bored near to tears and accept your order without ever looking at you. It is an utterly late-twentieth century phenomenon, but then so are professional hunters and journalists who meet over coffee instead of whisky.

It had been many years since I first met Harry Selby. That was back in the days when Safari South was the pillar of Botswana's hunting community and Selby was the cornerstone upon which Safari South was built. I had found him to be curiously less imposing than I imagined. I'm not sure what I was expecting then — a man seven feet tall with a piercing eye, I suppose. What I found instead was a gentleman of medium height with a reasonable handshake and a quiet laugh. At least the short, curly, black hair was still short, curly, and black. We stood in the dust outside Safari South's garage waiting for the mechanics to finish up. Selby gave the impression he would much rather be somewhere else. Having waited the better part of a lifetime to meet Harry Selby, with all the questions I wanted to ask and all the things I wanted to hear, I found myself commenting instead on the weather in Botswana and the slowness of mechanics the world over. Instead of the legendary Robert Ruark, we discussed the legendary endurance of the Toyota Landcruiser. And then he was gone.

Seven years later, fidgeting in Steers, looking out through the plateglass windows to the neat little sun-washed parking lot, where the Landcruisers and Hiluxes were parked mirror to mirror and khaki-clad denizens dashed in and out of Spar with plastic bags of whatever they put in plastic bags, there was the same feeling of waiting for a legend. And when Harry ducked in out of the sun and walked over to the booth where I was sitting, there was again the feeling that if he was indeed a legend, he was a reluctant one. And a suspicious one.

\* \* \*

*Coffee, sir? Tea, please. Yes, that will be fine, thank you. Welcome back. It has been a long time. Yes, it has. I've seen some of your articles. So, you are writing a book about Bob Ruark. Why?*

*Why? Why, indeed. How do you answer that?*

*You know, that fellow Hugh Foster wrote a biography of Bob. He wrote to me and told me he would be in Kenya and could meet with me at such and such a hotel on such and such a date. Can you imagine? That's two thousand miles away. Summoned me to meet him. Didn't go, of course. Then got another letter from him later, wondering why I hadn't turned up. You'd think it was just around the corner, and it's on the other side of Africa.*

*Well, I'm here in Botswana. I came halfway around the world to meet you and talk with you about Ruark on your own ground. You had to drive into town, of course.*

\* \* \*

"I really am rather uneasy about all this, you know," Selby said to me. "It was all so long ago. Some things are maybe best left as they are."

"You're free to refuse to talk about anything that is too sensitive," I said. "I'm not trying to pry open any old wounds. If there is something that is private, of course that's up to you. I just want to ask a few questions about Ruark's time in Africa, what he did, the influence he had. He's still the most influential safari writer, you know, and he's been dead for thirty-five years."

"Yes, well. I was with him, you know, on every one of his safaris in East Africa. I knew him better than anyone. I suppose you know I am writing my own memoirs. Joe and I — Joe Coogan, that is — Joe and I have been working on it for some time. I'm meeting him in Tanzania later this year, and we are going to do some more work on it. Put some more material on tape. I don't know if anything will ever come of it, actually. I am not very enthusiastic about it."

"I know about the book Joe's writing," I said. "I'm not trying to take anything away from it. As far as I can see, there's no conflict between your book and this one. If anything, they should complement each other."

"Bob Ruark would be a very small part of my book, you know," Selby insisted. "No more than a chapter, probably. There is no doubt Bob helped me a great deal, although I sometimes think I would have been better off...."

"He made you famous."

"Yes. Well, actually, I might have been better off if he hadn't."

"If you like, I can write down the areas that I would like to talk about. You can look at them, and think about them, and we can meet again later. Please believe me, I'm not asking you to reopen any old wounds."

"There aren't any old wounds. Nothing like that. Bob and I were friends. Then he found new friends. But there is nothing I'm bitter about."

"I'll write the questions down and bring them out to the house."

"Yes, that will be fine. I'll talk to Joe and see what he thinks about all this. There is my own book to consider, you understand."

\* \* \*

There is a sameness to a day in Botswana in May. It is clear and hotly crisp; if a cloud appears, you are justified in complaining to the tourist board. It is cool for sleeping, and the first cup of coffee is delicious in the chill of the morning, but by nine you are glad you wore shorts and by ten you'd like to take off your shirt. Late morning is not a busy time for any hamburger place, and Steers looks out onto the hot parking lot, wistfully awaiting the lunch-time crowd. Harry Selby was back. We were sitting in the same booth. We might never have left.

"Yes, well, I spoke with Joe and he thinks there is some conflict here," Selby began.

"He said that?"

"Yes."

"Where, exactly?"

"Well, you know, I'm just uneasy about this whole thing. There are some things I would not want to talk about. The old elephant at Illaut, for example. I will be talking about that in my own book."

"That's fine with me. The things I want to talk about are those areas you wouldn't include. Things about Ruark that are not related directly to you."

The four fine walls of Steers seemed to close in. It was a week later, at least I thought it was, and here we were going over the same things again. Maybe this was just a bad dream.

"Let me ask you something," I tried. "Do you think it's possible that Ruark was suffering from a terminal illness, and that he chose to drink himself to death rather than stretch it out?"

"Bob? No! He couldn't have kept it a secret, you see. You mean like cancer? No! If he had cancer he would have told everyone. He would have said, 'It looks like I'm going to die, so let's have a party.' He was very open, you know. He told me things — he told me things of an intensely personal nature, things you would never expect. He could never have kept something like that secret. Where did you ever get that idea?"

"Just a hunch. *The Honey Badger* is so autobiographical, and the hero ends up with prostate cancer, I wondered if perhaps there had been something similar with Ruark himself. Something he kept secret from the world, for whatever reason."

"No, his autobiography was *Poor No More*. He told me when it came out, 'Harry, that's my autobiography'."

\* \* \*

Robert Ruark and Harry Selby were close friends from the moment they met in 1951 on Ruark's first safari, until July of 1962 when Selby helped smuggle Ruark to Embakasi Airport outside Nairobi and put him on a plane out of Kenya, half a step ahead of a lawsuit launched by Chief James Gichuru, whom Ruark had mislabelled as a Mau Mau leader in his novel *Uhuru*.

"That was the last time I ever saw Bob," Selby said.

"He came back to Africa after that, though." I said. "He went hunting in Mozambique."

"Yes. By that time he didn't need me. He had new friends. He'd found a new country. 'Kenya's finished,' he said to me. 'East Africa's finished.' He went hunting in Mozambique, and the government there was so eager to make him happy they let him do anything he liked. He shot forty-some warthogs, or so I heard. He wanted the tusks for his friends, to make bottle openers. The game department in Mozambique let him do whatever he wanted. He thought he'd found a great new country, and he thought he could do for it what he'd done for Kenya."

"You don't think it broke his heart, not being able to go back to Kenya after independence?"

"No, not at all. He had a new country, and new friends."

\* \* \*

Ruark's new country, Mozambique, saw him briefly. His new professional hunter was Wally Johnson, a man Ruark described in various magazine articles in the same terms he had used to describe Selby a decade earlier. "Wally is First Hunter, Chief of Camp and the best hunter and tracker I ever knew," he wrote. There was a whiff of vindictiveness about the description, a touch of "I'll show you," directed at Selby.

"At the end there was nothing he did not know about Africa," Selby told me. "There was nothing you could tell him about the country, nothing you could tell him about the people, or about the animals. It became a little hard to take, when you were putting up a leopard bait and Bob was standing there telling you how it should be done. He idolized professional hunters. I think he really wanted to be a PH himself, and towards the end I think he convinced himself that he could be one."

In fact, although Ruark never claimed to have guided clients, he did write more than once that he had achieved a "semiprofessional" status, and that the PH would often allow him to hunt on his own or, if there was another client in camp, to go out with that client as if Ruark was the professional. He described instances of setting out leopard baits and shooting animals that had eluded the "top pros" for years. By the end, although his enthusiasm for Africa was still there, the tendency to brag, which had become such an irritation for his friends, was seeping into his written works as well. Ruark was very much the old Africa hand, telling how it was — a far cry from his first safari with Selby, when he portrayed himself as an awe-struck kid on the loose in paradise.

"In the early years, Bob was a joy to be with on safari. He was a wonderful man. Africa seemed to bring him alive. I'd meet him at the airport and he'd be grey and sick-looking, exhausted. But after two or three weeks in Africa, it was like he'd been completely cured. He looked younger, he'd be able to walk and hunt. I've never seen anyone react to Africa the way Bob Ruark did.

"Nothing fazed him, nothing got him down. I'd get the Land-Rover mired in a mudhole, and Bob would just take the bottle of gin and climb up on the bank and sit there and say, 'Okay, Selby, let's see how you get out of this one.' He was simply a joy to be with."

\* \* \*

By all accounts, the gin bottle was the truest friend Robert Ruark ever had, and the stories of his drinking are all-pervasive. There are few people left who knew Ruark well, but there are many who met him once or twice. Almost without exception those people recall only that, when they met, Ruark was drunk — at the Long Bar in the New Stanley, or on the terrace at the Norfolk, or the Muthaiga Club, or the Mount Kenya Safari Club, or at any one of a dozen watering holes throughout East Africa. Alcohol was a staple to Ruark in a way that very few writers use it. It was a catalyst for him, more than a crutch; it was a key that opened the door to his imagination, not just a barrier against the demons that are always waiting.

"Bob Ruark was the happiest drinker I've ever seen," Selby said. "I can honestly say that the only time I ever saw him despondent or depressed was when he *wasn't* drinking. One time we locked him in his room at the New Stanley and put a guard on the door while he dried out. Well, I won't go into that. But he ended up not drinking for about nine months, and all through that period he was unhappy and depressed."

At one point Selby sent Ruark to his own doctor in Nairobi, who prescribed a new regimen — no alcohol and a healthy diet being the main changes. For a while Ruark accepted the doctor's advice; then he reverted to form.

"He started drinking again, and suddenly it was all my doctor's fault," Selby recalled. "He told anyone who would listen that (the doctor) was a quack, he didn't know anything. For some reason he felt he needed to destroy the doctor to prove that he was all right."

"And that became your fault, too?" I asked.

"Of course."

Ruark's ability to function on a diet of gin and cigarettes, to cover thousands of miles and sit up until dawn in hotel rooms, writing columns and filing them from far-flung places, would be impossible to believe were there not so many witnesses to attest to the fact. A lifestyle that would cripple most people was, to Ruark, standing operating procedure, to use one of his favorite naval terms.

"It was amazing to see what he could do," Selby said. "He would be in the Long Bar, drinking away an afternoon and on into the evening. Hunters would come in, have a few drinks, and leave. Then others would come in. Bob would drink with them all, talking and listening. By the end of the evening, he would be so drunk you'd think he couldn't stand up. Then he'd go to his room, open his typewriter, and start writing down all the stories he'd heard that day in the bar. When you read the stuff later, it was all there — all the detail, all true. He had an amazing memory and ability to work when he was drinking."

More than one professional hunter who met Ruark said the same thing, that they would regale him with an anecdote when they thought he'd never remember it, only to have it show up in print months or years later, exact in every nuance and detail as they had told it. For a professional journalist, it was an exceptional and extremely valuable gift. It was an ability he shared with Ernest Hemingway, who also had an almost superhuman retention even during the direst of straits.

Ruark's drinking was more than merely a personal idiosyncracy, however. It reached out and affected two of the people who were closest to him during the 1950s: His wife, Virginia, and Harry Selby. "Ruark turned Selby into an alcoholic," one hunter told me bluntly. "It almost destroyed him. It damaged his family, and it took them years to get over it." Another told me how he had inherited some of Harry Selby's safari equipment after Selby left Kenya. Included was a notebook recording, in the old Ker & Downey method, the goods and services that had been purchased at outlying *dukkas* during various safaris. "The quantity of liquor they bought — gin, whisky, beer — it was truly astounding." As Ruark pointed out in "Far-Out Safari," however, "You cannot have too much gin or ammunition. The only thing drier on safari than a dry throat is a dry gun." As practical advice goes, it ain't bad.

\* \* \*

Shortly after Ruark and Selby first met, Harry Selby married a South African Airways stewardess named Miki, and he became a father. His son was named Mark Robert Selby, and Robert Ruark was both godfather and namesake. Or so Ruark said, in print, more than once.

"Actually, Mark was supposed to be named Mark Arthur," Selby told me, "But Bob insisted he was going to be the godfather. He insisted he be named Robert. He was to be named Mark Arthur, after my father, but he ended up Mark Robert."

"That shows how much Ruark cared about you and your family, doesn't it?"

"No, it doesn't. He did it so it would give him something to write about. He just wanted something to write about."

\* \* \*

The events of their first safari together in 1951 are familiar because they were so well documented in *Horn of the Hunter*. Although Ruark

372

and Selby made many more safaris together over the next ten years, none was chronicled in such detail, although several were mentioned in magazine articles and some of the incidents provided Ruark with exquisite subject matter. In the summer of 1960, for example, they made a journey into Uganda's Karamoja, a remote desert northwest of Kenya's own Northern Frontier District (NFD). It was only the second hunting safari in fifty years into that fabled, forbidden region. On that safari, Ruark carried a rifle, a .275 Rigby, that had belonged to Walter Dalrymple Maitland Bell — the famous elephant hunter Karamoja Bell himself. Another time they were elephant hunting on New Year's Day, with all the morning-after implications imaginable, when they encountered three pink elephants. Selby uttered the comment that Ruark made immortal: "Maybe if we shoot one, the other two will go away." There was also a camel-back safari into a newly opened, barely explored part of the NFD north of Marsabit, and there was the old elephant of Illaut, an ancient beast that Ruark hunted, then shot, then immortalized. His description of the life and death of that elephant in *The Honey Badger* is one of the finest pieces of writing that Ruark ever did.

One safari had nothing directly to do with hunting, however. In 1959, Robert Ruark arrived in Kenya on an extended assignment to write magazine articles and columns about emerging Africa for the Scripps-Howard news service. It was a tribute to his reputation as an authority on Africa that he was assigned the job, but it was also a severe test of stamina. By that time, a lifetime of drinking, smoking, and intemperate living had reduced Ruark to an almost frail condition, and five months of traversing emerging Africa all but finished him. His companion on this undertaking was Harry Selby. Travelling by airplane, Land-Rover, and any other means of transportation available, they covered Ethiopia, Somalia, all of East Africa, the apartheid regime in South Africa, and Southern Rhodesia. Ruark also made a long side trip into the Congo, but Selby did not accompany him on that leg.

Ruark used that lengthy assignment as the cornerstone of the last part of *The Honey Badger*, in which Alec Barr finally achieves many of his elusive goals in life, only to lose what he had ostensibly been searching for all along. For Barr, the journey took eighteen months, three times as long as Ruark's actual assignment, but Ruark's description of the demands of such an undertaking is a *tour de force* of boiled-down journalism. By the end of it, Barr was ready to wrap up the non-fiction book that was the focus of the assignment and get started on the big novel of his life. For Ruark, however, the aftermath was somewhat different: He was almost a basket case.

"We drove up to Somalia, and I had to do all the work," Selby recalled. "Bob was unable to do anything. When we stopped for the night I had to make camp, build the fire, do all the cooking. The next morning I'd break camp, clean up, and we'd set off again. He was so weak he could hardly function, and not do any of the work at all."

Journalistically, however, Ruark remained more than capable of doing the necessary work, with Selby's help. In *The Honey Badger*, Selby's role is played by Mike Denton, a professional hunter who never really develops a personality beyond that of Barr's chauffeur and errand boy. Ruark's description of how they dug up the stories behind the front-page political upheaval of the time rings true even after so many years:

*Mike's animal sensitivity came in very handy on more than one occasion. For one thing, he would work the other side of the street. He had large, trusting brown eyes; soft brown eyes that belied the keen brain behind. People talked to Mike where they were likely to be wary of Alec, whose press credentials were known...*

"At one point, when we were in South Africa," Selby said, "Ruark sent me up to Rhodesia to gather information. He was too weak to travel, so I went. I got what he wanted, I think."

At the time, Southern Rhodesia's government under Ian Smith was bearing down on its Unilateral Declaration of Independence, which would spark the fifteen-year brush war, and the situation there was electric. For his part, Ruark was in Johannesburg, a city he heartily disliked in the center of a country he described as being one step away from a fascist police state. Selby returned from his assignment in Salisbury with the necessary goods, and the team retreated, gratefully, to Kenya. There may have been drawbacks to life in Nairobi, but at least Ruark did not feel his room was bugged and his telephone tapped.

There were many more questions I wanted to ask about that journalistic odyssey, the particulars of which would have made a magnificent non-fiction book on Africa had Ruark taken the time (or been given the time) to write it. But, having made his comments, Selby rose and departed, leaving, as usual, more questions than answers.

* * *

Robert Ruark was married to Virginia Webb for thirty years. They met when he was a young reporter in Washington and stayed married until almost the end of his life — and hers. They were together on the first safari with Selby in 1951, and according to Ruark she fell as much in love with Africa as he did. Over the next ten years, however, while he returned to Africa regularly, Virginia went on safari with him only once or twice. Selby got to know her well, on those safaris as well as during a trip he made to New York City to visit them. That the Ruarks' marriage lasted as long as it did is a mystery. Robert Ruark's endless infidelities would have tested the forgiveness of a saint, and the fact that he was away, frequently and for extended periods, did not help. Or perhaps it did. A clue to the longevity of the marriage lies, once again, in *The Honey Badger*. Barr's wife, Amelia, is portrayed quite sympathetically(most women don't agree, but then most women don't read the book more than once, and then with rising irritation) and the relationship Ruark describes is one of mutual dependence. While Barr feels that he gets neither the love nor the understanding from Amelia that he wants in a wife, he finds repeatedly that he needs her for his work. He needs to have her there — someone "to run away *from*, and to run back to," as his friend Marc Mantell sardonically sums it up.

In Ruark's case, his dependence on Virginia, and her influence on his work, was far more direct.

"Bob was extremely dependent on Virginia," Selby told me. "Every idea he had he bounced off her first. Every piece of writing he did, he showed to her first. If she didn't like it, he dropped it. She was very important to his work in that way. That's why I was so surprised when I heard that they had divorced. How was he going to get along without her?

"Incidentally," Selby said as he left, "I asked my wife, Miki, about your idea that Bob might have had a terminal illness — prostate cancer or whatever. She agrees with me that it's impossible. He would never have been able to keep it a secret.

"Never!"

\* \* \*

In the end, Harry Selby decided he did not want to be involved in a new book about Robert Ruark — beyond what his own memoirs might someday say, of course. He gave various reasons for this. He went back and reread Hugh Foster's biography, and told me that since Foster had captured the Robert Ruark he had known quite well, there was no need to delve into the past any further. "I don't really see what there is to add," he said. I tried to explain that my goal was not to go over the same ground unnecessarily, or to dig up scandal about Ruark, or to damage his reputation in any way. What I wanted, I said, was to ask about those areas that were left curiously hanging by Foster — Ruark's actual times on safari, his influence in Africa, and above all, the influence of the books he left behind.

Selby listened to this and nodded, then shrugged, stood up, and walked out. I rose and went out with him. We stood outside Steers in the bright Botswana sunlight.

"No," Selby said, "I don't think so. I think I just want to remember the good times with Bob, and leave it at that."

\* \* \*

*Chapter Sixteen*

# A TUSK
# AND A BOOK

In the end, all that counts in a writer's life are the books he leaves behind. Nothing else really matters: not the drinking, not the women, not the ego, not the broken friendships, not the betrayals. Robert Ruark left a collection of books, the quality of which varied widely, from serious to almost trivial, and after his death a cottage industry grew up anthologizing his magazine articles, almost all non-fiction. The first appeared in 1966, and the most recent thirty years later. All have sold well, which is a testament to his continuing appeal as a writer, if not to the limitless depth of first-class material available.

Ruark would probably have wanted to be remembered as a novelist first and a newspaperman second. Michael McIntosh and others have noted that he was one of the best magazine writers who ever lived, but magazine writing has little status as an art form. The other major form of fiction in the twentieth century was short-story writing, but while Ruark wrote a few, they were not very good, and none was memorable. At least two have been included in the clutch of anthologies, but more as curiosities than as examples of Ruark's writing at its best.

\* \* \*

At the end of the twentieth century, hundreds of lists were compiled attempting to assign authors and their works a place in history. Depending on which list you read, either Marcel Proust's *Remembrance of Things Past* or James Joyce's *Ulysses* was generally acknowledged as the century's foremost novel, or the most influential, or both. The greatest American novel, according to most polls, was F. Scott Fitzgerald's *The Great Gatsby*. Ernest Hemingway and William Faulkner, both Nobel laureates for literature, appeared less than one might have expected, and Robert Ruark appeared not at all.

This is not surprising, and it is not my purpose to present a case for or against any of the above. To the best of my knowledge, Ruark's works of fiction do not comprise any part of any literature course; nor is he considered one of the serious novelists of the twentieth century, whether as a stylist or as an innovator. You are unlikely to find yourself embroiled in any discussion of his work in a modern-day New York literary salon, if such things still exist. There is, however, a phenomenon that grows up around significant works of art, and that is the small, devoted coterie of admirers, enthusiasts, and, at times, obsessive fans who live, eat, and drink a particular work. For example, Richard Wagner's *Ring of the Niebelungen* cycle of music-dramas is widely admired by critics, and generally acknowledged as a contender for the title of greatest work of art in history. At the same time it has a legion of Wagnerite fans who know the works inside out, have memorized entire passages, know the characters like family members, and endlessly attend performances. Similarly, there are people who have read and re-read Proust's *Remembrance* and can discuss the arcane foibles of even its more obscure characters. Hemingway and Faulkner have comparable followings, and annual festivals are devoted to examining and celebrating their works.

It would be hard to imagine three more disparate worlds than Wagner's Valhalla, Faulkner's Mississippi, and Proust's Paris, yet all three engender a remarkably similar reaction in the people who admire them: Somehow, in some sublime and unfathomable way, they strike a chord in certain people who read the work and become part of its extended family. Wagner, Proust, and Faulkner each created a unique world. Whether these worlds ever really existed as portrayed no longer matters: Because of these writers, those worlds will exist forever in the pages of their books and in the minds of their readers. Every writer dreams of achieving this goal, but remarkably few (considering the number of words written and pages published) ever do.

In his own way, Robert Ruark also created a unique world. While he never assembled a formal series of novels, linked by plot or characters or chronology, several of his books taken together do form a whole, although it is largely subliminal. *Horn of the Hunter, Something of Value, Uhuru,* and *The Honey Badger,* combined with some of his short non-fiction pieces, created a world of the modern African safari. This world owes its reality to the fact Ruark poured so much of his own genuine love of Africa into the pages of his books, and that reality continues to shine through, to inspire others, and to evoke a world many of us try to share and all of us envy.

\* \* \*

Toward the end of his life, Ruark wrote that "there are worse monuments to a life than a tusk or a book." To a writer — whether a newspaperman, poet, essayist, or hack — a book is the ultimate product, and a major novel is the ultimate book. Ruark left six novels; of these, three are major works (*Something of Value, Uhuru,* and *The Honey Badger*). *Poor No More,* while lengthy and serious, is really a potboiler, written to make money by cashing in on the success of *Something of Value,* and two can best be described as semi-comic curiosities (*Grenadine Etching* and its sequel). Most Ruark admirers feel *Something of Value* is the best novel. Certainly it was the foundation stone upon which his career as a novelist was built. It was a massive best-seller, book-club selection, and ultimately a motion picture with Rock Hudson and Sidney Poitier. It made Ruark a wealthy man and allowed him to live the life he wanted.

More than that, the novel had a wide impact politically, making people aware of what was happening in Kenya and helping to increase interest in Africa generally. And it was not just a best-seller; it was a long-seller. *Something of Value* stayed in print for many years, and today you can still find copies for sale in remote parts of Africa. From the Cape to Kenya, it is a rare bookshelf that does not have at least a paperback edition.

The same can be said of *Uhuru,* which was a loose sequel, although the names were changed so Ruark would not be limited by what he had already written about the characters. *Uhuru* is a more complex novel than its predecessor; there are more types of characters, and the characters themselves have more facets. In writing *Uhuru,* Ruark abandoned blacks and whites in favor of many shades of gray. This reflected his deepening knowledge and understanding of Africans and African life, and the realization that nothing is ever as simple as it first seems. By the time *Uhuru* was published, Ruark realized that not only did he not have all the answers to the desperate problems facing emerging Africa, but that there was almost certainly no one answer, and perhaps no answer at all — nothing that could apprehend the fate that lay in store not only for Kenya, but for all the former colonies that were lurching, stumbling, and occasionally slouching, toward independence.

Ruark's third major novel was *The Honey Badger*. The book has more detractors than admirers, but no one reading it can deny it is one of Ruark's major works. Finally, *Horn of the Hunter* is one of the foremost examples of a particular type of niche literature — the non-fiction account of a first safari. Between 1850 and 1999, literally hundreds of such books were published in Europe and America. Ruark's stands out as one of the very best because it combines a journalist's eye and devotion to accuracy and detail with a vivid, self-deprecating style and page after page of sheer enthusiasm.

After Ruark's death, his memory slowly faded and most of his books went out of print. Gradually, though, a market grew up for some of his titles among big game hunters and African travellers. By the late 1980s, there was a small but thriving market for early editions of his works, particularly *Horn of the Hunter* and the first anthology, *Use Enough Gun*. So great did the demand become, in fact, that Safari Press obtained the right to reprint both books, and they have sold steadily ever since. Among the novels, *Something of Value* carried the highest premium, followed at a distance by *Uhuru*. Except among the most devoted Ruark fans, however, his other books were in little demand and could be found for a few dollars in used-book stores and garage sales.

\* \* \*

One area to which Ruark could lay claim, almost as a specialty, is anthologies. He published four anthologies during his lifetime, and four more have been assembled since. This attests both to his prowess and production as a magazine writer and to the continuing appetite for his work among hunters and shooters.

There are two anthologies of his syndicated newspaper column (*I Did-n't Know It Was Loaded* and *One for the Road*) and two of the Old Man series of columns for *Field & Stream*. Ruark was barely in his grave before his survivors were hard at work assembling *Use Enough Gun*. This is a book about hunting, especially in Africa. The dust jacket has a photograph of Ruark at his world-weary best and includes excerpts from *Horn of the Hunter*, from his three major novels, and from various magazine articles. It was edited by Stuart Rose, with the introduction written by Ruark's close friend, Eva Monley. For the serious Ruark fan, there is little in the book that is not familiar, but it is certainly an excellent introduction to his work.

The second posthumous anthology was titled *Women*. It was edited by Joan Fulton and appeared in 1967. By that time Ruark's executors were trying to sort out his estate, which, between his divorce, expatriate living, and foreign exchange controls, was in considerable disarray. More to the point, there were bills to be paid, and the executors were eager to cash in on whatever market value still accrued to the Ruark name. As a columnist, Ruark made his first big splash attacking women's fashions and had used the war between the sexes as reliable dull-day copy for the rest of his career; it was his stock-in-trade as a mass-market columnist, so it was only natural to assemble some of his greatest hits in that direction and turn them into cash. The book was published in both hardcover and paperback. For those interested in Africa and hunting, there is little to *Women* except one piece extolling Virginia Ruark's virtues as an interior decorator, displaying Ruark's horns and hides to best advantage in the house in Palamós. Anyone with a sizable trophy collection and a recalcitrant spouse should obtain a copy of the book for that article alone.

After *Women*, Ruark's executors, including Eva Monley and his agent, Harold Matson, concluded the market had been saturated. By the end of his life, Ruark's celebrity as a syndicated columnist was largely gone anyway — the column was canceled by United Features because of low readership, and either indifference or outright hostility on the part of newspaper editors — and *The Honey Badger*, while a best-seller and book-club selection, received poor reviews. To all appearances, it was the end of the line. Although various of his books remained in print for several more years, in paperback at least, it was highly unlikely any general-interest publisher could be interested in further anthologies, even if they could be assembled.

The 1970s was a strange and depressing period for guns, hunting, Africa, and African literature. All appeared to be in terminal decline. The newly independent countries of Africa were flexing their political muscles and being courted by both East and West, who in turn were busy fighting the Cold War on all fronts. Ruark's political views, especially regarding self-governing African countries, were highly unfashionable. In London, the great English gunmakers were going out of business one after another, and the remaining ones were hanging on by the skin of their teeth. Africa's game herds were declining everywhere you looked, and both Kenya and Tanzania (the latter only temporarily) banned big game hunting. Other great hunting countries, including Mozambique, the Sudan, Rhodesia, and Angola, were all in a state of war, declared or undeclared. Under these circumstances, it is no wonder Ruark's literary reputation went into almost total eclipse.

In the 1980s, however, attitudes changed. African countries discovered there was considerable hard currency to be gained from big game hunting, and they needed it badly. A few conservation organizations came to the belated realization that regulated hunting was the best way to ensure the survival of species like leopards and elephants, and hunting groups like Safari Club International began to gain size and influence. A trickle of American hunters going to Africa became a flood, and with increased interest in Africa came a renaissance of Robert Ruark's reputation as a safari writer. The magazine world had also changed considerably in the interim, with a proliferation of smaller but more focused publications devoted to every aspect of outdoor life, from fine guns to wingshooting to art and literature. This evolution brought with it a new generation of magazine writers.

One of the best is Michael McIntosh, an expert on double guns who also happens to be a Shakespearean scholar and one of the most literate and graceful writers ever to adorn a masthead. Although he is a wingshooter and shotgunner almost exclusively, he is also a historian, admirer of good writing, and has an interest in Africa and hunting history. For many years he had been an admirer of Robert Ruark, primarily because of Ruark's *Old Man* articles and pieces on wingshooting. McIntosh decided there was room for another Ruark anthology, more focused than *Use Enough Gun*, drawing on Ruark's previously uncollected magazine works. With the Ruark estate's permission, McIntosh compiled *Robert Ruark's Africa*, published in 1990 by Countrysport Press. It has been a steady seller ever since and has helped rekindle interest in all of Ruark's works.

The articles McIntosh chose for the anthology range in quality, simply because he did not want to include anything that had already been collected. There is a law of declining quality in anthologies, because as each one appears the pool of remaining material grows smaller, and the material itself grows thinner. As well, the two *Old Man* books had already used the cream of that series. Still, there was enough first-rate material available for McIntosh to assemble an excellent overall collection. He also wrote a detailed introduction in which he recaps Ruark's life and career and offers insights into the state of his health, both physical and emotional. Harry Selby, who knew Ruark well, says McIntosh's analysis is very perceptive.

Unfortunately for the average reader, Countrysport Press published the work, as is its custom, in both a trade edition and a leather-bound limited edition at a higher price. Unlike some publishers, Countrysport makes a practice of including one or two pieces in the limited edition that are not in the trade, to make it more attractive to collectors. Because the higher-priced edition is limited to a small number of books (typically 250 to 1,000), this means the additional articles receive relatively little circulation. In the case of *Robert Ruark's Africa* this is doubly unfortunate, because the two additional articles are among the finest African pieces Ruark ever wrote. Both deserve far wider circulation than they have received.

The first, "Far-Out Safari," was a general piece on modern-day African hunting, commissioned by *Playboy* very near the end of Ruark's life; the second was one of the last *Field & Stream* columns, titled "A Leopard in the Rain." It is a short, heartfelt essay that shows more clearly and sincerely what safari life can and should be — beyond the killing of animals and the collecting of trophies — than any article I have ever read anywhere.

The success of this anthology helped spawn a second some years later. McIntosh has been closely associated with the magazine *Sporting Classics* almost since its inception. *Sporting Classics* is based in South Carolina, and its book reviewer, Dr. James Casada, is a university English professor and authority on southern hunting writers, including Ruark. In fact, he wrote an article about Ruark for the magazine in 1984. In the early 1990s, *Sporting Classics* decided to assemble a series of anthologies of "lost classics" — previously uncollected works by writers like Ruark and Jack O'Connor. Casada edited the Ruark book, which was published by Safari Press. In overall quality, it is not as even as McIntosh's — it suffers from the fact that there were simply not many articles left that had not been anthologized already, and Casada included a few odds and ends of the *Old Man* series that are frankly inferior. On the positive side, however, because he was not limited to pieces on Africa, Casada was able to include some fascinating articles such as Ruark's autobiographical piece, "The Man I Know Best," that appeared in *True* magazine in 1963. There are also three articles related to Ruark's assessment of Ernest Hemingway, published shortly after Hemingway's death. Finally, and fortunately, Casada included "Far-Out Safari" and "A Leopard in the Rain," on the (quite reasonable) grounds that, since they were not in the trade edition of *Robert Ruark's Africa*, they were not generally available and so could be considered "lost classics." If some of the other pieces are weak, or repeat themes Ruark handled better elsewhere, it does not detract from the overall value of the anthology. With this book, however, it is reasonable to assume Ruark's literary ore has been mined to exhaustion.

* * *

That so many anthologies have been published since his death is proof of one thing: Robert Ruark did not leave nearly enough behind. A shelf devoted to Ruark that includes everything he wrote, and everything that has been written about him, is tiny when put beside a comparable collection of Hemingway. This is understandable, however, when you consider Ruark's serious literary career lasted barely thirteen years, while Hemingway's spanned almost forty. There is no question

Ruark worked hard, produced a great deal in a short time, and made the very most of the limited time he was here, but the fact remains that he was only forty-nine years old when he died. By all rights, he should have lasted at least another decade or two had he lived a little slower and drank a little less. Well, drank a *lot* less.

At the end of *The Honey Badger*, Alec Barr is facing a shortened life expectancy due to cancer. But it will be a life unencumbered with demanding marriages, free to be devoted to literature. "Ten years, five books. That's a fair deal," he thinks to himself. Barr has a huge project in mind: a series of linked novels about Africa, similar to Galsworthy's *Forsyte Saga*, which Barr has tentatively titled *Dark Dawning*. Robert Ruark was projecting a similar series that, according to Eva Monley, was to be called *A Long View from a Tall Hill*, although the word "long" is usually omitted when the name is mentioned. The series was to embrace Ruark's two existing African novels, as well as one set in Kenya in the early years of the century and a concluding one that would take place after independence. Yet the first and last novels were never written. Unlike Ernest Hemingway, Robert Ruark left no huge treasure trove of material — no unpublished novels, no almost-completed manuscripts, no short stories in draft form. And so exactly what shape these novels were to take is a matter of conjecture.

That Ruark did not live long enough to write these, especially the last one, is a great loss. By the time he wrote *The Honey Badger*, his skill as a writer, both in his style and ability to structure a complex novel, was at its height, and it would have been fascinating to see what he produced — especially given the wide knowledge and understanding of Africa that he then possessed.

Two books that would have been naturals for Robert Ruark, given his background and interest in the subject, are a comprehensive non-fiction work on safaris and a journalistic non-fiction work on emerging Africa similar to the one Alec Barr wrote in *The Honey Badger*. To the best of my knowledge, he never considered writing either one. In a way, this is a greater loss than the uncompleted series of novels. Very few books have been written about safari life and organization from an objective standpoint, rather than from first-person experience. His friend Robert

M. Lee wrote *Safari Today* in 1960, and after Ruark's death several other such books appeared, most notably James Mellon's *African Hunter* (1975), and a history by Bartle Bull (*Safari*, 1988). Imagining what "Far-Out Safari" might have been if expanded to book length — honest, critical, and suitably world-weary — is enough to make a Ruark fan weep. As a writer, Ruark always leaves you wanting more, which is why he continues to enthrall us so many years after his death.

\* \* \*

In literature, there are various genres, and Robert Ruark made solid contributions to three of them. The two *Old Man* books fit into a niche shared with writers like Archibald Rutledge and Havilah Babcock. Generally speaking, it is a niche of short articles largely populated by bob-white quail, white-tailed deer, and white-haired elders; a lot of dogs sicken and die, and many memories are explored. At its worst, it includes tear-jerking stories about the autumns of our lives; at its best, it evokes memories of the important times in life, times which are never truly treasured until they are gone. Exactly which rung Ruark's work occupies on that particular ladder is a matter of opinion, with various authorities assigning Ruark either a very high position or putting him somewhere in the middle.

To me, the very fact that Ruark never resorted to the easy, maudlin approach sets the *Old Man* stories several notches above most of the others. Even in writing about the Old Man's death, for example, the story is simple and straightforward and, in the end, uplifting. You don't want to cry; you want to cheer. To some, this quality is somehow a detraction, as if anything so relentlessly upbeat cannot be any good. As any outdoor magazine editor will tell you, however, the most common submission he receives, from professional and amateur writers alike, is the "my old dog up and died" story. Most are rejected, a few are printed, and even fewer deserve to be. Almost none achieve lasting stature as literature. As Hemingway commented, the hardest thing to do is write honest prose about human beings. That is what Ruark attempted and, in large part, succeeded in doing with the *Old Man*. And he did so by avoiding clichés and almost never taking the easy way out. In the end, most of those articles look effortless. Perhaps for Ruark they were, although I doubt it;

making writing look smooth and effortless is very hard work. But that quality can cause critics to dismiss entire books as not being serious.

The second genre is the non-fiction safari book, of which *Horn of the Hunter* is an example. It was a spectacularly lucky work in several ways, not least of all in the fact that it was perhaps the last book of its type to appear before the Mau Mau Emergency erupted and swept away the old Kenya, along with our delusions about Africa. It captured a magical place at a precise moment in time, just before it ended, never to be regained.

Finally, the three major novels. They really should not be compared with books by Proust, Hemingway, Fitzgerald, or Faulkner, and I rather doubt even Ruark would suggest it. Their counterparts are works like Herman Wouk's *The Caine Mutiny*, or James Jones's *From Here to Eternity*.

The test for such a novel is not how many copies are sold but whether people are still reading it ten, twenty, or thirty years later. By that measure, Ruark's works must be placed in the solid second echelon of twentieth century novels, because they are still being read, still changing hands, and still being written and talked about many years after the novels finally went out of print. The reason lies not merely in the subject matter, but in what Ruark did with it: Like Proust's Paris of the *belle époque*, he created an Africa that may or may not have existed, but certainly exists now in the pages of his books. The Africa Ruark knew is gone, but the Africa he created for us will live forever.

❋ ❋ ❋

*Epilogue*

# A VIEW FROM
# A TALL HILL

On a sunny morning in May, 1994, I was riding in a Datsun pickup truck on a dusty road outside the town of Memel, a dot on a map on the high veldt of the Orange Free State. It was election day in South Africa, the first exercise of equal black and white democracy in the former strong-hold of apartheid, a day of momentous change, of world-shaking import — all in all, a day of journalistic hyperbole at its most outrageous. To acknowledge the significance of such a day, my Afrikaner friend Willem and I did what we did every other day: We went hunting.

On the road out along the Klip River, where the ducks flighted and the coots scurried, we encountered another pickup coming into town. It was loaded, shoulder to shoulder, with black farm workers and their wives and children. In front was another friend, a South African of established English pedigree and, by Willem's Afrikaner standards, of suspiciously liberal leanings. William and his wife, Sue, were driving their workers into town so they could line up outside the polling station to cast their votes for, in all probability, Nelson Mandela's African National Congress. They were participating in democracy their way, just as Willem and I were participating in ours.

During his time in Africa, Robert Ruark covered many conferences and elections — to say nothing of massacres, hangings, and highway rob-beries — and he noted that you never really learn anything from cover-ing a conference. What you need to do, he wrote in *The Honey Badger*, is go to the country that is affected and dig for the reaction there. He also said writing was mostly "exposure to the scene." Since I received my first grounding in the practical aspects of journalism from that book, I was following his instructions to the letter. The way to get a feel for what would become of South Africa under a new government, I believed, was to head for the vastness of right-wing Afrikanerdom — of which the eastern Free State is a bastion — and see what happened. Which is how I came to be in that truck, on that road, on that day. The one thing William and Sue and Willem and I all had in common was that we were armed to the teeth. Whatever happened, we were not going to go quietly.

As it turned out, Willem and his right-wing cohorts boycotted the election to a great extent, thereby helping to ensure an overwhelming ANC victory, which was the last thing they wanted. They knew what they were doing, but they did it anyway — a contradiction I am at a loss to explain coherently, even years later. William and Sue voted one way, their workers voted another. Then everybody went home, and life continued very much as it had for a century. While the foreign correspondents gathered in the press club in Johannesburg and fed off each other and political handouts, all predicting great and/or ghastly things, the impression I got in Memel was that everyone would take a guarded, but well-armed, attitude of simply waiting to see what would happen, and be ready for it when it did. Meanwhile, the cattle would graze, the sheep would go to market, William and Sue would drive their children to school, and the farm workers would cook their mealy-meal over the fires in their smoke-filled huts. It could have been 1894 as easily as 1994, and that was the real story out of South Africa that day in May.

* * *

The history of Africa since the great rush to independence in the early 1960s, and since Ruark's death in 1965, has been one of almost unremitting tragedy. So many of his dire predictions came true that it is almost pointless to list them. The continent became, and remains, the economic basket-case of the world. This happened for a combination of reasons, and there is no denying the roots of many of the problems lay in the legacy of colonialism — in the arbitrary borders that divided tribes on the one hand, or threw bitter enemies in together on the other; in the politicians who were ill-prepared to govern and people unable to read, much less vote rationally; in handing machine guns to warriors who still filed their teeth and drank menstrual fluid during tribal ceremonies. But that was just the starting point for Africa's troubles through the last thirty years of the twentieth century. The overwhelming factor that ensured these countries would stay on the road to ruin was the Cold War and the competition between the United States and the Soviet Union to draw third-world countries into their orbits, to attract allies who would vote the right way at the United Nations. To this end, Washington and Moscow fomented trouble, tolerated despots, and threw aid money at governments that were little more than thugs and thieves. The global chess game between the superpowers reduced the newly independent African countries to the role of expendable pawns, and the real losers in the game were the people of countries like Tanzania, Somalia, and the Congo.

Each of the colonial powers pulled out in its own way, and each left behind its own kind of mess. Belgium was by far the worst, judging by what happened in the Congo in the early 1960s, in the months leading up to independence — *l'indépendence* was the cry in Francophone Africa, as *Uhuru* was in Kenya — and in the three decades since. Robert Ruark saw the unfolding tragedy firsthand and wrote about it in his newspaper columns, and to a great degree it colored his view of emerging Africa. The Congo was one of Africa's largest and richest colonies with a treasure trove of minerals in Katanga Province. It was well worth fighting over, and the *Union Minière* was determined that, independent or not, it would keep its hands on the mineral wealth. The Congo was the setting for Joseph Conrad's *Heart of Darkness*, the definitive literary work on the evils of colonialism, and it provided the graphic images of raped nuns, castrated priests, slaughtered villages, colonial paratroops with their red berets, and ex-Foreign Legion mercenaries. The Congo was the United Nations' first real attempt at peacekeeping, and it was a disaster that almost destroyed the organization. It cost the life of the UN Secretary-General, Dag Hammarskjöld, in a still-unexplained plane crash. By the time the country lurched to independence, everyone in the civilized world was more than ready to welcome a strong man like Joseph Mobutu, a general who later took the name Mobutu Sese Seko and changed the Congo to Zaire. He then embarked on a systematic looting of the country, eventually salting away an estimated five billion dollars in Swiss bank accounts. Mobutu's reign in Zaire was one long rape-and-pillage, punctuated by periodic uprisings, civil wars, and massacres, all more or less tolerated by the West, which saw him as an anti-communist ally.

Of the fifty or so independent countries resulting from the scramble out of Africa in the 1960s, only one or two — literally — can be said to have enjoyed anything like a prolonged period of peace and prosperity. The two that spring to mind are Botswana and the Ivory Coast — and the latter is now starting to disintegrate. Angola, Mozambique, Rhodesia (Zimbabwe), and the Sudan have had civil wars that lasted for decades. Uganda and the Central African Republic were taken over by remarkably similar despots, Idi Amin and Jean Bedel Bokassa, who instituted reigns of terror. Ethiopia, Africa's one stable country of long history, was subjected to a military coup and a period of terror in which Emperor Haile Selassie was murdered, and the country descended into a perverted Marxist hell not unlike Cambodia. In recent years, notable slaughters have occurred in Rwanda and Burundi.

When most Americans think of Africa — if they think of it at all — the dominant images are of herds of animals on the Serengeti Plain, or starving Ethiopians perishing in the latest famine. Yet Africa is far from poor. It has vast oil reserves, not just in the north (Libya and the Sudan) but also in Nigeria and Angola. The Congo and South Africa have some of the richest mineral deposits to be found anywhere. The soil is generally fertile, and provided the rains come, people can feed themselves almost effortlessly. And, if the rains fail in one area, other regions are more than capable of producing food for everyone given the opportunity. South Africa, for example, is in some ways one of the most advanced agricultural countries on earth. During the dark days of the 1970s, the prime minister, John Vorster, argued that his country could become the aid basket for black Africa, given the opportunity and provided those countries backed off on their demands for the dismantling of apartheid. It may have been a blatant attempt at bribery, and it was dismissed without a second thought, but it was a valid observation nonetheless.

In 1971, I was in Uganda at the time Idi Amin first seized power, while he was still popular and the country was still "the garden of Africa," with a cheerful and well-fed (if somewhat barbarous) population. I met a truck driver who was South African by birth, who had left his homeland for the independent north to experience life in a black-ruled country where he was any man's equal. He had been in Uganda for nine months when we met, and he was completely disillusioned. There was no work to be had, and his savings were gone. I bought him a beer, and we sat on the terrace of the Speke Hotel, a delightful colonial relic, and talked about Africa. All he wanted to do was go home and find a job. But that avenue was closed to him. He was now independent, whether he liked it or not. Were it not for Idi Amin and various crackpot Marxists, Uganda should be a quite prosperous little country. It is almost oppressively fertile in most areas, and it has coffee, tea, some minerals, and excellent potential for tourism. Yet, almost forty years after independence, it is only now clawing its way to anything approaching prosperity, and it is doing so against the tide of Africa's newest scourge, Aids.

A better example of a potentially great nation squandered for no good reason is Nigeria, the largest black country by population and one of the wealthiest. With about one hundred million people, a generous mass of productive land, and vast oil reserves, Nigeria was touted in the 1960s as a potential superpower of Africa. It did not turn out that way. The country's boundaries confined several hostile tribes together, which led to the disastrous Biafran war and an endless succession of military dictatorships. Each new ruler borrowed against future oil production, then either squandered the money or embezzled it. Nigeria became famous for one thing only: *baksheesh*, or *dash*. By whatever name, it was life by bribery. Its largest city, Lagos, is an overpopulated, polluted, traffic-congested slum — a true hardship posting for any diplomat. As I write this, the *Financial Times* reports the current government (a laudable attempt at democracy) has had the Swiss bank accounts of the former ruler, General Abacha, frozen. They contain about 650 million U.S. dollars. Not much compared to Mobutu, I suppose, but then Abacha was only in power for six years. Had a heart attack not snatched him in the bloom of youth, he might have been a contender. Thanks to the legacy of Abacha and his predecessors, Nigeria has gone from being a beacon of hope to a symbol of hopelessness — conclusive evidence that an African country cannot be trusted to prosper even when blessed with substantial, valuable, dollar-producing resources.

Not all colonies rushed to independence in the 1960s. Southern Africa stood apart — the Republic of South Africa, Rhodesia, and the two Portuguese colonies, Mozambique and Angola. With South Africa as the anchor, they steadfastly resisted the tide of black rule and watched as one newly independent country after another descended into chaos. Portugal took the position that Mozambique and Angola were not colonies at all, but overseas provinces of Portugal — integral parts of the country. This argument was futile, and Portugal was forced to pull out; since then, both countries have had blood-soaked histories.

Rhodesia (Southern Rhodesia as it was originally) had a substantial white population, estimated at a quarter-million in 1964, with a black population of about six million. This was a substantially higher ratio of white to black than in Kenya, and the economy of the country was quite different. As well, of course, it had close ties with South Africa. The prime minister, Ian Smith, decided black rule was not an option and chose instead a unilateral declaration of independence in 1965. In spite of urgings by its former colonies in Africa, Great Britain refused to use military force to bring down Smith's government, and Rhodesia embarked on a fifteen-year odyssey of defiance. Several black guerrilla movements sprang up, based mainly in neighboring Zambia and Mozambique. The long bush war that ensued drained the country's treasury, and international trade sanctions did the rest. In 1980, a black government under Robert Mugabe took power, the name of the capital was changed from Salisbury to Harare, many of the hard-line white colonists fled to South Africa, and Zimbabwe became an independent country. Mugabe was a self-styled Marxist who followed the general line of most African Marxist leaders, which is that Marxism should be imposed on the common people but not on themselves or their friends and colleagues. If George Orwell had been alive to see it, after writing *Animal Farm*, he would be amazed, gratified, and horrified at the way life imitates art.

Trade sanctions contributed to Rhodesia's capitulation, but they were not without their benefits. Rhodesia was a naturally rich country, with a prosperous agricultural sector (there were huge white-owned ranches and farms, similar to South Africa) and substantial mineral resources. The tourist trade all but dried up, of course, but the potential was still there. Unable to import most basic consumer items, Rhodesia became self-sufficient in a surprising number of areas. Mugabe inherited a country that should have been largely immune to the problems facing countries like Ghana, for example, which had commodities to export, but were forced to import goods using the hard currency.

In twenty years of Mubage's rule, however, Zimbabwe has gone steadily downhill. All but about 60,000 white people have left the country, and those who remain are hanging on tenuously. Land reforms have been threatened, implemented, then threatened again. The justification is the age-old African refrain of a few people having too much land, while the majority has none. Farms have been seized, with and without compensation. The Mugabe government has sometimes insisted that compensation should be paid by Great Britain, since it had been a British colony, most of the whites are of British descent, and Britain caused the problem in the first place. That aside, many of the confiscated farms have been handed over, intact and operational, to Mugabe's friends, cohorts, and relatives. This pattern occurred also in Kenya and Tanzania, and it is one white South African farmers now fear. At the beginning of the twenty-first century, Zimbabwe is facing bankruptcy, with inflation spiralling, and the government grasping at ever-smaller straws in the hopes of an economic miracle.

In an earlier era, before the Cold War ended, Mugabe & Co. could have counted on Washington or Moscow to ride to the rescue, with loans or guarantees to prop them up, in hopes of acquiring another acolyte at the United Nations. Unfortunately for them, the era of easy aid is over. With Washington's support, the International Monetary Fund is calling the shots to a great degree, and one by one African countries are being forced into fiscal line. Had this been the case from the moment they became independent, the recent history of Africa would be considerably different.

The United Nations declared that January, 2000, would be the Month of Africa — a period in which the organization and its member states would focus on the problems facing the Dark Continent. Judging by the headlines, the problems today are depressingly like the problems of forty years ago, magnified and multiplied. Once again, the world is viewing events in the Congo (the name having been restored after Mobutu's demise) with a mixture of fascination and disgust. Mobutu's successor is a man named Laurent Kabila, who made the usual promises of honesty, fairness, and good government. After three years in power, albeit tenuously, he has come to be regarded as from the same mold as Mobutu. Kabila was barely in office when rebellions sprang up in various parts of the country, with some of his neighbors supporting him, others supporting his opponents, and still others supporting rival groups of rebels battling each other. In the northwest, Uganda, Rwanda, and Burundi are supplying arms and assistance to rebel groups; elsewhere, Zimbabwe, which does not even border on the Congo, has sent some 11,000 troops to help Kabila, and is maintaining them at its own expense and in defiance of the IMF, as its own economy sinks without a trace.

Journalists' descriptions of conditions in the Congo are depressingly familiar. A correspondent for London's *Financial Times*, a newspaper not given to hyperbole, describes crossing from Zambia into Katanga as "passing through the gates of Dante's Inferno." Reports from the northwest list atrocities on both sides — the latest being women buried alive. Exactly what any of the participants is trying to accomplish is not really clear. The only fact acknowledged by all sides, including the IMF, is that none of them can afford the high cost of what they are doing. Uganda has still not recovered from the Idi Amin era and is ravaged by Aids; Rwanda was the human-rights horror story of the 1990s; Zimbabwe is facing economic collapse. Yet still they fight a costly, endless war in the Congo. It has reached a point where no one can even suggest what a solution might be.

\* \* \*

For its part the Republic of South Africa, with its four million whites, its relatively modern economy, its gold and diamond mines and commercial ties to London, and its three hundred years of white history, watched what was happening elsewhere and dug in to resist black rule to the end. To many, the resistance was futile and gained them nothing but increased acrimony, but in retrospect it appears that the time bought by the Vorster government and its Afrikaner-dominated successors may have paid off. And, except for the most radical Old Testament right-wingers, every white South African with whom I have ever spoken, right from my first visit in 1976 at the time of the Soweto riots, admitted black rule was inevitable. What they accomplished by resisting for so long was to allow the object lessons of other countries time to unfold and sink in. By the time the ANC took power in 1994, Nelson Mandela and his colleagues, who were far from stupid, realized they had two choices: descend into hell, like Nigeria, or cooperate to make South Africa work. So far, having chosen the latter, the results have been surprisingly positive.

None of this would have surprised Robert Ruark. Most of it he predicted, publicly and in print, one way or the other. He was not an optimist about black Africa's prospects after independence, not because he was unduly critical of black Africans, but simply because he knew they were ill-prepared to govern independently in the modern world and were hopelessly out of their depth dealing with the realities of Cold War geopolitics. What would have surprised Ruark, however, was what happened in Kenya, the country he knew and loved best. Against all odds, it has come through the last thirty years as well as any country in Africa, and far better than most. Certainly, far better than anyone expected. Had anyone made a prediction about Kenya's future at the height of the Mau Mau Emergency in 1953-54, it would likely have envisioned a history not unlike the Congo with its ravished nuns and rivers of blood. That this did not happen is due, in the opinion of many white Kenyans, to the influence of Jomo Kenyatta, the man they had feared as the devil incarnate with his hooded eyes and blood-red ring. Tony Archer, a former professional hunter and one of the anti-Mau Mau "pseudo-gangsters," attended a meeting shortly after independence at which Kenyatta addressed the crowd, both black and white. He asked them to put the past aside, to forget the bitterness, and not attempt to even old scores. According to Archer, that is generally what happened. The most bitter or fearful white settlers left the colony, many of them emigrating to South Africa and Rhodesia. Those who remained seemed intent on making the best of the situation.

\* \* \*

If Ruark were to walk down Kenyatta Avenue today, he would not recognize his old haunt. The New Stanley is still there, as is the Thorn Tree Grill. And across town the Norfolk Hotel is expanded, renovated, and playing host to a new generation of diplomats, tourists, and aid workers. Now, though, a Hilton dominates the downtown skyline next to the Nairobi conference center with its round, black office tower. Like all cities in Africa, Nairobi has grown beyond all recognition, most of the growth being in slums and pollution. The sparkling, white-washed colonial town of 1953 has been replaced by a sprawling network of roads clogged with automobiles. Beggars and street hawkers walk up and down the traffic jams, tapping on car windows and offering to sell everything from stereos to framed photographs of the current president, Daniel arap Moi.

Moi was vice-president to Jomo Kenyatta from independence until Kenyatta's death in 1978. Kenyatta's rule can be condemned or praised, depending on your point of view. On the positive side, he did not encourage tribal divisions. The Kikuyu were dominant, of course, but the country did not descend into serious tribal conflict or anything like a civil war. There were one or two abortive attempts at military coups, but they were quickly put down with British assistance. Overall, Kenya was a stable political entity by African standards. Unfortunately, it was not immune to the major disease of African politics: corruption. Kenyatta himself became a major landowner. At one point, he reportedly owned twenty-seven large farms around Nairobi. His family also benefited. When the British left, Kenya had a functioning infrastructure that was largely neglected for the next three decades. The telephone system, for example, the finest in Africa in 1963, was treated by a succession of ministers like a cow to be milked, and in 1993 the equipment in place was virtually the same as it had been thirty years earlier. Even a cross-town Nairobi telephone call was all but impossible, with endless delays, and any kind of overseas call or fax was a hit-or-miss proposition. Mostly miss.

Daniel arap Moi succeeded Kenyatta in 1978, and at this writing is still in power. His government has become a byword for corruption and mismanagement in some circles, and he fights a running battle with the IMF over loans and aid money. Unemployment is high, and the Nairobi stock exchange is stagnant.

The real change in Kenya, though, seen through the eyes of a visitor who first went there in 1971 and has been returning on a more or less regular basis ever since, has less to do with conventional measurements of government and prosperity than it does with what is revealed by a casual walk through the center of Nairobi. Each visit saw changes. In 1971, Nairobi still retained the vestiges of colonial rule. The streets were clean and well-kept; the white walls of buildings were still white. Begging was not rife. A tourist could walk at night from the New Stanley to the Norfolk without fear. The available cuisine was the best in Africa — Indian food at the Three Bells, seafood at the Lobster Pot, and cheeseburgers at the Thorn Tree. There was even Africa's very first Japanese restaurant, newly opened at the Inter-Continental Hotel. On Sundays we would drive up to the Ngong Hills to find a cluster of Mercedes and Peugeots and Asian families out for a walk. Kenyatta Avenue was lined with shops dealing in skins and hides and horns, the products of legitimate hunting and government control work; ivory carving was a big industry, and whole tusks were sculpted into elaborate set-piece displays showing everything from the wildebeest migration to the procession of the Sirdar. Even the smell was different: Every breeze brought a waft of fresh-tanned hide, a hint of the Serengeti, and a whiff of curry. It was exhilarating then just to be alive and in Nairobi.

Joe Cheffings, a professional hunter who arrived in Kenya from England one week before the Mau Mau Emergency was declared, and who has lived there ever since, recalled that during that one period everyone who lived in Kenya, black and white, was proud to be Kenyan. "It seemed that life would always be good," he said. "There was a real sense that the country was going somewhere. Now...." As it turned out, Kenya was going somewhere, but not where anyone hoped. In 1976, under pressure from international anti-hunting organizations, Kenya banned big-game hunting and ushered in a period of game poaching such as has never been seen. The black rhino was poached to the brink of extinction, and elephant numbers were reduced to a fraction. Kenyatta's family and high members of the government were implicated in a sophisticated large-scale ivory-smuggling operation. Meanwhile, the country's population was growing at an alarming pace; for several years, according to U.N. figures, it had the fastest rate of increase in the world. Pressure on available land became ever greater, as well as on land set aside for game preserves and parks. Preservation of wildlife in Kenya became a major concern for everyone, it seemed, except for those in a position to do something about it; for their part, they used the international concern to line their own pockets at the animals' expense.

Tourism, however, grew to become the dominant industry. Zebra-striped minibuses became the symbol of a new Africa in which people watched animals, rather than shooting them for their horns. A nice symbol in some ways, if you ignore the fact that such encroachment can be far more damaging in the long run than a lone trophy hunter, on foot, taking one or two old bulls out of a herd. Horror stories of rings of minibuses, driving predators off their kills and literally causing them to starve, never seemed to leak out into the mainstream press, which regarded Africa as one big theme park. At the height of the tourist rush in the 1980s, whole plane loads of tourists invaded Kenya on package tours. Many of the former professional hunters, Joe Cheffings included, switched in 1976 from hunting to photographic safaris, with a little wing-shooting, which was still allowed by law. The most famous safari firm of all, Ker & Downey Safaris, became a major photographic outfitter.

Oddly enough, one of the factors that took the air out of the tourism balloon was the Gulf War of 1991. Iraq's invasion of Kuwait, and the threat of terrorist strikes against Americans, caused a downturn in the tourist industry, from which it never really recovered. Safari companies set up to service an endless stream of tourists found themselves scrambling for clients. Nairobi in 1990 was noticeably different than it had been twenty years earlier. The white walls were grimy; roads were pock-marked with potholes; you could still walk from the Norfolk to the Thorn Tree for lunch, but if you were returning after dark, you were strongly advised to take a cab and not carry much cash. The Thorn Tree was still there, but the red tablecloths sported cigarette burns and stains, and the waiters' contemptuous response was merely to turn it over and allow you to enjoy a different set of cigarette burns and stains. For the first time the prostitutes who hung around on the fringes of the New

Stanley would march into the Thorn Tree and sit down, unbidden. Ten minutes of desultory and unwelcome conversation later, they would demand money for their time and leave. If you argued, the waiter (who got a cut) sided with the woman. According to reports, the HIV rate among Nairobi prostitutes was ninety-eight per cent. Lunch at the Thorn Tree was not the unalloyed pleasure it once had been. The whole town seemed cynical.

Three years later, more of the same, except the Kenya shilling was going through the floor, the Norfolk was accepting payment in foreign currency only, you were advised not to walk anywhere downtown, and to deposit all but the barest amount of cash in the hotel safe. The city's buildings were dingier, the potholes bigger. There were bargains to be had for anyone with a few dollars, pounds, or marks. The streets were lined with hawkers, each trying to sell you something. If you paused to be polite, two or three shoeshine boys would jostle to get at your defenseless feet. Now I knew how a wildebeest felt if it slowed down and looked back. It was a mistake you only made once. On the bright side, at least they were selling something, not merely demanding money because they were poor, or deprived, or missing a limb, or, as Robert Ruark once reported an encounter with a prostitute in the Congo, simply "because I am black."

By 1993, Kenya was a stark contrast to Tanzania, its neighbor to the south where big-game hunting was once again a major industry. Under Julius Nyerere, Tanzania embarked on a thirty-year experiment in crackpot socialism that nearly bankrupted the country and turned it into a professional beggar at every level — from the finance minister pleading with the IMF to the leper clawing at your pant leg with his two remaining fingers. After a week or two in Tanzania, returning to Kenya was like home and mother. In 1993, I got to see Kenya from that point of view twice, once returning from Addis Ababa and once from Tanzania. That, perhaps, is the way anyone who might presume to judge it should see it.

Ethiopia was just then emerging from its period of Marxist military dictatorship, followed by a civil war. Addis Ababa (literally "new garden") was once again pleasant to visit, at least judging by the view from the Hilton Hotel terrace. You learned to ignore the beggars, some of whom were armed with AK-47s. That is taking begging to levels of sophistication unknown in Nairobi. And the Ethiopian money was worthless, even in Ethiopia. About all you could buy with it was a bag of sugar from a street vendor. The bag looked like it had changed hands many, many times. Getting back to the Norfolk after a stay in Addis Ababa, to a hot shower and a bartender who smiled, to a dining room with crisp tablecloths and a well-prepared steak and a bottle of Burgundy, was better than home and mother, by far. Similarly, getting back to Nairobi from Tanzania was an escape from the extortion kingdom of the world, where the consensus was that you — you, personally — owed them a living. All of them.

\* \* \*

For all of that, however, each successive visit to Nairobi produced more of the same, only worse. Which is not surprising. That is the way most of the world has gone since we were young, and things were all so much better. But the last time was different.

By 1999, Kenya was into serious difficulties with the IMF, and President Moi was doing his best to stall, to make cosmetic changes, to go just far enough to get the next loan instalment or have the lid taken off the aid jar. Not just the IMF, but that gaggle of sugar daddies known as the "donor countries" were insisting on some real changes. Blah, blah, blah. The telephone system seemed marginally better, and Kenya even had internet connections, which operated at a speed slightly greater than the average carrier pigeon.

On a visit to downtown Nairobi, I walked from a parking lot near the courthouse, up past the Hilton, down Kenyatta Avenue, and back through the government section to Haile Selassie Avenue. This was my old haunt thirty years ago. The street vendors were less aggressive, and the beggars were relatively few. The fundamental change from years past, however, was the complete absence of white faces on the streets. It took me a few minutes to realize it. I passed beggars and loiterers, men in business suits, women dressed to the nines in platform shoes, and others wrapped in colorful *kangas*. There were, presumably, lawyers and bankers and storekeepers and housewives and lady diplomats, and every single one was black. Once I realized this, I began consciously to look for white faces, or brown ones. In the old days, Nairobi was a multiracial town. Now it was a black city in a black country. It was at that moment I fully realized, and maybe acknowledged, that the old Kenya was dead.

A few days later I took a drive with Joe and Antony Cheffings on a duck-hunting expedition up past Nairobi to what is known as the "rice project," an expanse of flooded paddies where the duck population ravages the crops and a few local hunters like Joe have special permission to hunt as a form of control shooting. A far cry from shooting on control like J.A. Hunter, clearing Cape buffalo and lions from prospective farmland, but it is hunting on control nonetheless. On the entire drive up to the rice project, all day driving around, and then back into Nairobi and on to Langata, I saw not one other white face driving a car. Kenya is truly a black country now, fundamentally different than it was in Ruark's day. The old "white highlands" area, with Delamere's Equator Ranch, is mostly black-owned farms and plantations now. The white population, which numbered about 60,000 in 1963, is today no more than 20,000. That is the estimate, at least; no one knows for certain because there is no census breakdown by race.

When I was there in early 1999, the mostly white suburb of Langata had just won a court battle with the city of Nairobi. Langata had, in effect, seceded. Its citizens — people like Joe Cheffings and other former professional hunters, including Tony Archer and, until his death, John Sutton — live in houses set well in from the road, screened by high hedges. The security is not obvious, but it is substantial. They have (and pay for) their own security force, which camps out on a corner of Cheffings's property. They run their own waterworks. In effect, they operate as an independent town and saw no reason to pay taxes to Nairobi for services they did not receive. The battle went up the judicial chain to the high courts, which ruled in favor of Langata. Karen, the other favorite suburb that includes a large proportion of wealthy black people, is in a similar situation.

In Langata, the residents have a security system of short-wave radios and check in with each other on a nightly basis. Across a valley is a black community. In South Africa it would be called a township. Here it is a suburb. In the evening you can hear the deep throbbing bass of the ghetto blasters that pervade the place, and occasionally night-time intruders rouse Langata's guard dogs. Doors are routinely chained shut and a late-night alert brings the hired guns running with their dogs. The crime is mostly economic — smash-and-grab robberies as opposed to murders and muggings — but the residents' precautions and reactions are strangely reminiscent of the Mau Mau Emergency. The sea-change in the life of Kenya Colony that took place in October, 1952, has never really relaxed its grip. Joe Cheffings is one of the few who still own firearms. He was allowed to keep them when the police conducted their sweep after hunting was banned, in which all hunting rifles were confiscated and either destroyed or shipped out of the country. "I told them these were not for hunting, they were for self-defense," Joe told me. It is a bizarre twist on gun-control arguments in other countries, where some sort of sporting purpose is the one defense of a particular gun. At any rate, while Kenya does not have the routine bloodshed that characterizes crime in South Africa today, it is still a fearful society by European or American standards.

The simple truth is that the Kenya Ruark knew no longer exists. The country has not merely moved along, it has been transformed. Today, tourism is a major industry, but the United Nations is an even bigger industry. Since 1963, Nairobi has become the center for several U.N. agencies, who pour money into the local economy and provide thousands of jobs. Nairobi is no more the hunting capital of old than modern-day Dallas is a cowtown.

\* \* \*

For most hunters May, 1976, was a turning point in the history of Africa. That is the date when Kenya bowed to the demands of international animal-welfare groups and outlawed big game hunting. At a stroke, the traditional safari industry was crippled; Kenya, "the cradle of safari," was no longer the hunting capital of Africa.

Since that time, Safari Club International, among others, has worked to persuade Kenya to reverse the decision. While Kenya has periodically seemed to be on the brink of restoring big game hunting, for a variety of reasons it has never happened, and is now less likely than ever, as we shall see. May, 1976, was certainly a turning point, and it can be argued that it was the historical low for hunting in Africa, but in some ways it was actually a blessing for hunters — certainly more so than for the game animals it was intended to protect.

What is sometimes forgotten is that Tanzania had already closed hunting and showed no signs of reopening. Since Tanzania was then, and is now, the greatest storehouse of game on the continent in terms of wild conditions and number of species, its closure in 1974 was a considerably greater blow. And while Kenya was still the spot to hunt certain animals peculiar to the region, such as bongo in the Aberdares, it was not as significant a hunting area as its neighbor to the south. Tanzania closed hunting ostensibly as an anti-poaching measure, although part of the motivation was that hunters and hunting were viewed as colonial relics that had no place in a modern socialist state. Tanzania reopened hunting in 1984 because it found poaching actually increased without regulated hunting and a well-trained, well-funded game department. As well, Tanzania realized its experiment in socialism was failing miserably. The country was counted regularly among the very poorest in the world, and there was a huge pot of hard currency to be made from big game safaris.

Tanzania stands alone in one respect, which is the dedication and imagination it has brought to the art of squeezing every last dollar out of visiting sportsmen. A hunter on a flight out of Kilimanjaro Airport has every right to feel like a well-wrung sponge. From bribes to taxes on firearms and even, at one time, on individual rounds of ammunition, to "conservation surcharges" and trophy fees on any creature that can walk, crawl, slither, or fly, Tanzania has done its best to take much of the fun out of safari, even while providing the greatest hunting on the continent. That hunters continue to flock to Tanzania in spite of this legalized shakedown is testimony to the quality of the hunting and the animals to be found there.

In 1963, when Kenya achieved independence, there was a general exodus of professional hunters, many of whom settled in southern Africa. A group led by Tony Henley and Harry Selby went to Botswana and helped turn the Okavango Delta and the Kalahari Desert into southern Africa's answer to the Serengeti. In the mid-1970s, with Tanzania and Kenya both closed, there was another movement out of East

Africa, as professionals looked for new fields to hunt. With no chance of taking a bongo in Kenya, for example, attention turned first to the Sudan and Central African Republic, and in later years to even more remote areas where the western bongo can be found, such as Congo Brazzaville and Cameroon.

All these developments pale, however, in comparison to what has happened in South Africa since 1965, the year Robert Ruark died and also the period when James Mellon was hunting all over Africa, compiling material for his classic, *African Hunter*. In game terms, the Republic of South Africa was a wasteland at that time, although this was hardly a recent development. During the fifty years from the time William Cornwallis Harris first hunted there and wrote *The Wild Sports of Southern Africa*, until the second Boer War in 1899, the game of southern Africa had been systematically exterminated. The vast migrating herds of springbok were virtually wiped out; several animals, including the *blaubok* and the quagga, became extinct. Elephants, rhinoceros, hippopotamus, giraffes, and lions were unheard of in the provinces of South Africa (Cape Province, Orange Free State, Natal, and Transvaal) after 1900. The Afrikaners are farmers, who traditionally viewed wild animals as predators to be destroyed, or as a source of meat to be killed at will to feed the hands, or as competition for their grazing herds which must be eradicated. The decimation of the game in southern Africa during the last decades of the nineteenth century rivalled the despoiling of the American West, and was the main factor that led to the Convention for the Preservation of Wild Animals, Birds, and Fish in Africa. This international convention was signed in London in 1900 by representatives of Great Britain, France, Germany, Spain, Italy, Portugal, and the Congo (which was then ruled by Belgium).

While parks were established in South Africa, notably Kruger National Park, to provide a sanctuary for the remaining game, land that had been given over to agriculture remained largely devoid of game animals right up until 1965. When Mellon hunted there, you could take peculiar species like the black wildebeest or *blesbok* on some ranches whose owners looked upon them more kindly than most, but that was about the extent of big game hunting in South Africa. Over the next thirty-five years, however, there was a radical change. South Africans discovered game ranching. Kruger became the greatest concentration of animals anywhere on the continent, bursting at the seams with everything from elephants on down. Under South African law, a landowner owns the animals and birds on his property, and there is virtually no public land where you can hunt for free. Farmers discovered that a herd of blesbok could be a valuable source of income, and the game departments took to auctioning breeding stock of many different species from the surplus animals that needed to be culled in the parks. Rather than going in and shooting a few hundred and giving the meat away, they began trapping the animals and auctioning them. Pretty soon, the sight of herds of blesbok on pasture land in the Free State was as common as pronghorns in Wyoming — and for many of the same reasons.

Johannesburg became a gateway to hunting, not only in South Africa but to countries like Botswana, where lions and Cape buffalo were staple game animals, and Zimbabwe, which has a mix of both ranches like South Africa and wild tribal areas like Botswana.

Late in his life, Robert Ruark made the somewhat rueful claim to be the father of the modern safari industry, and there is no doubt his influence was considerable. Partly because of his writings, more and more Americans wanted to hunt in Africa, which meant there was more money to be had, which led to the growth of safari industries in a far wider variety of countries than ever before. Ruark was one of the very first Americans to hunt in Mozambique; although that colony ceased to be a viable destination soon afterward because of post-colonial civil wars and insurrections, it still has great potential. Today, with a surprisingly good government in Maputu (formerly Lourenco Marques), Mozambique is starting to open up to hunters again.

The key to all this change is hard currency. The American dollar is the single most important factor in preserving hunting in Africa. Tourism is one of the greatest global industries, and hunters are really just well-heeled tourists. Unlike the average sight-seer, however, if there is good hunting to be found, hunters will visit countries that otherwise have little to offer in the way of attractions or amenities. Again, Tanzania is a perfect example: While it has a few scenic areas like Kilimanjaro and the Ngorongoro Crater, which draw the zebra-striped minibuses, much of the country is as drab, remote, and unscenic as Africa gets. Yet hunters flock to areas like the Selous Reserve in the south because it is a treasure trove of game.

A second factor is the realization that while foreigners may view game conservation and preservation as laudable goals in themselves, local people who are eking out a living on a meagre plot of land, having their goats killed by leopards or their crops trampled by elephants, view wildlife decidedly differently. While laws against poaching are useful, and an influx of funds from international animal-welfare groups can play a role as well, the key to providing real protection for animals lies in making them an economic asset to the people in their immediate area. Zimbabwe, with its Campfire Program, has been a leader in this. The principle is no different than giving a South African farmer an economic reason to tolerate, or foster, herds of blesbok on land that otherwise might support cattle.

An interesting object lesson occurred in the 1970s when the U.S. Congress decided in its wisdom to do its bit to protect leopards. The importation of leopard skins was prohibited. At the time, leopards may have been threatened in a few specific areas, but they were never an endangered species. They are intelligent animals — wary, and capable of living in close proximity to man without even being detected, much less eradicated. At any rate, thanks to Congress, they became a non-game animal. That meant they had no commercial value in countries like Tanzania and Zambia. Since the locals could not realize anything from leopards as trophies, they were declared vermin in many areas, and the natives embarked on programs of trapping and poisoning them, just to keep the numbers down. A measure that was intended to protect the animals in fact put them in serious danger.

Two animals that became wildlife symbols during the 1980s were the elephant and the black rhinoceros. Both were poached relentlessly, the rhino for its horn, which is made into ceremonial dagger handles in Arab countries and ground up into aphrodisiac powder in the Far East, and the elephant for its ivory tusks. At one point, black rhino numbers dropped to about 2,500 in total. While elephant numbers never declined to anywhere near those levels, and elephants as a species have never been endangered, the commercial trade in ivory became an international *cause célèbre*. In Kenya, the wife of Jomo Kenyatta and other high-level government people were implicated in an ivory-smuggling ring, in which aircraft of the state airline were used to transport the ivory out of the country. A ban on commercial ivory sales in the 1990s was instrumental in reducing the trade to a fraction of what it had been. Elephant numbers have stabilized in East Africa. Today, you can legally hunt elephant in several different countries. Tanzania is the foremost elephant-hunting country, but Botswana reopened elephant hunting in 1996 after more than a decade, because elephant numbers in the Okavango and other areas were outstripping the ability of the land to support them.

The various aspects of elephant conservation are too complex to discuss at length here. The point is, at one time in the 1970s it appeared elephant numbers were irreversibly declining, and that recreational hunting would soon be a thing of the past; yet today elephant hunting is becoming more widespread, not less, even though it is hideously expensive everywhere. The cost is not the point, however; the availability and long-term viability is.

Ironically, while the economic and conservation benefits of big game hunting are being at least recognized (if not actively embraced) elsewhere, one country that is highly unlikely ever to do so is Kenya — but not for the obvious reasons. Kenya was targeted by international animal-welfare groups in the 1970s because it was a very high-profile country internationally. An obscure state like Tanzania could close hunting and few would notice, but if Kenya closed hunting it would give the international anti-hunting movement a burst of publicity and a significant boost. Millions of dollars went into the campaign, and promises were made that if Kenya put an end to hunting, these groups — and some donor countries were included — would move heaven and earth to ensure that the financial shortfall would be made up by so-called non-consumptive tourism. As well, there was outright bribery. So hunting was closed.

Since then, pro-hunting groups have tried to have it reopened. At times, especially when Kenya's economy has been at its rockiest, they have appeared to be on the verge of succeeding. But it never actually materializes. Partly this is due to Kenya's fear of offending both the animal welfare groups and donor countries they see as being largely anti-hunting, but there is more to it than simply fear of reprisals. Joe Cheffings, the ex-professional hunter who ran a very successful photo-safari operation after hunting was closed, is not optimistic that hunting ever will return. More surprising, however, is the fact that he is quite sure he does not want it to return.

The reasons for the first view are that Kenya has simply moved past the hunting stage in its development. Hunting is no longer part of its culture. Mention hunting to the average black Kenyan and you receive a blank stare. "We know that the subject has come up in cabinet meetings," Cheffings told me, "and it is always turned down. Quite frankly, the idea of a bunch of guys running around the country with guns and short-wave radios frightens them." Economically, he estimates, big game hunting would be worth no more than forty or fifty million dollars a year — about one tenth or less what the country realizes from conventional tourism. Overall, Cheffings sees no economic advantage that could outweigh the possible negative effects. More than that, though, Cheffings is not sure that big game hunting, the way it is done today, is good or right or desirable. And certainly it is nothing he would work toward.

"A few years ago I did one last safari in Tanzania, working on contract," he told me. "I won't mention the professional hunter's name. I arrived in camp and was met by a South African hunter who looked like a young Harry Selby, right out of central casting. We were talking about lion hunting, and he began to tell me how they did it — running the lions down with safari cars, and shooting them from the back of the vehicle. He saw nothing wrong with it. It is sickening to me to see what goes on today. If that is big game hunting, then we are better off without it."

* * *

Hunting is one of the oldest of human activities, and one of the most fundamental. It has the power to bring out the very best in a person, and also the very worst. In 1965, in his finest overview piece on hunting, "Far-Out Safari," Robert Ruark talked about many of the questionable aspects of hunting existing even then, from trophy hunters obsessed with record books who will stop at nothing to get a record head, to cowardly or lazy clients who have their professionals kill their animals for them, to people who just like to kill, to those who become so competitive that they ruin the safari for themselves and everyone around them. None of these is a recent development, however. Questions of ethical behavior in Africa go back to the last century, when recreational hunting in its modern sense first began. There have been game hogs and murderers of animals from the beginning. And almost from the first time airplanes and cars became available, they have been used in hunting and have given rise to debates about where convenience ends and unethical behavior begins.

The advent of the hunting car spelled the end of the old foot safaris with long lines of porters, but cars also opened up country that would never have been accessible otherwise and made safaris affordable for hunters of average means. Even such icons of hunting as Denys Finch Hatton and Bror Blixen used aircraft to locate and evaluate game, often flown by their friend and mutual mistress, Beryl Markham. Rules were eventually formulated, outlawing some of these practices and regulating others. In East Africa, it became an iron law that you could not shoot unless the safari car was several hundred yards away from where you shot. These rules of fair chase found their way into literature: "No one shot from cars," Robert Wilson tells Margot Macomber coldly in *The Short Happy Life of Francis Macomber*, and the ethical aspects of hunting cars became part of Hemingway's complex plot. Those of us who grew up reading this and other stories from East Africa's golden age find it difficult under any circumstances to shoot from a vehicle, although it is now standard practice from Texas to Zimbabwe.

Speaking of Margot Macomber, Ruark wrote at some length about women on safari and the good and bad effects they had — mostly bad. Some involved young wives of rich older men making a play for the handsome young professional hunter. This has been a Hollywood staple for decades. There is also the necessity for the aforementioned older men to go to extraordinary lengths to impress their young wives. Although safaris today are more egalitarian and accessible than they have ever been, there is still a considerable portion of the industry that is geared to very wealthy people, and both safaris and record heads are viewed as status symbols in some circles. When he was shooting editor of *Outdoor Life*, Jack O'Connor wrote about receiving letters from comely young things offering to provide all sorts of personal services if he would take them on his next safari. A combination of Rock Hudson and big safari moons in the velvety African sky tend to bring out that aspect of womanhood.

There are a few serious female hunters around — women who sincerely like hunting and respect the animals. But there are more, it seems, of the variety that feel they can impress Daddy or their ex-husband or otherwise prove themselves equal to men by hunting and taking bigger heads, or more heads. You combine this with a pair of batting eyelashes and a voice you could use for pie filling, crawling all over total strangers at the Safari Club Convention to get a free hunting trip, and you realize that the more things change in some ways, the more they remain the same in others.

Safari Club International has done more than any other organization to change international hunting. Since its founding in 1969, SCI has become a major force in game conservation around the world, and its annual convention is a highlight of the hunting year. It can be argued equally, however, that its record book and the awards it gives to its members make them focus on a few inches of horn — and forget that, in hunting, what you get is not nearly so important as how you get it. For both men and women, big game hunting is a way of proving something. The problem is, the only person worth proving anything to is yourself.

\* \* \*

In October, 1971, I walked out of a small house on the outskirts of the Ugandan town of Kasese, crossed through some long grass to the foot of a steep hill, and began to climb. It was a bright, clear morning. The sky was deep blue, the clouds were fluffy and far away, the plain stretched away to the southeast, and the hill was like a wall before my eyes, never changing as I slowly planted one foot in front of the other and the plain fell away behind me.

Every so often I would look back down. At first I could see each house clearly, with its windows and bougainvillea and banana trees. Then the houses became neat white boxes and the lots fell into place, forming a patchwork of gardens. As I got higher, the gardens became a mozaic —

*414*

an indication of human life without the complications. And of course, the higher I got, the farther out I could see, to where smoke from distant fires gathered in a haze on the horizon, and the breeze carried the faint whiff of burning that, in Africa, is never far away.

I sat down under a small acacia that clung to the hillside and looked out over the plain for a long, long time, enjoying the smell of smoke without the crackling desecration, the neat shambas without the squalor, the beckoning distance that promises secret things, if you could only ever get there. That morning is as close as I will ever get to seeing Africa the way Robert Ruark saw it. But as long as there are tall hills and Ruark's books, it is a view of Africa that will always exist.

❋ ❋ ❋

# BIBLIOGRAPHY

## Books by Robert Ruark

*Grenadine Etching, Her Life and Loves.*
Doubleday & Company, Inc., Garden City, N.Y., 1947.

*I Didn't Know It Was Loaded.*
Doubleday & Company, Inc., Garden City, N.Y., 1948.

*One for the Road.*
Doubleday & Company, Inc., Garden City, N.Y., 1949.

*Grenadine's Spawn.*
Doubleday & Company, Inc., Garden City, N.Y., 1952.

*Horn of the Hunter.*
Doubleday & Company, Inc., Garden City, N.Y., 1953.

*Something of Value.*
Doubleday & Company, Inc., Garden City, N.Y., 1955.

*The Old Man and the Boy.*
Henry Holt & Company, New York, N.Y., 1957

*Poor No More.*
Henry Holt & Company, New York, N.Y., 1959

*The Old Man's Boy Grows Older.*
Henry Holt & Company, New York, N.Y., 1961

*continued*

*Uhuru.*
McGraw-Hill Book Company, Inc., New York, N.Y., 1962

*The Honey Badger.*
McGraw-Hill Book Company, Inc., New York, N.Y., 1965

\* \* \*

## Anthologies of Ruark's Work Published Posthumously

*Use Enough Gun.*
Edited by Stuart Rose, Introduction by Eva Monley.
The New American Library of World Literature, Inc.,
New York, N.Y., 1966

*Women.*
Edited by Joan Fulton.
The New American Library of World Literature, Inc.,
New York, N.Y., 1967

*Robert Ruark's Africa.*
Edited by Michael McIntosh, with illustrations by Bruce Langton.
Countrysport Press, Traverse City, Michigan, 1991.
The Deluxe Edition contains two additional articles: "Far-Out Safari" and "A Leopard in the Rain."

*The Lost Classics of Robert Ruark.*
Edited by James Casada.
Safari Press, Long Beach, California, 1995

\* \* \*

## Biography of Robert Ruark

Foster, Hugh. *Someone of Value.*
Trophy Room Books, Agoura, California, 1992

# *Related Works*

Literally hundreds of books about Kenya, its people and its history, as well as the Mau Mau Emergency, have been published over the last century. The following is a list of works which are of particular interest, or of relevance to Robert Ruark's time in Africa.

Bull, Bartle.
*Safari: A Chronicle of Adventure.*
Viking Penguin Inc., New York, N.Y., 1988

Cullen, Anthony.
*Downey's Africa.*
Cassell & Company Ltd., London, 1959

Edgerton, Robert.
*Mau Mau - An African Crucible.*
Macmillan, Inc., 1989

Hemsing, Jan.
*Ker & Downey Safaris - The Inside Story.*
Sealpoint, Nairobi, Kenya, 1989

Hemsing, Jan.
*Then and Now - Nairobi's Norfolk Hotel.*
Sealpoint, Nairobi, Kenya, 1975

Huxley, Elspeth.
*The Sorcerer's Apprentice - A Journey Through East Africa.* Chatto & Windus Ltd., London, 1948

Huxley, Elspeth.
*A Thing to Love.* (Novel of the Mau Mau Emergency).
Chatto & Windus Ltd., London, 1954

*continued*

Huxley, Elspeth and Curtis, Arnold, Editors.
*Pioneers' Scrapbook - Reminiscences of Kenya 1890 to 1968.* Evans
Brothers Limited, London, 1980

Huxley, Elspeth.
*Out in the Midday Sun - My Kenya.*
Chatto & Windus Ltd., London, 1985

Huxley, Elspeth, Editor.
*Nine Faces of Kenya.* Anthology.
Collins Harvill, London, 1990

Lander, Cherry.
*My Kenya Acres.*
George G. Harrap & Co. Ltd., 1957

Pakenham, Valerie.
*Out in the Noonday Sun — Edwardians in the Tropics.*
Random House, New York, N.Y., 1985

Pakenham, Thomas.
*The Scramble for Africa.*
Random House, New York, N.Y., 1991

Trzebinski, Errol.
*The Kenya Pioneers.*
William Heinemann Limited, London, 1985

Wieland, Terry.
*Spiral-Horn Dreams.*
Trophy Room Books, Agoura, California, 1995

\* \* \*

## The North Atlantic Convoys

Terraine, John.
*Business in Great Waters - The U-Boat Wars 1916-1945.*
Leo Cooper Ltd., London, 1989

* * *

# INDEX

## A

*Across the River and into the Trees* (Hemingway), 110; Ruark's review of, 259-60
*Act of God* (projected novel), 241, 317
Adkins, Charlotte, 1, 2, 5, 92, 306
Adkins, Capt. Edward Hall, 1, 2, 5, 7, 8, 92, 306
*Admiral Scheer* (German pocket battleship), 40
*Afoundria*, S.S., 65
African Boot Company, 98
*African Game Trails* (Roosevelt), 109, 117
*African Hunter* (Mellon), 388, 408
*African Story, An* (Hemingway), 265-6
Ahamed Brothers, 98
Alaska, hunting trip in 1958, 222
"All He Left Me Was The World," 7, 307
Annabel, Russell, 294, 298-9
Arbuthnot, Dr. Thomas S., 136
Archer, Tony, 160, 181, 196; as pseudo-gangster, 216; 405
*Ark Royal*, H.M.S., 42
Armed Guard (branch of U.S. Navy), 33, 50-1
Aschan, Kris, 160
*Athenia*, S.S., sunk by U-boat, 38
Atlantic, Battle of, 34-50, 53-66
*Atlantic Monthly, The*, condemns *Something of Value*, 213
Australia, 69, 95; kangaroo hunting, 298
"Authors and Ulcers," 86

## B

Baker, Sir Samuel, 120
Bari (Italian port), 63-4
Baring, Sir Evelyn, 165, 176
Barr, Alexander, *xxii-iii*, 7, 12, 16, 51-2, 65-6, 76, 88-90; and Mau Mau, 173;
    African odyssey, 238-9; 249; on Hemingway, 265-7; 278, 310, 324, 337-363
Barr, Amelia, 29, 88-90, 337-363; modeled on Virginia Ruark, 357
Barr, Emma, 6
Barr, Penny, 91
Bartlett, Fred, 160
Belgian Congo, 125; Ruark's first visit, 236; independence, 243; refugees, 243-4;
    Katanga secedes, 245; Lumumba assassinated, 250; after independence, 393
Bell, W.D.M. (Karamoja), 270, 373
*Bismarck* (German battleship), 40-2
black people, Ruark's attitudes towards, 8, 171, 174, 207-8
Blixen, Karen, 133, 192
Blixen-Finecke, Baron Bror von, 134, 139, 413
Block, Jack, 160, 224, 271
Blundell, Michael, 182, 243
Boedeker, Dr., 131
bongo, 271-2, 407-8
Book-of-the-Month Club, 188, 213, 275
Botswana, 100
Bowker, Eric, murder of, 167
Bowman, Frank, 102, 160
British Empire, disintegration of, 142
Burrows, Brian, 231, 348
*Burnt Offering* (original title of *Uhuru*), 241, 247, 251
Burton, Capt. Sir Richard Francis, 120-4
*Business in Great Waters — The U-Boat Wars 1916-1945* (Terraine), 55, 421
"But Not On Opening Day," 307

423

# INDEX

## C

*Caine Mutiny, The* (Wouk), 211
*Campi a Simba* (Lion Camp), 176, 216
Cape buffalo, 114
Cape Fear River, 3, 7
Capote, Truman, 353
Caras, Roger, 112-3
Cardigan, Lord, 81
*Carrion Men* (original title for *Something of Value*), 203
Cartridges: .220 Swift, 113, 297, 301; .244 H&H, 299-301; .275 Rigby, 270, 373; .30-06, 113, 277, 297; .375 H&H, 113, 297; .450 No. 2, 139, 297-8; .470 Nitro Express, 113, 297; .505 Gibbs, 139
Cary, Lucian, 295
Casada, James Dr., x, 300, 386
Cheffings, Joe, 401-2, 405-6, 412
Cholmondely, Hugh — see Delamere, Lord
Churchill, Sir Winston, 59; urges accord with Mau Mau, 216
Churchill shotgun, 297
*Clarissa Radcliffe*, S.S., 55
Cloete, Stuart, 289
Coffin, Skipper, 13-4
Cole, Berkeley, 223
Cole, Lady Florence, wife of Lord Delamere, 130
*Collier's*, 83, 178, 294
Coogan, Joe, 102, 116, 367
Corbett, Jim, 162
Corfield Report, 151, 244
Countrysport Press, 385
Cumming, Roualeyn Gordon, 124

## D

*Daily News, The* (New York), 218
*Daily News, The* (Washington), 21, 23-4, 27, 30, 50, 74
*Death as a Way of Life* (Caras), 112
Delamere, Hugh Cholmondely, Lord, 130-2, 135, 192
Destro, Reggie, 117, 160
Doenitz, German Admiral Karl, 39, 54, 56
*Dorsetshire*, H.M.S., 42
Doubleday & Company, 85, 91, 209, 214; break with, 215
Downey, Sydney, 158-161
*Downey's Africa* (Cullen), 419
*Dreadnought*, H.M.S., 36
Dugmore, John, 102, 160; at *Campi a Simba*, 216-7; in Botswana, 217-8
Dyer, Tony, 102, 115, 160

## E

East African Protectorate, 131
*East African Standard*, 151
Edgerton, Robert (historian), 154, 163-6, 175; references to Ruark, 179; and *Something of Value*, 195; assessment of Mau Mau military losses, 204; on Operation Anvil, 206; casualty estimate, 224; assessment of Corfield Report, 244
elephants, hunting, 265-7; 272-3; status of, 410-11
*Eli Whitney*, S.S., 51-3, 61-5
Equator Ranch, 130
Erskine, Gen. Sir George, arrival, 182; impression of settlers, 182, 207; begins military operation, 203; and Operation Anvil, 205; forest operations, 215-6; replaced, 216
Ethiopia, and emerging Africa, 235; today, 403-4
*Evening Star, The* (Washington), 21, 23, 30

**F**

*Facing Mount Kenya* (Kenyatta), 152
"Far-Out Safari," 300, 325, 372, 385-8, 412
Faulkner, William, 281
*Field & Stream*, ix, 1, 92, 171, 173, 199, 207, 248, 270, 293-302, 305, 308, 385
Finch Hatton, Denys, 134, 139, 159, 413
*First Footsteps in East Africa* (Burton), 124
*Flame Trees of Thika, The* (Huxley), 192
Foster, Hugh, x, xi, xxiii, 3, 13, 30, 77, 88, 91, 105, 170, 202, 210, 227, 239, 246, 274, 319-20, 323, 328, 366, 376
Fournier, Lew, 25
Francis Scott, Lady, i
Freeman, John, 82

**G**

*Garden of Eden, The* (Hemingway), 265
German colonial policy in Africa, 129
Ghana, achieves independence, 232
Gichuru, Chief James, xxi; sues Ruark, 315; 369
*Gneisenau* (German battle cruiser), 37, 40
Gordon, General Charles George "Chinese," 126, 129-30
*Graf Spee* (German pocket battleship), 37, 39
*Grand Safari* (Arbuthnot), 137
Great Britain, as colonial power, 125
*Green Hills of Africa* (Hemingway), 110, 138, 265, 270
*Grenadine Etching, Her Life and Loves* (Ruark), 84, 111, 170, 381, 417
*Grenadine's Spawn* (Ruark), 200, 381, 417

**H**

Hadley, Leila, 77
Hamlet, N.C., 14-6
Happy Valley Set, 134
*Harper's*, 213
Harris, William Cornwallis, 109, 408
"Harry Thuku Affair,"(1922), 151
Heiskell, Andrew, 172-3
Hemingway, Ernest, ix, xvii-xx, xxiii-iv, 2, 15, 25, 102, 107, 109-17, 134; safari, 137-9; second safari, 183; in Pamplona, 201; work compared to *Something of Value*, 213; suicide, 251-2, 263-7; Ruark's relationship with, 255-67; 297, 307, 330-2, 334, 341; and Alec Barr, 350
Henley, Tony, 100-2, 115, 160; on Ruark, 335; 407
Henry, Skipper, 13, 28
Hesselberger, Kitty, 177
Hill, Gene, 302
Hinde, Maj.-Gen. W.R.N., 176, 180, 182
*H.M.S. Ulysses* (MacLean), 47
Holden, William, 223-4, 264
Holmberg, Andrew, 102, 115, 160, 174, 196
Holt, Henry & Co., 215, 251, 273
Home Guard (Kikuyu), 180
*Honey Badger, The* (Ruark), xi, xix, xxi-iii, 3, 4, 6, 7, 14, 51, 60, 87, 92, 171, 173, 209, 212, 264, 319-27; assessment, 337-63; reviews, 337-8; 381-2, 391, 418
*Hood*, H.M.S, 35, 41
*Horn of the Hunter* (Ruark), xix, 60, 98, 106-7, 109-17, 160-1, 170, 202, 207, 209, 297-8, 372, 381-2, 389, 417
"House Comes Home, The," 3, 92
Howard, Roy, 74, 218, 227; approves African series, 234; death, 325
Hudson, Rock, 215, 217
Hunter, J.A., 100
*Hunter's Life in South Africa, A* (Cumming), 124
hunting block system, 98-100

Hurt, Roger, 217
Huxley, Elspeth, 192
HX 229 and HX 229A (Atlantic convoys), 54-7
hyena, killed with .220 Swift, 113

**I**

*I Didn't Know It Was Loaded* (Ruark), 86, 111, 383, 417
Illaut, Old Elephant of, 272-3, 354, 368
India, 275-8
*Islands in the Stream* (Hemingway), 341
"It Takes a Gentleman to Approach Another Gentleman," 309
ivory trade, commercial, 127

**J**

James, Jimmy, 29, 60-1
*Jervis Bay*, H.M.S., 40
Jesperson, Ken, 247-8
Johnson, Wally, 369
Johnstone, K.N. — see Kenyatta, Jomo
Jones, James, *vii*

**K**

Kaggia, Bildad, 154, 166
Karamoja, safari to, 269-70
Kasese (Uganda), 414
Katanga Province (Congo), 236-7, 398
Kenya, 97; exploration and settlement, 119-144; game conservation, 139-40; race relations in, 139, 143; impact of second world war, 142-4; postwar immigration, 148; independence, 319; army mutiny, 322; today, 399-408; bans hunting, 406; efforts to reopen hunting, 411-2
Kenya African Union (KAU), 153-5; and Mau Mau "action group," 155
Kenya Central Association (KCA) 152-3
*Kenya*, H.M.S., 166
*Kenya Pioneers, The* (Trzebinski), 420
Kenya Police Reserve (KPR), 165, 176
Kenya Regiment, 166
Kenyatta, Jomo, 141; origins and name, 151; education, 152; return from England, 153; and Mau Mau, 155, 162-3; arrested, 166; Ruark's attacks on, 179, 183; plea for reconciliation, 196; release, 319; 400; and ivory poaching, 411
Ker, Donald, 97-8, 159-61
Ker & Downey Safaris, Ltd., 97, 104, 115-7, 158-61, 372, 402
*Ker & Downey Safaris — The Inside Story* (Hemsing), 419
Ker, Downey & Selby Safaris, Ltd., 117
Kiambu, meeting at, 162
Kidepo National Park (Uganda), 100
Kikuyu, 131; social structure, 141-3, 149-51; resist colonization, 149; and mission schools, 150; circumcision, 150; land issue, 154
King's African Rifles (KAR), 142, 165
Kingsley-Heath, John, 160
*kipande* (pass) system, 150-1
Koinange, Chief, 163-5
Kruger National Park, 408-9
Kubai, Fred, 154-6, 166
kudu, greater, 114, 270

**L**

*Lake Regions of Central Africa, The* (Burton), 124
Lancashire Fusiliers, 166
Lancaster House Conference, 238
Lander, Cherry, 177-8
Langata, 205; today, 405

# INDEX

Lari Massacre, 180
Lartéguy, Jean, 288
Lathbury, General Sir Gerald, 216
Lawrence-Brown, Stan, 160
Lea, Ben, 356
Lee, Lt.-Gen. John C.H. (Courthouse), 80-3
Lee, Robert M., 271-2, 275, 387
"Leopard in the Rain, A," 248, 301, 385
leopards, 115; Ruark attacked by in India, 275-8; status of, 410
Lettow-Vorbeck, Gen. Paul von, 134
*Liberty*, 83
Liddell Hart, B.H., 45
*Life*, 82, 85, 91, 94, 172-3, 178, 262-3
"Life Among The Giants," 15, 309
Livingstone, Dr. David, 121
*Long View from a Tall Hill, A* (projected series), 241, 316-7
*Look*, 184
*Lost Classics of Robert Ruark, The*, x, 300, 386, 418
Luciano, Charles (Lucky), 78-9
Lumumba, Patrice, 246, 250
Lunatic Line — see Uganda Railway
Lütjens, German Vice-Admiral Günther, 40-1

## M
*Macomber Affair, The*, 159
Mahdi, The, and defeat at Omdurman, 129
*Man-Eaters of Tsavo, The* (Patterson), 130-3
Mantell, Marc, 73, 89, 90, 348
Masai, 126, 131
Masai Mara, 159
*Mathew Luckenbach*, S.S., 57
Matson, Harold, 89, 90, 201-2, 209, 211, 241, 251, 270, 273, 321-2, 326-9, 348, 383
Mau Mau, origins, 154; oathing ceremonies, 154; origin of name, 156; early violence, 157; first violence against settlers, 164; Christmas killings and murder of Ruck family, 175; Communist links, 179; attack on Naivasha, 180; Lari massacre, 180; Nyeri battles, 204; losses by end of 1953, 204; activity in Nairobi, 204; total casualties, 224; activity renewed in 1960, 244
*Mau Mau - An African Crucible* (Edgerton), 154, 195, 419
Mau Mau Emergency, 97, 147-84; state of emergency declared, 165; enforcement and penalties, 168-9; effect on tourism, 183; Erskine's campaign, 203-7; and *Something of Value*, 213; and Alec Barr, 345
Mayfield, Fran, 13-5
Mboya, Tom, 205
McGraw-Hill, 251, 273-5, 320, 323-4, 326-7
McIntosh, Michael, x, 73, 105, 112, 300, 325, 379, 384
McKenzie, Peter, xx, 188-97
Mediterranean, Battle of, 61
Meiklejohn, Cdr. Ian and wife, attacked by Mau Mau, 169
Meinertzhagen, Col. Richard, 149-51, 156
Mellon, James, 388, 408
*Moby Dick* (Melville), xix
*Modern Warfare* (Trinquier), 168
*Mogambo*, 162, 177, 209
Monley, Eva, xxiii, 92, 208, 246-7, 323-5, 328, 347, 362, 383
Monsarrat, Nicholas, 288
Mozambique, 271, 300, 325, 369, 409
Mungai, John, 155
Murmansk Convoys, 43-9
*My Kenya Acres* (Lander), 177-8, 420

# INDEX

## N

Nairobi, 97, 102-3; founding, 131; and Operation Anvil, 205-6; 234; Ruark's last departure from, 315; today, 401, 404-5
Nderi, Chief, 166
Nelson, Derek (military historian), 64-5
*Nelson*, H.M.S., 36
New Stanley Hotel (Nairobi), 102, 160, 401-2
*New York Times, The*, xxii, 1, review of *Something of Value*, 213; and *Uhuru*, 286; and *The Honey Badger*, 337
Newland & Tarlton, 159
*News-Messenger, The* (Hamlet, N.C.), 14-6
Newsom, Louis Norman (Buck), 26-7, 344
*Newsweek*, xxii, 82, 85, 202; review of *Poor No More*, 228; compares Ruark to Hemingway, 258; review of *The Honey Badger*, 337
Ngengi, Kamau — see Kenyatta, Jomo
Nigeria, 395-6
Nightingale family, 209, 246
Nile, search for source of, 120-7
*Nine Faces of Kenya* (Huxley), 420
"Nobility is Wrecking the Country," 311
*Norfolk*, H.M.S., 41
Norfolk Hotel (Nairobi), 102, 160
Norman, Nan, 13-4
North Atlantic Convoys, 42-50, 53, 344
North Cape, Battle of, 49
North Carolina, ix, 1, 275, 305
Northern Frontier District, safari to, 269, 373

## O

O'Connor, Jack, 160, 293-4, 296-8, 414
*Old Man and the Boy, The* (anthology, Ruark), xix, xxiii, 1-3, 7, 92, 215, published in 1957, 220; assessment, 305-12; 343, 388, 417
"Old Man and the Boy, The" (magazine series), ix, 92, 171; begins in *Field & Stream*, 173, 215; series ends, 274; 295-6, 299, 305.
*Old Man and the Sea, The* (Hemingway), 110; Ruark's review of, 261
*Old Man's Boy Grows Older, The* (Ruark), x; assessment, 308-12; 417
Olsen, Capt. Karl Peder, master of the *Eli Whitney*, 63
*One for the Road* (Ruark), 27, 86, 383, 417
ONS-2 (Atlantic convoy), 59
Operation Anvil, 205
Operation Jock Scott, 166
Oswell, William Cotton, 124
*Out in the Midday Sun* (Huxley), 192, 420
*Out in the Noonday Sun — Edwardians in the Tropics* (Pakenham), 420
*Out of Africa* (Blixen), 134
*Outdoor Life*, 160, 293-4

## P

Page, Warren, 296
Pakenham, Thomas (historian), 125
Palamós, xxi, 172, 193, 200-1, 209-10, 330-5,
Pamplona, 201, 330-2, 349
Paris, *xviii*
Paton, Alan, 289
Percival, Blayney, 101
Percival, Philip, 101, 111, 140, 159
Petzal, David, 295-6
*Pioneers' Scrapbook — Reminiscences of Kenya 1890 to 1968* (Huxley and Curtis), 420
*Playboy*, 299, 300, 325-7, 385
pocket battleships, 37

Poole, Peter, 241, 244-6, in *Uhuru*, 283
*Poor No More* (Ruark), xx, 3, 92, 220-2; 226-9; reviews, 228; 233, 338, 349, 381, 417
Pound, Ezra, 26
PQ 17 (Murmansk convoy), 48
PQ 18 (Murmansk convoy), 49
Price, Craig, xx, 229
Price, Victor, 15
*Prince of Wales*, H.M.S., 41
*Prinz Eugen* (German cruiser), 40
professional hunters, 99-101
"pseudo-gangsters" (anti-Mau Mau units), 181, 216
Pulitzer Prize in National Reporting, 82

**Q**
Queen, James, 23, 29, 60-1

**R**
Raynes-Simson, Dorothy, 177
*Reader's Digest*, 202
rhinoceros, poaching of, 410
Rhodesia, 135, 237, 325, 374, 396-8
Rigby, 297
Riley, Galbert Rockford (Rocky), 24-8, 86
Ritchie, Alan, hired by Ruark, 201; 333
"Robert Ruark Among The Mau Mau," 178
Robert Ruark Foundation, 92
*Robert Ruark's Africa* (film documentary), 322
*Robert Ruark's Africa* (posthumous anthology), x, 112, 300, 385-6, 418
*Rodney*, H.M.S., 36
Rolls-Royce, 214, 218-20
Roosevelt, Theodore, 109; safari in Kenya, 133
Rowbotham, Mike, 117
Royal Inniskilling Fusiliers, 204
Ruark, Caroline, 3-5, 13
Ruark, Charlotte Adkins, 2-6, 13, 92-4, 274, 324
Ruark, Hanson Kelly, 3, 5, 7, 306
Ruark, Robert Chester Sr., 2, 4-6, 9, 92-4, 274, 309; death of, 317
Ruark, Virginia Webb, xxi-ii, 28-31, 72, 86, 87-91, 97, 105-6, 203, 212, 214, 248, 275, 277, divorce, 317-20; 325; death, 333; on *The Honey Badger*, 339, 357-8, 375
Ruck family, murder of, 175
Rundgren, Eric, 160
Ryan, Bill, 160

**S**
*Safari: A Chronicle of Adventure* (Bull), 388, 419
Safari Club International, 384, 406, 414
safari life, 136-7, 412-4
Safari Press, 382, 386
Safari South, 100, 217, 365
*Safari Today* (Lee), 387
Safariland, 159
San Fermin, Fiesta of, 258, 331-2
*Saturday Evening Post, The*, 83, 91, 178, 207, 294-5, 316
Sauer shotgun, 297
SC 122 (Atlantic convoy), 54-7
*Scharnhorst* (German battle cruiser), 37, 40, 49
Scramble for Africa, 125
*Scramble for Africa, The* (Pakenham), 125, 420
Scripps-Howard News Service, 74, 82, 169-70, 174, 199, 200, 327

Selby, Harry, xx, xxii, 90, 97-8, 101, 106, 111-7, 159-60; in New York, 170; 173-4, 176; model for Peter McKenzie, 188; 194, 196, 207; forms Selby & Holmberg, 223; 228, 264, 269, 272, 297, 320, 324, 338, 347, 362, 365-76, 407
Selby & Holmberg, 117, 223
Selby, Mark Robert, 372
Selby, Miki, 375
Selous, Frederick Courteney, 109, 125, 134
"Sentimental Safari," 270
Seth-Smith, Tony, 213, 217-8
settlers, temperament, 132; reaction to Mau Mau, 158; and Baring, 166; life under siege, 167, 176; Ruark's sympathy with, 179, 183, 208, 226; antipathy toward government, 182; divisions among, 182; in Uhuru, 283
Short Happy Life of Francis Macomber, The (Hemingway), 138-9, 265, 413
Sicré, Ricardo, 201, 270, 331
Sinatra, Frank, 78-80
slave trade, 126-9
Snows of Kilimanjaro, The (Hemingway), 139, 265
Soldier Settlement Scheme (1920), 134
Somalia, Ruark and Selby visit, 235, 374
Someone of Value (Foster), x, 3, 418
Something of Value (motion picture), 215, 217
Something of Value (novel, Ruark) xix-x, 155, 176-7; assessment of, 187-97; origin of title, 189; reviews of, 191, 213; reaction of Kenyans to, 191, 213-4; and A Thing to Love, 192-3; reaction of black Kenyans, 195; and Tom Mboya, 205; 208; publication of, 211-2; paperback and motion picture rights, 214; 353, 381-2, 417
Sorcerer's Apprentice, The (Huxley), 192, 419
South Africa, Republic of, 237, 391-4, 398-9, 408-9
Southport, N.C., 3, 5, 7, 91-3, 211, 228, 306, 329
Spain, 172, 199
Speke, John Hanning, 120-4
Spiral-Horn Dreams (Wieland), 420
Sporting Classics, 386
Sports Afield, 293-4
Stanley, Henry, 120
Stein, Gertrude, xviii
Stone, Walker, 74
Sudan, 126, 134; independence and civil war, 235
Suez Crisis, effect of, 232
Suffolk, H.M.S., 41
Sun Also Rises, The (Hemingway), xix, 332
Sundance, S.S., 15-6
Sutton, John, 102, 115, 117, 160, 251, 322, 405
Swan, Capt. Praxiteles, 59

T
Tanganyika, 97-8; becomes British, 134
Tanzania, 403, 407, 409
Tarlton, Leslie, 159
Taylor, Harry, 240; killed in Kasai, 246; model for Larry Orde, 350
Taylor, John (Pondoro), 101
Terraine, John (military historian), 55-6
Then and Now — Nairobi's Norfolk Hotel (Hemsing), 419
Thing to Love, A (Huxley), 192-3, 419
"This Is New York," 86
Thornburg, Dick, 74
Thuku, Harry, 151-2
"Tiger Doesn't Stand A Chance, The," 207
tiger hunting, 207
Time, xxii, 82, 85, 200

# INDEX

*Tirpitz* (German battleship), 44-50
*Torrents of Spring, The* (Hemingway), 85
Transvaal, discovery of gold in, 127
*Travels and Researches in South Africa* (Livingstone), 121
Trinquier, Col. Roger, 168
*True*, 82, 262, 337
Tsavo, man-eaters of, 130
Turner, Myles, 160

## U
Uganda, 98, 134, 394-5
Uganda Railway, 129-30
UGS 42 (Mediterranean convoy), 62
*Uhuru* (Ruark), *xxi*, 209, 240-3, 251, 273, 275; assessment of, 281-91; reaction to, 286-8; banned in
    South Africa, 287; paperback rights, 288; Gichuru named in, 315; 320, 326, 353, 381-2, 418
United Features Syndicate, 82, 95, 214, 227, 249-50, 321; Ruark fired from, 326; farewell column, 328
University of North Carolina (Chapel Hill), 9, 11-6, 259
*Use Enough Gun* (posthumous anthology), 113, 316, 382, 383, 418

## V
*Vulcania*, S.S., 174

## W
Waruhiu, Chief, 163; murder of, 165
Washington Naval Treaty of 1922, 35
*Washington Post, The*, 21, 23
Webb, Benton, 28
Webb, Jack, 30
Webb, Polly, 28
Webb, Virginia (see Ruark, Virginia Webb)
*White Hunter* (Hunter), 100
"white man's country," explanation of term, 132
*White Man's Country* (Huxley), 192
*Wild Sports of Southern Africa, The* (Harris), 109, 124, 408
Williams, David, 159
Williams, Verity, 159
Wilmington, N.C., *xxi*, 1-7, 12, 92-3; Ruark's return, 219; 228, 306
Winchester Silvertip, 300
wolf packs (U-boat), 39
Wolfe, Thomas, 12
*Women* (posthumous anthology), 71, 383, 418
"Women Drive You To The Poolrooms, The," 5
Wood, Rev. J.G., 121
Works Progress Administration (WPA), 15
*World-Telegram, The* (New York), 74
Wouk, Herman, *vii*, 211

## Y
Young Kikuyu Association, 151
"Your Guns Go With You," 178

## Z
Zimbabwe, 398, 410

* * *

431